WHEN VIOLENCE WORKS

WHEN VIOLENCE WORKS

Postconflict Violence and
Peace in Indonesia

Patrick Barron

CORNELL UNIVERSITY PRESS ITHACA AND LONDON

First published 2019 by Cornell University Press

Library of Congress Cataloging-in-Publication Data

Names: Barron, Patrick, 1977– author.
Title: When violence works : postconflict violence and peace
    in Indonesia / Patrick Barron.
Description: Ithaca : Cornell University Press, 2019. | Includes
    bibliographical references and index.
Identifiers: LCCN 2018035597 (print) | LCCN 2018036920 (ebook) |
    ISBN 9781501735455 (pdf) | ISBN 9781501735455 (epub/mobi) |
    ISBN 9781501735448 | ISBN 9781501735448 (cloth)
Subjects: LCSH: Violence—Indonesia. | Peace-building—Indonesia. |
Conflict management—Indonesia. | Ethnic conflict—Indonesia.
Classification: LCC HN710.Z9 (ebook) | LCC HN710.Z9 V534 2019 (print) |
    DDC 303.609598—dc23
LC record available at https://lccn.loc.gov/2018035597

Contents

Tables

Figures

Preface

In 2006, I was living and working in Aceh, tasked with developing programs for the World Bank that would support a recent peace agreement in the Indonesian province. After almost three decades of civil war, the first year of Aceh's postconflict era had gone well. An international peace-monitoring mission had had relatively little to do and both the government and former rebel GAM leaders appeared committed to making the peace accord work. There was talk that the Indonesian president, Susilo Bambang Yudhoyono, could be up for a Nobel Peace Prize. Analysts were already declaring Aceh a rare story of peace-building success. I was also optimistic and saw much progress, but it was also clear that violence had not completely ceased. The monthly conflict monitoring updates we produced were starting to pick up incidents of many types—land conflicts, vigilante attacks, and most noticeably, a worrying upsurge in violent crime. It did not seem likely to me or others that a return to civil war was in the cards. But nor did Aceh appear to be as peaceful as some made out.

Trying to understand what was going on, I started to work my way through the academic and policy literature on why some peace settlements are successful while others are not. The books and papers I read sought to explain why civil wars often reoccurred after peace agreements or military victories had (temporarily) halted hostilities. But I found little that helped me understand why other forms of violence could emerge.

The ideas in the literature on the sources of postconflict violence also did not seem to fit with what I saw. If violence was the result of failed elite bargains, as some proposed, why was it occurring so frequently in Aceh even as leaders from both the rebel movement and the Indonesian government seemed so committed to the peace accord? If postconflict violence was the result of societal factors such as tense intergroup relations, another major focus in the literature, why was violence occurring even as surveys I commissioned were showing high levels of social cohesion? How could I square arguments that postconflict violence was a result of weak state capacity with the observed reality that Aceh was governed by a strong, and strengthening, Indonesian state? Existing theories were ill equipped to provide an explanation of what was happening in Aceh.

My interest in these questions strengthened as the first data came in from another project I was managing. Colleagues and I had been building a database of incidents of violence reported in local newspapers across Indonesia.

Turn-of-the-century Indonesia had seen intercommunal conflicts in many provinces and the data provided an empirical picture of just how affected different regions had been. As I started to sift through the information on provinces such as Maluku and its close neighbor North Maluku, stark differences emerged. Both had seen horrific conflicts that killed thousands before peace agreements and fatigue had brought them to an end. Yet the data showed that Maluku had continued to see frequent outbursts of deadly violence while North Maluku had not. And many of the incidents in Maluku were having far greater destructive impact than that of the postconflict violence in Aceh. What could explain the differing postconflict trajectories of different Indonesian provinces?

This book seeks to answer three questions. What causes postconflict violence to occur in some places emerging from large-scale escalated violent conflict and not in others? Why do episodes of postconflict violence take different forms? And what causes violence to escalate into larger renewed and extended violent conflict?

In doing so, I develop a new theory of postconflict violence. Such violence is often not directly caused by failed elite bargains, dysfunctional intergroup relations, enduring grievances, or a lack of state capacity. Rather, it flows from the incentives that three sets of actors—local elites, local violence specialists, and national elites—have to use violence as a political or economic strategy. Violence is used when it works—when it is beneficial, noncostly, and other opportunities for getting ahead do not exist. How postconflict resources are deployed, the degree to which those who use violence face sanctions, and the availability of peaceful means to achieve goals shape incentives and hence patterns of violence.

Where only local violence specialists support violence, the book finds, postconflict violence will take small-scale forms. Where local elites also support violence, escalation to larger forms of episodic violence tends to occur. In countries where the state has sufficient capacity, extended violent conflict occurs only where national elites linked to the state also have reason to use or allow violence to occur.

The arguments are based on a comparative analysis of the diverse postconflict experiences of Indonesian provinces and changes in national-level institutions and politics. But the same factors that explain variation in postconflict trajectories within Indonesia will also likely do so in other areas emerging from large-scale violence around the world. The ideas presented in this book have consequences for how we conceptualize, study, and understand the drivers of postconflict violence. They also have important implications for policymakers and practitioners working on and in postconflict areas.

The debts I have incurred writing this book are numerous. The ideas that underpin it have evolved slowly over the course of a decade living and working in

Indonesia. Special thanks are due to Scott Guggenheim and Michael Woolcock who brought me to Indonesia and who have served as mentors *extraordinaires* since then. Other colleagues from my years at the World Bank in Jakarta and Aceh have been intellectual sparring partners as together we sought to understand the logic behind Indonesia's violence: Muslahuddin Daud, Sana Jaffrey, Dave McRae, Adrian Morel, Blair Palmer, Sri Kusumastuti Rahayu, Didit Setiawan, Joanne Sharpe, Amy Sim, Andi Tama, Rob Wrobel, and Matt Zurstrassen. Adrian provided particularly helpful comments on the book's case chapters. Thanks also to the two anonymous reviewers commissioned by Cornell University Press for their many helpful comments and to my editors at Cornell.

Other friends and colleagues, too many to list in full, have shaped my understanding of Indonesian violence, politics, and society. Thanks to Paul Adams, Aguswandi, Ed Aspinall, Vic Bottini, Raihana Diani, Rachael Diprose, Byron Good, Jesse Grayman, Suprayoga Hadi, Sandra Hamid, Sidney Jones (who also reviewed early write-ups of some of the chapters), Sri Kuntari, Karrie McLaughlin, Kharisma Nugroho, Ben Olken, Tom Pepinksy, Erman Rahman, Joanne Sharpe, Claire Smith, Matt Stephens, Sudarno Sumarto, Zulfan Tadjoeddin, Yuhki Tajima, Michael Vatikiotis, and Andrea Woodhouse. Dewi Fortuna Anwar provided useful comments on a draft paper outlining early findings.

The project really took flight during my time at the University of Oxford. Richard Caplan and Anke Hoeffler were a constant source of ideas, critical feedback, and encouragement. In Oxford, others provided useful comments on drafts or otherwise stimulated my thinking. Thanks to Nancy Bermeo, Christine Cheng, John Gledhill, Julien Labonne, Alex Scacco, and Maya Tudor. Gerry van Klinken also provided useful feedback.

Samuel Clark and Chris Wilson both went well beyond the duties of friendship by commenting on most of the chapters of the book. Conversations over coffees and beers with Sam and Chris also shaped my thinking at many points in the research and writing. While I did not incorporate all of their suggestions, and neither will agree with everything I have written, their testing questions about my findings and theoretical and methodological assumptions have made this a far stronger book than it would otherwise have been.

Beyond Indonesia, conversations and exchanges with many people have provided comparative perspectives that have enriched my thinking. Thanks to Bobby Anderson, Adam Burke, Sarah Cliffe, Nat Colletta, Macartan Humphreys, Stathis Kalyvas, Markus Kostner, Rob Muggah, Ben Oppenheim, Tom Parks, Gordon Peake, James Putzell, Nigel Roberts, Pam Tansanguanwong, Ashutosh Varshney, Ingo Wiederhofer, and Susan Wong.

The quantitative data I use in the book are from the Indonesian National Violence Monitoring System. Ashutosh Varshney and I originally cooked up the idea to build a comprehensive violence dataset on Indonesian violence. Sana Jaffrey, Imron Rasyid, and Blair Palmer helped make it happen, and their distinctive intellectual interests and experiences shaped the decisions we made on data collection methods and coding choices. Sana and her team deserve credit for turning an idea into the largest single country violence dataset worldwide. Thanks to the World Bank and USAID for providing funding, to JRI Research for building the dataset, and to the Indonesian government's Coordinating Ministry for People's Welfare for agreeing for the data to be made publically available. My fieldwork was financed in part by the World Bank's Conflict and Development team under the leadership of Sonja Litz. Within that team, Inge Tan was a continual source of administrative and logistical support.

Colleagues from the Center for Security and Peace Studies at Universitas Gadjah Mada helped with the Maluku and North Maluku field research. Najib Azca led the research in Maluku and Imron Rasyid, Jacky Manuputty, and Hilda Rolobessy supported the data collection and drafted initial case study write-ups. Special thanks to Najib whose deep knowledge and sharp analytic thinking I drew on continually as the Maluku chapter took shape. Tri Susdinarjanti helped lead the North Maluku fieldwork and Achmad Muhammad Nur, Muhammad Asyikin, Adrian Morel, Blair Palmer, Syahril Sangaji, and Didit Setiawan participated in the research. Titik Firawati and Nurul Aini helped me translate many of the interview transcripts, and Fransiskus Agustinus Djalong provided research assistance.

In Aceh, I conducted most of the new fieldwork with Muslahuddin Daud. Over the course of eight years, Mus was my guide and coconspirator in Aceh as we set up and developed the World Bank's program of support to the peace process. The Aceh chapter builds on many studies I conducted or managed between 2005 and 2009.

The interviews we conducted with more than three hundred people in Maluku, North Maluku, Aceh, and Jakarta constitute the core of the case study chapters. Because of the sensitivity of the research, and to encourage openness from informants while limiting risks to them, I have largely chosen to keep informants' identities anonymous.

While the World Bank funded much of the data collection, other Oxford grants helped finance my visits to Indonesia and living expenses. The Clarendon Fund provided me with three years of support, and two grants from the Politics Department helped pay for research trips. Nuffield College also contributed research expenses. In Jakarta, I benefited from my time as a visiting fellow at the Center for Security and International Studies Jakarta. Thanks to Rizal Sukma and his colleagues for making me feel so welcome.

I was also fortunate to be able to present my findings as they emerged in seminars and conferences. Thanks to Ed Aspinall for organizing our panel at the 2011 Indonesian Council Open Conference in Perth, Australia; Kirsten Schulze for inviting me to present at Chatham House; Edo Mahendra for asking me to speak in the Oxford Southeast Asian Studies seminar series; and Asep Suryahadi for giving me the opportunity to run my ideas by Indonesian government personnel and civil society activists in a talk hosted by SMERU as part of the Forum Kajian Pembangunan seminar series. Other talks I gave in Jakarta, Bangkok, Manila, and Providence helped me to refine and better articulate my ideas.

I made the bulk of revisions to the original manuscript while working for The Asia Foundation, managing their peace-building work across Southeast and South Asia. The job afforded me an opportunity to see Indonesia in a comparative perspective, learning much more about a range of places that are experiencing, or have emerged from, protracted violence. Myanmar, Nepal, the Philippines, Sri Lanka, and Thailand's Deep South are not discussed much in this book. But time spent working with the Foundation's teams in these places helped me refine the ideas presented here. Thanks to Matthew Arnold, Bill Cole, Kim Joliffe, Bryony Lau, Steve Rood, and George Varughese for valuable conversations.

My two children, Kiara and Seamus, were born while I worked on the initial manuscript. It is to them that I dedicate this book.

WHEN VIOLENCE WORKS

INTRODUCTION

11 September 2011. As much of the world remembered the toppling of New York's twin towers a decade before, the people of Ambon, the capital of the poor eastern Indonesian province of Maluku, had other things on their minds. The previous evening Darfin Saimin, a Muslim motorcycle taxi driver, had been found dead in Gunung Nona, a Christian part of town.[1] The official story was that the death was accidental. It had been raining, the road was slippery, and motorcycle crashes were frequent in this area. But not everyone was convinced. When the police returned the body to Darfin's family later that night there appeared to be a stab wound on his back. His motorcycle was largely undamaged. What is more, his helmet was full of blood despite the absence of any major head wounds. Rumors started to spread, aided by anonymous text messages, that the driver had been tortured to death by Christians.

The next day hundreds gathered for Darfin's funeral. Tensions soon turned to violence as mourners left the cemetery. A mob set fire to a Christian motorcycle taxi base. A Christian man and two of his grandchildren got caught in the middle of another mob and were attacked with one of the children injured. Claims that the child had been killed spread (she had not) and some Muslim houses were set on fire. Soon text messages were circulating saying that the landmark Silo Church and Mukhlisun Mosque had been attacked. Violence continued until late evening. Early on 12 September, violence flared up in another part of town on the border between Muslim and Christian residential areas. More homes were torched and groups fought through the night. By 14 September, when clashes had largely subsided, eight people, including Darfin, had lost their lives, almost two hundred had been injured, more than three hundred houses had been burned, and over three thousand people were displaced.

Communal passions were ignited but these large episodes of violence did not appear to be entirely spontaneous. Many among the local political elite were under suspicion of corruption and would benefit from a show of violence that might deter investigators. Criminal *preman* (thug) groups in Ambon often caused trouble, sometimes at the behest of local politicians. The actions of the local police and military were also strange. Troops had been withdrawn from Ambon before the violence began despite the obvious potential for unrest. Seven of the deaths were from the bullets of the police and military personnel who were sent in to restore peace.

Outbreaks of violence were not new to Ambon city or Maluku Province. In January 1999 interreligious riots erupted following a clash between Muslim and Christian youths in the city. Before long, violence had spread, first to other areas of Ambon Island and then to neighboring islands. By the time a central government-sponsored peace agreement was signed three years later, almost 2,800 people had died during the extended violence—half of them in Ambon city—more than 15,000 buildings were damaged, and half a million people, one-third of the province's population, had been displaced.[2] The region's economy contracted by one-quarter; access to health, education, and other services deteriorated severely; and trauma was widespread.[3]

After the accord was signed, violence dropped sharply but did not disappear. From the end of large-scale hostilities in February 2002 until the end of 2012, Maluku saw an average of seven large incidents of violence—riots, group clashes, and large one-way attacks—per year, and smaller-scale episodes have also been common.[4] Extended violent conflict, where violence continues for a long period of time at a large scale, has not reemerged in Ambon or Maluku. Yet the "postconflict" period has hardly been peaceful.[5]

Maluku was but one of seven Indonesian provinces that experienced large-scale extended violence in the early years of the country's transition from General Suharto's authoritarian New Order regime to a more democratic polity. Following unrest in Jakarta and other cities in May 1998, a series of extended ethnic and religious violent conflicts erupted across the archipelago—from Indonesian Borneo, to Sulawesi, to the Moluccas. Secessionist conflicts also heated up. East Timor demanded and received independence but 1,400–2,600 lives were lost in the process. The long-running civil war in Aceh escalated sharply as demands for independence were met by a military clampdown. In six Indonesian provinces that experienced large-scale extended violence in the early post-Suharto years, more than eighteen thousand people were killed between 1998 and 2003.[6]

More than a decade on, all of Indonesia's extended violent conflicts are over: peace agreements, security responses, and conflict fatigue brought large-scale hostilities to an end. Yet the levels and dominant forms of postconflict violence differ significantly from place to place. North Maluku Province experienced its own massive extended intercommunal conflict with more than three thousand killed in less than a year from August 1999. However, from July 2000, when large-scale violence ended, until the end of 2012, in annual per capita terms it has seen only one-third as many violent deaths as has Maluku and very few large violent incidents. The postconflict experience of Aceh Province differs again. Since the signing of a peace agreement between rebel insurgents and the Indonesian government in August 2005 violent incidents have been common. However, almost all of these have been small disputes with minimal human or material impact per incident.

Postconflict Violence: Three Puzzles

The short sketch of the postconflict experiences of Maluku, North Maluku, and Aceh illustrates the central puzzles this book seeks to answer. Each experienced an intense extended violent conflict, and in each place large-scale hostilities came to an end. Yet patterns of postconflict violence are very different in the three provinces. In Maluku, large episodes of violence have continued to occur frequently as have smaller incidents; in postconflict North Maluku, violence has been largely absent; in Aceh, large outbreaks of violence are absent but smaller-scale incidents commonly occur. As I will show in chapter 3, such divergence in both levels and forms of recent violence is also noticeable within and between Indonesia's other postconflict provinces: West and Central Kalimantan, and Central Sulawesi.

Two puzzles immediately stand out. First, why do levels of postconflict violence vary between areas within states? Existing explanations have focused on national-level conditions that make violence more or less likely, with factors such as a country's political institutions and social and economic structures seen as determining whether or not postconflict violence occurs. In Indonesia, however, these factors do not differ greatly across areas, yet there has been a clear divergence in levels of postconflict violence. Why then have some of Indonesia's former conflict zones remained susceptible to episodes of violence while in others peace appears to have taken hold?

Second, why does postconflict violence take larger more destructive forms in some areas and forms that result in smaller impacts in others? Previous studies have typically viewed postconflict violence in binary terms: it is either present or absent. Explanations of the causes of different types of violence following peace settlements—on civil war recurrence, on large episodes of violence (such as ethnic riots), and on smaller-scale forms of violence (such as crime and inter-personal violence)—have been developed in isolation with few points of connec-tion. To what extent are these differing forms of postconflict violence driven by similar factors? Under what conditions does violence escalate into larger forms and conflagrations?

The patterns of violence sketched out above also point to a third puzzle: Why has large-scale extended violence not recurred anywhere in Indonesia since the early years of this century? Globally, such recurrence is common; states that have been affected by civil war have a 40 percent chance of seeing war reoccur within a decade.[7] We might have expected extended violence to recur in at least some of Indonesia's postconflict areas. Factors identified in the literature as heighten-ing the risk of recurring civil war are present in Indonesia. These include the presence of abundant natural resources,[8] high levels of poverty,[9] ethnic hetero-geneity,[10] large areas of mountainous terrain,[11] and the fact that Indonesia has been experiencing a transition from authoritarianism to democracy.[12] And yet Indonesia has not seen large-scale violence recur. Analyzing why this is so can improve our understanding of the causes of recurring extended violent conflict.

These puzzles are of academic interest, but unraveling them is also key for those seeking to build consolidated peace. Large-scale extended violent conflict, whether in the form of civil war or intercommunal violence, has massive human, material, and social impacts.[13] Using Indonesia's experience to improve our un-derstanding of how recurring extended violent conflicts can be prevented, even in unpromising circumstances, can help policymakers work out how to break such tragic cycles of violence.

Beyond this, the book can help policymakers develop approaches to prevent episodic violence in postconflict areas. Such violence is of concern because it is so common and because its collective impacts can be great. Nicaragua, Guate-mala, and El Salvador, for example, have not reverted to civil war but episodic postconflict violence has led to fatality rates above those experienced during their wars.[14] Of the 740,000 deaths from armed violence across the world each year, 490,000—two in three—are outside of war zones,[15] and a sizeable proportion of these occur in "postconflict" places where wars have formally ended.[16] In 2006, violence in Central America, where the majority of countries have emerged from civil wars, is estimated to have resulted in losses of US$6.5 billion, or 7.75 per-cent of GDP.[17] Indeed, armed violence outside of war zones has larger economic impacts than in areas where wars are ongoing, with losses in productivity of US$95–163.3 billion.[18]

Limiting the incidence and impacts of postconflict violence is thus vitally important both for domestic policymakers in affected countries and for the international agencies who spend vast resources trying to secure the peace in postconflict areas. However, efforts to support peace are often stymied by a lack of understanding of the causes of postconflict violence. Why does postconflict violence occur in some places but not in others? What explains when it erupts, why it takes different forms, and why it sometimes escalates? In this book, I aim to answer these questions by building a new theory of postconflict violence.

The Approach

The book adopts a different methodological and analytical strategy than previous studies of postconflict violence. Studies have typically compared the experience of different countries. This has meant that we cannot understand why some postconflict areas within countries see continuing violence while others do not. Studies have usually only looked at the violence that occurs after civil wars, where the state was an active party to the conflict, with little consideration of violence that occurs after other types of enduring intrastate conflict, such as extended intercommunal violence. Most work has focused on explaining why civil war reoccurs (or does not) rather than why episodic violence—the riots, group clashes, and attacks that can be so common in postconflict areas—emerges in some places. The few studies that have investigated these types of violence have not systematically compared areas with and without postconflict violence. Not examining relatively peaceful cases means that we have less confidence that the factors identified are actually causing violence.

My approach differs in significant ways. First, I explore why experiences of postconflict violence differ within countries. The presence of considerable variation in the impacts and forms of postconflict violence across different parts of Indonesia suggest that local-level factors are important. A single country research design is appropriate for isolating what such factors are. While studies of violence have increasingly focused on subnational variance, to my knowledge there have been almost no attempts to date to systematically investigate within-country variation in postconflict violence.[19] My approach is to compare areas within Indonesia that experienced large-scale extended violence but which have seen differing patterns of postconflict violence. Comparing subnational cases with similar initial conditions—that is, extended violent conflicts with similar impacts—but that diverge in postconflict experiences can help us identify the causal factors that lead to differences in postconflict violence.

A second difference is that I explain why postconflict violence takes different forms. Past work has tended to either assess only one type of violence (recurring civil war) or has lumped all forms in together (postconflict violence). Yet some postconflict areas experience frequent episodes of violence that result in high fatalities, injuries, or damaged buildings in each incident, while in others violence is smaller in scale. The book develops a taxonomy of violence, distinguishing extended violence from episodic violence and large-scale episodes of violence from smaller-scale ones (table 1). This allows us to assess the extent to which different types of postconflict violence are driven by similar or different causal processes, and the ways that different forms of violence are linked.

The book uses both qualitative and quantitative methods. With colleagues, I constructed a dataset containing information on more than 158,000 incidents of violence in Indonesia, the largest single country violence dataset anywhere in the world.[20] The data allow for a fine-grained mapping of patterns of violence and how they differ between areas and over time.

Based on differences in patterns of violence between areas, I chose six districts in three Indonesian postconflict provinces for deeper study. Each experienced extended violent conflict, but they vary in terms of both the levels and predominant forms of violence they have seen in the postconflict period. Drawing on interviews with more than three hundred people, and analysis of secondary sources, I develop a narrative for each province in chapters 4–6, combining an account of the recent postconflict history of the area with deeper analysis of why violence has occurred with frequency or not. Structured comparative analysis of these narrative accounts is used to build and refine a theory that explains why postconflict violence occurs where and when it does, why violence takes different forms, and why some areas are peaceful.

To assess why extended violent conflict has varied over time, our third puzzle, I turn in the penultimate chapter to the national level, drawing primarily on secondary source accounts of national elite politics and a more limited number of interviews.

TABLE 1.   Types of violence

TYPE OF POSTCONFLICT VIOLENCE	CHARACTERISTICS	FORMS OF VIOLENCE
Episodic (small-scale)	Temporally isolated incidents of violence, resulting in relatively small physical and human impacts	Vigilante attacks Small-scale one-on-one fights Small-scale group clashes
Episodic (large-scale)	Temporally isolated incidents of violence, resulting in larger physical and human impacts. Often have level of organization	Riots Large one-way attacks Large group clashes
Extended violence	Where related incidents of violence occur frequently with few temporal gaps, resulting in very large physical and human impacts	Civil wars Long-lasting intercommunal violent conflicts (e.g., interethnic wars)

The Argument

Patterns of postconflict violence can be explained by the incentives of three sets of actors—local elites, nonstate violence specialists, and central state elites—to use, tolerate, or resist violence. These incentives are shaped by the extent to which the allocation of resources and power following a peace settlement makes the use of violence a profitable tactic. Where postconflict resources are deployed in ways that reward those who use or threaten violence in the early postconflict period, where those who use violence are not disciplined by the state or others, and where institutional channels do not exist whereby groups can access power and resources through nonviolent means, postconflict violence occurs more frequently. Conversely, where violent behavior is not rewarded, and where channels exist to pursue political and economic goals peaceably, there will be limited postconflict violence.

The predominant types of postconflict violence in an area depend on the combinations of actors supporting the use of violence. Frequent smaller-scale episodic postconflict violence is most likely when groups within society who have experience using violence (violence specialists) continue to see benefit in using violence to capture resources or power. Escalation to frequent larger-scale episodic violence requires the support of local elites. In the absence of such support, postconflict areas are likely to be peaceful or see only smaller-scale episodic violence. Escalation to extended violence will only occur when elements of the central state support or allow such escalation. In the absence of this, violence will remain episodic in its smaller and/or larger forms. In peaceful postconflict areas there will be little support for violence from local elites, violence specialists, or from the central state.

The theory also explains when both extended violent conflicts and episodes of postconflict violence are likely to occur. In contexts where groups believe that violence works as a strategy for accumulation, levels of postconflict violence tend to rise when there are changes to the perceived costs or benefits of using violence or when other opportunities for accumulation that do not require violence diminish. Postconflict violence often increases when it is expected that there will be an increase or decrease in the level of resources that can be captured, when there are expected changes to who will control resources, or when it is expected that the rules of the game governing access to resources or power are about to change.

STUDYING POSTCONFLICT VIOLENCE
Approaches and Methods

Studying postconflict violence is a recent enterprise. After an earlier focus on understanding why countries go to war with each other, researchers turned their attention to forms of violence internal to states. The second half of the twentieth century saw the production of vast shelves of books, articles, and policy papers seeking to explain why civil wars, rebellions, and more localized episodic violence such as ethnic riots occur. But it was only as that most deadly of centuries drew to a close that scholars started to pay serious attention to the violence that can emerge after the formal end of extended intrastate violent conflicts.

This new focus was driven primarily by policy concerns. From the end of the Cold War, international groups—United Nations agencies, regional bodies such as the European Union, international financial institutions, international NGOs, and foreign militaries and diplomats—started to play an ever-expanding role mediating peace agreements and providing financial and technical support to their implementation. Yet this growth in policy ambition was matched by a growing realization that many peace settlements fail and that even where wars are brought to an end violence can continue and even increase in their aftermath. New puzzles started to capture researchers' imaginations: Why do some civil wars recur while others do not? Why are some war-to-peace transitions largely peaceful while others are marked by violence? What types of policies are most likely to lead to the consolidation of peace in places scarred by previous extended violence?

This chapter and the next assess this new and growing literature on the causes of postconflict violence. In chapter 2, I consider the findings of various studies and the arguments and theoretical claims they make. But before doing so I will examine the methodological and analytic approaches that have been employed to date. Unfortunately, these have often not been well suited for providing a deeper understanding of why postconflict violence occurs with frequency in some places and not in others.

Previous Approaches to Studying Postconflict Violence and Their Limitations

Researchers of postconflict violence have tended to follow one of two paths. The first group of explorers, made up of economists and quantitatively oriented political scientists, has focused on explaining why civil wars recur in some countries and not in others after peace settlements or military victories. Large-n cross-country datasets, which code countries as being either in civil war or at peace, are used with a range of environmental factors (such as the type of war; how it ended; political, economic, and social structures; and geographic characteristics) employed as explanatory variables to test. Econometric analyses isolate the correlates of renewed civil war, and case material is sometimes used to show how such factors are indeed causing renewed civil war, although this is not always deemed necessary. The focus has been to develop and test parsimonious explanations that account for a significant share of the variance in the likelihood of civil war recidivism.[1]

The second group, a diverse mix of social scientists (qualitative political scientists, sociologists, historians, anthropologists) and lay researchers (journalists, policy analysts, development practitioners), have taken a different approach. Arguing that each country needs to be understood on its own terms, researchers have provided in-depth examinations of peace processes and postconflict transitions, seeking to identify what went wrong or, less frequently, why the war-to-peace transition was successful. Where such pieces are gathered together in edited volumes, introductory or concluding chapters draw out commonalities and differences, although the ambition to use the cases to develop or test any theory is usually limited.[2] Postconflict contexts are seen to be exceptionally complex and the search for regularities may be fruitless. As Berdal, in his concluding reflections to one recent volume of case studies, writes:

> Post-war environments do display common features and this has naturally stimulated work on more general studies or "approaches" aimed at explaining post-war violence. While these have undeniably provided valuable insights, bringing to the fore new and potentially significant

points of analytical emphasis, the case material collected here makes it clear that *the heuristic value of such general theories is often limited and problematic.*[3]

Despite the differences in approach, most researchers in both traditions have tended to share a number of problematic assumptions.

The Unit of Analysis

Almost five decades ago, Przeworski and Teune noted that comparative analysis does not require comparisons between countries. Rather, the choice of the unit of analysis (the state, the region, the village, the household) should depend on "an a priori assumption about the level of social systems at which the important factors operate."[4]

Scholars of violence have taken heed. Snyder's assertion that "subnational units of analysis play an increasingly important role in comparative politics"[5] certainly applies to the study of violence. Blattman and Miguel in their summary of advances in understanding civil war argue that "the most promising avenue for empirical work is on the subnational scale."[6] Others have reached similar conclusions when studying different forms of violence. Varshney and Wilkinson, for example, look at how local factors lead to variations in ethnic rioting in India, while Straus assesses sources of local variation in genocidal violence in Rwanda.[7] Econometric papers have also increasingly employed subnational data to assess sources of within-country variation in violence.[8]

However, the study of postconflict areas has not followed this trend in violence research or comparative political science. Case-based and large-n studies have overwhelmingly used countries as the unit of analysis with both the outcome to be explained (the presence of postconflict violence) and the factors or mechanisms that explain it measured at the national level. Sorpong Peou thus talks of Cambodia's postwar violence and situates his explanation of it in the fragility of national democratic institutions;[9] Collier, Hoeffler, and Soderbom identify issues such as the presence or absence of national elections and national levels of economic development as the reasons why some countries see renewed civil war while others do not.[10]

This is problematic for two reasons: first, extended violent conflicts tend only to affect some areas of countries; and, second, postconflict violence usually varies in incidence and form within these areas. This variation means that factors or mechanisms at the subnational level must be important.

The majority of civil wars and other extended violent conflicts do not affect all areas of a country. Even in such national civil wars, where groups fight over control of the central state, many areas of a country will be only minimally affected.

Until recent years, northern areas of Afghanistan were relatively untouched by violence.[11] Providing a catalogue of examples across countries as diverse as Spain in the 1930s, Vietnam in the 1960s, and Yugoslavia in the 1990s, Kalyvas persuasively shows that civil war violence, as opposed to civil war presence, is a localized phenomenon.[12]

Furthermore, subnational extended violent conflicts, which include secessionist insurgencies and localized extended intercommunal violence, are at least as frequent as civil wars where combatants aim to control the central organs of the state. Weinstein argues that more than half of all civil wars since 1945 have been national in scope with rebel groups seeking to control the state accounting for 56 percent of all belligerent groups, but this overstates the amount of wars that are truly national.[13] In South and Southeast Asia alone, there have been twenty-six active subnational conflicts affecting ten countries since 1992. Since 1946, such conflicts have killed more than 1.35 million people with almost 100,000 dying between 1999 and 2008. Between 1999 and 2008, subnational conflicts killed more people in Asia than every other form of conflict combined.[14]

In nations affected by such conflicts, violence has little direct impact in large swathes of the country. In Uganda, the Lord's Resistance Army operated in provinces covering 44 percent of the country while other provinces remained untouched by war.[15] Mindanao, the location of a series of secessionist civil wars, accounts for just one-quarter of the Filipino population, but these conflicts have only affected around 6 percent of the national population.[16] The conflict-affected Deep South of Thailand houses less than 3 percent of the country's population,[17] a similar level to the proportion of the UK population that lives in Northern Ireland, which was wracked by decades of unrest.[18]

Similarly, Indonesia's bouts of extended violence have affected just some locales. The province of Aceh, which saw three decades of civil war, includes less than 2 percent of Indonesia's population. Aside from a single terrorist attack on the Jakarta stock exchange building in September 2000, Indonesians in other parts of the country saw little impact from the civil war, one reason why it took so long for a conflict resolution process to emerge. Indonesia's intercommunal extended violent conflicts were also concentrated in a relatively small number of areas, with fifteen districts and cities, containing just 6.5 percent of Indonesia's population, experiencing 85.5 percent of all deaths from communal violence between 1990 and 2003 according to one count.[19] Describing Uganda, the Philippines, Thailand, the UK, or Indonesia as being either "in conflict" or "at peace" is not particularly illuminating, for it masks the extreme variation in levels of violence within each country.

Within countries that have experienced extended violent conflicts that have come to an end, there also tends to be marked differences in the incidence of postconflict violence across areas. As I show in chapter 3, there has been significant variation in levels, impacts, and forms of postconflict violence between areas of Indonesia affected by different violent conflicts and, indeed, between areas affected by the same conflict. But this is by no means only the case for Indonesia. One may compare levels of postconflict violence in, say, Bosnia with other postconflict countries and conclude that postconflict Bosnia presents "an encouraging exception" in that it has been largely violence free.[20] Yet such cross-national comparisons draw attention away from the fact that some areas of the country have seen continuing violence while others have not.[21]

The presence of subnational variation in both extended and postconflict violence means that theories of postconflict violence that are built solely on national-level factors are at best insufficient. One issue is methodological and affects all of the large-n cross-country studies. These studies have developed explanations using variables measured at the national level: the strength and characteristics of central state institutions, nationwide levels of poverty, the ethnic makeup of a country, and so on. Yet national measures of mountainous terrain, GDP per capita, or ethnic fractionalization, which are deemed to predict civil war recurrence, may be poor proxies for conditions in the areas that actually experienced civil war.[22] Even if ethnic makeup at the national level co-varies with the likelihood of a country experiencing civil war recurrence, if such diversity is similar in areas of a country that saw renewed violence and those that did not then it cannot be deemed to be causing recurrence. If a large proportion of a country that sees renewed violence is mountainous, but the actual areas that experience new violence are not, then terrain is not a convincing explanation.[23]

Beyond these methodological problems, which can be addressed through the use of better measures,[24] there is a broader point to be made. Logically, national factors cannot be the source of differences in violence within countries. The presence of a set of environmental factors might explain the propensity of a given country to experience extended violence or high levels of postconflict violence within its territory. But it cannot explain why some areas of the country are affected while others are not, for, by definition, national-level factors do not vary across regions of a polity.[25] To understand such local variation, we need to build theories based on factors that differ from area to area. This requires research designs that use disaggregated subnational data, that turn their analytic focus to local factors and mechanisms, and that compare areas within a country.

Forms of Extended Violence

A second assumption is that civil wars are distinct from other forms of extended violent conflict. Past work in the quantitative and case study traditions has focused overwhelmingly on postconflict violence that emerges after the end of civil wars where the central state is one of the warring parties. Little attention, however, has been paid to the violence that can occur after the end of other forms of extended violent conflict, such as long-lasting collective intercommunal violence.[26]

Five of Indonesia's seven recent extended violent conflicts were of this type: violence in Maluku, North Maluku, Central Kalimantan, West Kalimantan, and Central Sulawesi was between population groups rather than between the state and an armed nonstate group. Extended violence in parts of Colombia, Brazil, and South Africa also falls into this category.[27] Insights from the post–civil war literature *may* have applicability to these areas; but the exclusion of areas that experienced extended intercommunal violence from studies means that it has not been possible to determine whether or not this is the case.

Civil war violence is traditionally studied in isolation from other forms of collective political violence, such as long-lasting ethnic riots or pogroms, because it is viewed as distinct in two aspects. It is assumed that the causes of civil war are different from those of other forms of violence. Scacco posits that "the incentive structures and dynamics at work in civil and interstate wars are quite different from those we observe in shorter, more localized but no less deadly episodes of ethnic rioting."[28] Weinstein argues that patterns of, incentives for, and collective actions associated with civil war recruitment differ from mobilization for other forms of violence.[29] Because root causes differ, it is argued that it does not make sense to address both in the same study. It is also assumed that the impacts of civil war are greater than that of other forms of extended violence. Gurr, for example, highlights differences in the scale of destruction, and Varshney notes that civil wars are more likely to affect rural areas whereas ethnic riots are an urban phenomenon.[30] One consequence of viewing civil war and other types of violence as distinct is that the literatures on civil war, ethnic violence, and violent crime have developed independently, with few points of connection.[31]

Yet, as Blattman and Miguel argue in their extensive survey of the civil war literature, "the distinction between civil wars and other types of political instability has been largely assumed rather than demonstrated."[32] Observations of differences in causes and impacts are indeed salient when comparing civil wars with Horowitz's episodic "deadly ethnic riots"[33] or localized forms of smaller-scale violence. However, the differences between civil wars and other forms of escalated enduring violent conflict are less clear. Tilly, for example, argues that the motivations driving other forms of "coordinated destruction" may be similar to those fueling civil wars and treats both civil war and other forms of highly organized violence with large impacts as one type of contention.[34] In a recent special edition of *Perspectives on Politics*, contributors called for the inclusion of a wide range of forms of political violence within the same research studies and agendas to allow for an assessment of the ways in which they are related.[35]

Indeed, the similarities in patterns of violence in areas affected by civil war and those affected by large-scale extended intercommunal violent conflict are often greater than the differences. As the Indonesian cases explored in the book show, extended communal violence, where the state is not a central conflict party, can result in thousands of deaths and have serious impacts on physical, human, and social capital. It can be multiyear in duration, may be spread over a large geographic expanse, and a large share of deaths may be concentrated in rural areas. Levels of organization can be similar to that of armed groups in civil wars. The state is often unable to ensure order for long periods of time and sometimes is involved in backing different factions.

Stathis Kalyvas, who has done more than any other contemporary scholar to highlight the conceptual ambiguities and problematic assumptions in commonly accepted definitions of civil war, notes that nonstate extended violent conflicts can be viewed as being a subset of the broader family of civil wars.[36] In typologizing cases of civil war, he identifies "symmetric non-conventional wars" as one category. These involve irregular armies on both sides battling for control of territory and take place in places where the state has imploded. While he cites failed state examples such as Somalia and the Central African Republic,[37] such wars may also occur in transitioning states, where the state is unable, or unwilling, to impose order. Using Kalyvas's taxonomy, the distinction between secessionist civil wars, such as that which occurred in Aceh or Timor, and the intercommunal wars of other areas of Indonesia is largely related to the degree of asymmetry in fighting capabilities between warring parties.[38]

Excluding areas that saw extended communal violence that does not meet the restricted criteria that many scholars use to define civil war means that it is not possible to analyze the differences (or similarities) between postconflict violence in areas that experienced differing kinds of large-scale intrastate violent conflict. Comparing violence patterns in areas that experienced classically defined civil war and in areas that experienced highly organized enduring intercommunal violence allows for an assessment of whether and how differences in the kinds of extended violence impact on the likelihood of postconflict violence occurring and the forms it takes.

Episodic Postconflict Violence

Past work has focused primarily on identifying why civil war recurs rather than why other forms of episodic postconflict violence occur. Such studies treat civil war as a binary condition: countries are either at war or peace. To be counted as experiencing war, a country must have suffered at least one thousand battle deaths in a given year. If this threshold is not met, the country is recorded as being "peaceful."[39]

This is problematic. Small fluctuations in death totals can provide a misleading picture. A relatively small rise in battle deaths, for example from nine hundred per year to a thousand per year, would result in a country being coded as having gone from peace to war, even though there may be substantively little change on the ground. The difficulty of capturing precisely the number of deaths during wars, particularly in rural areas, means that changes that put a country over (or below) the threshold may be a function of measurement error. This risk is particularly great given that English language news sources, written far from where violence is occurring, are generally used when determining the fatality counts, leading to significant underreporting of levels of violence.[40] The problem is compounded by a lack of clarity, and indeed consistency, in coding procedures.[41]

The use of absolute death totals is also problematic given that countries have very different populations. A conflict that kills less than 1,000 people in a small country may have a far higher per capita impact than one that leads to over 1,000 deaths in a larger state.[42] If we examine impacts at the subnational level (focusing only on affected regions), per capita death tolls can jump significantly and a strong case can be made to categorize conflicts with lower annual death tolls as civil wars. Homicide rates in Thailand's Deep South, for example, have hovered around 30 deaths per 100,000 people per year, close to Afghanistan's national homicide rate of 33.5 between 2007 and 2012.[43] Regression results are also extremely sensitive to the coding of when wars start and end, one reason why different scholars have reached such different conclusions on factors associated with civil war onset.[44]

Beyond these issues, such approaches are not able to solve the book's puzzles for they do not allow for an assessment of *why other forms of postconflict violence occur*. If a dichotomous war/peace distinction is employed, what Suhrke and Berdal call the "peace in between" and Nordstrom terms "not-war-not-peace," where war has not recurred but violence continues, will go undetected and cannot be investigated.[45]

The country case studies help fill this gap by highlighting a range of forms of postconflict violence such as revenge killings,[46] sexual violence,[47] violent gang battles,[48] and violent crime.[49] Yet by focusing on one kind of episodic postconflict violence, we again face the problem that we cannot tell whether or not the drivers of violence differ for different types. Ascertaining this requires more work in developing theoretically and empirically grounded taxonomies of violence and then carefully comparing the causal processes behind each type. There have been few attempts to systematically typologize forms of postconflict violence and even fewer attempts to use such distinctions to assess variation across countries or areas.

Explaining Variation

A final issue affects much of the case study work. Where studies have considered episodic postconflict violence, methodological strategies have usually not been used that carefully match areas with differing patterns of violence. Studies have typically not compared "successful cases" (where postconflict areas have seen little violence) with cases where violence reemerged.

Without such variation in outcomes, it is difficult to determine whether factors identified as being associated with violence, or a lack of it, are actually causing violence or peace. Suppose X represents violence and Y represents its absence. Many explanations of violence have taken the following form: if (a) high levels of migration, (b) income differences between ethnic or religious communities, and (c) poor governance are present in X, they have been treated as the causes of violence. Methodological discussions inspired by King, Keohane, and Verba have shown the limitations of this kind of causal reasoning.[50] Factors (a), (b), and (c) may "cause" X if one can show that they are *not* present in Y. But if (a), (b), and (c) are present in both X and Y, then something else is leading to the divergence.[51] Studying appropriately chosen cases that vary along the spectrum of postconflict violence is important to tease out the contribution of different factors to different outcomes.

Concepts

In seeking to understand and explain postconflict violence, I make a number of conceptual distinctions. First, I differentiate violent from nonviolent contention. Second, I distinguish extended violent conflict from postconflict periods. Finally, I disaggregate the forms of violence that can occur in the postconflict period.

Conflict, Crime, and Violence

The focus of this book is to explain why postconflict violence occurs (or does not) rather than why some areas see postconflict tensions that do not take violent form. Peaceful conflicts are essential features of functioning societies, economies, and polities across the world.[52] In areas emerging from extended violence, too, nonviolent conflict may play a productive role. Moving toward consolidated peace requires transforming the economic and political structures and distri-butions of power that gave rise to earlier violence and which often solidified during periods of extended violence. Such transitions often create tensions with groups who benefited from past violence rejecting change; but the presence of tensions may be a sign that postconflict transformation is indeed occurring. Lev-els of postconflict tensions are hence not a good measure of the extent to which peace is consolidating. The challenge for policymakers is not to limit conflict and tensions but to ensure that they do not erupt into violence. In ascertaining the strength or fragility of a postconflict environment, violence is a better, although by no means perfect, measure than nonviolent conflict.

I use postconflict violence as my outcome measure. I define violence as any incident between individuals or groups (including the state) that results in direct physical impacts such as deaths, injuries, rapes, or the destruction of property. There are a number of elements of this.

First, I focus solely on violence that has observable physical effects and hence do not include what Galtung has influentially termed "structural violence."[53] Sec-ond, I include not only violence involving groups but also that between individu-als. Researchers have generally differentiated collective and individual violence, sometimes calling the former violent conflict and the latter violent crime. While violent conflicts involve an incompatibility of interests between groups, violent crime is viewed as being driven by private motives. As such, it is assumed that violent conflict and violent crime have different causes. Yet this dichotomy has considerable conceptual weaknesses. Using the presence of a group actor as a proxy for violent conflict (as opposed to violent crime) is problematic because it conflates the parties directly involved in the violent incident with the nature of the contestation that underlies the violence. Violent incidents between indi-viduals are often manifestations of deeper underlying contention. Incidents of violence involving only individuals often stem from deeper-rooted intergroup struggles over material or psychological resources.

Table 2 sets out the logic. Incidents of violence can be differentiated not only by the parties directly involved in the act but also by the nature of the cleavage that underpins it. The bottom-right quadrant contains an example of what is commonly thought of as collective violent conflict: the violence involves groups and violence is driven by intergroup contestation. Yet incidents in the top-right quadrant are also motivated by intergroup differences, even though individuals participate in the unrest. In postconflict contexts, where tensions between groups tend to be high, such incidents can be common. Excluding such incidents from any study of postconflict violence risks biasing analyses.

The types of incidents set out in the two left-hand quadrants are typically thought of as crime. Yet in practice, determining whether an incident fits in the

TABLE 2. Different forms of violence

		CLEAVAGES UNDERPINNING VIOLENCE	
		INTERPERSONAL	GROUP
Parties involved in the violent incident	Individual participants on both sides	Two people fight over a debt = individual expression of interpersonal incompatibility	A local kills a migrant = individual expression of a group conflict
	Multiple participants on at least one side	Individual hires thugs to beat another individual = conflict or criminal act committed by a group	Interethnic riot = mass expression of group conflict

left- or the right-hand column can be difficult because it requires information that identifies the motives driving a particular incident of violence. This is often hard to obtain. Violence is often fueled by a combination of private and group-based motives, ranging from pecuniary interests to efforts to protect a group's cultural heritage or political position.

Because of this, I include incidents typically thought of as violent conflict and those thought of as violent crime in my primary outcome measure: postconflict violence. As discussed later, I do attempt to distinguish between the two, based on an interpretative reading of the extent to which a preexisting cleavage is used as a justification for the violent act: where such a cleavage is implicated, the incident is coded as being violent conflict; where it is not, the incident is coded as violent crime. Yet the difficulty in establishing this with any precision means that for general purposes a more encompassing category (postconflict violence) has greater utility. And, as I discuss below, there are other more theoretically and practically useful ways to disaggregate postconflict violence than to distinguish between conflict and crime.

The Extended Violent Conflict and Postconflict Periods

Studying postconflict violence requires determining when a given conflict period ends and hence when the postconflict period begins. One way to do this is to look at when a prominent event such as a declared military victory or a signed peace accord occurred with the postconflict period starting at this point. Yet as the experiences of Iraq and Afghanistan illustrate all too clearly, these points do not always coincide with a major change in the dynamics of violence. Instead, I define the violent conflict and postconflict periods by the prominent types of

violence that occur in each. The *violent conflict period* is when extended violence occurs, which may take the form of civil war (armed battles for control of
the central state or for territory within the state) or extended communal violent
conflict (large-scale collective violence between communal groups that endures
over a long period). During the extended violence period, large-scale violence
with large physical impacts is ongoing with violent incidents, framed as part of a
master conflict narrative, occurring frequently. The *postconflict period* is defined
as the time after large-scale extended violence has ended.

Two issues require discussion. First, conflict (and indeed violence) may continue in the postconflict period. As Suhrke has observed, "Taken literally, 'postconflict violence' is an oxymoron."[54] Indeed, this book shows how pervasive
violence can be in some "postconflict" areas. Yet such violence differs from that
which occurs in periods of extended violence. While underlying drivers and the
actors involved may remain the same, although not necessarily so, incidents of
violence tend to be *episodic*, lasting for shorter periods of time. Impacts are usually (although not always) lower per incident, the nature of organization of violence tends to be different, and there are longer gaps between sets of incidents.[55]
Extended violence, in either its civil war or extended communal violence forms,
may reemerge during postconflict periods. But when this happens, as in Iraq, it
no longer makes sense to call such places "postconflict." I thus define postconflict
violence as the episodic violence that occurs in areas emerging from extended
violence where extended violence has not restarted.

A second issue relates to the length of time for which an area can be viewed
as being postconflict. Strictly speaking, anywhere that has ever experienced extended violence is postconflict. Yet such a conceptualization has little practical
utility. Using this definition, all societies where large-scale extended violence is
not ongoing are postconflict—that is, the vast majority of places.[56] A more useful
definition puts temporal bounds on the postconflict period. Collier and Hoeffler's ten-year period, the time they argue when places are particularly prone to
the reemergence of extended violence,[57] makes as much sense as any, although it
should be noted that the remnants of war (and its associated risks) can endure
long beyond this. The earliest of Indonesia's postauthoritarian extended violent
conflicts (in West Kalimantan) ended in April 1999, the latest (in Aceh) in 2005.
The postconflict periods analyzed in this book are between seven and thirteen
years in length.

Types of Postconflict Violence

Postconflict violence may be classified in a number of ways. One option is to
separate out incidents that appear to be driven by different *issues*. Such an approach may, for example, distinguish postconflict violent incidents over land

from those that relate to political competition and those where identity issues appear to be more important. Another approach is to differentiate incidents by the *actors* involved in incidents of postconflict violence. Thus state-inflicted violence can be separated from that instigated by civilians or violence committed by former combatants. A third approach is to differentiate incidents by the *motives* of those involved with those driven by greed distinguished from those that seek to address grievances.

In general scholars and practitioners have tended to include issues, actors, and motives in their typologies of postconflict violence. Muggah, for example, includes elements of all three in developing a taxonomy of five types of post-conflict violence: political violence, routine state-led violence, economic and crime-related violence, community and informal justice, and property-related disputes.[58] The World Bank's 2011 World Development Report distinguishes between local intergroup conflict, "conventional" political conflict, gang violence, organized crime and trafficking-related violence, and local conflicts with transnational ideological connections.[59] Other classifications of violence differentiate types using more than one of the three factors. Horowitz and Sambanis, for example, distinguish between ethnic and nonethnic violence.[60] This classification is built on both actors (ethnic groups and groups which have their basis in another form of identity) and issues (relating to intergroup ethnic differences).

Such typologies have a number of weaknesses. One issue is that the categories are not mutually exclusive. Muggah's property disputes, for example, could be driven by political or criminal motives; the World Bank's gang violence may be identifiable by the involvement of criminal groups, but the actions of gangs may be driven by local intergroup tensions or, indeed, by the inflow of money from political parties or leaders. The typologies are also not exhaustive. Where, for example, does nonroutine state-led violence fit within Muggah's classificatory schema? Under which category of the World Bank's typology would nonlocal intergroup conflicts fall? The lack of obvious discrete rules for assigning an episode of violence to a type means that different analysts may choose to place different incidents in different categories, leading to different findings. This is a result of trying to use too many variables to distinguish cases.

Ultimately the heuristic value of typologies lies in their ability to parsimoniously identify the *key* elements of a given phenomenon that vary across types. In ascertaining which elements are of most importance, and hence which should be used to classify postconflict violence (or, indeed, any other outcome variable), one must assess which aspects of a phenomenon are most important in determining why important causal variables have differential effects. Different types, in other words, should be identified based on differing casual processes; the greater the difference between causal processes across types, and concomitantly the greater similarity in causal processes underlying incidents within types, the more useful the typology is.

In constructing a simple typology of postconflict violence I follow Tilly's argument that more important than motives, actors, or issues is the level of damage caused by an incident and the degree of organization that underlies it.[61] The next chapter makes the case for this. I argue that incidents of postconflict violence that result in greater human and physical impacts tend to have a higher level of organization, with larger groups usually involved and elites orchestrating the violence; I argue that the factors that explain smaller (less destructive) and larger (more destructive) incidents of postconflict violence differ to a large extent. As such, I differentiate incidents of postconflict violence with large impacts—defined as those leading to three or more deaths, ten or more injuries, or fifteen or more damaged properties—from those with smaller impacts.[62]

Other things such as issues (what the violence was ostensibly about) and the form of violence (the way in which it was expressed) are also important. But, at a deep level the causes of violent incidents driven by contestation over say land or ethnic animosity tend to be more similar than the causes of incidents that result in large-scale or smaller-scale damage.

Based on these distinctions, table 3 presents the taxonomy of violence used throughout the book.

I aim to identify and explain differing patterns of episodic violence—in both aggregate levels and in levels of the two "types": larger-scale and smaller-scale—in

TABLE 3. A taxonomy of violence

DIMENSION	EXTENDED VIOLENCE (CONFLICT PERIOD)	EPISODIC VIOLENCE (POSTCONFLICT PERIOD)	
	I. CIVIL WARS/EXTENDED COMMUNAL VIOLENCE	II. LARGE-SCALE EPISODIC VIOLENCE	III. SMALL-SCALE EPISODIC VIOLENCE
Common forms	Civil wars, extended interethnic violence	Riots, large group clashes, terror attacks, large one-way attacks	Violent crime, vigilantism, small-scale groups clashes
Level of destruction	Very high	High per incident	Low per incident
Organization of violence	Highly organized groups on both sides	Usually show a high degree of organization	Usually little organization
Duration	Long, usually multiple years	Short per incident	Short per incident
Geographic concentration	Over wider areas (although some areas less affected)	Concentrated	Concentrated

areas that experienced extended violence. Comparisons of areas with high and low levels of postconflict violence (type II plus type III) can help us identify the factors that lead to such divergence. Comparisons between areas experiencing larger-scale episodic postconflict violence (type II) and those seeing small-scale incidents (type III) can illuminate the extent and the ways in which the causes of the two are similar or differ.

Methods

Using Different Research Methods to Understand Postconflict Violence

Both quantitative and qualitative approaches have advantages and limitations when used to understand postconflict violence. Large-n datasets typically allow for two kinds of analyses: identification of broad patterns and trends and establishment of correlations between independent and dependent variables. Econometric work has greatly added to our knowledge on postconflict violence, for example by identifying factors that coexist with the recurrence of civil war. This can help policymakers ascertain the risk that a country or an area with a certain set of structural characteristics will see renewed fighting.

Econometric work alone, however, is rarely able to supply fully satisfying causal explanations for why postconflict violence occurs. Quantitative analyses can rarely move beyond giving us a good assessment of causal effects (what is the effect of X on Y?), to an understanding of causal mechanisms (*how* and *why* did X cause, or lead to, Y?)[63]

One problem is that there are generally multiple observationally equivalent pathways through which a purported causal variable may shape the outcome variable, that is, the presence of violence. Kalyvas, in his review of papers on the Maoist insurgency in Nepal, considers the common finding that poverty is correlated with high levels of fatalities. While there does appear to be a robust correlation between the two, it is unclear why this is the case:

> It may be, for instance, that insurgents recruit poor individuals who join to seek justice (the "grievance theory" of civil war); or that individuals in poor areas (which is not the same as saying poor individuals) see joining as a job in places where job opportunities are nonexistent (the "greed theory" of civil war); or that the government invests more resources to prevent the conflict in wealthier areas which is why the conflict is "fully expressed" in the rural countryside; or that the opportunity

costs of violence are lower for the state in poor areas; or that people in poor areas may be less able to protect themselves from violence, including its "collateral damage" dimension.[64]

Of the three papers he assesses, only one recognized the different possible ways in which poverty and violence might be linked but it was unable to distinguish between them.

Understanding these links, or the processes by which causal variables impact outcomes, is of great importance for policymakers. The various possible pathways linking poverty to violence that Kalyvas identifies each have different implications for those seeking to reduce violence. If the link is a grievance-based mechanism, policymakers should invest in building institutions to deliver redistributive or retributive justice. If the link is a greed-based mechanism, efforts should focus on providing licit employment opportunities and boosting the local economy. Applied social scientists should seek not only to provide evidence of the factors associated with violence but also develop logically sound but empirically grounded theories that show the causal mechanisms through which these factors have an impact.[65]

Qualitative historical case study work has considerable comparative advantages when trying to understand such processes or mechanisms. Tracing a case over time can help identity how and why causal factors actually produced an outcome; in so doing, it can help refine a previously hypothesized mechanism or identify new mechanisms that link cause and effect.[66] Process tracing also allows for a deeper consideration of how agency and contingency works in producing violence. Econometric studies tend to measure a set of structural factors (be they economic, social, political, or geographic) and to assess how these co-vary with levels of violence. Yet, ultimately, structures do not directly produce violence. Violence is undertaken by people: it is men (sometimes women) who kill and maim each other. Structures may shape their motives, interests, beliefs, and opportunities, but they do not directly inflict violence.

Many scholars have made the case that future advances in understanding the causes of violence will be built on generating a deeper understanding of its microfoundations—why individuals choose to rebel or take part in violence or not—and I fully agree.[67] Approaches that look to the local level are more likely to be able to discover how such agency functions and how local structures create or constrain it. Process tracing can help identify the ways in which, for a given case, structures shape the choices of individuals, and how this then leads to violence or to nonviolent interaction.[68] Well-constructed case studies can be used to develop causal stories (or theories) that outline how and why the presence of a set of conditions makes postconflict violence more or less likely in a given place. I follow

Tilly's proposal for comparative politics to focus on lower levels of analysis and on identifying microlevel processes that contribute to outcomes.[69]

One limitation of developing or testing theory using only case methods is that it is difficult when studying a single case to establish that a factor or mechanism deemed to cause violence actually has a causal rather than spurious relationship; it is necessary to also establish that the identified factor or mechanism is absent in a comparable case where violence did not erupt. For understanding postconflict violence, this means comparing areas where violence has frequently erupted with areas where it has not.

It is also difficult to know how representative cases studies are. Different areas, and different incidents of violence, may have idiosyncrasies that can lead the analyst away from identifying common causal processes. Quantitative methods can be used to test whether the causal factors and mechanisms identified are also evident in other places. Combining the insights from, and comparative advantages of, both quantitative and qualitative methods is preferable when trying to understand violence.

Quantitative Data: The National Violence Monitoring System

The book draws extensively on a new dataset of incidents of violence in Indonesia.[70] The version of the National Violence Monitoring System (NVMS) dataset used in this book contains information on violence in sixteen Indonesian provinces, including all of those that experienced extended violent conflict, with reports primarily coming from local newspapers. The dataset, which covers the 1998 to 2012 period, contains 158,363 discreet incidents of violence: 40,176 incidents of violent conflict, 96,387 incidents of violent crime, 14,299 incidents of domestic violence, and 7,510 incidents of violence by security forces. Almost 50,000 of these incidents occurred in the six provinces that experienced extended violent conflict that are the focus of this book. The NVMS is the largest dataset of violence created for any country.[71]

For each incident, a series of variables were coded, including when and where it took place, its physical impacts, the actors involved, the issue that appeared to drive the violence, the form violence took, the weapons used, and what interventions were made to try to stop escalation and how successful they were. The dataset allows for a disaggregated analysis of patterns of violence in different areas over time.

I use the new data in three ways: to map incidents of violence in both the extended violence and postconflict periods for each of Indonesia's postconflict provinces; to select case studies for deeper investigation; and to generate descriptive statistics that are used throughout the book to illustrate elements of the cases and the extent to which findings are representative of a larger set of cases.

District Case Studies

Six district case studies in three Indonesian provinces were chosen for deeper study.[72] Each experienced extended violent conflict that came to an end—two saw civil war, four extended communal violence. Yet levels and types of post-conflict violence vary across districts. Comparing districts that had similar experiences of large-scale extended violence, but that have seen very different postconflict trajectories, can help to identify what has caused such divergence.

I gathered two distinct types of data for each of the district cases. Information was collected on a range of issues that I hypothesized at the outset of the study could impact on the likelihood of postconflict violence occurring. My reading of the literatures on postconflict violence helped identify some areas where I should focus, such as how elites reached bargains, the role of the security forces, and the ways in which patronage networks function, and previous experience researching violence in Indonesia provided some ideas on issues that might be of importance. However, as I became more familiar with the district cases, new issues emerged. Subsequent rounds of research were able to focus in greater depth on a more limited set of issues than initial field trips, which involved surveying a much wider range of topics. The theory built in this book thus relies on both deductive and inductive reasoning. The former led to initial hypotheses; but these hypotheses were iteratively amended as I became more familiar with the cases allowing for deeper theory development.

In each case district, I also selected a number of incidents where violence either erupted or where tensions were present but violence was averted. Some were identified through the NVMS; others were the result of tips from people I met in the regions. I process-traced each of these incidents building up a historical story of events. These incident-level case studies were particularly useful for identifying the role of different actors in producing violence and are incorporated within chapters 4–6.

I meld the two types of material into analytic narratives focusing largely on the postconflict period for each district. These narratives combine stories (of incidents of violence, of attempts at conflict resolution, of people's and groups' actions) with analysis of why events turned out the way they did. They weave together empirical and theoretical materials, looking at the extent to which actual events conform or not to the suppositions of theory.[73] The book's case chapters are narrated in a way that combines "stylized facts" with Geertz's "thick description," with the text interweaving facts and analysis.[74]

Building the cases involved a process of "soaking and poking."[75] This required time in the field. The case studies are primarily built on fieldwork conducted in each district and provincial capitals. Around three hundred people, including government officials, journalists, (former) rebels, conflict leaders and foot soldiers, civil society activists, police and military men, traditional leaders, rural villagers, men and women, were interviewed. Interviews were conducted with Muslims, Christians, those who had supported secessionist groups, and those of conflicting ethnic groups. Some had been involved in violent action, some in trying to stop it, others had been on the receiving end. In addition, dozens of informal discussions—in taxis, on the roof of boats, and on the back of motorbikes; in coffee houses and the sitting rooms of friends' houses; in government offices, waiting rooms, and hotel lobbies—gave me a better sense of local conditions. The district case studies also draw on a range of secondary sources, including past writings on conflict in the regions I studied. Most of these studies focus on the years when violence was at its peak rather than more recent developments. But the availability of careful historical accounts of the chronology of the extended violent conflicts provided important background information to help me interpret patterns of postconflict violence.

Generating a National Narrative

While the core empirical chapters concentrate on provincial and district-level dynamics, the penultimate chapter of the book focuses on the evolution of central state elite bargains and institutions. Understanding this required generating a historical national-level analytic narrative. My analytic approach in the chapter is similar to that employed in the chapters on Maluku, North Maluku, and Aceh provinces. However, given the relatively rich body of material already published on national political change, the chapter primarily uses secondary sources rather than newly collected primary information.

In the next chapter, I turn the focus from methods to the causal claims made in the existing literature. I build on these to develop a theory of why postconflict violence occurs and takes the forms it does. Subsequent chapters then test and develop the theory by examining different postconflict areas of Indonesia.

EXPLAINING POSTCONFLICT VIOLENCE
Evidence, Theories, and Arguments

Previous studies have identified three sets of issues that lead to postconflict violence: failed elite bargains, the impact of past violence on societal relations, and weak state capacity or inappropriate state structures. Each provides insights, but no existing theory can adequately explain why postconflict violence occurs—in Indonesia or elsewhere. In focusing on the role of only one set of actors—elites, groups within society, or the state—previous theories have failed to recognize that violence is coproduced, that in most instances no single group has the agency to instigate violence alone. A singular focus on elites, society, or the state also limits our ability to explain why postconflict violence takes *different forms*, for different actors are important to varying degrees in producing different types of postconflict violence. A useful theory of postconflict violence must consider all three sets of actors, specify how their attitudes and actions interact with those of others, and how this produces or limits different types of postconflict violence.

The first half of this chapter surveys the existing literature, noting contributions, limitations, and proposing extensions. The chapter then builds on this to develop a new theory that can help us understand, first, why postconflict violence occurs (or does not) and, second, why it sometimes escalates into larger, more destructive forms.

Alternative Frameworks for Understanding Postconflict Violence

Elite Bargains

A first body of work sees the sources of postconflict violence in the difficulties that former belligerent leaders have in finding and sustaining agreements whereby both sides agree to renounce violence. While we might expect such bargains to be frequently reached and maintained—war, after all, is destructive and risky—in practice bargains are often illusive or weak with the result that violence continues or recurs after periods of calm.[1]

Bargaining theorists have two explanations for the failure of agreements to be reached or stick.[2] The first is information asymmetries. Each party has private information on their side's ability and willingness to use violence that is not shared with their opponents. In the absence of accurate information on the other side either party may choose to use violence. Where past extended violent conflicts endured for longer, it is argued that the relative capabilities of each side should be clearer and hence bargains should be easier to reach and maintain.[3] Cross-country studies have found a relationship between the duration of violence and the likelihood of civil war not recurring.[4]

Second, parties can have difficulties in credibly committing to settlements. Renouncing violence creates vulnerabilities for former conflict leaders. In an environment where trust is lacking, actions to disband can be suicidal, *even* where both sides would prefer that violence ceased. A leader of a conflicting group can see the benefits of peace and may want to agree to give up arms. However, a positive payoff from committing to a cessation of violence is contingent on his former adversary also taking similar substantive actions. In the absence of an arbiter-enforcer, such as the state or a strong third party, this can result in a "security dilemma" with elites on both sides choosing to retain their coercive apparatuses and continuing to use violence to signal strength.[5] Researchers have emphasized the importance of third-party guarantees that can help reduce the uncertainty former conflicting parties have in committing to peace.[6] How the violence was ended is also deemed to be important. Where extended violence ceases because of a military victory, a single party can impose the terms of peace, which will usually include the demobilization of the losing party. This removes both information asymmetry and commitment problems making postconflict violence less likely.[7]

Bargaining theories thus view postconflict violence as occurring because of the failure of peace settlements to stick, which is a result of the actions of elites. Violence emerges when the leaders of one or both sides think that their old adversaries will renege on the terms of the settlement, for example, to dispose of their arms or to share power.[8] Because leaders do not trust each other, violence can recur where there are not effective mechanisms to ensure contract enforcement. Postconflict violence is deemed to be a product of fear and a lack of trust and the information gaps that drive these.

However, there are limits to the ability of bargaining models to explain why some forms of postconflict violence occur. The first is that elites may not wish to cease using violence not because of fear or a lack of information but because violence may be profitable. The bargaining literature assumes that renouncing violence is the optimal outcome for a previously warring party, contingent on the other side also doing the same. Because violence destroys multiple forms of capital, the resources available will be larger in its absence. Yet this is often not the case. The development of wartime economies can mean that violence can be very profitable for those who organize it.[9] Large-scale violence creates space for rent-making activities, including the provision of protection, the monopolization of economic sectors (licit or illicit), and trade in drugs or minerals. This can create predatory motives that, over time, may become more important drivers of conflict than the grievances or ideologies that led to initial unrest.[10] David Keen thus reaches a different conclusion to many of the bargaining theorists, arguing that "the longer a civil war, the more likely that people will find ways to profit from it."[11] This makes it harder to bring such wars to an end or to ensure they do not recur after periods of calm.

Even where elites accept that they are better off without extended violence, either because of the costs incurred or because of the material benefits provided as part of a peace settlement, they may see continued utility in using other forms of violence. Episodic violence, or the threat of it, can be used to affect decisions over the allocation of resources and rent-making opportunities. Riots may be instigated to demonstrate enduring coercive capacity to those who make decisions on how public funds are used. Attacks, or threats of them, can be used to ensure that former conflict elites and their underlings receive state or donor largess. Violence may be used to consolidate ethnic or religious support bases for political reasons. Wilkinson, investigating the causes of ethnic riots in India, argues that they are provoked by local politicians who use them to enhance their chances of election. Riots, he argues, "are best thought of as a solution to the problem of how to change the salience of ethnic issues and identities among the electorate in order to build a winning political coalition."[12] This can lead to what Brass has called "institutionalised riot systems," controlled by local politicians and elites, which allow small events, such as neighborly quarrels, to develop into larger episodes of violence such as communal riots.[13] Such instrumental uses of violence for political gain are also common elsewhere.[14]

Episodic postconflict violence can also be employed to increase the size of the resource pie. This can work for a simple reason: violence attracts peace-building and reconstruction funds. These resources, often massive in scale compared with the size of local economies, can be a boon for former conflict leaders. In a post-conflict context, large-scale incidents of violence can send a signal that tensions remain, and this may be an effective means of attracting further funds from the government or international donors, money that can then be captured by former conflict leaders and other elites.

Bargaining theories also do not explain why supposed adversaries some-times collaborate in producing violence. Civil wars, as Staniland has usefully ob-served in his work on wartime political orders, are not always best understood as a "straightforward struggle [between the warring sides] for a monopoly of violence."[15] Indeed, many accounts of extended violent conflicts are replete with examples of warring factions working together, in particular when economic interests are at stake. Andreas, for example, describes how Serbs, Croats, and Bos-niaks in Sarajevo collaborated to profit from the smuggling of goods and people:

> While the Bosnian Serb leadership played the front-stage role of or-chestrating the siege of the city under the official balancing of ethnic grievance and animosity, backstage they profited from the siege through clandestine business dealings that included cross-ethnic economic ex-change across the frontlines. Similarly, some of the city's key defenders played the formal role of repelling Serb military incursions while also engaging in illicit trading with their counterparts.[16]

Political and military elites and businessmen from all sides would meet in a bar to make their deals. The vast profits that could be made created incentives to prolong the violence, one reason why the siege of Sarajevo lasted so long.

Such bargains sometimes involve the toleration of certain kinds of violence but not of others. Rules of the game emerge regulating acceptable "wartime" behavior. In Sarajevo, for example:

> It was against the rules for the besiegers to shell public places where large groups of people gathered (such as breadlines and marketplaces), but it was within the rules to shell the rest of the city and terrorize civil-ians with sniper fire (the former had a greater media shock effect, and thus could provoke NATO air strikes, while the latter prompted only routine international condemnation).[17]

As in times of extended violence, postconflict areas also vary in the levels and types of collaboration between former adversaries. Postconflict violence can be the result of a tacit agreement between former conflicting parties whereby vio-lence is, at a minimum, accepted, or at extremes, even coproduced. A sustained absence of violence following a peace settlement will tend to lead to a decrease in levels of postconflict funding. To avoid this, formerly warring leaders may in cases agree to violence of certain types continuing. Tolerating the use of violence by others can legitimize its use by oneself.

The bargaining literature points us to the importance of the security dilemma as wars come to an end. This may lead to violence in some cases but such violence is more likely to take the form of continuing or recurring extended violent conflict than episodic violence. In many places, postconflict violence will not be the result of fear and mistrust but will be employed opportunistically for material gain, and may involve collaboration between elites who were ostensibly on opposite sides of the extended violent conflict.

Society

A second approach focuses on the structures of postconflict societies and how these lead to violence. The roots of postconflict violence are viewed as lying in the motivations of individuals or groups within society rather than elites.

One focus is on the impact of extended violent conflict on group identities and intergroup relations and the extent to which new, less divisive identities can be forged in its aftermath. Large-scale violence often essentializes identities that previously played a more limited role in structuring social, political, and economic life; ethnic identity, for example, is often a product of war and state failure rather than a cause of it.[18] Extended violence, in creating or strengthening a commonly shared master narrative that simplifies group boundaries and patterns of interaction, can reify divisive identity categories that then sustain into the postconflict period, making future conflict and violence more likely. This, it is argued, tends to be particularly common following ethnic conflicts.[19] By extension, ethnically divided societies emerging from extended violence are deemed by some to be more prone to postconflict violence than those where group differences are constructed around other axes.

What is needed to overcome this are crosscutting ties. Varshney, in his study of Indian cities, found that where civic associational structures that cut across identity divides are present, riots are less likely.[20] International donors frequently fund peace-building activities in areas emerging from conflict that seek to build relationships between people across old conflict divides. Others have emphasized the importance of "reconciliation" activities that help forge new, less divisive identities. What reconciliation means will differ from context to context. But it requires, as Bräuchler argues in her study of postconflict Maluku, "(re)creating symbols, narratives, and rituals that enable former enemies to distance themselves from the past and imagine themselves as a unity."[21] In postconflict contexts, it can be expected that violence will be less common where such cross-identity group institutions and organizations exist and where effective reconciliation activities have been pursued.

The extent to which grievances are redressed may also affect levels of postconflict violence. Early work on the determinants of civil war and rebellion emphasized intergroup economic and social disparities as a source of unrest.[22] Using a cross-country dataset on horizontal inequalities, Cederman, Weidmann, and Gleditsch show that distributional asymmetries are strongly linked to civil war onset,[23] and other forms of violence are also more likely to occur where intergroup inequalities are marked.[24] Where the peace settlement or postconflict policies do not address the underlying issues and grievances that led to the extended violence, postconflict violence should be more likely. Indeed, this logic underpins many of the common responses of the international community in postconflict areas. Truth and reconciliation commissions and other transitional justice mechanisms aim to deal with past wrongdoing to ensure grievances do not reemerge.[25] Postconflict growth, it is argued, must be "balanced" to avoid reigniting grievances.[26]

The emphasis on the societal bases of postconflict violence provides a welcome complement to elite-based accounts. Not all incidents of postconflict violence will be instigated by former conflict elites; many forms of localized violence do not require organization by elites and can occur when elites do not condone violence. Even where elites do instigate violence, they need to mobilize others.[27] Critiquing overly elite-centered explanations for riots in India, Varshney and Gubler write, "One should not assume that just because it is in the interests of the ruling party to inflame riots, it will be possible for it to do so."[28] The motivations of members of society to participate in and condone violent action can therefore be an important determinant of postconflict violence. The literature summarized above would suggest that differences in such motivations and attitudes is contingent on the strength of exclusionary identities, the weakness of intergroup relations and institutions that promote cross-group collaboration, the effectiveness of reconciliation activities, and the extent to which past grievances endure into the postconflict period.

Yet, as with the bargaining theories, society-focused explanations also have limitations. The first is the failure to see the extent to which societal preferences, norms, and relations are shaped by elites. Elites can play an important role in emphasizing and essentializing old conflict cleavages for political or economic purposes.[29] Elite provocation, exaggeration of previous incidents, and the dissemination of propaganda can change societal attitudes almost overnight.[30] The likelihood that new narratives that promote reconciliation will be promulgated by elites will often depend on whether they find it politically advantageous to do so.

A second problem with many of the society-focused theories is that they are more likely to explain tensions and conflict than violence. The level of enduring grievance, for example, may account for the extent to which resentment is present in a postconflict area. But it does not alone explain why people would choose to use violence to seek redress. A fuller explanation requires diagnosing what leads people to decide that using violence is the best way to achieve their goals. This will often be a calculated choice. It is a mistake to assume that it is only elites who partake in violence for instrumental purposes and that the societal bases of violence are less rational. Scacco, in her assessment of the motivations of rioters in Nigeria, criticizes the tendency of many studies to assume "that elites are highly strategic, if not implausibly cunning, while masses are non-strategic and easily manipulated."[31] Petersen argues that "social scientists should not assume that participants are ignorant dupes of elites."[32] We need to identify what translates discontent into violent action.

A third issue is that the attitudes and incentives of members of society at large are often less important than those of the people who actually participate in postconflict violence. In most contexts, including those where wars are ongoing, the majority will not support violence. Extended violence inflicts vast costs on people who live in the areas where it occurs. Beyond the risks of being killed or injured, people typically cannot send their children to school, farm their fields, or access adequate health care. Even in the most divided of societies most people will not be supportive of postconflict violence because this raises the risk of costly extended violence recurring.

Why then do people participate in violence? One strand of research has focused on the provision of selective incentives to help overcome Olson's free-rider collective action dilemma.[33] For example, promises of disproportionate access to resources or power in exchange for fighting muscle may be provided.[34] Others have identified how participation in violence may create cognitive satisfaction.[35] Riots may be "performative," almost festival-like in nature.[36] Petersen's study of Eastern European violence highlights the role of a range of emotions—fear, hatred, and resentment—each of which can serve an instrumental purpose whereby "emotion drives the individual to reach a recognizable goal."[37] Such goals may include the desire for revenge, a desire to help prevent a preemptive attack, or the wish to put another group "back in their place."[38]

Given the associated risks and moral sensibilities, it will usually be a minority who take part in violence—during or following conflict. Indeed, recent work has explained variation in postconflict violence through the actions of members of armed groups after peace settlements and the ability of armed group organizations to control their fighters. Sarah Zukerman Daly, in her impressive study of armed groups in Colombia, and Michael Boyle, who compares different postconflict countries, emphasize the importance of organizational cohesion to prevent groups remilitarizing[39] or factions using violence strategically.[40]

Yet, as the Indonesia cases that follow show, it is not only former combatants who engage in violence once conflicts end. Criminal gangs, some active during the extended conflicts, some not, have been involved in many incidents of post-conflict violence in Indonesia and the same is true elsewhere.[41] I find Charles Tilly's broader conception of "violence specialists," those who are predisposed to use violence to achieve their goals, more useful for it includes both those who were part of organized combatant or militia movements and those who were not, both those who fought in the extended violence and those who did not.[42] It will be useful to focus not only on broad societal attitudes but on the conditions under which violence specialists are able and willing to use violence.

The State

A third literature turns its gaze from elite or societal motivations to the institutions and organizations of the state that sustain order. The human impulse to use violence is omnipresent. It follows that states are needed to allow an escape from Hobbes's "war of every man against every man." Only with a strong *leviathan* that monopolizes the use of force and coercion can violence be tamed.[43] The primary task in areas emerging from extended violence is thus to build a state capable of controlling violence. This, it is argued, should be the major focus for the international agencies aiming to prevent a return to violence in war-scarred areas or the emergence of frequent episodic violence. A vast literature has developed in the last decade arguing for state building as a postconflict peace-building strategy and providing advice on how to do it.[44]

State strength is clearly important. Cross-country evidence shows the symbiotic, mutually enforcing relationship between state fragility and violence. Besley and Persson, for example, discuss "the observed tendency for effective state institutions, the absence of political violence, and high income per capita to be positively correlated with one another," both across countries at a given point in time and across time within a country.[45] Of the seventeen countries ranked by the World Bank as being fragile in the 1980s, and which remained fragile between 1990 and 2008, sixteen experienced civil wars.[46] Where the coercive arms of the state, such as the police, military, and judicial system, have limited capacity, civil war violence becomes more feasible.[47] Other forms of collective violence also tend to be more common in places where the state is weak. Postwar violent crime, for example, is less likely if strong control mechanisms, such as a well-functioning security and justice apparatus, exist.[48] Effective states are also more likely to pursue policies that improve well-being, undermining desires to use violence in the aftermath of conflict.[49] Growth leads to higher incomes, which lower the risk of civil war recurring.[50] It can improve government legitimacy, reducing grievances.[51] More effective states are more likely to invest in public goods that benefit large sections of the population, reducing grievances. This should bring down risks of violence recurring in the postconflict period.

Yet state strength is not the sole determinant of postconflict violence. Stronger middle- and high-income states such as those in the Balkans, Lebanon, Guatemala, the Philippines, Indonesia, and the United Kingdom all have functioning states that collect revenues, build roads, and fund armies. None makes most state fragility lists. But all have seen substantial violence after their extended violent conflicts have ended.[52] This raises a question which the state strength theories cannot answer: Why is postconflict violence a problem in many countries where the state has strong coercive capacities, where functioning bureaucracies are in place, and where state service delivery penetrates even the most rural of areas?

Others have focused on the institutional design of states with three areas receiving attention. The first is regime type. Democracies may be better placed to handle sensitive postconflict transitions where they have mature institutions for dealing with disputes in nonviolent ways; authoritarian regimes may be more able to provide the control necessary to ensure peace settlements stick. In contrast, states with hybrid regimes, containing elements of democracy and authoritarianism, see higher levels of civil war, and this correlation also seems to stand for "social" forms of violence such as violent crime.[53] In such hybrid regimes, or where transitions to democracy are occurring, it may be more difficult for states to impose order in areas emerging from extended violent conflict.[54] Efforts to rush democratization, for example by holding quick elections after the end of extended violent conflicts, may make areas more prone to postconflict violence.[55] Yet the effect is by no means deterministic. Many countries do manage to go to the polls after large-scale violence ends without violence reemerging. In Asia at least, there is very weak evidence that regime type is a predictor of violence.[56]

Second, federalism or decentralization could impact on the risk of postconflict violence. Devolving funds and powers can satiate the needs of separatist groups and may quell emerging violence in multiethnic states. There is some evidence that federalism is associated with a lower incidence of rebellion but the evidence is not conclusive.[57] Similarly, there is not strong evidence as to whether decentralization following the end of conflicts leads to more or less violence.[58]

A third focus has been on the rules that shape the division of state resources and positions across the groups who fought in the past. Call observes that civil wars are more likely to reignite where a formerly warring group is politically marginalized in the postconflict period.[59] Yet in some places where a military victory ended the conflict with the losing party locked out of power, northern and eastern Sri Lanka is one example, there has been relatively little postconflict violence.[60] Even among those who prioritize the need for power sharing in the postconflict polity, there is debate over how best to ensure this. Lijphart has argued that in divided societies there is a need to allocate positions in government to ethnic groups, with each forming part of a grand coalition.[61] Others have observed that such group-based democratic institutions can lock in divisive identities, raising the risks of postconflict violence. In Bosnia, for example, the Dayton agreement has merely led to "a frozen conflict . . . [setting] in concrete the ethnic apartheid it sought to overcome."[62] For such reasons, some prefer rules that incentivize moderation and cooperation across ethnic groups through electoral engineering.[63] Unfortunately, there is little empirical evidence on the impacts of these different types of power-sharing rules on violence.[64] The theories also have less relevance to areas emerging from subnational civil wars, such as Aceh, where identity divides within the local population are not marked.

A further problem with both the state strength and state structure arguments is that they are unable to show why postconflict violence varies *within* a country. Whether a country is democratic or autocratic (or somewhere in between) is a national-level phenomenon. Rules of electoral competition and constitutional structure are set at the center and tend to be applied equally across a country's subnational units. As such, the state-focused arguments do not help us understand why some areas of Indonesia that were affected by large-scale conflict have seen postconflict violence while others have not.

In understanding the role of states in either preventing or facilitating postconflict violence, we need to move beyond state strength and structure to delve deeper to assess why states act in the way they do. This requires disaggregating the state by the actors who embody it. The state is usually conceived of as a single body, modeled as a unitary actor that interacts with society.[65] However, North, Wallis, and Weingast make the important observation that treating the state as one actor or body "assumes away the fundamental problem of how the state achieves a monopoly on violence."[66] This is a function of the interests and strategic interaction of different elites. In much of the world, states are not autonomous impersonal bodies but a "dominant coalition [of individuals] whose members possess special privileges."[67] Understanding the incentives of these state-based actors to either allow violence or prevent it is key.

In short: the state-building literature focuses on the importance of the state's coercive capacity, its ability to promote growth and development, and the ways in which the state structure shape the likelihood of postconflict violence. Yet the theories do not explain why in many cases states do not prevent or manage conflict in ways that stop it turning violent when they have the capacity to do so. The ability of formal structures and rules to explain the presence or absence of violence is also undermined by the fact that postconflict violence may vary within states that have the same formal institutions in place across regions. It is more useful to disaggregate the state by the actors that embody it to understand why states act the way they do and how this facilitates or prevents postconflict violence.

When Violence Works

The rest of this chapter outlines the building blocks of the book's theory. The starting point is three assertions. I argue first that the actions and interests of local elites, members of society, and state-based actors are each important in explaining why postconflict violence occurs or does not but that different actors are important to varying degrees in producing different forms of postconflict violence. The predominant forms of postconflict violence an area sees will depend on the combinations of support for violence from these different groups. Second, postconflict violence often serves instrumental purposes related to the protection or accumulation of resources or power. The presence (or absence) of postconflict violence is shaped by the ways in which the terms of the peace settlement (re)distributes access to power and resources in ways that variously incentivize and disincentivize support for violence. Third, spikes in postconflict violence are related to expected changes in the level of resources that groups can access, expected changes to who will control resources, and expected changes to the rule of the game governing access to resources.

Support for Violence and Different Forms of Postconflict Violence

Variance in levels and types of postconflict violence are rooted in differences in the attitudes of three sets of actors to the use of violence:

- *Local elites*, defined as those residing in postconflict areas with extensive power. They may hold formal political positions or have informal bases of authority. Examples include politicians in the regions, other powerful agents of the state (such as local police or military chiefs), traditional and religious leaders, and those who commanded conflicting parties during the extended violence period. The makeup of the local elite will differ between places. But common across all local elites is that they have support bases that they can mobilize. Local elites are subject to the authority of central state elites.

- Nonelite civilian *violence specialists*. This group can include those who fought during the extended violence (ex-combatants or militia members) and other thugs with experience of using violence. They may use violence at the behest of elites or for their own purposes.
- *Central state elites*. National elites play a role in determining the ways in which the state's coercive power is exercised, for example where and when the military and police are deployed. They also control how central state funds are distributed. This group may include those in national government, other influential politicians, and senior figures in the security forces.

The likelihood that postconflict violence will occur is determined by the level of support for it from each set of actors. Different combinations of support for or rejection of violence from these groups determines not only whether postconflict violence is likely to occur but the extent to which it will escalate into larger forms of violence. This is because different kinds of postconflict violence require the active participation or acquiescence of different sets of actors. The theory leads to the following hypotheses.

LARGE-SCALE EPISODIC VIOLENCE

> H1. Necessary conditions: support for violence from local elites and violence specialists.

Where local elites support violence, observable by tracing their participation in instigating violent incidents, and where violence specialists have motivations and opportunities to use violence, large episodic violence will occur frequently.

Large-scale episodes of violence generally involve local elites. Tambiah, for example, in his survey of ethnic riots in Sri Lanka, India, and Pakistan, points to the role of local politicians and other elites in instigating violence and encouraging its escalation: "In country after country, police, army, other security forces, paramilitary groups recruited by the state, and even some public officials participated in riots, either as onlookers slow to take preventive action or as vigorous participants favoring the cause of one side."[68]

Local elite support for violence tends to be required for such violence to occur for three reasons. First, riots, group clashes, and large one-way attacks all require organization and hence leadership. Local elites can help organize such violence in a variety of ways, including by spreading suspicions or rumors and hiring thugs to participate in violence.[69]

Second, violence usually only escalates to frequent large episodic forms when local state security agencies either do not have the capacity to prevent such escalation or when they consciously allow it to occur. In middle-income states such as Indonesia, the latter is often more important. Indonesian security bodies possess an intelligence apparatus and technology—water cannons, tear gas, strategies for quick deployment—to prevent such incidents from occurring. Where riots or clashes occur frequently it is often a result of the coercive powers of the state being applied only selectively. A key strategy for local elites who want violence to occur can be to influence the performance of the local police or military, preventing them from acting on intelligence or responding once unrest has begun. There is evidence from many places that this dynamic is common. Wilkinson argues that "abundant comparative evidence shows that large-scale ethnic rioting does not take place where a state's army or police force is ordered to stop it using all means necessary," and the same can be true for other forms of escalated unrest such as two-way group clashes.[70] Wilson, in explaining riots in the Indonesian province of North Maluku in Indonesia, argues that incitement by elites only led to instrumentalist violence after the security forces were immobilized.[71]

Third, even where large episodes of postconflict violence are not led by elites but by groups within society, where they occur frequently there is usually some level of elite acquiescence. Local elites, who are defined by the power they exercise over the local society, should be able to rein in groups who have an interest in perpetrating violence. Frequent large incidents thus indicate a degree of acceptance or support from at least some in the local elite for violence, even where elites are not leading the organization of such violence. Where local elites do not use or support such violence, violence that occurs is likely to be smaller in scale, involving fewer participants with more limited impacts.

Elite support for violence is, however, not enough to produce large-scale episodic violence. In almost all cases, local elites themselves will not directly engage in violence. Local elites need to be able to mobilize nonelites for this purpose. There thus needs to be support for the use of violence by others who are willing to participate in violent action.

In contrast, frequent large-scale violence does not require the support of central state-based actors. In all but the most centralized of countries, the central state will devolve authority to control episodic violence to local elites and branches of the state. It is only where episodic violence threatens to spiral out of control, raising the risk of escalation into extended violence, that central states will tend to get involved.[72]

SMALL-SCALE EPISODIC VIOLENCE

H2. Necessary condition: support for violence from violence specialists.

Small-scale episodic violence will occur when civilian nonelites have incentives to use violence to achieve their goals but where elite support for the escalation of violence into larger forms is absent.

Not every incident of small-scale violence will involve specialists in violence. Interpersonal squabbles can get out of control and take violent form. Communities may mobilize to respond (violently) to threats from other communities. As I show in the next chapter, and discuss in greater depth in the three case study chapters that follow, forms of violence such as popular justice, which often involve largely spontaneous violent reactions to perceived offences committed by others, have been prominent in postconflict areas of Indonesia.

However, where episodic postconflict violence is endemic, much of it will usually be committed by violence specialists such as former combatants or criminal thugs. Where small-scale violence is common, the ranks of violence specialists are likely to swell. Communities will often turn to young men to provide protection or use violence to represent their interests. Those who previously just dabbled in violence can over time become experts in it, with strong demand for their services, meaning the rewards they receive for using violence accentuate incentives for them to specialize in it.

In contrast, local elite support for violence is not necessary for smaller-scale episodes of violence to occur with frequency. Violent incidents with smaller impacts tend not to require the same level of organization as larger-scale incidents. Nor is immobilization of the local security apparatus necessary. Smaller-scale incidents of violence will often be harder to prevent than larger episodes, because they tend to last for a shorter time, because (by definition) they do not escalate beyond a certain level, and because they usually involve smaller numbers of people: each factor makes detection and response more difficult. In some instances, elites may be involved in instigating small-scale episodic violence, using it to increase their credibility by showing that they have an ability to engage in violence if necessary. However, the support or tolerance of local elites is not a *necessary* condition for small-scale postconflict violence to occur. Indeed, where elites support the use of violence for their own purposes it is likely that smaller-scale incidents will be accompanied by larger-scale ones that send a clearer signal of strength. Where small-scale incidents exist alone it is unlikely that elite machinations are driving them.

Likewise, small-scale episodic violence can occur with frequency even where the central state does not support it occurring. If the central state is usually not overly concerned with large-scale episodic violence occurring, as long as it does not reach a certain threshold where further escalation is likely, it will be even less concerned with incidents of small-scale violence.

EXTENDED VIOLENT CONFLICT

H3. Necessary conditions: support for violence from central state actors, local elites, and violence specialists.

For large episodes of postconflict violence to escalate into (renewed) extended violent conflict, the support or acquiescence of national state-based elites is necessary in states that have a sufficient degree of control.[73]

The theories outlined above on failed bargains and fractured social relations tend to view the scale of violence as being a function of the depth of support for violence from, respectively, local elites and societal groups. The former theories predict that places where there is deeper animosity or less trust between local elites on either side of the conflict divide would see escalated renewed extended violence rather than more episodic outbursts. The latter predict that places marked by deeper intergroup hatreds or grievances will be those where there will be renewed extended violence rather than episodic forms of violence. This reasoning is built on an assumption that local elites and citizens have the agency to produce extended violence if they are motivated to do so.

However, in middle- and higher-income states this will often not be the case. In such places, the central state usually has the ability to control violence before it escalates into extended violence, through coercive means (sending in the troops), by buying off belligerents, or through a combination of such tactics. Most extended violent conflicts in such countries will be nonconventional, fought between either two nonstate groups, for example, religious or ethnic groups, or between a guerrilla movement and a state army. In the former symmetrical conflicts, the central state can act as an arbiter and enforcer, stepping in when things get out of hand. In the latter conflicts, which can be characterized by the asymmetric capacity of the two sides, the state will likely have disproportionate power, allowing it to shape to a large extent how violence evolves.

As discussed earlier, most central states will tolerate a certain level of episodic violence in the regions. But they will usually not support extended violent conflicts where their power is seriously challenged, where the cost to the state is significant in lost revenues or postconflict reconstruction costs, and which may result in a loss of international prestige and investment. As such, given moderate central state capacity, local elites and/or citizens will only be able to produce extended violence—in its communal or civil war forms—where there is support for or acquiescence to this from the central state.

SUPPORT FOR VIOLENCE AND FORMS OF POSTCONFLICT VIOLENCE

Figure 1 summarizes the argument, showing how different combinations of support for violence shape the predominant forms of violence that are likely in different postconflict areas. The different types of violence can usefully be conceptualized as escalated forms of each other. Escalation of violence to more destructive types (from small episodic to large episodic violence, and from large

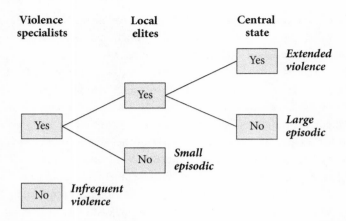

FIGURE 1.   Support for violence from different groups and types of postconflict violence.

episodic to extended violence) requires support from those with higher levels of authority and hence agency to produce violence.

When Groups Support Postconflict Violence

The presence of different forms of postconflict violence is determined by the extent to which different groups support it. The follow-on question is what determines such support. I argue that the ways in which the terms of conflict resolution shape access to resources and power is key. Different sets of actors will be more likely to use or support violence in the postconflict period where access to resources and power is structured in ways that make the use of violence an effective instrumental strategy

People may use or support the use of violence for a number of reasons. Sometimes, violence will be emotive, an uncalculated outburst of frustration. Yet more often violence serves instrumental purposes for those who employ it (or who allow it to occur). Violence will be most common when it works—when people think it is a useful tactic for achieving their goals.

These goals are likely to be diverse, varying across conflict, place, and individual. As Roger Petersen has argued, people desire a range of things in life, including safety, wealth, status, and self-esteem.[74] Emotions such as fear (that these are under threat) or resentment (that they have not been reached) can play an instrumental role, triggering individuals to take actions to achieve such goals. Violence may be employed for reasons related to both the material and nonmaterial interests of individuals and of groups.

Particularly prominent, however, in most postconflict areas—and indeed elsewhere—are the goals of securing resources or power and shaping the rules of the game on how they are allocated. In part, this is because wealth and status, to use Petersen's categories, loom large in people's lives. However, beyond the goals of self-enrichment, access to resources, or to the positions that control their allocation, can serve instrumental functions: they can be important in enhancing the agency of individuals and groups to control other areas of their lives.

An individual or group may seek power to ensure that their customary land rights are not lost. An ethnic group may fight for sizeable representation in the police or military to ensure that they are not threatened. A rich man can buy protection from prosecution or extortion. The control of positions and resources is thus both an end in itself but also an important means to achieve other desired ends. Individuals and groups compete for power and resources to enrich themselves but also to safeguard the wide range of their interests.

Competition over resources and power is particularly important in countries like Indonesia that are "patronage democracies," characterized by a concentration of political and economic power and an overlap between conceptions of the public and the private spheres. Here, "the state has a relative monopoly on jobs and services, and . . . elected officials enjoy significant discretion in the implementation of laws allocating the jobs and services at the disposal of the state."[75] State offices are regarded as "prebends," with it seen as legitimate for officeholders to appropriate material benefits to pass on to those in their patron-client network.[76] In such places, "personal relationships, who one is and who one knows, form the basis for social organization and constitute the arena for individual interaction, particularly personal relationships among powerful individuals."[77] The importance of controlling positions or resources is thus increased because one cannot rely on impartial legal institutions to protect the rights and interests of those who do not have direct connections to those in power. With the relative absence or ineffectiveness of impersonal institutions, and where there are few checks on those in power, control of political positions and/or resources is important both for group- or self-enrichment and because it can provide a bulwark against exploitation and violence from others.

THE TERMS OF CONFLICT RESOLUTION
AND ACCESS TO POWER AND RESOURCES

Peace settlements, whether formal peace agreements or informal arrangements following the end of extended violent conflicts, shape access to power and resources. Postconflict areas typically see an influx of resources: to reconstruct infrastructure, to speed economic recovery, to reintegrate former combatants and facilitate reconciliation. In the 1990s, more than US$100 billion of international aid was pledged by donors to support countries recovering from violent conflict.[78] In 2007 alone, more than US$630 million was spent on international programs to disarm, demobilize, and reintegrate ex-combatants often as a means of generating support from potential spoilers.[79]

These resources, as well as those from the state, are often deployed with the intention on ensuring buy-in to peace agreements. The provision of postconflict reconstruction funds, including funds targeted at former combatants and their organizations, can be used as a carrot aimed at shifting cost-benefit calculations and leading to an acceptance of a peace settlement. One function of the provision of such a peace dividend can be to buy out "spoilers" whose interests and powers may be threatened by an emerging peace.[80] Conflict-era economic structures can be allowed to endure into the postconflict period, meaning that conflict elites do not lose wartime sources of rent.[81]

Access to power will also typically change with an end to extended violence. As discussed earlier, peace agreements are often followed by elections and/or power-sharing deals aimed in part at incorporating former belligerents into the state. Where one side to the conflict has won, they may be able to take control of the local state and the opportunities for patronage that affords.

Support for violence from each set of actors will be stronger in the postconflict period where violence proves to be a useful way to capture these resources and power. In particular, it can be expected that support for and use of violence will be greater under two conditions: (a) when the expected gains from using violence to access power and/or resources are high and outweigh the risks associated with using it (in terms of being killed, injured, arrested, or otherwise sanctioned); and (b) when there is a lack of peaceful ways to access power or resources.

THE EXPECTED BENEFITS OF USING VIOLENCE

Violence is more likely when groups and individuals expect it to be profitable, that is, when they perceive the benefits of using violence to outweigh the costs. How do individuals and groups make these cost-benefit judgments? In deciding on whether to initiate, participate in, or support violence (or not), each set of actors will rely in large part on the signals that past acts of violence, and responses to it, have generated.

Nancy Bermeo's concept of political learning is useful in helping us understand how attitudes toward violence may evolve in postconflict settings. Focusing on the creation or reconstruction of democracy after periods of dictatorship, she argues that cognitive change is key. Elites, both incumbents and challengers, learn the lessons from past failures and may change their goals or tactics accordingly. "The reconstruction of democracy," she posits, "almost always requires some form of prodemocratic learning."[82] It is these changes in beliefs that lead to discontinuities in regime types and the elite strategies that shape them.[83]

Similarly, political learning is required in postconflict areas if violence is not to reemerge. Only where beliefs about the utility of violence change will violence subside after extended violent conflicts end. Individuals and groups use violence during periods of communal or civil war if they think that, strategically or tactically, violence is the best means of achieving their goals. The ending of an extended violent conflict provides a critical juncture where individuals and groups, elites and nonelites alike, can reevaluate whether violence still serves their purposes in a radically changed environment. At such points, uncertainty is rife: leaders, former combatants, and civilians do not know whether peace will hold, whether the terms of an accord will be applied, whether the continuing use of violence will be beneficial in achieving goals, and whether it will be sanctioned by the central state, peacekeepers, or others with authority. In such information-scarce environments, individuals will look closely for signals that reveal whether or not violence will continue to be an efficient and relatively risk-free strategy.

An important source of such information is whether the use of violence in the early postconflict period results in benefits without significant costs for those who employ it. Particularly important will be the extent to which extra postconflict peace-building and reconstruction funds are distributed to those who continue to use, or threaten to use, violence. As discussed earlier, peace processes are typically accompanied by additional resources, and these are sometimes used to try to co-opt those who had been fighting. Channeling funds to such individuals and groups can help incorporate them into peace settlements. However, if access to these funds is contingent on the use or threat of violence *after* the extended violence has ended, this can inadvertently signal that continuing use of violence is acceptable and profitable.

We can expect that responses to violence in the early postconflict period will play a more important signaling role than responses when the extended violent conflict is still ongoing. This is because peace settlements—whether they take the form of mediated agreements or the forced terms of a military victory or third-party military intervention—will be expected to change the rules of the game with regards to the use of violence. Militia members, for example, may have been rewarded handsomely by political leaders during the extended violence but may find that their activities become a nuisance for those same elites in the postconflict period. A militia member trying to work out whether the continuing use of violence will be profitable or not in the postconflict period will get a far stronger signal from analyzing what happened when another member used violence following a peace agreement than from assessing responses and success during the extended violence period. Developing Bermeo's idea, we can thus predict that the period *following* a shock such as a peace settlement will be more important in determining whether and what kind of political learning with regards to violence will take place than the time before the critical juncture.

Where early postconflict violence leads to the securing of rents or positions, and where those with authority to provide sanctions instead give active or tacit support to this, individuals and groups are more likely to use violence as a political-economic strategy. In contrast, where responses to postconflict violence show how risky it is (for example, when perpetrators were arrested), or where it has failed to result in benefit, postconflict violence will be less likely. The ways in which those with authority respond to acts of violence is thus key. Where violence is rewarded, by providing preferential access to resources or positions for those who perpetrate it, future violence is more likely. In contrast, where the use of violence does not result in rewards, those who may have been tempted to use violence to pursue their goals will be less likely to do so.

These processes apply to civilian violence specialists, local elites, and to central state elites in their decisions on whether or not to use or support violence. This leads to the following hypotheses:

> H4. Where resources or positions are given out based on the use of, or threats of, violence in the postconflict period, more future postconflict violence will occur.

> H5. Where authorities do not impose costs on those who use violence, more future postconflict violence will occur.

THE PRESENCE OF PEACEFUL MEANS FOR ACCUMULATING RESOURCES AND/OR POWER

Even where the expected benefits of using violence outweigh the expected costs, each set of actors may prefer not to use it if other ways to achieve their goals exist. This is because, even when costs are expected to be low, violence is still risky and because most people will have a natural tendency to prefer peaceful to violent interaction and to act on the "better angels of our nature."[84]

What these peaceful means are needs to be distinguished by different actors. For civilian violence specialists, who are often un- or underemployed, the availability of well-remunerated jobs may be sufficient to limit the support of many, if not all, for violence. We can predict that where local economic growth is stronger, and where this translates into employment opportunities for young men, fewer will engage in violence. Leaders of criminal or ex-combatant groups may also have political ambitions. Where they are able to fulfill these, without resort to using violence in doing so, they may be less likely to support or participate in violence.

Local elites typically have both economic and political goals. With regards to the former, environments with high levels of growth or where decentralized public funds are large and expanding may provide more opportunities for local elite accumulation. However, in environments where patrimonial relations determine who benefits, it will be important that some elite groups (and their patronage networks) are not locked out. Where collaboration across elite groups on economic projects is possible, support for violence from local elites will thus be less likely. Similarly, local elites will be more likely to participate in peaceful politics where the costs of losing are not too great—that is, where there is some degree of power sharing across elite groups. As discussed earlier, the formal rules of the game, for example, different electoral system designs, will shape the extent to which such power sharing occurs. However, informal norms, which lead to cross-elite collaboration or not, will also be important.[85]

For central state elites, a similar logic applies. Where different elite groups have opportunities to profit, and where they perceive an ability to access and maintain political power without resort to violence, they will be more likely to support a political order where extended violence is not deemed legitimate. We can thus hypothesize the following:

> H6. Where opportunities exist to achieve political or economic power through peaceful means, each set of actors will be less likely to use violence in the postconflict period.

From Incentives to Norms

The political learning that takes place in the early postconflict period can have path dependent effects on longer-run patterns of violence.[86] This is because where violence proves beneficial and not costly, the same individuals will choose to use it as a tactic again and others will also see that it has utility. As violence is used more frequently, and by a wider number of people, norms about the legitimacy of using violence to achieve desired ends can also change. Robert Axelrod has argued that norms are often a product of learning: "What works well . . . is likely to be used again while what turns out poorly is likely to be discarded."[87] Where people see that violence works, more will engage in it; after a threshold is reached, a "tipping point" can occur with violence legitimized as a mode of political or economic interaction.[88]

This can lead to more violence through two different causal mechanisms. First, individuals' calculations change. As more information becomes available showing that violence is not costly, the perceived level of risk of using it will decrease. At the same time, cost-benefit calculations may become less important.

This is because violence can change people's conceptions of their goals. Divisive identities or ideologies can harden; destroying, disadvantaging, or achieving victory over "the other" can become a goal in itself. This can lead to what Varshney has called "value rationality" where, in contrast to "instrumental rationality," individuals or groups will continue to pursue goals despite the high costs and low expected probability of achieving them.[89] Both changed instrumental rationality and value rationality can become drivers of violence.

This in turn leads to feedback effects that can be reinforcing. Where violence is socially sanctioned—where it becomes legitimized under the rules of the game that govern competition between individuals and groups—the likelihood that violence will occur frequently rises substantially. Such social norms can lead people to support the use of violence even when it is not in their immediate best interests. Over time, such norms may be difficult to shift, requiring another shock that results in a significant change to the costs or benefits of using violence.

Why Postconflict Violence Varies Over Time

The theory points us to time periods when levels of postconflict violence will heighten within a given area. If postconflict violence is a function of the expected gains of using violence, the degree of perceived risk, and the absence of peaceful means for reaching goals, changes to each of these may alter the propensity of an area to experience violence. Violence is more likely to be used when there are changes to the perceived costs or benefits of using violence or when other opportunities for accumulation that do not require violence diminish. Such changes can operate for any of the three sets of actors—violence specialists, local elites, and national elites—hence affecting levels of different forms of violence.

For each set of actors, incentives to support or participate in violence may be strengthened, and hence levels of violence may rise, when there are either (a) expected changes in the level of resources that can be captured, (b) expected changes to who will control resources, or (c) when it is expected that the rules of the game governing access to resources are about to change. This leads to the following hypotheses:

> H7. Where resource levels are expected to increase sharply, postconflict violence may rise.

Expectations of greater future resources, for example when the state or international donors are about to provide postconflict funds, may raise the willingness of different groups to use or support violence if it is seen as a potentially fruitful strategy to capture these. In such situations, individuals and groups will tend to trade off the risks of using violence against the expected benefits to be gained from it. However, we would expect any increases in violence to be conditional on a lack of peaceful opportunities being available for accessing such resources.

H8. Where levels of resources are perceived as being about to drop significantly, postconflict violence may rise.

Violence can also be used as a means to secure a share of a diminishing resource pie. This effect is likely to be stronger where violence was the means used previously to access resources. Where violence was not used for this, because of high risks or because other channels for accumulating resources were available, reductions in resources will be less likely to correlate with higher levels of violence.

H9. Where there is heightened competition over who controls resources, or occupies powerful positions, violence will rise.

In democracies, one key time period is when elections are about to be held. We can expect elections to be more tense (and potentially violent) in areas where electoral institutions are the main means through which resources and power are allocated. In places where other means of politicking (for example backroom deals facilitated by the illicit exchange of money or favors) or coercion are more important than elections, elections will be less likely to correlate with spikes of violence.

H10. Where there are expected changes to the rules by which resources or power are allocated, violence will rise.

Such changes may relate to the structure of the state. The literature on violence and democratic transitions, for example, has shown that the two often coincide. They may also relate to more microlevel changes in the practices of the state. For example, a decrease in the discretion elites have in allocating resources (e.g., where there is increased monitoring of the use of funds and sanctioning those who engage in corruption) may lead to an upsurge in violence. This is because violence can be a useful means to shape the formal and informal rules of the game as they are (re)forged. At these times, bargains need to be renegotiated. When violence is deemed legitimate or normal, there is the potential for it to be used to shape the content of such agreements.

This chapter has developed a theory that explains where postconflict violence is likely to occur, the forms it will take, and when there will be increases in violence. The following chapters turn to the Indonesian cases to assess its efficacy and to further develop it.

VIOLENCE AND INDONESIA'S DEMOCRATIC TRANSITION

This chapter provides an overview of violence in Indonesia since the beginning of the country's democratic transition in 1998. A necessary first step to explain why postconflict violence varies between areas and over time is to map out the extent and nature of this variance. Only after we comprehend the broader patterns of violence can we turn our attention to explaining them.

Such patterns can be seen most clearly if we take a bird's eye view and look at the large-n of violence in Indonesia. The chapter draws primarily on Indonesia's National Violence Monitoring System (NVMS) dataset, introduced in chapter 1. The NVMS provides the most comprehensive and accurate quantitative picture to date of the spread, nature, and impacts of violence in postauthoritarian Indonesia. The version of the dataset used in this book records incidents of violence reported in more than one hundred local newspapers for around half of Indonesia's provinces, including all of those that were previously affected by large-scale extended violent conflict around the turn of the century. This allows us to consider how violence is distributed across the country and how it has changed in incidence, destructive impact, and forms over time.

Violence in Early Post-Suharto Indonesia

Violence was a defining feature of the three-decade New Order regime. General Suharto came to power on the back of the massive anticommunist killings of

1965–66 when more than half a million people lost their lives.[1] Throughout the New Order years, the security arms of the state used violence extensively to retain control, build power, and scare off challenges.[2] Large-scale, state-sponsored violence included the *petrus* (or "mysterious") killings of alleged criminals from 1983–85, when as many as two thousand may have died.[3] The military, which only received a small share of its budget from official state sources, also used violence to generate income. At times state repression and coercion led to armed resistance. Separatist violence ebbed and flowed in Papua from 1963 and in East Timor and Aceh from 1976, resulting in harsh counterinsurgency operations that killed many more. Communal rioting also occurred, in particular in the late Suharto period, with outbreaks in Situbondo and Tasikmalaya in Java and Banjarmasin and Makassar in Kalimantan and Sulawesi.[4]

The violence that accompanied the fall of the New Order was new, both in its scale and nature. The period from 1998 to 2004 was one of major national-level political and socioeconomic change driven by parallel transitions from authoritarianism to democracy (*reformasi*) and from a centralized to decentralized polity (*desentralisasi*) as well as changes to the structure of Indonesia's economy following the Asian financial crisis (*krismon*). These years undoubtedly saw the highest levels of violence since the 1965 killings. In the seventeen provinces for which we have data, 21,495 people lost their lives between 1998 and 2003.[5]

Forms of Violence

The upsurge in violence was a national phenomenon. It is no coincidence that aggregate levels of violence increased as the Indonesian polity and economy was undergoing rapid change. Globally, as a host of scholars have shown, violence often emerges during authoritarian breakdowns and when rapid economic changes are taking place.[6] Studies of violence in this period of Indonesian history have pointed to the ways in which the uncertainty caused by such changes motivated groups to use violence.[7]

Yet the violence of Indonesia's transition was also inherently local. Violence did not encompass the whole country: some regions of the country experienced high levels of violence while others remained largely peaceful. There was no common master narrative driving the violence in different areas. Changes at the national level interacted with local concerns and goals. As a result, transition-era violence took diverse forms, with different parts of the country affected by varying types of violence. Four different forms of violence emerged, which can be distinguished by scale and duration (figure 2).

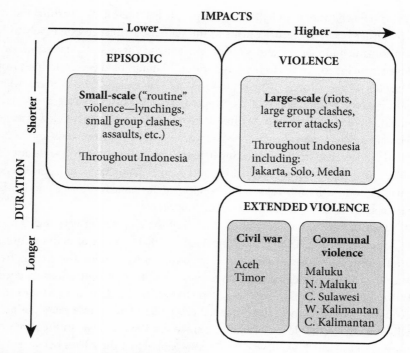

FIGURE 2. Forms of violence in early transition Indonesia.

In seven provinces scattered across the archipelago, there was extended violent conflict, highly organized with large physical impacts in terms of lives lost, people injured, buildings damaged, and economic effects (map 1).

In two provinces, long-running civil wars gained new momentum. In Aceh, the war between the secessionist Free Aceh Movement (GAM) and the Indonesian military heated up with at least 8,775 killed in the province between 1999 and 2003 and a further 1,521 losing their lives in 2004. In East Timor, 1,400–2,600 were killed as the province parted from Indonesia, adding to the tens of thousands of deaths during the Indonesian occupation.[8] Papua also saw separatist violence although this was much more sporadic than in either Aceh or Timor.[9]

Other provinces saw escalated, extended communal violence, new to modern Indonesia. The New Order era had certainly not been free of interreligious and interethnic unrest, but episodes were usually short-lived, burning out after a day or two often after the arrival of the military. In contrast, new communal violence in five Indonesian provinces continued for months, even years with resulting large destructive impacts.[10]

MAP 1. Indonesian provinces affected by extended violent conflict

In Central Sulawesi and Maluku, the cleavage was primarily religious; in North Maluku, ethnic violence morphed into interconfessional battles. Violence in each place started with small-scale clashes between community groups but later escalated into much larger armed confrontation. Violence was not short-lived: in North Maluku it endured for almost a year; in Maluku and Central Sulawesi for multiple years. Extended communal violence also broke out in In-donesian Borneo. For around three weeks from late 1996 to early 1997, while Suharto was still in power, ethnic Dayaks in West Kalimantan attacked the mi-grant Madurese community; a second round of violence two years later set ethnic Malays against the Madurese. In February 2001, Dayaks in Central Kalimantan attacked the Madurese over the course of a few weeks, resulting in 90 percent of the Madurese population fleeing the province.[11] While the violence in West and Central Kalimantan was shorter than that in Maluku, North Maluku, and Central Sulawesi, there were similarities. Fatalities were high (over a thousand in each province, except Central Sulawesi—see table 4), violence was highly organized, government services halted, and clashes spread over large geographic areas.

Early transition violence was not confined to the provinces that experienced extended violence. Episodic violent incidents rose across Indonesia. The larg-est of these were the massive riots that engulfed Jakarta in mid-May 1998 that preempted the fall of Suharto. Further anti-Chinese riots hit other Indonesian

TABLE 4. Extended violence by province in transitioning Indonesia

PROVINCE	FORM	PERIOD OF EXTENDED VIOLENCE	DEATHS	INJURIES	BUILDINGS DAMAGED
Aceh	Civil war	Jan 98–end July 05[a]	10,613	8,546	9,230
North Maluku	Communal	Aug 99–end June 00	3,257	2,635	15,004
Maluku	Communal	Jan 99–end Feb 02	2,793	5,057	13,843
East Timor	Civil war	Jan 98–end Dec 99[b]	1,485–1,585	?	?
West Kalimantan	Communal	Jan 97–end Feb 97 / Feb 99–end Apr 99	1,103	646	3,830
Central Kalimantan	Communal	Feb 01–end Apr 01	1,031	77	1,998
Central Sulawesi	Communal	Apr 00–end Dec 01	517	579	6,004
Total			20,799–21,799	17,540+	49,909+

Source: NVMS. Timor data from CAVR (2005a).

a Best estimates are that 1,574–6,074 people were killed in Aceh in the 1976–1998 period. These figures are calculated by subtracting deaths in Aceh for the 1999–2005 period (as reported in NVMS) from Aspinall's (2009a, 2) estimate of the number of deaths over thirty years of violence in Aceh.

b Timor figures are calculated from The Timor-Leste Commission for Reception, Truth, and Reconciliation (CAVR 2005a). They report 17 killings by Fretelin/Falantil in 1998 (p. 244), 29 such killings in 1999 (p. 244), 39 killings by the Indonesian military in 1998 (p. 233), and 1,400–1,500 military killings in 1999 (p. 245). Across the full period of Indonesia's occupation, there were an estimated 18,600 unlawful killings and disappearances (CAVR 2005a, 2) and another 84,200 people died due to excess mortality (hunger and illness) as a result of the conflict (CAVR 2005b, 2).

cities such as Medan in North Sumatra and Solo in Central Java.[12] Death tolls and other impacts were large. An estimated 1,193 died in Jakarta;[13] the riots in Solo led to Rp. 457 billion (US$46 million) of damage in a city of just 400,000 people.[14] However, such incidents differed from the communal violence of the Moluccas, Sulawesi, and Kalimantan, and the secessionist violence at either end of Indonesia's archipelagic stretch. Violence was shorter in duration. The large-scale violence in Jakarta, for example, only lasted for two days. Other high-impact episodic violence included terror attacks on international targets. The 2002 Bali bombing killed more than two hundred people, while the Australian Embassy in Jakarta was attacked in 2004 and the Marriot Hotel in Jakarta in 2003 and again in 2009.

The incidence of other forms of smaller-scale episodic violence also appears to have risen in the early transition period, although we have less data on this. Welsh, using local newspapers, found that more than 5,500 people were the victims of lynchings between 1995 and 2004 in just four Indonesian provinces, although this figure appears high when compared with other studies, and it is not clear if such victims include those who were injured as well as those killed.[15] Other case studies have found significant levels of "routine violence" over a multitude of issues, including land and other natural resources, administrative squabbles, and elections.[16]

Peace Settlements: Reduced Levels of Violence

The big wave of violence that followed the fall of Suharto eventually subsided. Figure 3 shows deaths from violence in fifteen provinces for which we have time series data until 2009.[17] Violent deaths peaked between 1999 and 2001 with more than 4,500 people killed each year. Deaths then dropped substantially in 2002, when 3,227 were killed, and 2003, when 2,484 died.

This reduction in violence was largely a consequence of the extended communal violent conflicts coming to an end. In Kalimantan, violence dropped sharply after the displacement of almost the entire ethnic Madurese population. In Central Sulawesi and Maluku, peace accords mediated by the central government played an important role. In North Maluku, a mixture of conflict fatigue and the imposition by the national government of a state of civil emergency, resulting in new security operations, helped reduce violence. By February 2002, each of the five extended communal conflicts had officially ended, although, as we will see, violence did not disappear.

From 2002 until 2005, most deaths from violence in Indonesia were a result of the civil war in Aceh, where violence had escalated sharply in 2001 after a

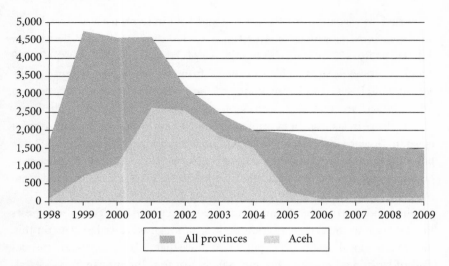

FIGURE 3. Deaths from violence in fifteen Indonesian provinces, 1998–2009.
Source: NVMS and UNSFIR-2.

failed peace agreement. In August 2005 a new peace accord was signed by GAM (the proindependence rebel group) and the Indonesian government. From August 2005, deaths from violence in Indonesia have continued to occur but these have largely been the result of episodic violence, both in postconflict areas and other parts of the country.[18]

Postconflict Violence in Indonesia

Determining levels of postconflict violence requires us to define the temporal bounds of the postconflict period. These vary for each province because the extended violent conflicts ended at different times. I use two approaches to generate cutoff points for the end of the extended violence and beginning of the postconflict period. First, I look at when key interventions aimed at ending the conflicts, such as peace agreements and interventions from national-level security forces, occurred. Not all such agreements and interventions were successful. As such, I use the NVMS data to assess when the timing of these interventions correlates with reduced levels of violence. Only where there appears to be a close relationship between the timing of the intervention and a sustained decline in violence is the date of the intervention used as the cutoff point.[19] Table 5 gives the dates used for the postconflict period for each province.[20]

TABLE 5. Postconflict periods by province

PROVINCE	POSTCONFLICT PERIOD	INTERVENTION
Aceh	Aug 05–end Dec 12	Helsinki peace accord
North Maluku	July 00–end Dec 12	Declaration of civil emergency
Maluku	Mar 02–end Dec 12	Malino 2 peace accord
West Kalimantan	May 99–end Dec 12	Departure of Madurese
Central Kalimantan	May 01–end Dec 12	Departure of Madurese
Central Sulawesi	Jan 02–end Dec 12	Malino 1 peace accord

TABLE 6. Postconflict violence by province

PROVINCE	TOTAL POSTCONFLICT PERIOD			PER YEAR/PER MILLION PEOPLE			LEVEL POSTCONFLICT VIOLENCE
	DEATHS	INJURIES	BUILDINGS	DEATHS	INJURIES	BUILDINGS	
Maluku	529	4,305	2,300	34	280	150	Higher
C. Sulawesi	718	3,666	1,529	27	139	58	Higher
C. Kalimantan	547	2,833	166	22	114	7	Medium
Aceh	597	3,345	704	19	108	23	Medium
W. Kalimantan	929	10,730	1,559	16	188	27	Medium
N. Maluku	139	1,356	827	12	115	70	Lower

Source: NVMS. Population data are from the Indonesian Bureau of Statistics and are for 2008.

Varying Levels of Postconflict Violence

Using these cutoff dates we can examine patterns of postconflict violence by province. While violence declined in all the provinces that experienced extended violent conflict, there are large differences in the extent of the decline. Table 6 shows the number of deaths, injuries, and damaged buildings in the postconflict period for each province. Provinces have been categorized by whether they have seen high, medium, or low levels of postconflict violence, putting particular emphasis on fatality rates.

Examining annual per capita impacts provides a better indication of levels of postconflict violence. Of the six provinces, postconflict West Kalimantan has seen the greatest number of people killed and injured and the second highest number of buildings damaged. However, this is a result of its postconflict period being longer than elsewhere (extended violence subsided in 1999) and of its population being larger than most of the other provinces.[21]

Using annual per capita impacts, we can see that Maluku has seen more violence than elsewhere. Violence levels in postconflict Central Sulawesi are also high. North Maluku is notable for the relative lack of violence in its postconflict period with just twelve deaths per million people per year.

Varying Forms of Postconflict Violence

Forms of violence also vary between the different postconflict provinces. In some, episodes of violence are frequently large in scale. In other provinces, violent episodes tend to have more minimal impacts per incident.

Table 7 divides episodes of postconflict violence in each province into large and small incidents. Large incidents are defined as those where three or more people are killed, ten or more injured, and/or fifteen or more buildings were damaged. (Small incidents are all incidents with lower impacts.) In every province, the majority of deaths come from smaller incidents of violence. After controlling for the length of the postconflict period and the population size, the provinces do not greatly differ in the number of deaths from such incidents with the exception of North Maluku. Across the provinces, one-quarter of the 2,514 deaths from small-scale, episodic postconflict violence came from violent crimes rather than conflicts, another 12 percent came from domestic violence, and 7 percent from security force violence. This share was similar across the provinces.[22]

There is much greater variation between provinces in both the incidence and impacts of large episodes of violence.[23] In the postconflict periods in the six provinces, there have been 214 large incidents. The most common form such violence has taken has been assaults involving small groups (67 incidents), two-way group clashes (63 incidents), riots (23 incidents), and terror attacks (15 incidents).

Large episodic violence has been much more common in postconflict Maluku and Central Sulawesi than elsewhere. Seventy-three of the large incidents (over one-third of all such incidents in the postconflict periods across the six provinces) have occurred in Maluku. This equates to seven large incidents per year. Postconflict Central Sulawesi has also seen relatively frequent large incidents with forty-seven such incidents (four per year) in its postconflict period. Death tolls from large incidents of violence are also much higher in these two provinces,

TABLE 7.   Forms of postconflict violence by province

PROVINCE	LEVEL POSTCONFLICT VIOLENCE	LARGE EPISODIC VIOLENCE (PER YEAR/PER MILLION PEOPLE)			SMALL EPISODIC VIOLENCE (PER YEAR/ PER MILLION PEOPLE)	
		INCIDENTS	DEATHS	LEVEL	DEATHS	LEVEL
Maluku	Higher	4.7	10.8	Higher	23.6	Higher
C. Sulawesi	Higher	1.8	5.2	Medium	22.0	Higher
C. Kalimantan	Medium	0.4	1.1	Lower	20.9	Higher
Aceh	Medium	0.9	1.4	Lower	17.9	Medium
W. Kalimantan	Medium	0.6	1.8	Lower	14.4	Medium
N. Maluku	Lower	1.5	3.0	Lower	8.8	Lower R

Source: NVMS. Population data used is from the Indonesian Bureau of Statistics and are for 2008.

especially Maluku. In Maluku, other physical impacts from large episodic violence in the postconflict period are also much higher than elsewhere.[24]

Understanding Variation: Six Contrasting Districts

There are thus substantive differences between provinces affected by extended violent conflicts in both the levels of postconflict violence and in the types of postconflict violence that are occurring. In this book, I aim to explain the variation in both. To do so, I look more closely at areas that differ on these two dependent variables. If we studied all six provinces we would only be able to do so in a cursory way. As such, I chose to focus on three provinces.

Provinces

Maluku is the first selected province. It has seen not only the highest levels of violence in its postconflict period but also the greatest number of large incidents. Of the Indonesian cases, it is as an example of an area where peace has not fully consolidated. The second provincial case is North Maluku, which stands out from the others with its relative lack of postconflict violence. The third province chosen for deeper study is Aceh. Since the end of its extended violence, Aceh has seen middling levels of violence. However, almost all of the violence has been the result of small-scale incidents.

Studying these three provinces allows for a number of comparisons. Comparative analysis of Maluku and North Maluku (cells A and C in table 8) can help us understand why violence occurs with frequency in some postconflict areas and not in others. Comparing Aceh with North Maluku (cells B and C) allows us to assess why small-scale violence occurs in some postconflict areas and not in others. Comparing Aceh with Maluku (cells B and A) allows us to assess why violence takes smaller rather than larger forms in some postconflict areas.

TABLE 8. Levels of postconflict violence by form in selected provinces

SMALL-SCALE EPISODES	LARGE-SCALE EPISODES	
	HIGHER	LOWER
HIGHER	A. Maluku	B. Aceh
LOWER		C. North Maluku

Districts

Within each of the three provinces, I selected two districts for deeper study. I chose to focus on the district level for several reasons. In common policy and scholarly parlance, each of Indonesia's extended violent conflicts is usually referred to by the name of the province in which it took place. Yet such descriptors mask the extent to which violence was concentrated in a limited set of areas within many of the affected provinces. This was particularly the case in the two Kalimantan provinces and in Central Sulawesi.[25] Violence was not so concentrated in the provinces chosen for deeper research, yet, even there, some districts saw much more violence than others.[26] Selecting (high extended violence) districts to study rather than provinces ensured I focused on geographic areas that had actually experienced extended violence before—that is, that are actually postconflict.

A second reason to focus on districts is their importance as a level of political administration and economic activity. The New Order state was highly centralized but *reformasi* soon resulted in a rapid and radical transformation of subnational powers. Importantly, Indonesia's decentralization laws devolved authority to rural and urban districts (*kabupaten* and *kotamadya*) rather than to provinces. The provinces were bypassed because of fears that empowered provinces, in particular those with significant natural resource wealth, could be tempted to try to secede from the country. Districts, in contrast, with an average population of around 300,000 outside of Java, were hardly feasible as independent states.[27] Almost overnight, the revenues of district governments increased massively in one "big bang."[28] Following the reduction of national-level oil subsidies in 2006, the level of funds available to districts again increased greatly, with an average 64 percent increase in the general allocation across the country.[29] Indonesia is now one of the most decentralized developing countries in the world with 36 percent of all public expenditures in 2011 made by subnational governments; of these expenditures, three-quarters are by district governments and one-quarter by provincial governments.[30] The importance of the district, both as a locus of competition and (potentially) as a source of policies that could minimize violence, makes it fruitful to focus at this level.

Within some provinces, especially Aceh, there is variation in levels of postconflict violence between districts that saw high levels of extended violence. Studying districts allows us to examine variation in postconflict violence at this level, holding constant provincial-level factors.

I used three criteria to select districts. First, the districts must have experienced significant levels of extended violence. Second, the districts should be broadly similar to those chosen in other provinces to allow for controlled comparisons to be made. Third, patterns of postconflict violence in the selected districts should

TABLE 9.   Impacts of extended violence in the ten most-affected districts

RANK INDONESIA (WITHIN PROVINCE)	DISTRICT	PROVINCE	DEATHS	INJURIES	BUILDINGS
1 (1)	**North Halmahera**	**N. Maluku**	**2,016**	**1,804**	**5,901**
2 (1)	North Aceh	Aceh	1,989	1,955	1,601
3 (2)	**East Aceh**	**Aceh**	**1,511**	**1,695**	**2,032**
4 (3)	Bireuen	Aceh	1,443	888	867
5 (1)	**Ambon**	**Maluku**	**1,413**	**2,957**	**3,733**
6 (4)	**South Aceh**	**Aceh**	**904**	**357**	**454**
7 (1)	East Kotawaringin	C. Kalimantan	857	23	1,133
8 (4)	Aceh Besar	Aceh	838	508	262
9 (5)	Pidie	Aceh	737	440	1,118
10 (2)	**Central Maluku**	**Maluku**	**557**	**632**	**3,714**
35 (6)	**Ternate**	**N. Maluku**	**76**	**94**	**961**

Source: NVMS. Impacts reported are for the periods of extended violence, as outlined by province in table 5. Districts in boldface are those selected as case studies.

be driving overall provincial patterns, except in Aceh where I deliberately chose an outlier to allow for an intraprovincial comparison.

Table 9, which ranks districts by the number of deaths experienced during extended violent conflict, shows the districts selected. Five of the six selected districts are within the ten most affected districts in Indonesia.

In Maluku Province, I chose Ambon and Central Maluku districts. Both were at the epicenter of the province's extended violent conflict: collectively, the two districts account for 71 percent of the deaths that occurred. Ambon is the provincial capital, a bustling town of just more than 200,000 people. Central Maluku, its more rural neighbor, includes parts of Ambon Island outside of Ambon city, as well as the middle swath of Seram Island and a number of smaller islands. Demographically, both districts have an almost equal number of Christians and Muslims.[31]

In North Maluku, I selected North Halmahera and Ternate districts. Almost two-thirds of deaths across the province during the extended violence period were concentrated in North Halmahera. Indeed, North Halmahera saw more people killed than any other Indonesian district. That the extended violence in North Maluku lasted for only eleven months makes this even more tragic. The district in many ways resembles Central Maluku. It is predominantly rural, religiously balanced (Protestants make up 54 percent of the population, Muslims 45 percent), and regional GDP is similar (Rp. 2.1 million per capita in North Halmahera compared to Rp. 1.5 million in Central Maluku). Ternate saw lower, although still significant, impacts from extended violence: 76 people were killed, 94 were injured, and 961 buildings were damaged. However, Ternate was, and remains, the center of political competition in the province and thus shares many similarities with Ambon in Maluku.[32] Further, while extended violence was rela-tively short-lived in Ternate, political competition in the city was a major factor in fueling subsequent unrest elsewhere in the province. Many of those mobilized to fight on Halmahera Island were residents of Ternate and most returned there after fighting subsided. As such, we might have predicted that Ternate would remain vulnerable to violence in the postconflict period.

In Aceh, I selected East Aceh and South Aceh districts, two rural districts with similarities to Central Maluku and North Halmahera. The regional GDP of both is close to that of Ambon. The two districts saw among the highest numbers of deaths from extended violence of the Acehnese districts. They were both GAM strongholds and the structure of the economy and poverty levels are similar in both places. However, as shown below, the two vary in levels of postconflict violence.

Postconflict Violence in the Six Districts

Tables 10 and 11 show that the provincial-level variations in levels and forms of postconflict violence also apply to the districts selected. Ambon and Central Ma-luku have by far the highest levels of postconflict violence of the six districts. In-deed, in per capita terms, Ambon has seen more than twice as many postconflict deaths as has Maluku as a whole. North Halmahera and Ternate both have much lower levels of postconflict violence, although levels of postconflict violence in the latter have been above the provincial average with high numbers of injuries occurring there. In Aceh, there has been a divergence in levels of postconflict vio-lence between the two selected districts. Patterns of postconflict violence in South Aceh are similar to those of North Halmahera in North Maluku. In contrast, in

TABLE 10. Impacts of postconflict violence in selected districts

DISTRICT	TOTAL POSTCONFLICT PERIOD			PER YEAR/PER MILLION PEOPLE		
	DEATHS	INJURIES	BUILDINGS	DEATHS	INJURIES	BUILDINGS
Maluku	529	4,305	2,300	34	280	150
Ambon	218	2,656	1,011	74	902	343
C. Maluku	163	685	948	38	159	220
N. Maluku	139	1,356	827	12	115	70
N. Halmahera	19	98	35	8	42	15
Ternate	40	884	236	19	425	113
Aceh	597	3,345	704	19	108	23
S. Aceh	15	84	20	10	55	13
E. Aceh	65	275	41	28	120	18

Source: NVMS.

TABLE 11.   Large-scale postconflict violence in selected districts

DISTRICT	TOTAL POSTCONFLICT PERIOD				PER YEAR/PER MILLION PEOPLE			
	INCIDENTS	DEATHS	INJURIES	BUILDINGS	INCIDENTS	DEATHS	INJURIES	BUILDINGS
Maluku	73	166	1,148	1,568	4.7	10.8	74.6	101.9
Ambon	34	78	713	748	11.5	26.5	242.0	253.9
C. Maluku	17	43	162	670	3.9	10.0	37.6	155.3
N. Maluku	18	35	236	528	1.5	3.0	20.0	44.7
N. Halmahera	4	5	26	21	1.7	2.1	11.1	9.0
Ternate	8	0	144	91	3.8	0	69.2	43.7
Aceh	29	42	153	229	0.9	1.4	4.9	7.4
S. Aceh	0	0	0	0	0	0	0	0
E. Aceh	2	3	11	0	0.9	1.3	4.8	0

Source: NVMS.

yearly per capita terms, East Aceh has seen higher numbers of people killed from violence than any of the other selected districts except those in Maluku.

Our two districts in Maluku together account for fifty-one of seventy-three large incidents of postconflict violence in the province. In contrast, none of the selected districts in North Maluku or Aceh have seen frequent large episodic postconflict violence.

This chapter has shown that there is substantial variation in postconflict violence across areas of Indonesia that previously experienced extended violent conflict. The observed variation was used to select six districts in three provinces, which differ in both overall levels of postconflict violence and in the types of postconflict violence that are occurring. The next three chapters use case materials from Maluku, North Maluku, and Aceh to test and develop the book's theory on why some postconflict areas continue to see frequent violence while others do not, and why such violence takes larger or smaller forms in different places.

LARGE EPISODIC VIOLENCE IN POSTCONFLICT MALUKU

In a Catholic settlement outside of Ambon, people have recently prepared an escape route to a safe place in case the conflict erupts again. They expect something to happen. It may be a small trigger: a drunken man, something wrongly said, someone out of his mind. But it could escalate quickly. In Maluku now there are many small clashes. If these are between Muslims or between Christians, it is not a big problem, even if there are impacts. But if it is between [people of different] religions, then there is a big problem. People say they are just waiting for the moment, then they want to take revenge.

—Priest, Ambon

Every time investigations of corruption are held, psychological terror emerges from thugs or people from the same region as the elites who are going to be investigated . . . for example, there are threats of murder through telephone calls, by text message.

—Muslim youth, Ambon

Maluku is the most violent of Indonesia's postconflict provinces. After controlling for the length of the postconflict period and population size, there have been more violent deaths, injuries, and buildings damaged than in any other province that emerged from extended violent conflict. Violence in postconflict Maluku frequently takes larger, more destructive forms such as intergroup clashes and riots. The deadly clashes of September 2011 in Ambon city, a discussion of which opened this book, were not isolated events. In annual per capita terms, large episodes of violence have been three times more common in Maluku than in any of Indonesia's other postconflict provinces except Central Sulawesi.[1]

The roots of Maluku's postconflict violence lie largely in the material incentives of local elites rather than in societal hatreds or a state lacking capacity. Large episodic violence has been frequent because it has proven to work for many in the local elite—including politicians, security force personnel, and thug leaders—as a strategy for accessing resources and power. Elites have nurtured local grievances and consolidated conflict-era networks. Over time, incentives to use and support violence have translated into elite and societal norms that legitimize the use of violence. The result is that violence has become an important and licit modus operandi in Moluccan political and economic life.

Violence in Maluku

The Extended Violence

On 19 January 1999 a riot broke out between Muslim and Christian youths in Ambon city.[2] Unrest soon spread encompassing other parts of the Moluccan archipelago. By the end of 1999, 1,460 people had lost their lives, 2,738 had been injured, and 7,795 buildings had been damaged. Violence continued through the year 2000 with another 1,025 people killed. The following year saw lower levels of violence (294 were killed) although 109 people died in June alone. By the time a peace accord was finally signed in February 2002 after three years of communal war an estimated 2,793 people had died, 5,057 were injured, 13,843 buildings had been damaged, and one-third of the provincial population had been displaced.

The violence pitted Muslims and Christians against each other, but the causes of the conflict had more to do with local political and economic competition than primordial hatreds. Historically, Christians had dominated political and higher-level bureaucratic positions in the province.[3] Nationwide, the rise of ICMI, the Indonesian Muslim Intellectuals' Association, which was established in 1990, coincided with and contributed to a push for Muslims to play a larger role in public life.[4] This included a drive for Muslims to capture a greater portion of civil service jobs in the regions. Christians perceived a growing Islamization of Ambon as progressive Muslims argued for a more equal religious composition in local governments at the provincial and district levels.[5] A shift in the local demographic balance from the 1970s due to the migration of tens of thousands of Muslims from Sulawesi Island heightened concerns among Christians that past access to resources and positions would be threatened.[6]

Such concerns were particularly salient because of the local economy's dependence on the public sector. In 1990 Maluku, which still included what was to become North Maluku province, had nearly fifty-five thousand civil servants, more than the province of East Java, which had a population seventeen times larger.[7] In the absence of a robust private sector, civil servant employment was one of the few means by which citizens could ensure a stable income and the security of a pension after retirement. Control of higher-level bureaucratic and political positions was key in determining the allocation of such jobs. State development resources, too, tended to be allocated through patronage networks structured along religious lines. Competition over state positions and the control of resources and jobs this afforded was fractious.

Local tensions were compounded by two national dynamics. The first was the transition from Suharto's authoritarian New Order regime, which fell in May 1998, to a more democratic polity. This created uncertainty on what the new rules of the game would be and who they would favor.[8] That Suharto was succeeded by B. J. Habibie, who had headed ICMI throughout the 1990s, only served to accentuate Christian worries. Second, the decentralization of powers and resources from Jakarta to the regions increased the importance for religious groups of accessing key political and bureaucratic jobs. While the decentralization laws came after Maluku's extended violence had started, it had been clear before that radical devolution was imminent. In November 1998, a special session of the MPR, Indonesia's upper house, adopted a decree calling for regional autonomy.[9] In this environment, violence became a means by which political goals were pursued and, with no effective intervention from Jakarta, episodic violence soon escalated into all-out war.

Local elites emphasized religious difference and the threat of other confessional groups to mobilize masses in violent actions, often for self-serving purposes. Many of those organizing the violence were local politicians. Christian leaders came largely from the secular-nationalist PDI-P, while Muslim conflict leaders were mainly attached to Islamic parties such as PAN and PPP as well as the secular party of Suharto, Golkar. Violence was used to signal strength in an attempt to build power in the local political and economic arena. In the words of one of the mediators of the peace accord for Maluku: "It was not a religious conflict—it was a conflict of interest using religion to incite unrest."[10]

Political leaders formed close alliances with criminal and militia groups. Violence escalated significantly with the arrival of Laskar Jihad, a radical Salafi group who sent more than three thousand militants to Maluku from April 2000, and who introduced order into the local Muslim militias.[11] Other groups of jihadis also arrived, sometimes collectively referred to as Laskar Mujahidin.[12] These militants worked with local political and religious figures to plan and execute attacks. Local criminal groups also emerged, sometimes to defend their communities, sometimes to take advantage of the new economic opportunities that war provided. In Ambon city, for example, preman (thugs) from Haruku Island made profits occupying the houses of fleeing Christians, then selling them on or renting them out.[13] On the Christian side, gangs such as Coker, Agas, and Laskar Kristus had links to elites in local politics, the Church, and the security forces.[14] Other community members supported and participated in the violence, sometimes because of the opportunities it afforded for local score settling and accumulation. Local economic motivations related to the use of land explain the participation of many rural villagers in the extended violence.[15] In many parts of Ambon and

Central Maluku, the land of those fleeing was taken over by others who remained in the village or by groups who arrived.[16] John Sidel argues that "it is difficult to escape the conclusion that the violence served as a means of effecting displacement, rather than displacement coming as a by-product of violence."[17]

Local political and religious elites and militia groups also collaborated with members of the Indonesian security forces. Christian and Muslim personnel often took the sides of coreligionist fighters.[18] Soldiers and police rented out their weapons and sold bullets; many security force members deserted, joining the ranks of the *pasukan siluman* (phantom forces) who fought alongside religious militia. The regional police chief, Firman Ghani, admitted that 10 percent of his forces were missing: "I don't know their location, whether they have deserted or joined the rioters."[19] The army had facilitated the entry of the Laskar Jihad militia to the province, shipping them from Java and providing them with weapons on their arrival; the police were seen as being close to the Christians. From the end of 2001 until mid-2002, some Kopassus (military special forces) troops cooperated with Coker, the Christian militia, in planning attacks.[20] In June 2000, the Indonesian president, Abdurrahman Wahid, declared a state of civil emergency for Maluku and North Maluku, bolstering the powers of the local security forces. However, this had little impact on the violence in Maluku or on the performance of the police and military.[21] The causes of such ineffectiveness related more to financial and political calculations than technical capacity. A larger police and military presence would bring bigger budgets and would allow for the generation of off-budget resources through local businesses and extortion.[22] It would also demonstrate the need for a strong military and police force as the newly democratic Indonesia took shape.

The Malino Agreement and Postconflict Violence

On 12 February 2002, three years after the initial outbreak of violence, a peace agreement was signed in Malino, South Sulawesi. The accord, which followed a similar December 2001 agreement for Central Sulawesi, signaled a new commitment to peace from Jakarta. Jusuf Kalla, then coordinating minister of people's welfare and later Indonesia's vice president, brought together Muslim and Christian leaders to sign an eleven-point agreement.

The accord led to a significant drop in violence but violence did not disappear. From March 2002 until the end of 2012, at least 529 people were killed in Maluku, 4,305 were injured, and 2,300 buildings were damaged. Ambon city and Central Maluku district, the epicenters of the extended violence and the focus of this chapter, have been particularly affected by postconflict violence. Seventy-two percent of the violent deaths, 78 percent of injuries, and 85 percent of damaged buildings in postconflict Maluku have occurred in these two districts.[23]

Large episodes of postconflict violence have also continued in postconflict Maluku. Fifty-one of seventy-three such incidents that occurred from March 2002 until the end of 2012 took place in Ambon city (thirty-four incidents) or Central Maluku (seventeen incidents).

Following a series of small incidents that collectively killed 3, injured 20, and damaged 2 buildings in February and March 2002, the first large episode of violence occurred on 3 April. A bomb was thrown from a passing car on Jan Paays street in a busy part of Ambon's Christian sector killing 7 people and injuring 56. On 28 April, the Christian village of Soya in Ambon was attacked: 12 were killed, 21 injured, and 27 buildings were damaged, including the old church that dated from the seventeenth century. In the following days, snipers attacked boats in Ambon Bay, and there were attacks near the borders of the Christian and Muslim sectors in Ambon.[24] An interreligious clash in May on Haruku Island in Central Maluku killed 5. In all, 24 people were killed in April 2002 and another 23 died in May. June, July, and August were quieter—a total of 7 people died—but on 5 September a bomb explosion in a sports field in Ambon killed 4 schoolgirls. Many of these attacks were later revealed to have been perpetrated by men linked to radical Muslim groups.[25]

Such incidents started to recede in late 2002. There were seven large interreligious incidents between 2002 and the end of 2012, the same number as occurred between the signing of Malino and the end of that year. However, the group clashes and riots of September 2011 in Ambon, which led to 8 deaths, hundreds of injuries and damaged buildings, and the displacement of 3,295 people, and a series of smaller incidents in the months that followed that led to at least 15 injuries, showed that religious identity could continue to be mobilized in violent ways.

Over time, clashes between Muslims and Christians have often been recast as being between defenders of Maluku's place in the Indonesian state and those in favor of separation from Indonesia, supporters of the Republic of South Moluccas, the RMS.[26] These identities mapped conveniently onto the old interreligious conflict cleavage. The old RMS rhetoric was revived with the establishment in December 2000 of a new Christian militia group, the Front for Moluccan Sovereignty (FKM), which aimed to continue the RMS struggle. FKM has never had more than a few hundred members, and neither the organization nor its cause has much support among Christian Moluccans. Yet its presence, even after it was banned by the Indonesian government in 2001, has allowed for the generation of a narrative that Christians are separatists whose actions must be contained. Many Muslims continue to be suspicious of RMS/FKM activities.

In April 2004, the largest episodes of violence since the end of the extended violence broke out around the anniversary of the RMS's formation. Including smaller incidents that month, 34 people were killed, 162 were injured, and 135 buildings were damaged, with close to 15,000 people displaced. Since 2004, there have been no large incidents of violence related to RMS but smaller episodes have continued. In 2007, six such incidents injured 10 people and a further four incidents in Ambon and Central Maluku in 2009 and 2011 killed 1 and injured 14.[27]

Other large incidents of postconflict violence have less obvious links to the earlier extended violence. Across the province, these include 13 large land conflicts (which resulted in 14 deaths, 196 injuries, and 242 damaged buildings), a 2006 clash between *kaki lima* (street food sellers) over access to markets that led to 200 damaged buildings, and eight cases of mobs running rampage in response to insults from other groups or in revenge attacks (11 dead, 58 injuries, and 170 damaged buildings).

Local Elite Struggles

Many of these incidents of large episodic postviolence—both those directly flowing from interreligious divisions and those with a less clear link to the past extended violence—can be traced to continuing support for and use of violence from members of the local elite. Local elites have played a range of roles from actively organizing violence to turning a blind eye to groups who instigate it. They have done so primarily for two reasons.

First, local elites have found that the use of violence works—it pays dividends and is relatively risk free. Particularly important was the ways in which resources and positions were distributed in the early postconflict period, which sent a strong signal that violence pays; this also strengthened patron-client networks between local political elites and criminal groups. With the local security forces tolerating the use of violence, often for pecuniary reasons, local elites have been able to mobilize groups to partake in violence when it is in their interest to do so.

Second, the nature of the local political system, with lasting collaboration across old conflict divides difficult, has meant that opportunities to use other more peaceful channels for accumulating resources and power have been limited. These two factors have combined to make the use of violence a common strategy for elites in postconflict Maluku.

The Benefits of Violence: The Peace Settlement, Cooptation, and Signaling

Efforts to find and sustain peace in Maluku focused on satiating the desires of local elites: politicians and senior bureaucrats, security chiefs, religious leaders, and those who had led militia groups. Many individuals fitted into more than one of these categories.

The Malino peace agreement itself said very little about the issues local elites were most interested in—how power would be shared and how resources would be distributed. Only clauses 8 and 11 mentioned elliptically resources or the distribution of power in postconflict Maluku.[28] The first said that public infrastructure should be rehabilitated by the Indonesian government; the second addressed recruitment to Pattimura University, the preeminent state higher education institution in Ambon, stating that it should be "implemented based on the principle of fairness while upholding the necessary standards." This was interpreted as an agreement to balance the composition of the faculty and students between Muslims and Christians.

Yet while the accord had little specifics on the distribution of resources, positions, or power, it soon became clear that this would be the focus of Malino's implementation. The clauses that focused on peace building were not fully implemented. The two *pokja* (working groups) that were to monitor progress on law and order and to oversee social and economic conditions were never established. The reason commonly given was that the provincial government did not provide office space.[29] However, given the small costs involved, it is clear that this was a political decision. The local government was reluctant to have others provide unwelcome oversight of their tasks or to share the discretion they held in allocating postconflict money. The independent team that was mandated to investigate the causes of violence was set up but the results of the investigation were never published.[30]

Elites focused instead on how the promised postconflict resources due to follow from the central government would be divided. The Malino agreement was not just between the warring Muslim and Christian groups but between the two of them and Jakarta. Acceptance of the terms of Malino would allow for an inflow of substantial funds, ostensibly for postconflict reconstruction.[31] The provision of such resources was contingent on a degree of calm reigning in the province. For this to happen, the groups and individuals who had resisted the peace process—some for ideological reasons, some because they had been profiting from the violence—would have to be brought onboard.

PROVIDING JOBS

Attempts at cooptation took a number of forms. Jobs in the civil service were provided to some who did not agree with the Malino process. Such jobs were valued; even though wages were low, civil service positions came with job certainty, a pension, and usually some side benefits such as cuts on contracts.

On the Muslim side, those responsible for the early wave of postconflict inter-religious violence were targeted. To a greater extent than for Christians, Muslim leaders were split on whether peace was in their interests. On 14 February, Laskar Jihad released a statement arguing that Malino was premature and that the Muslim delegates had not been representative of the Muslim ranks.[32] In the days following Malino, a group of eleven local leaders, calling themselves the Maluku Muslim Meeting Forum, announced their rejection of the accord. The Team of Eleven, as they subsequently became known, was led by Husni Putuhena of the Maluku chapter of the Islamic Defenders Front (FPI) and included other prominent figures.[33] Putuhena traveled to Jakarta to meet with the coordinating minister for political and security affairs, Susilo Bambang Yudhoyono, who along with Kalla had been instrumental in arranging the Malino talks. His attempt to garner support for the team's stance was rejected, but Yudhoyono and Kalla remained in touch.[34]

While the motivations of many within groups such as Laskar Jihad who disagreed with Malino were in part ideological, those who supported a continuation of violence were often influenced by material considerations. One Muslim delegate to Malino reflected: "There were hardliners when the conflict was happening but later they became soft. Maybe they had another motivation. For example, they wanted to occupy positions in the government. After this aim was reached, then their attitude that had been merciless suddenly changed and they became soft."[35] Another Muslim delegate noted that "the radical groups ended up agreeing with Malino because . . . they had conditions and needs. When their needs were fulfilled, they changed their minds."[36]

The example of Ustadz Mohammad Attamimi, a lecturer at the Islamic College in Maluku (STAIN), illustrates. Attamimi had been the main local counterpart to Laskar Jihad during the conflict and was a strong opponent of the Malino process as a member of the Team of Eleven. Over time, however, his position altered. He was appointed director of STAIN, allegedly at the instruction of the central government, despite strong opposition from students and many others. Yudhoyono and Kalla maintained contact with Attamimi after Malino and brought him to Jakarta several times.[37] STAIN was provided with additional facilities and funding. In 2005, the police found a cache of weapons hidden on the campus. It was unclear whether Attamimi had sanctioned the weapons or whether they were placed there by others. While he was questioned by the police no further action was taken.[38] He was subsequently appointed chief of the Religious Affairs office of Maluku Province, a job with plenty of opportunity for rent making given its responsibility for organizing hajj visits, its oversight of religious schools, and its role in managing the rebuilding of houses of worship that had been destroyed in the earlier violence.[39] Other former members of the Team of Eleven also did well in postconflict Maluku.[40]

At lower levels, former fighters and militia leaders on both sides were also given jobs. M. J. Papilaya, Ambon's mayor from 2001 until 2011, outlined the reasoning:

> Commanders during the conflict had no role after the conflict and they became a source of problems. They were nothing before the conflict but they became popular, in both Muslim and Christian communities. Some of them like Ongen Pattimura [a Muslim militant] were a big source of problems. After thinking about what to do with them, we decided to give them jobs. Some were recruited as public order officers (Satpol PP) and were given support to become disciplined. Some were given jobs as a parking officer. For instance, those from Kailolo managed the parking area being the Amplaz [Ambon mall], while those from Aboru were in Mardika [the market]. We did this to facilitate them to adjust to the postconflict situation.[41]

Militia leaders like Ongen would not have been satisfied with a low status, low pay, parking attendant job. But using militant leaders as intermediaries— allowing them to select who would be hired and to control local rackets—gave them status, strengthened their role as patrons of former militia groups, and cemented relationships with political elites that could later be used profitably.

FUNDS: CIVIL EMERGENCY AND *INPRES* 6/2003

A second mechanism for cooptation was the deployment of special postconflict assistance. Initial emergency funding to the province followed the declaration of civil emergency for both Maluku and North Maluku on 26 June 2000 under Presidential Decree (*Keppres*) 88/2000. With the emergency came resources under the control of the provincial governor in coordination with the local heads of the police and military. Smith argues that monitoring the use of such funds was not a priority for the central government and that "it was in the direct interests of central government to unofficially enable regional government elites' access to these funds as doing so 'bought back' regional support to the centre at a time of great unrest."[42] As emergency funds, money from Keppres 88/2000 lay outside the regular budget, did not require national parliament approval, and central government monitoring procedures did not apply.

Civil emergency funds were widely used to pay off those who supported continuing violence and they did succeed, to an extent, in domesticating the hardline militias and their supporters in the political elite on both sides of the religious divide. Muslim and Christian groups received funds for "security enforcement" projects. Sarundajang, the acting governor from late 2002 to August 2003, was "very adept at dealing with Muslim radicals, particularly by understanding their economic requirements and providing them with appropriate assistance."[43] Christian militia leaders who had organized violence, such as Femmy Souisa and Emang Nikijuluw, both of whom had been signatories to Malino, also received funds and projects.[44]

Money also went to senior individuals in the security forces who played a major role alongside the governor in managing funds.[45] Civil emergency funds were allegedly provided directly to the head of the military and police to bind them in to the agreement:

> In the time of Governor Saleh Latuconsina [1997–2002], the security apparatus were very late in responding to conflict incidents. But these conditions changed drastically when the position of governor was held by Sarundajang. Saleh Latuconsina was too stingy in using money, but Sarundajang was not like that. During the time of civil emergency, Sarundajang gave big funds [out]. For example, he gave an incentive to the governor [himself] of Rp. 100 million, gave the head of police and military Rp. 75 million. Maybe the money also made the security forces move fast.[46]

While such funds were relatively small they played an important signaling role. Acceptance of the use of emergency funds by local elites for personal benefit, to fuel patron-client networks, and to buy off potential challengers demonstrated the extent to which development effectiveness was not the main priority of the central state. They also indicated that using or threatening violence could be an effective tactic to receive a piece of the postconflict resource pie.

The Malino agreement promised funds for rehabilitation. A large chunk of this money was to be spent on the repair of large-scale infrastructure, a sector where funds could be relatively easily skimmed.[47] Money started to arrive in large volumes with Presidential Instruction (*Inpres*) 6/2003 after civil emergency had been lifted in September 2003. These funds became available in the 2005 fiscal year and totaled Rp. 2.2 trillion (around US$220 million) from 2005 until 2007 in Maluku.[48] This was a major component of the development funds available to the province. The Rp. 663 billion of Inpres funds in 2005, for example, was equivalent to around one-quarter of Maluku's total revenues, which had to cover personnel and capital expenses as well as development expenditures.[49] Beyond their volume, Inpres funds were important because of the level of discretion that was afforded to local political elites in allocation and implementation. Despite being central government funds, executed through line ministries, proposals for fund use came from the provincial level, and the provincial executive and legislative (as well as the powerful local military and police chiefs) worked with the line ministries to implement projects. Unlike most subnational resources in postdecentralization Indonesia, Inpres funds were largely controlled by the province rather than the districts.

Funds were used to consolidate political power and support for the Maluku accord. Money was allegedly spent on building official residential buildings for the Maluku deputy governor, a new house for the Pattimura XI military commander, a new provincial building in Jakarta, and on the local representative board's office.[50] None of these buildings had been damaged during the extended violence. Beyond mismanagement, substantial resources were corrupted. Money allegedly went to individuals within the security forces.[51] Local politicians and senior bureaucrats reportedly made billions of rupiah during the tender of reconstruction contracts.[52]

SIGNALING THE BENEFITS OF VIOLENCE

The provision of funds and positions to satisfy elites and to co-opt those who might disagree with the peace was widespread in Maluku, and it did help reduce support for a continuation of, or return to, communal war. Religious radicals, militia leaders and their followers, criminal gangs, security force chiefs, and local politicians: all benefited from postconflict resources. This reduced the incentives of key groups to support a return to extended violence for it was clear that people could do well in times of "peace."

But giving jobs, funds, and projects to groups and elites in response to threats or acts of violence in the early postconflict period had the effect of showing that using *episodic* violence could continue to be profitable. Former militia and gang leaders realized that continuing to use or threaten violence was both an effective and acceptable way to access resources. Emang Nikijuluw, the Christian thug leader, notes that "pressure, or the threat of violence, has been common in accessing and getting development projects. Those who fail to get projects often use this threat and pressure. If we are getting involved in the process of accessing the projects, others are forcefully 'stepped back' [prevented from getting funds]. This is our way of feeding our children."[53] Emang and Femmy Souisa collaborated in developing an "economic empowerment project," employing, in the words of Emang, around 140 "bad boys" with funds from the government. Each established a company, initially receiving projects of around Rp. 500 million (US$50,000), but later projects of up to Rp. 2.5 billion (US$250,000) from the Department of Public Works. Emang admits that threats and blackmail were used by both to get projects with others "forced out."[54]

The success of such tactics revealed to others that violence could be useful as a way to access political or economic benefits. As a result, other gangs emerged. On Haruku Island, Central Maluku, new gangs sprung up in Pelauw, Kabua,

Rohomoni, and Hulalui villages.[55] Other organized groups that used violence and coercion included the Baguala Muslim Youth Forum (FPMB) and the street vendors' association (APKLI Maluku), which has around four thousand members in Ambon, both led by Sulaiman Latupono.[56] Latupono has strong ties to the military, especially intelligence, and political figures.[57]

Providing resources and jobs to criminal groups also had the effect of cementing patron-client links between these groups and elites in the local government and bureaucracy and religious leaders. In an environment where there was an influx of resources—both from postconflict funds and from increases in subnational revenues due to decentralization—elites increasingly utilized these relationships with criminal groups in the local political and economic sphere. Violence, or the threat of it, was frequently used when there were resources to compete for. M. J. Papilaya, Ambon's mayor for most of the postconflict period, acknowledged the pervasiveness of such tactics: "Currently students cause many conflicts in Maluku, especially those who come from East Seram and Buru. They generally come from poor neighborhoods in their area and can be paid by the elite to stage political actions such as demonstrations. . . . There are elite interests involved. And economic interests, too, related to projects, behind the demonstrations."[58] The Ambon police chief agreed, arguing that many brawls and intergroup clashes are the result of elite actions. "Elites," he noted, "can easily provoke people and they do so to become popular." The provincial police chief thought the same: "Clashes that happen within society are usually related to interest groups or political interests."[59]

Elites have used such networks because they prove to be effective. The initial distribution of the postconflict spoils to those who continued to use or threaten violence indicated that involvement in nasty acts would be an asset rather than hindrance. Groups soon learned that violence continued to be a useful strategy in capturing a piece of the pie, and local elites found it beneficial to use the handout of cash, projects, and jobs to such groups to cement patronage relationships with local violence entrepreneurs. Violence became an important currency in local politics.

Low Costs: Security Sector Tolerance of Violence

The use of episodic violence by criminal leaders and local elites proved not only to be useful but also largely risk free. This is because the local police and military have tolerated, and sometimes supported, such violence. There have been clampdowns on violence when it is perceived to be linked to transnational terrorism, a result of pressure from Jakarta. After the attack on a police station in Loki in 2005, for example, there was a rapid response from the police. But such operations were almost always led by national-level police, especially the elite

Indonesian counterterrorism squad, Detachment 88. Where there has not been a strong signal from Jakarta, local police and military have taken little action to investigate incidents of unrest.

During Maluku's extended violent conflict, many police and military took sides, working with local leaders and militia groups. As Indonesia's polity stabilized, the motivations and ability of security forces to stoke large-scale extended violence greatly diminished.[60] However, elements of the local military and police force in Maluku continued to have incentives to allow *episodic* violence to occur.

In large part, motives are financial. In the civil emergency period, and when Inpres funds were still flowing (until late 2007), BKO troops (extra nonlocal forces stationed in the province) received salaries from multiple levels of government. Police BKO have been fully withdrawn but two battalions of military BKO, totaling around eleven hundred personnel, remain.[61] These troops no longer receive extra salary payments but many are active in the informal economy generating rents that benefit individual personnel and that are channeled upwards through the military structure. Business activities allegedly include running internet cafes, car washes, small cinemas, illegal mining, drugs, running *kosts* (boarding houses), gambling, and renting cars.[62] The police are said to be involved in similar businesses.[63] These financial benefits created incentives for the military and police to retain high numbers in the province. Allowing a certain level of violence was a means by which the police and military could justify their large numbers.

According to the former mayor of Ambon, M. J. Papilaya, military and police intelligence sometimes spread false reports of shootings or attacks to justify the presence of BKO forces.[64] Indeed, as one influential peace activist argued, "Security has become a commodity in Maluku. If violence occurs, more security personnel are deployed. And then more budget is needed!"[65] A local representative of the National Commission on Human Rights (Komnas HAM) was not alone in stating that the BKO troops tend to create more problems in communities than they solve. The commission has called for a removal of the nonlocal troops from the province.[66]

Lack of effective responses to violence are thus a product of the incentives of law enforcers rather than weak state capacity. This has limited the costs to local elites and criminal groups of using violence. Links between individuals within the police and military and large incidents of violence can be drawn in a number of cases, including Maluku's most deadly episodes of postconflict violence.

Security Sector Involvement in the RMS Riots of 2004

On 25 April each year a celebration is held in Ambon to commemorate the separatist RMS's anniversary. In 2004, three hundred people gathered at the house of Alex Manuputty, FKM's leader. The police soon arrived, arresting FKM's secretary-general, Moses Tunawakotta, and hauling down UN and RMS flags.

Moses was brought to the provincial police office on foot. Around two hundred people followed and another thousand later joined the procession, marching three kilometers to the police headquarters. The large crowd led many onlookers to believe that this was a FKM/RMS parade. Rally participants again raised the RMS flag. While the police took away the flag, another appeared. After a short time outside the office, the group left with a police escort.

When they passed through the stretch of road from Tugu Trikora to Pohon Pule in central Ambon they were blocked by a group flying Indonesian flags. A clash ensued. Snipers in multistory buildings shot eight people, six of whom died. All of the dead were Muslims. Violence then escalated. Houses, a church, and the Christian university were burned. In retaliation, SMA Muhammadiyah, an Islamic senior high school that had been a pilot project for multiculturalism in Ambon accepting Christian students, was burned. Shootings by snipers and burning took place sporadically until 30 April. Violence only ceased after the central government sent in extra troops.

The clashes could be viewed as a natural consequence of continuing tensions between the Christian and Muslim communities of Ambon in the early post-Malino years. Yet the violence appeared to be organized. The snipers seemed to be professionals or to at least have significant experience. How had they been able to access the buildings and why were none arrested? Suspicions soon emerged about the conduct of the security forces. Why had the police allowed for a procession of FKM supporters through Muslim areas of the city? Why were there no efforts from the security apparatus to stop the early violence? Why did it take the arrival of forces from outside of Maluku to deal with the violence, despite the long experience the military and police had in dealing with riots and violence in Maluku?

One factor was the need for the military to demonstrate that large numbers of personnel were still required in Maluku. The previous year had been relatively quiet—28 people had been killed in Maluku in 2003 compared to 101 in 2002. In the months leading up to the riots there had been plans to pull out BKO troops.[67] Indeed, both during and following the extended violence, the RMS issue had been consistently exaggerated by the military as a way to receive additional funding. The RMS issue was particularly effective for this because of the concerns of the Indonesian state about the vulnerability of the country to secessionist threats. Taking harsh actions against supposed RMS separatists was also a sure way for individuals within the military to get fast-tracked promotion.[68] Over time it emerged that some of the snipers were most likely former military men, including some who had joined the pasukan siluman but who had retained close contact with other security personnel.[69]

Limited Opportunities for Peaceful Politics

Violence has thus proven to be both beneficial and relatively risk free for local elites including politicians, security force leaders, and the heads of criminal
groups in postconflict Maluku. The rewarding of those who have used or threatened violence, and lack of action taken by security forces, sent out a signal that
episodic violence paid. However, the decision by local elites to use violence in
political and economic competition in Maluku is also a function of the percep-
tion that there is a lack of other options. The structure of local politics, where it
is extremely difficult for elites to make lasting deals with those from other faith
backgrounds, has limited opportunities for peaceful collaboration.

Edward Aspinall has observed that the political saliency of ethnicity in Indonesia has subsided as democracy has consolidated: "Elites' dominance has been
accompanied by a culture of deal making and compromise that in the arena
of ethnic politics, as well as in some areas of political life, has had important
conflict-ameliorating effects. In Indonesia, patronage networks on the whole
tend to cross ethnic lines rather than harden them, and to blunt ethnic competition rather than intensify it."[70] Patronage is indeed the dominant logic of Moluccan political life. Yet patron-client networks in Maluku continue to be structured
along confessional lines.

In national and local legislative elections, Muslim voters tend to vote for Muslim parties while the candidates and supporters of PDI-P, the dominant party in
postconflict Maluku, are almost entirely Christian. Collaboration takes place at
election time. From the end of the extended violence, all pairs of candidates for
the provincial governor and district head (*bupati/wali kota*) elections have contained both a Christian and a Muslim on the ticket.[71] Such informal power sharing has minimized tensions during elections. Across Maluku Province, there have
been 107 violent election-related incidents in the postconflict period, leading to
5 deaths, 114 injuries, and 80 damaged buildings, with most of these relating to
district-level contests.[72] This compares favorably with levels of electoral violence
in many other provinces in Indonesia.[73]

Yet while joint tickets limit violence around elections, such collaborations
tend to be but electoral marriages of convenience, merely preceding within-ticket
battles over the distribution of resources after election results are announced.
The case of M. J. Papilaya and Syarief Hadler, mayor and deputy mayor of Ambon from 2001 to 2006, illustrates. Papilaya was a Christian PDI-P politician
while Hadler led the Islamic PPP in the province. While at first they worked well
together, their relationship soon soured. Papilaya promoted a policy to build a
new business center in Passo village, a Christian area. Hadler opposed the policy on the basis that more Christians than Muslims would benefit. The project

continued and, as a result, the two went their own ways during the later period of their term, with little to no collaboration. They did not stand together in the next election.[74]

Continuing efforts by Muslims to balance jobs in the bureaucracy also demonstrate the extent to which resources tend to flow through religiously based patronage networks: "The equalization of power [is a big issue]. This can be done in the government or the bureaucracy. For example, if the governor is a Christian, then the deputy governor will be a Muslim, if the head of local ministry A is Muslim, then the head of ministry B will be Christian."[75] As with joint electoral tickets, attempts at religious balancing have played a role at generating adherence to the post-Malino political settlement, for they have ensured that neither side would lose out completely. However, the allocation of jobs and resources by religion has also reinforced systems of religious-based patronage, in so doing cementing networks that have been mobilized for violence. It has ensured that religious identity continues to be emphasized by those seeking positions of power. This is the risk of such "consociationalist" arrangements,[76] which, in their fullest form, have formal mechanisms for allocating positions of power by ethnic or religious identity. In Maluku, there has not been a formal institutional pact on sharing power between groups. But informal norms around balancing have developed, accentuating conceptions of politics as a zero-sum game and one that is structured by the same divides that were mobilized in the extended violence.

BALANCING AND VIOLENCE AT UNPATTI

The series of clashes in the postconflict period over the balance between Muslim and Christian faculty and students at the state Pattimura University (Unpatti) can be explained by this.[77] Under the colonial Dutch, Christians dominated the formal education sector, and this has continued to the present at Unpatti. In 1998, before the extended violence broke out, Christians made up around 70 percent of the teaching staff, students, and administrative officials. As violence escalated from mid-1999 to the year 2000, Unpatti was controlled by the Christians. A rumor circulated among Muslims that there was a weapon repair shop for Christian soldiers in the polytechnic building at Unpatti. Muslim troops attacked Unpatti in early July 2000 and burned most of the buildings.

Religious imbalance in the composition of Unpatti was included as one of the items in the Malino accord.[78] This item is frequently cited by Muslims as providing a basis for their demands for "proportionality," both in the recruitment of teaching staff, students, and administrators, as well as in the replacement of officers at the faculty and university levels. While the seat of the Unpatti rector has traditionally been allocated to a Christian, his leadership team always included Muslims. As such, contestation relates to which seats in the leadership team Muslims win. Muslims have tried to ensure they receive the position of first vice rector (responsible for academic affairs) or second vice rector (administrative and financial affairs), which they see as being more important than that of the third vice rector (student and alumni affairs). Tellingly, the opportunities for spreading largess are greater for the first and second vice rector positions. In many cases, Muslims have ended up with only the unpopular position.

Tensions between Muslims and Christians, on and off the campus, crystalize each time a rectoral or faculty-level election is held. In March 2010, there were small clashes and a riot during the election of the dean of the faculty of economics. Following this, a mediation team was finally created with ten members of both Muslim and Christian teaching staff chaired by a former Unpatti rector. The team produced a number of recommendations yet problems continued. In July 2011 riots erupted again amidst a heightened political situation that flowed from two developments: the ongoing selection process of the Unpatti rector; and conflict over control of the student union. Contestation in both areas ran along polarized religious lines. Another trigger, the announcement of the admission results for the new cohort of students, with Muslims rumored to only account for 15 percent of new students, created more heat.[79] The resulting riot did not result in casualties but it damaged many of the campus buildings.

LIMITS TO COLLABORATION AND PEACEFUL COMPETITION

Voters' choices, the nature of patronage networks, and struggles within Unpatti all show the extent to which competition for power and resources within Maluku continues to be structured along religious lines. Efforts at balancing—in the makeup of the Unpatti faculty and student body and by ensuring there are joint Christian-Muslim tickets for local executive elections—can defuse tensions in the short run. But collaboration and power sharing are usually superficial. While executive political power at the provincial and district levels is shared between Christians and Muslims, the constructed nature of the tickets means that heads and their deputies have their own power bases and networks, each built on a different religious community. After elections are over, and decisions on the distribution of resources and positions start to be made, tensions between the two often rise sharply with each seeking to satisfy their own group. There is little space for the development of deeper political alliances that cross old conflict divides.

In this context, coercion and violence can be a more effective political strategy than building support around policy positions. When promoting and negotiating ideas and interests through conventional political processes and institutional mechanisms, leaders often find themselves in a cul-de-sac with no way forward. With deep and mature political alliances difficult to develop and sustain, violence, or the threat of it, becomes a useful strategy.

Violence Specialists and Societal Support for Violence

The use of violence by elites in postconflict Maluku has been facilitated by local conditions that create willingness among many community members to condone and sometimes participate in violence. Religious divisions are marked and structure life, in large part because it is in the interests of local elites to continue to emphasize such differences and identities. Continuing segregation, and a lack of effective local-level reconciliation, ensure that suspicions remain. In this environment, some perceive violence to be in their own interests; these conditions also make it easy for elites to prey on fears and prejudices to get people to participate in violence. The continuing presence of criminal preman groups with strong ties to political elites, many of which draw on militia structures from the extended violent conflict, means that there is a large pool of labor that can be easily mobilized for violence.

Violence Specialists

Many of the incidents of large episodic postconflict violence in Maluku have involved local preman groups. During the extended violence, Coker, Laskar Kristus, FKM, and Agas played active roles on the Christian side. Other organized criminal groups, including a gang of young Muslims from the Hatuhaha area on Haruku Island, worked with outsiders from Laskar Mujahidin and Laskar Jihad in perpetrating violence. These groups did the bidding of local political elites and received support from elements of the police or military. By and large, they have remained active in postconflict Maluku.

On the Muslim side, many of the outsiders who arrived in Maluku to take part in jihad were arrested, killed, or drifted away. Laskar Jihad was formally disbanded in October 2002, a result of internal conflict and pressure from the central government. A few hundred ex-Laskar Jihad remained in Maluku but most now criticize violent jihadi ideology and the use of violence.[80]

However, links between some in the local political elite and members of the outlawed militant jihadi organizations persisted. Former Laskar Jihad members have developed close links to government officials and community leaders.[81] Members of the other outsider jihadi groups who remained in Maluku operate in more covert ways, making it hard to detect their extended networks. Many suspect they are protected by local political figures.[82]

Local militants such as Ongen Pattimura have also worked closely with political elites. Ongen commanded men from Latu village on Seram Island during the extended violence, and he subsequently formed a large urban gang in Ambon.

Reportedly receiving training from a member of the terrorist Jemaah Islamiyah organization, his group was involved in terror attacks, including the 2002 Jan Paays bombing and an attack on the 2004 Villa Karaoke café that killed two. Yet despite an arrest warrant being issued in April 2002, and his reported escape to hide in Sulawesi, he was able to continue to cultivate political links. This culminated in his standing for the Islamic PKS party in the 2004 Ambon elections.[83] The PKS needed a local boy like Ongen who had a large network at the grassroots level. Ongen, in turn, needed an Islamic political party to transform his influence among youngsters into political currency. It was only after the attack on a police post in Loki on Seram in 2005 that he was finally arrested.[84]

Many of the other local Muslim gangs who emerged during the extended violence also consolidated because of their links with local politicians and other elites. Such groups have been active in violence in the postconflict period:

> There are groups who try to create issues because they will benefit in the event of conflict. These are the people from Hatuhaha: Pelauw, Kailolo, Rohomoni, and Kebau. During the height of the conflict, these groups looted abandoned shops. They also occupied homes left by residents. The houses were then rented to someone else. If the owners wanted their house back, they had to pay because that group said they were looking after the houses that had been long abandoned. . . . Before the conflict, communities in the four areas had a poor standard of living. But after the conflict, they became suddenly rich with a nice big house and many cars.[85]

On the Christian side, too, many of the old conflict-era gangs and militias remained strong in the postconflict period.[86] The relationship between elites and the militia led by Femmy Souisa and Emang Nikijuluw has endured. Both continued to live in Maluku and have close relationships with Christian elites in both the bureaucracy and the church. Their groups continue to be used by local politicians around election times and when other key political events, such as the launch of corruption investigations, occur.

The ongoing presence of militia and criminal gangs is an alternate explanation for why large incidents of violence have been frequent in postconflict Maluku. Could it be that the endurance of such groups alone explains why violence has been so common?

It is certainly the case that these groups have played a prominent role in acts of postconflict violence and that if they were absent postconflict violence would likely occur with less frequently. However, their enduring strength is best explained by the incentives and actions of local elites. As we have seen, local leaders have supported and provided protection to thugs. The provision of jobs, contracts, and resources, combined with tolerance of their activities by political and religious elites and the security forces, explains their organizational continuity. Politicians and other local elites have allowed such groups to flourish because having them around is very much in their own interests. In contrast to efforts to clampdown on radical Islamic groups with links to transnational terror organizations—which have been led by Detachment 88, the national antiterrorist arm within the police, and which have led to many arrests—there have been few efforts by security agencies to deal with local gangs.

Community Support for Violence

The use of large episodic violence by local elites and violence specialists is supported by community tolerance of, and sometimes active support for, violence. Three factors—historical conflict, ongoing segregation, and a lack of effective reconciliation activities—have shaped societal attitudes toward violence.

Historically, Maluku has been prone to local conflicts stretching back at least to the arrival of the colonial powers.[87] The Portuguese and the Dutch supported some local leaders at the expense of others, sowing the seeds of future contention. Traditional communities (*negeri*) developed *adat* (traditional unwritten) laws determining their boundaries but different communities often had different and conflicting adat.[88] The encroachment of the modern state in the New Order era, and in particular Law 5/1979 which standardized village governance structures, weakened such traditional systems. In recent years there has been a resurgence of adat in Maluku and elsewhere, a result of decentralization that has created greater space for the recognition of local customs and identities in public life. This has reinvigorated customary systems of land tenure, which often conflict with private land rights as determined by the state.[89] This has led to a rise in conflicts between villages over the location of their borders. Such long-standing tensions have contributed to postconflict violence both directly and indirectly. Between March 2002 and the end of 2012 there were nine large land conflicts in Ambon and Central Maluku.[90] Historical tensions have also reduced interethnic solidarity, which could have acted as a counterbalance to religious animosity.

A second issue is the continuing segregation of Muslim and Christian communities in postconflict Maluku. The province, and in particular Ambon Island, remains heavily segregated with Muslim and Christian communities living in distinct areas.[91] Day-to-day interaction is common and Muslims and Christians generally feel free to venture into each other's areas during the day, although there are few mixed residential communities. However, when tensions rise, as they did in the aftermath of the September 2011 riots, interaction drops markedly. Ongoing segregation has led to a lack of trust and fear between groups with the result that small-scale incidents of violence, often between youth groups, are frequent, especially in Ambon city where segregated communities live in close proximity to each other. From March 2002 until the end of 2012, there were 151 incidents of popular justice violence in Ambon, leading to 11 deaths, 187 injuries, and 85 damaged buildings.[92] Small disagreements frequently turn violent, especially when the youths involved are drunk. Such clashes in turn solidify inter-religious suspicions and tensions.

A third factor that has kept societal tolerance of or support for violence strong has been the limited effectiveness of local-level reconciliation efforts in Maluku. Both during and following the extended violence, there were hundreds of initiatives aimed at building peace and reconciliation, including those from local nongovernmental organizations as well as international development agencies.[93] Many of these, and especially those driven by local actors, focused on using traditional adat institutions as a basis for creating new identities and trust that crosses confessional divides. Yet these activities often covered small areas, sometimes became formulaic, and were often ill equipped to make progress in the light of broader problems such as continuing segregation and local and national political interests.[94]

The presence of deep and continuing societal tensions points to another alternative explanation for the continuing high levels of postconflict violence in Ambon and Central Maluku. It could be that local tensions—between villages and between Muslims and Christians—are more important in accounting for postconflict violence than elite motivations and behavior.

Such an analysis ignores the extent to which grievances and mistrust are in large part a product of elite actions in the postconflict period. This can be seen if we explore why segregation has continued. Fear of return and difficulties associated with the occupation of land are certainly factors. Yet these have not been overcome because of a lack of support from the local government for the repatriation of people displaced by the conflict. The overwhelming focus of government postconflict programming has been on building infrastructure and paying off potential spoilers rather than repatriating displaced persons or local-level reconciliation activities. Where funds were used for displaced people, they were used to help them resettle in new areas rather than to facilitate their return. The widespread corruption of Inpres funds for displaced persons certainly did not help.

The presence of segregation, fear, and mistrust means that communities are prone to provocation or to elite manipulation. Indeed, it is commonly argued that ensuring that communities remain segregated has been a conscious political strategy of elites. A Christian leader noted:

> I don't like segregation. It provides a bigger chance for provocation to work. It can be misused by actors who play a negative role. . . . The

government has not done much to make people safe. . . . They have not done much because they are busy with other things [said in a scornful tone]. . . . It's all about politics! I think the government prefers segregation so they can potentially utilize it later. I really see that. Otherwise, why would it be kept like this?[95]

Similarly, the lack of government attention to reconciliation and peace-building activities can be explained by the advantages that having separated and tense communities can afford. Government-sponsored peace-building activities, such as the creation of a network of local traditional leaders (Majelis Latupati) and the activities of the state-mandated Inter-Religious Harmony Forum (FKUB), have focused more on strengthening patronage networks, which run along religious lines, than supporting reconciliation.[96]

Explaining Spikes in Violence

Large episodes of postconflict violence occur frequently in Maluku because local elites have continuing incentives to strategically use violence and to tolerate its use by others. The ability of elites to "play" in this way has been bolstered by the presence of organized violence specialists and continuing tensions between religious communities. Over time the frequent use of violence, by elites and violence specialists alike, has translated into norms where violence is deemed an acceptable strategy in political and economic life.

However, large episodic violence has varied over time in postconflict Maluku. Figure 4 shows that incidents of large episodic postconflict violence—and their destructive impacts—have been concentrated in 2002, 2004, 2008, and 2011. These years account for 78 percent of the deaths from large incidents of violence across the eleven postconflict years, 68 percent of injuries, and 58 percent of damaged buildings.[97]

The book's theory predicts that there will be upsurges in postconflict violence at times when key actors have heightened incentives to support violence. Given that large episodes of violence require the involvement or support of local elites, we can expect that changes to the incentives of such elites will be most important in determining changes in levels of such violence over time. The theory predicts increases in levels of violence: (a) when resources are expected to sharply increase or decrease; (b) at election times, when there is heightened competition over resources; and (c) when there are expected changes to the rules that govern the allocation of resources. The Maluku evidence provides support for some but not all of these hypotheses.

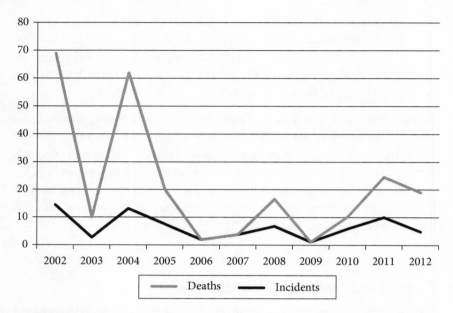

FIGURE 4.   Large incidents of postconflict violence in Maluku over time.
Source: NVMS

Changing Levels of Resources

The relationship between changing levels of resources and large-scale episodic violence is not straightforward. As table 12 shows, there is no correlation between either levels or increases in subnational resources and large incidents of violence. Revenues increased most sharply in 2006. We might expect that there would have been higher levels of large episodic violence in 2005 and early 2006 as competition rose over the allocation of such resources. Instead, levels of large-scale episodic violence were lower in those years.

There is a closer relationship between levels of special postconflict funds and large episodes of postconflict violence. The 2004 uptick in violence can be partly explained by the expected arrival of Inpres funds, which are not counted in subnational revenues as they are executed through national line ministries. In 2004 these funds were not yet flowing but elites knew that the funds would be coming and bargaining over their use began.[98] Elites, including criminal leaders, used violence as a means to ensure that they would receive a good share of the resources that started to disburse in 2005. Both Muslim and Christian leaders had incentives to incite violence. Pictures of Ambon in flames again would likely speed the arrival, and potentially increase the volume, of postconflict assistance to the province. The FKM mobilization can be interpreted as a show of strength

TABLE 12.   Subnational revenues in Maluku and large episodic violence over time

YEAR	SUBNATIONAL REVENUES (RP. BILLION)	INCREASE ON PREVIOUS YEAR (%)	LARGE EPISODES OF VIOLENCE (#)	DEATHS FROM LARGE EPISODIC VIOLENCE (#)
2002	189.5	25%	14	55
2003	249.2	31%	3	7
2004	Data not available	—	13	49
2005	309.2	—	8	12
2006	427.7	38%	2	0
2007	544.4	27%	4	0
2008	621.5	14%	7	10
2009	721.3	16%	1	0

Source: World Bank subnational dataset (2012). Data for Maluku are available only until 2009.

by some elites in the Christian community. The responses of Muslim groups can be understood in part as local Muslim elites signaling their own strength as the pie was to be divided.

Once funds started to flow again in 2005, levels of violence again reduced. No one was killed from a large violent incident in Ambon or Central Maluku between 2006 and the end of 2007. The availability of plentiful resources, combined with police operations targeting jihadi groups, in particular following the attack on a police station in Loki, reduced levels of violence. However, Inpres funds had been fully disbursed by 2008 and many groups who had benefited (both elites and gangs who supported their agendas with muscle) saw resource channels closed off. M. J. Papilaya, Ambon's former mayor, reported that groups who had been involved in the conflict and who had subsequently received assistance in the form of jobs, money, or projects began to cause trouble again as Inpres funds tailed off: "They were angry with me. They asked why some received assistance in the past but many did not get this assistance now. I told them that now the situation was back to normal so everybody should follow the rules. Previously the situation was not normal so I could do this or that. But whenever the situation is normal, I am no longer able to do so."[99]

Papilaya's statement points to the reason why there is a stronger relationship between levels of large episodic violence and Inpres funds than with the overall levels of subnational resources. The difference lies in the level of discretion available to local elites in the deployment of the special postconflict funds. As we have seen, at the time they were spent there were few checks and balances on how these funds were used and the central government was happy to ignore any allegations of corruption for the sake of peace. In contrast, there are more constricting rules and accounting procedures in place for regular government funds. This meant that competition over special postconflict money was particularly fierce.

Changing Rules of the Game: Corruption Investigations

Another factor that contributed to the rise of large episodic violence in 2008 was the initiation of investigations of the misuse of Keppres and Inpres funds. Violence has been frequently used by elites to deter such investigations.

In 2002, the Indonesian parliament established a Corruption Eradication Commission (KPK), which became active in 2004.[100] While the KPK issued just two indictments in 2004, this had increased to thirty-seven by 2007 and thirty-eight people were indicted the following year. Until October 2011, the agency boasted a 100 percent rate of successful convictions for those indicted.[101] This contrasts with a successful conviction rate of 51 percent between 2005 and mid-2009 for indictments initiated by the Attorney General's Office. Further, the average sentence for those indicted by the KPK and tried under the Anti-Corruption Court was 4.8 years compared to 6.2 months for those found guilty in the general courts.[102]

The changing tolerance of corruption impacted Maluku. Whereas in the early post-Malino period the central state was not concerned with ensuring that postconflict or other development funds were distributed cleanly, this began to change. A series of corruption investigations from 2008 included investigations of the use of 2006 provincial funds, which were to be distributed to those displaced by the conflict, and 2007–8 education and sports funds in Central Maluku.[103] The director and treasurer of the displaced persons project and the head and treasurer of the Central Maluku education department were arrested and convicted. After another scandal emerged relating to graft in provincial-level social department projects, the head of the department, his treasurer, and the tender committee were all arrested in mid-2010. Corruption investigations grew even more frequent in 2011.

No higher-level politicians have been prosecuted despite many alleged cases of corruption. An investigation by the prosecutor with regards to funds allegedly skimmed during the building of the Maluku provincial parliament office in 2006 began in 2007. Another project with alleged corruption was the construction of the Maluku provincial guesthouse in Jakarta where there was reportedly a markup of Rp. 13.5 billion (US$1.35 million). Allegations about corruption in the building of an official house for the governor of Maluku also persisted. In both cases, KPK sent a team to Maluku to investigate. Yet there was no follow-up following the visits.[104]

One reason why many corruption cases stall is the use or threat of violence by local elites as a strategy to prevent investigations. While it is usually possible for people to pay off the local branch of the Attorney General's Office to prevent an investigation being conducted, it is much harder to use this tactic to stop

KPK investigations.[105] As such, elites often use other approaches. The overturning of the conviction of the Aru district head on corruption charges came after a series of violent demonstrations. Even the latest Unpatti riot, discussed earlier, coincided with the issuing of a permit from the Indonesian president and the Ministry of Home Affairs to undertake an investigation of several local officials for corruption.[106] Two cases illustrate how violence or the threat of violence is often used to deter investigations.

THE BURNING OF LETWARU

On 9 December 2008, the village of Letwaru in Masohi, the capital of Central Maluku district, was attacked with fire devouring seventy-one houses, ten *warung* (food stalls), and the local church. The mixed Muslim-Christian village had been attacked during the extended violence on the last day of 1999 but was rebuilt. While trauma remained, Muslims and Christians started to interact again. Few expected violence to return.

Two weeks before the latest attack, rumors spread that a Christian teacher in a local elementary school had told her students that polygamy was a sin.[107] Some Muslim parents took offence and this spread to the broader community, with Asmara Wasahua, a candidate for the local parliament, stirring up emotions. On 25 November, in neighboring Amahai subdistrict, rocks were thrown at buildings and a house was torched. A Christian house on the border between Letwaru and the Muslim village of Lehane was attacked. The incident was reported to the Central Maluku police intelligence but no action was taken. Many Christians started to feel that local politicians and security personnel were deliberately stalling despite the risk of violence escalation.

On 8 December, Asmara issued an order to Muslims in Masohi to demonstrate against the schoolteacher and demand her firing. The protest, held the next day, started at the district head office, continued to the education department, and then moved on to the district police headquarters. Security forces were drawn from around the town to the city center. While the demonstration was ongoing, groups equipped with machetes formed in several parts of Masohi. Metal drums and tree trunks blockaded the main road of the town. Before long, smoke was billowing from Letwaru.

The case was puzzling. The offending teacher was not from Letwaru and did not live there. The demonstration was in the city center. So why was Letwaru burned? The Central Maluku police, the chief of which boasted when interviewed of the quality of their local intelligence operations, had information that violence was likely to erupt.[108] Yet both the police and military were strangely absent from the streets when violence started to escalate. Security bases were only five minutes away but help did not arrive until after the houses were on fire. Those who came did little but watch. The day before the burning of Letwaru there had been a co-ordination meeting between the security forces, local authorities, and religious leaders. However, the local police chief and military commander left the meeting early. Before the riot there was an order from the police chief to close the armory, which meant that officers who arrived in Letwaru were not equipped with weapons.[109] No legal action was taken against anyone involved in the riot, with no arrests or subsequent investigation.[110]

People pointed to the riot as being deliberately perpetrated by local elites. Information leaked in mid-November that the KPK would visit Masohi to investigate corruption in the use of health and education projects financed through Inpres funds. Many informants, including community members, senior policemen, local bureaucrats, journalists, and activists, said that those who were concerned about the impending visit of the KPK had planned the violence.[111] The violence was alleged to be a deliberate strategy aimed at making Jakarta think twice about investigating such sensitive issues. If the environment was tense, then surely such an investigation could do more harm than good.

Following the riot, Abdullah Tuasikal (the Central Maluku district head) and Karel Albert Ralahalu (the provincial governor) appeared on television. The talk show was a vehicle to communicate the message to Jakarta that conditions were unsafe and that a visit by the KPK would be harmful. In such a situation, national standards on corruption should not be applied to Maluku. The KPK visit was subsequently called off. This was not the first time violence had led to the KPK abandoning a visit. Several years before, a riot had broken out in Pelauw in Central Maluku just before the KPK was due to visit. The planned visit was also canceled.[112]

Other motivations may also have played a role. Asmara Wasahua, the organizer of the demonstration, was standing for the local parliament and many people argued that mobilizing anti-Christian sentiment was aimed at bolstering his electoral chances.[113] The head of the local military intelligence was apparently very close to the district head and other senior local leaders and has been known to create incidents at their behest. A very senior civil servant in Central Maluku boasted: "Intelligence is close with the district head and with me . . . which means if I have a problem, I can ask the Intel to create a small turmoil as a diversion. . . . After that, they would create provocation."[114]

PROVOCATIVE TEXT MESSAGES

In late November 2010, an anonymous text message was sent out across Ambon claiming that Muslim villages had been attacked.[115] The message came shortly after the KPK had started an investigation of the use of Inpres funds. In early November, five staff from the KPK came to Maluku for a week. Beyond suspicions of corruption of Inpres funds, the mission was also a response to the finding of the state auditing agency (BPK) in the first quarter of 2009 that Rp. 1.7 trillion (US$170 million) of funds were not accounted for. Cases to be investigated included the building of the governor's mansion, the misuse of Inpres funds for displaced people, and the construction of the Maluku government guesthouse in Jakarta and the Maluku local parliament building. Shortly after the message was sent out, a decision was made to suspend the investigations. Although it is unclear who distributed the text message, informants saw the logic behind it for many in Maluku's political elite who could have been implicated in the corruption cases:

> Suddenly the SMS circulated saying that there would be riots so KPK decided not to follow up. It seems that terror is an effective strategy to prevent the eradication of corruption. Currently the governor is a Christian, while the deputy governor is a Muslim. If the governor was arrested for corruption, this would cause a big problem. So sectarian issues are blown up to resist the efforts of the KPK to investigate. In the end, Jakarta got scared.[116]

Indeed, many saw the potential for violence being an effective way to fend off investigations:

> Regional leaders use their power, as do those in Jakarta. If they are to be inspected then they create an issue. This is to test the power of Jakarta. Will they still be inspected? The rumor [spread by text message] was meant as a signal to the center that this region needs extraordinary special treatment. What can deter the inspection is a *force majeure*, like a natural disaster. In Maluku, social unrest plays this role. Therefore, it was initiated to avoid the inspection. . . . Jakarta also thinks, if the inspection follows through what then will be the consequences? If they receive only Rp. 2 or 3 billion, but this ultimately leads to losses of trillions [because violence restarts], then they will be against this. This causes the regional rulers to do as they please, to use the funds to their benefit.[117]

> The governor is a Christian while his deputy is a Muslim. If the governor is checked by the KPK, then automatically the deputy will assume the position. The people of Maluku will also automatically think the governor is guilty [if he is investigated]. The Muslims will demonstrate to ask for the governor to be checked and brought to justice while the Christians will undertake retributive demonstrations to support the governor. If the deputy becomes governor, then there will be a lot of Muslims who will hold important positions in the regional government.

> The strategic positions will change, triggering jealousies from the Christians. Both groups, Muslims and Christians, can play this issue for their benefit. Therefore, after calculation, the investigation is too risky, both for people from the capital and the region.[118]

Violence has proven to be a useful way for local elites to prevent corruption investigations. As the strategy has proven to work, it has been adopted more widely.

Heightened Competition: Elections

In contrast to expectations, there have not been upsurges in violence in postconflict Maluku around election times. As we saw earlier, levels of electoral violence have been lower in Maluku than in many other Indonesian provinces. The reason for this is that the informal norm of ticket sharing has limited both the costs and benefits of gaining elected office for each religious group. This has made elections less hot. However, such power sharing has only served to displace such contestation to periods after elections are over and bargaining over power and resources begins.

Other Factors: Identity and Ideology

The theory, focused as it is on competition over resources and power, is less able to explain the spike in violence in the year following the signing of Malino accord. The year 2002 saw twelve large episodes of mainly interreligious violence. Some of these episodes were perpetrated by militants aiming to either ensure payoffs or to provoke a continuation of the communal war because of the personal economic benefits this would bring. Yet it is certainly not the case that all of those involved in these incidents were driven by such pecuniary concerns. Many members of outsider jihadi groups, and some radicalized locals, favored a continuation of violence because their initial goal—to purify Maluku of heathens and infidels—had not been achieved. Violence was in part strategic, sending a signal of strength to the other side. Yet it was also sometimes emotive and symbolic, driven by hatreds and a desire for revenge. Patricia Spyer, in her discussion of the violence that followed the Malino accord, observed that while people suspected the violence was "orchestrated by those who profit" from it, past violence has deepened the religious definitions of opposing parties and led to "concentrated pools of resentment and bitterness."[119] This helped legitimize the actions of some hardliners who continued to use violence. Over time, however, such emotive violence became less prominent. In part, this was due to security operations to rid Maluku of outside jihadis in the context of declining tolerance from Jakarta of actions that were increasingly framed as being terrorist.

Changes in leadership, for example, when a moderate was elected as head of the synod of the Protestant church, were also important, as was a loss of enthusiasm from some local combatants as they felt those emphasizing religious difference were manipulating them.[120]

A Toxic Mix: The September 2011 Riots

The September 2011 riots, the largest outbreak of violence since the RMS violence of 2004, shows how the factors I have identified in this chapter can combine to form a toxic mix. The riots, summarized in the opening chapter, left eight dead, almost two hundred injured, led to the burning of more than three hundred houses, and displaced more than three thousand people.

It is still not clear who or what caused them.[121] Some theories emphasize societal motivations. Communities remain segregated and there is a lack of trust. This explains how easily people could be mobilized to participate in violence once tensions erupted. Criminal preman groups are also active in postconflict Ambon and were undoubtedly involved.

Others have emphasized local elite goals. One theory sees the source of the riots in intra-Muslim power battles. The Hatuhaha federation of five villages in Haruku Island, Central Maluku, has traditionally produced provincial leaders. However, this elite has declined in recent years and now occupies few prominent positions. Ambon is the last area of Hatuhaha influence in the province. The decline has produced resentment and some have allegedly tried to use the Islamic card, emphasizing Christian political dominance, to win over other Muslims. A preman leader from Hatuhaha urged friends to take cover before the rioting began. The implication may be that he, or others, took advantage of the motorcycle driver's death to instigate rioting that fitted with their anti-Christian narrative, in the expectation of later electoral or financial dividends.[122]

Another theory points to the role of corruption investigations. In July it emerged that the governor was being investigated by the state Financial Transactions Reporting and Analysis Center (PPATK) because of four suspicious financial transactions related to his account in 2009 and one in 2008.[123] He was not the only member of the local elite fending off investigations. In the months before the riots the Ambon high court had been considering several cases of alleged corruption against senior figures. Those under pressure included the south Buru district head and figures in West and East Seram, Southeast Maluku, and Tual districts. There were almost daily demonstrations, some pushing for prosecutions, others for the investigations to be canceled. Groups from outside of Ambon were mobilized when their leaders were being investigated with (sometimes violent) demonstrations occurring.[124] As with the November incident of the previous year, anonymous text messages provoked both religious communities after the driver's death. It was in this environment that violence erupted again.

Other theories point to collusion from the local security apparatus. Two truck-loads of police were moved out of Ambon just before the riots broke out and information that riots were planned at the funeral of the motorcycle driver did not lead to an increased security presence. Seven of those who died were killed by the bullets of the police and military personnel sent in to restore peace. The riots also came just as the National Human Rights Commission released a report recommending that the nonorganic BKO troops be withdrawn from Maluku.[125] In the months leading up to the September riots, the provincial police chief had also been pressuring the civilian government to increase police resources in Maluku, requesting extra resources due to the province's archipelagic nature and high living costs.[126] The outburst of violence could strengthen the police's claims for extra resources. On the other hand, police passivity and slowness could simply be a function of a lack of capacity.

It is difficult to adjudicate between the different explanations of the events. Indeed, the search for a single cause may inevitably be fruitless. In all likelihood, a combination of the different factors contributed to the September riots. However, the outburst of violence is consistent with the theory proposed in this book. There were many reasons why members of the local elites might want fresh violence to occur. Violence also served the interests of some nonelites, including criminal groups with links to elites. Tolerance or support for violence from some within the security forces created an enabling environment for violence to occur. Threats to interests help explain the timing of the outbreak of violence.

This chapter has shown that the book's theory is useful in explaining why large episodic violence has been frequent in postconflict Maluku. The theory suggests that for large episodic violence to occur frequently local elites and violence specialists should support the use of violence.[127] Maluku provides ample evidence of this. The theory suggests that support for violence from each set of actors is, to a significant degree, a function of the extent to which they perceive violence to be a viable and effective strategy for accumulating or protecting wealth or status. The Maluku evidence shows that this has been the case for local elites, including politicians and security force leaders, and for violence specialists. Both have used violence to advance their material interests. Decentralization and, particularly, the arrival of postconflict funds meant that there was much to compete over and violence has been used to this end.

The theory highlights the ways in which responses to past acts of violence, in particular in the early postconflict period, provide information on the expected costs and benefits of using violence. Where past acts of violence were rewarded with resources or state positions, violence is more likely. Again, this has explanatory power in postconflict Maluku. Providing jobs, contracts, and other funds to those who used or threatened violence sent out a signal that violence paid. Local elites used violence to protect and advance their own interests. This was a relatively risk-free strategy with security agencies tolerating the use of violence.

The theory suggests that the propensity to use violence is driven in part by the absence of other channels for accumulation that do not require the use of violence. We would thus expect to observe barriers, real or perceived, for elites and others to gain elected office, jobs in the bureaucracy, or to grow licit economic businesses. This has indeed been the case in Maluku. The focus on the balancing of religious groups in the political sphere has made it difficult for relationships that cut across conflict divides to be sustained. Patronage networks are constructed within religious groups, accentuating conceptions of difference and raising the temptation for leaders to mobilize followers to use violence for their purposes.

The theory also suggests that violence is more likely at times when revenues increase or decrease sharply and when there are changes in the rules about how they can be allocated. In Maluku, changes in the resources available were important, in particular where there was significant local discretion on how funds could be allocated. In Maluku, violence has also risen at times when corruption investigations have been launched or are ongoing.

Maluku, which has seen regular incidents of large episodic violence, thus appears to provide solid evidence for the theory. However, the fact that many of the factors hypothesized as contributing to postconflict violence are present in Maluku does not, in and of itself, provide solid proof that they are indeed causing postconflict violence. Our confidence in the theory will increase if we can show that they are not present in a similar place that has not seen frequent large episodes of postconflict violence. North Maluku is one such area. It is to an analysis of that province's postconflict peace that we now turn.

NORTH MALUKU'S PEACE

Now there are no real problems anymore. There are still people feeling bitter, but just one or two. Kao and Makian people interact in peace. Anyway, the problem was never about the Makian who live here, we don't have a problem with them, the problem was the government!

—Former Christian militia leader, Pediwang, North Halmahera

Sometimes now, there are small incidents. People also try to provoke others, for example through text messages. The youth still play! They say, "He's Christian, he's Muslim." But people already understand how to deal with this and are not provoked anymore. Problems are quickly solved by the community leaders.

—Muslim community leader, Mamuya, North Halmahera

The postconflict experience of North Maluku stands in stark contrast to that of Maluku, its close neighbor. Both provinces were devastated by extended violent conflicts with Christians and Muslims murdering each other en masse. Similar dynamics of heightened local political competition in a time of national transition contributed to the outbreak of violence. Yet since fighting ceased in North Maluku in June 2000 its postconflict trajectory has been very different to that of Maluku. Per capita violence fatality rates are one-third of Maluku's and significantly lower than in any of Indonesia's other postconflict provinces. Large episodes of violence, of the type that have afflicted postconflict Maluku, have occurred infrequently with just eighteen such incidents scattered across the province in more than eleven postconflict years.

In this chapter, I explain why North Maluku's postconflict period has been relatively peaceful. I focus in on two districts. North Halmahera saw the most destructive extended violence anywhere in Indonesia. Ternate, the former provincial capital, was the seat of many of the players who led the extended violence and who shape the province's postconflict economy and politics. Both districts are now peaceful.

I argue that just as issues related to the expected benefits and costs of using violence, and the availability of other opportunities for accumulation, explain

Maluku's continuing violence, these same factors allow us to understand why postconflict North Maluku has been largely peaceful.

Violence in North Maluku

The Extended Violence

North Maluku's extended violent conflict began in August 1999 with clashes between the indigenous ethnic Kao and migrant Makian populations in Malifut, a rural area in the north of Halmahera Island.[1] The violence related to the proposed establishment of a new subdistrict in the area where the Makians lived. The Kao opposed this, claiming the area as their traditional ancestral land. The recent discovery of gold in the area made the issue more contentious. On 18 August, a Makian attack destroyed two villages. Two months later, after calls from the Kao for compensation from the government were ignored, several thousand Kao attacked Malifut, bombing or burning every house in sixteen villages and driving the entire community from Halmahera.

After riots on the islands of Ternate and Tidore in November, violence escalated sharply with Christian-Muslim clashes in North Halmahera from December. More than 1,300 people were killed in December 1999 alone, with 1,167 of these deaths occurring in North Halmahera. Violence continued until late June 2000 when the imposition of a state of civil emergency, conflict fatigue, and a stalemate between the two sides led to a sharp fall in violence.

As in Maluku, the roots of North Maluku's extended violence lay in heightened political competition in a time of uncertainty on the future rules of the game. During the New Order years, the institutions of Golkar (Suharto's ruling party) and the bureaucracy (controlled by Golkar) allowed for control of the region from Jakarta and created a relatively cohesive local elite that benefited from center-to-periphery patron-client networks. As in Maluku, the urban middle class was dependent on the state for civil service jobs and contracts. In the final years of the Suharto era, local factionalism increased as different leaders, and their networks, saw the potential for new political opportunities in a time of change. In Ternate, new challenges to existing power structures arose as groups from northern parts of the city, aligned around the traditional sultan of Ternate, tried to reassert power at the expense of "southern" groups, the ethnic Makian, Tidore, and Sanana, who had served as the New Order's regional functionaries.[2] Competition was heightened by the promise of the establishment of a new province for North Maluku, which had previously been governed from Ambon. This increased the rewards of capturing power. Many in the local elite believed that if the sultan became governor he would give bureaucratic positions to his support-ers, Ternateans and Halamaherans, including Christians, at the expense of others.

The new province was inaugurated in October 1999 just as violence escalated in Malifut. While the initial violence was over local issues, a slow response from district elites, who were preoccupied with the formation of the new province, re-sulted in escalation culminating in the displacement of the entire ethnic Makian migrant population. At this point, escalating violence was in large part a result of sins of omission from local elites who could feasibly have prevented it, although the conflict was taken advantage of by the sultan and his political adversaries. But violence was soon to be used as a more overt and conscious political strategy.

As around fifteen thousand displaced Makians arrived in Ternate city, the administrative heart of North Maluku, some Muslim political figures reframed what had been an ethnic dispute as an interreligious one. While religion was peripheral to the outbreak of violence in Malifut, the fact that the Makians were Muslim and the Kao largely Christian set the scene for the development of the interreligious narrative that defined later stages of the conflict.[3]

The Makians had become one of the more important groups in regional poli-tics and many potential candidates for the new governor position were either Makian or closely linked with the group. Bahar Andili, the *bupati* (district head) of Central Halmahera, was one front-runner. While not ethnically Makian, he had close ties with Ternate's Makian community and was backed by the stu-dent organization, Makayoa, who led protests against the Kao and who may have played a role in instigating violence in the Kao-Malifut area. A second contender, Thaib Armaiyn, a senior bureaucrat, was Makian. Both leaders supported violent protests by Makian groups against their displacement, which soon took on more political anti-sultan tones as he was viewed as having supported the Kao in the earlier violence. Local political entrepreneurs started to reframe the violence as being religious in nature, a means of undercutting support for the sultan who, de-spite being Muslim, was seen by many to be sympathetic to Christian causes. This was also a way for Makians to rally support from other Muslim ethnic groups. (Many of North Maluku's ethnic groups, including Muslim ones, were resentful of the Makians' rise to power in past decades and had no particular sympathy for them.) Reframing the Malifut conflict as interreligious allowed Makians to garner support beyond their own group, from the Tidore and others who might field challengers in forthcoming elections. The spread of rumors and provocative pamphlets were used to shift the discourse, with the violence now viewed as being driven by, and expressed in terms of, religious difference.[4]

Anti-Christian riots in Tidore and Ternate in early November displaced the local Christian population with most fleeing to Halmahera. Ethnic Makian Muslims, now residing in Ternate, and Muslims from Tidore left for central and southern Halmahera. These Pasukan Putih (White Forces, so called because of the color of their headbands) attacked Christian communities there.[5] Displaced Christians fleeing to Tobelo, the center of northern Halmahera, brought with them stories of Muslim atrocities. In late December, Christian militias responded. In northern Halmahera, hundreds of Muslims died in attacks on villages by the Christian Pasukan Merah (Red Forces). Battles between villages devastated the subdistrict of Galela and most Christians fled to Tobelo. The interreligious carnage taking place in neighboring Ambon and Seram islands increased suspicions and fears between religious communities in North Maluku. In contrast to the violent political battles in Ternate, the escalation of violence was largely the result of the insecurity felt by both the Christian and Muslim communities that allowed violence to spiral out of control.[6]

While Christians and Muslims were fighting across the province, political conflict came to the fore in Ternate. On 27 December, a fight broke out between members of the Pasukan Kuning (Yellow Forces, a militia group supporting the sultan of Ternate) and the Pasukan Putih. The latter group was made up of many who supported other Muslim leaders such as Andili and Armaiyn. Over the coming days, clashes spread throughout the city, ending with the defeat and surrender of the sultan. He subsequently fled the province after calls spread from figures including the sultans of Tidore and Bacan for his arrest, his gubernatorial hopes in tatters.

As in Maluku, elites organized violence for political purposes, which led to an escalation of violence that soon began to spiral out of control. As the Ternate fighting drew to a close, groups of Muslim warriors (Pasukan Jihad), built on the networks of the Pasukan Putih, were dispatched to Halmahera, resulting in rapid escalation as Christian and Muslim groups committed a series of atrocities.

As in Maluku, the security forces also facilitated the escalation of violence. Little was done to prevent violence in Tidore and Ternate during the riots of November 1999 or to stop violence reaching Halmahera. Once the conflict had spread, the role of security forces was limited to offering protection to displaced people in camps and assisting their evacuation to other areas, sometimes taking advantage of the situation to extort them. There are widespread suspicions in North Halmahera that as tensions were building in December 1999 the military fueled these by circulating fabricated rumors of impending attacks. Manipulations were aimed at securing benefits of various forms: military units posted in conflict areas receive greater funding, higher remuneration, and better career opportunities, and conflict situations also offer many opportunities for racketeering, extortion, or looting.[7] A Christian leader in North Halmahera remembered: "In 2000, you could be sure that if the military was stationed in a village, not even a week later the village would be destroyed . . . the TNI [Indonesian military] was only after security money. If you didn't pay, they would be the ones burning down houses."[8] However, some units, in particular nonlocal battalions brought in to secure the border between Tobelo and Galela, successfully deterred Muslim and Christian fighters from crossing over the front, preventing further escalation.

The Peace Settlement and the Absence of Postconflict Violence

Large-scale fighting in the province drew to a close in June 2000. An estimated 3,257 people had been killed in less than a year. At least a quarter of a million people had been displaced, and much of the province's infrastructure had been destroyed.[9]

There are a number of reasons why the extended violence came to an end. First, there was a stalemate. By 19 June, with the fall of Duma village, all Christians had been expelled from Galela. Christians remained in and around the local regional capital, Tobelo. But an attack on Tobelo by the Muslim militias was not feasible given Christian numbers and weaponry and protection by military troops. Second, many militiamen had spent months in the field and were exhausted. These ad hoc troops had left jobs and families behind for what they thought would be a short period and were keen to get back to ordinary life. In contrast to Maluku, there had not been a large influx of fighters from outside of North Maluku. Third, the imposition of civil emergency on 26 June, which had so little impact in Maluku Province, had a positive effect in North Maluku, emboldening the security forces to take more forceful action despite no increase in troop numbers.[10] Christian and Muslim communities were cantoned, separated by military troops, preventing tit-for-tat violence. Finally, there was pressure for peace from local elites. Political leaders in Ternate, having achieved their initial goal of ruining the sultan's electoral chances, met with Christian and Muslim militia leaders, explaining to them the importance of the implementation of civil emergency.

North Maluku's peace settlement was largely made up of a series of informal meetings. There was no government-mediated peace accord like those signed in Malino for Poso and Maluku. Yet, in stark contrast to Ambon and Central Maluku, peace held. Large incidents of postconflict violence have been infrequent in Ternate and North Halmahera. Of the twelve incidents that had occurred by the end of 2012, only two (both in Tobelo, the capital of North Halmahera) had their primary basis in interreligious issues. The first, in which one person was killed, took place in August 2002. A second incident occurred on 25 October 2003 when a bomb exploded in a house in Gamsungi village, killing four members of the Muslim Javanese family who lived there. This was not long after Muslims had returned to Gamsungi having fled at the height of the conflict. Before the Javanese family had moved in, the house had been occupied by displaced Christians from Payahe in South Halmahera. A rumor spread that the Christian family had left the bomb behind in their house to kill Muslims. This led to newspaper headlines, tensions, and the risk of retaliatory attacks. Some Muslims sent their wives and children away for protection. Things, however, eventually calmed down.[11]

The largest case of postconflict violence in North Maluku related to the contested 2007 gubernatorial election.[12] After a disputed vote count, two candidates claimed victory: the incumbent governor, Thaib Armaiyn, and the losing challenger from 2002, Abdul Gafur. As legal challenges reached the Constitutional Court, both sides mobilized supporters and thugs in an attempt to influence the final verdict. While no one was killed during the dispute—more by luck than anything else, given that bullets were fired and bombs exploded—at least fifty people were injured and thirty-four buildings damaged.[13] Yet the case did not escalate any further and by late 2010, when my research in North Maluku began, few people felt that there was much potential for new large-scale violence in the province.

Tensions, sometimes resulting in violence, are still present in the province. Gang fights in Ternate and Tobelo are fairly frequent, land conflicts occur, and elections have sometimes been tense. Yet fighting is usually not along religious or ethnic lines, and there is little link to the extended violent conflict from before.

Local Elite Support for Peace

In contrast to Maluku, the use of violence by local elites for political and economic purposes has not been common in postconflict North Maluku, and elites have tended not to support or tolerate the use of large episodic violence by others. Three factors are particularly important in explaining why this is the case.

First, the peace settlements in North Maluku did not focus on the split of power and resources between elites. Postconflict funds arrived long after the end of the extended violence, meaning that early peace talks, and subsequent implementation, did not focus on dishing out the spoils of peace, concentrating instead on locally important issues such as the return of displaced people. Unlike Maluku, few local elites used violence, or the threat of it, to try to access jobs or funds in the early postconflict period.

Second, on the occasions when people tried to use violence for political and economic purposes it backfired. The signal that violence does not pay was very different to that in Maluku. Local elites in both Ternate and Halmahera found it more beneficial to be seen as champions of peace.

Third, there were plentiful opportunities to compete for power through nonviolent institutional processes. The establishment of new districts in some of

North Maluku's former violence hot spots, including North Halmahera, created opportunities for aspiring elites. The pragmatism of elites, who often collaborated across formerly hot confessional or ethnic lines, meant that old conflict cleavages did not sustain in the way they did in Maluku. Political competition in North Maluku has not been characterized by a zero-sum logic as has been the case in Maluku. Rather, political life in postconflict North Maluku closely resembles that elsewhere in Indonesia, where patronage and money politics tend to be the preferred tools of influence rather than violence.

Peace Settlements: Reconciliation Rather than Payoffs

Peace came from the people. . . . It was a natural process; there was little intervention or engineering by local government as happened in Ambon and Poso.

—Catholic priest in Ternate, 9 December 2010

The peace process in North Maluku was very different to that in Maluku. Rather than having one central Malino-like process, a number of localized efforts were initiated in different areas of the province. Reconciliation in North Maluku was the product of various initiatives, limited in scope to a particular region, and largely uncoordinated between them, led by local elites and communities rather than the central, provincial, or even district governments.

It was decided early on that North Maluku would not have a formal mediated peace agreement. A combination of the largely successful imposition of civil emergency and the leadership of local political, religious, and ethnic leaders who took the initiative to start their own peace talks meant that there was little need for the central government, or indeed any other third party, to start a formal process. Large-scale violence in North Maluku ended eighteen months before the Indonesian government first experimented with using a mediated peace accord to end the intercommunal violence in Poso, Central Sulawesi. Of the key figures behind the use of that strategy, Jusuf Kalla was not in the government at the time civil emergency was imposed, and Susilo Bambang Yudhoyono was minister of mines with no remit to work on security or peace issues. Although Vice President Megawati attended a peace meeting in Galela in late 2000, the peace process in North Halmahera was already well underway and was being led by local Christian and Muslim leaders.[14] In Ternate, too, there was no formal accord, which did not necessary mean that the losers of the conflict (Christians and followers of the sultan) were in no place to demand concessions.

The North Maluku peace talks did not involve negotiations over the distribution of benefits—in the form of assistance packages, cash transfers, political access, or other forms of preferential treatment—to militia leaders. North Halmahera illustrates this process. Following the declaration of civil emergency for Maluku and North Maluku on 27 June 2000, a series of local reconciliation efforts were held.[15] The beginnings were inauspicious. On 9 August, the local military unit (the Banteng Raiders 401) held a meeting with local Christian leaders just before it was rotated out. Only Christians attended because most Muslims from the area were still displaced in other parts of the province. It was agreed that a meeting would be held the next day, facilitated by the navy, which would bring together Muslim and Christian leaders. The subsequent meeting, held on a military vessel off the Galela coast, failed with Muslim leaders, under pressure from their grassroots followers, deciding not to attend. A fresh attempt was made with the organization of an October meeting in Mamuya, a small town on the Tobelo-Galela border. Facilitated by the military, and in the presence of the district government, the meeting was attended by thirty Christians (led by Hein Namotemo) and ten Muslims (led by Samsul Bahri Umar). Two contiguous halls housed the delegations and were tightly protected by security forces. Both sides exchanged declarations of good will, and Christians agreed to let Tobelo Muslim refugees return for the fasting month.

A second meeting was held in Mamuya a month later. This time more than two hundred Muslims and Christians from Tobelo and Galela attended, joined by leaders from the district government and military. Dialogue took place in two rounds with each side making a number of demands. While differences remained, there was agreement that people should be given access to their relatives' graves ahead of Ramadan and Christmas. It was also agreed that small groups from each side would be formed to evaluate the security situation and that further talks should be held. A third Mamuya meeting on 24 December brought together six hundred Muslims and Christians and was marked by the presence of Indonesian vice president Megawati and officials from the national government and other parts of North Maluku.

Over the next four months a series of smaller follow-on meetings were held involving religious and traditional leaders as well as civil society organizations.[16] Primary topics of discussion were the return of displaced people, weapons surrenders, and how to consolidate support for peace at the grassroots level. They were followed with an eleven-day meeting in January in Tobelo of two hundred Christian community leaders, known as Halmahera Baku Dapa 1. Attendees enjoined the government to investigate the responsibility of elites in the conflict and agreed to advocate for the formation of a new North Halmahera district. It was agreed that reconciliation efforts should be based on community practices and draw on cultural adat traditions that crossed religious divides.

On 19 April 2001, a peace declaration was held in Tobelo at the *hibualamo* (traditional adat) field, with religious, cultural, and community leaders from both sides as well as commanders (*kapita*) from the conflict attending. A traditional hibualamo ceremony was held with cultural symbols such as betel and areca nut, tobacco, and clove cigarettes used. A cultural procession involved both Christians and Muslims and was followed by the reading of a peace declaration in the local language.[17] Further peace declarations were signed in Morotai on 29 May 2001 and in Galela on 30 June 2001. On 12 January 2002, an event involving Muslim and Christian leaders from Tobelo, Galela, Morotai, Kao, and Loloda—the five regions of North Halmahera—was held in the hibualamo field to underline the need for the establishment of a new administrative district. It was agreed that everyone would work together for this and that a prerequisite for the formation of the new district would be the (re)building of traditional bonds of solidarity between the area's different groups.

In the early postconflict days, decision makers in North Halmahera made sure that former militia leaders were included in the processes of reconciliation and postconflict rebuilding. However, this was not attached to the provision of targeted funds or positions. Rather, the focus was on acknowledging people's earlier conflict role:

> The way to smooth reconciliation with the field-level actors [*aktor lapangan*] was to involve them in the process. Every time there was a meeting, we would invite them, make them feel important. Benny Doro [former head of Pasukan Merah, the Christian militia]: we had to make sure to tame him [*kita harus reda*]. For example, we had this meeting with Ibu Mega [then vice president of Indonesia] and the head of the TNI [the Indonesian military], Widodo. I introduced Benny and Widodo and said: "This is the *panglima* [commander] of the Indonesian army, and this is the *panglima* of the North Halmahera army." This made Benny feel important. We invited him to all the meetings.[18]

The contrast between the peace talks and agreement in North Halmahera and in Maluku is clear. The Halmahera talks focused largely on practical local issues, for example the acceptance of the return of displaced people in a given village or set of villages and how to guarantee sufficient security to allow farming to begin again. There was little, if any, discussion of resources, spoils distribution, or power sharing.

WHY WAS THE PEACE SETTLEMENT SO DIFFERENT TO MALUKU?

North Maluku's peace process was different than Maluku's for two reasons. First, there was wide acceptance that peace was necessary. This meant that among the local elite there were few dissidents who would need to be co-opted. Second, the level of government assistance was much lower in the early postconflict period, meaning that peace discussions could focus on repairing relations rather than carving up resources.

As North Maluku's extended violence drew to a close, few in the local elite supported a continuation of violence. At the provincial level in Ternate, and in stark contrast to Maluku, one side, the incumbent elite, had won. The sultan had been removed as a potential challenger to the southern faction for the leadership of the new province. The ethnic Ternateans could have potentially been spoilers. But with their patron, the sultan, forced to leave the province, they were politically weak. With the absence of any alliance with other ethnic groups, they realized that violence would not take them far and thus efforts were not necessary to co-opt them. For provincial elites, violence had served its purpose of consolidating the political status quo.[19] Other political channels could be used for achieving power in the postconflict era. While the Ternate elite was by no means completely cohesive, as demonstrated by tensions between different challengers in the 2002 and 2007 gubernatorial contests, these cleavages did not map onto those that had been mobilized during the extended violence. There was little political capital to be gained from continuing to emphasize the differences that had been accentuated during the earlier violence, especially given that, as discussed below, conflict fatigue was widespread.

In North Halmahera, where the worst Christian-Muslim violence had taken place, most elites also had little motivation to instigate violence in the early postconflict period. In contrast to Maluku and Ternate, where violence throughout had been largely driven by elite pecuniary and political incentives, the extended violence in Tobelo and Galela can be better explained as a consequence of a security dilemma, with both religious communities arming and initiating attacks to prevent themselves from being killed or exploited. Throughout the first half of the year 2000, when violence was still raging, Christian and Muslim leaders were in regular contact making preparations for peace.[20] It was decided that "enough blood had been shed" and that the peace process must focus on genuine reconciliation.[21] By June 2000, the conflict had reached a stalemate with neither side capable of military victory and support for ongoing violence waning. In such an environment, local elites such as Hein Namotemo (a Christian leader who later became the head of the new North Halmahera district) and Samsul Bahri Umar (a former jihadi leader who later became chairman of the North Halmahera district parliament) presented themselves as champions of peace. In Ambon and Central Maluku, elites focused on distributing the spoils of peace and buying off those who might threaten their arrival. In contrast, the lack of support for continuing violence from local elites in Ternate and North Halmahera meant that there were few dissidents in North Maluku who threatened peace to be bought off.

Equally important in explaining the different peace settlement was the relative absence of postconflict funds in North Maluku, and especially in North Halmahera, in the immediate years after the extended violence ended. This meant that decisions on the distribution of funds did not become the core of elite-level peace negotiations. Reconciliation activities were not colored by attempts to capture postconflict money. The province received civil emergency funds of a similar level to those in Maluku.[22] However, this was dwarfed by the funds to finance the start-up costs of the new province, and little money flowed to areas such as North Halmahera where the violence had been the most intense. The far more substantial Inpres funds totaled around Rp. 1.6 trillion (US$160 million) for the province.[23] This makes them slightly higher in per capita terms than in Maluku. But, importantly, they arrived in North Maluku a full five years after the extended violence had ended. In Maluku, Inpres funds arrived three years after Malino. However, the actual Presidential Instruction, which indicated that funds would arrive, was issued just one year after Malino, and at a time when large incidents of violence continued to occur in Maluku. Further, the Malino agreement contained a specific clause on the provision of funds by central government. From the start the implementation of Maluku's peace focused on how expected funds would be allocated. In North Maluku, many of the remnants of the extended violence, such as widespread displacement and destroyed public and private infrastructure, had largely been dealt with by the time funds arrived, and there was little desire from local elites or communities to risk a return to violence by squabbling over the distribution of assistance.

SEEKING POWER AND RESOURCES IN POSTCONFLICT NORTH MALUKU

To be sure, among some local elites who had helped to organize the violence—for example, by running jihadi coordination posts, poskos, in Ternate and Tidore—there were expectations of rewards in the postconflict period and many did benefit. However, the peace deal in North Maluku did not include access to resources and positions, and many other former militia leaders did not benefit materially in the postconflict period. Rather, those who had been active in the extended violence who benefited later did so through the processes of collaboration and coalition building that characterize many other areas of Indonesia.

Some examples illustrate. Muhammad Albar was a key organizer on the Galela-Tobelo front. Before the extended violence he ran a library in Tobelo and acted as an intermediary for Ternate businessmen running projects in northern Halmahera. After the end of the violence his stature rose, and he now has large stakes in agricultural and other businesses. He won a seat in the provincial parliament in 2009, heading the PBB-Gerindra fraction. His rise was built on his ability to cultivate a wide range of political networks, and he played a role in securing support for Thaib Armaiyn in the 2007 gubernatorial election. Other prominent leaders or supporters of the militia who have done well in the postconflict period include, but are by no means are limited to, Zadrak Tongo-Tongo and Alex Supelli, Christians who became members of the provincial parliament in 2004; Imran Jumadri, a leader in the anti-sultan clashes of December 1999 who became a member of the provincial parliament for the 2004 and 2009 terms; Abdul Gani Kasuba, a Muslim preacher who helped organize the recruitment and transportation of jihadis to Tobelo and who is now deputy governor; and Wahdah Zainal Imam, one of the organizers of the jihad and anti-Christian riots, who was already a member of the Ternate legislature and who gained reelection in 2004. Others such as Muhammad Selang, another posko jihad leader, have not entered politics but have seen their careers advance. Selang, a former teacher, became head of a department in the provincial Ministry of Social Affairs and allegedly does well from facilitating contracts.

The rise of such figures, however, tended to be a result of regular processes of political patronage and networking rather than the handout of postconflict resources or preferential access to jobs based on people's role in the conflict: "Many conflict leaders became politicians, were in the bureaucracy, but this was not because there was deliberate concessions or compensation for them. There are also many people in politics who did not play a role in the conflict. The conflict actors did not get privileged access."[24] Some figures did use their conflict-era networks and their proven ability to utilize street power to gain political office or business contracts. The capacity of former militia leaders to mobilize masses for demonstrations and to collect votes made them useful to politicians during elections. As a result, some militia leaders were adopted by political parties in the 2004 legislative elections and secured seats. Yet the militia leaders who managed to pursue successful careers as political or business figures in postconflict North Maluku tended to be the organizers who handled recruitment, logistics, and fundraising. Their success relied less on the threat of resumed violence than on their ability to adapt to the postconflict context by converting the organizational capacity and support networks they had acquired or further strengthened during the conflict into a political commodity that could be exchanged for favors, such as parliament seats, bureaucratic jobs, or government construction contracts. As one activist remembered: "After the conflict a lot of people got suddenly wealthy. But it was not so much that the conflict leaders became rich. Rather, it was bureaucrats who were in a position to divert funds."[25]

DIMINISHED MOTIVATIONS TO USE VIOLENCE

This different type of peace process—driven by elite desires for a genuine reconciliation in North Halmahera, the consolidation of the status quo in Ternate, and the absence of extensive postconflict resources to argue over—lowered the risk of postconflict violence through its impact on the motivations of local elites and members of society to use violence.[26]

Local elites—almost all of whom did not support renewed extended violence— saw more benefit in championing peace than preaching ethnic or religious hatred. In North Halmahera, because talks did not revolve around the distribution of power or resources (zero-sum issues) but on the return of displaced people and reconciliation (agreement on which would provide simultaneous benefits to both communities), there was little temptation to use violence to affect outcomes. Similarly, in Ternate the incumbent elite had won and the sultan's followers were marginalized, meaning that violence was not necessary (for incumbents) or possible (for potential challengers). As we will see later, this also meant that old conflict networks did not sustain.

Indeed, leaders from both sides of the conflict attribute the relative success of North Maluku's peace process to the absence of discussion of how resources should be used: "If the government or military had got involved, it would be all about money, not from the heart . . . the government approach would fail. So we built from the bottom instead."[27] A retired academic and politician in Ternate, reflecting on why the postconflict period was more peaceful in North Maluku than elsewhere, argued that the financial dividends that accompanied peace processes in those places incentivized a continuation of violence. In Aceh and Papua, he argued, "conflict was maintained as a way to keep assistance flowing."[28]

The Costs of Using Violence: Responses to Threats

Most local elites, including militia leaders, were not motivated to continue to use violence, and, as such, levels of violence in the early postconflict period were low. However, there were some cases where violence was used by those who did not agree with the peace. The responses to these incidents by local leaders and security forces sent a signal that, in contrast to Maluku, the costs of using violence would be high.

Until 2003, isolated incidents of violence continued in North Halmahera. Some violence was triggered by local leaders who had been involved in the earlier fighting and who were not supportive of peace and reconciliation. In 2002, bombs went off in Morotai, Tobelo, Galela, and Kao.[29] One former Pasukan Merah fighter remembered, "Whenever a reconciliation meeting was held, you could be sure there would be an attack the next day."[30] While a large reconciliation meeting was ongoing in Togawa, Galela, in early 2001, a group of Muslims who did not agree with Christians returning to Galela started chopping down clove, nutmeg, and coffee plants and coconut trees in nearby fields. The fields were then set on fire. Yet local elites on both sides told attendees of the meeting not to respond. As one community leader put it, "We decided just to let them show their anger. To let it be. If the Christians wanted to respond seriously, then the conflict would happen again. And we did not want that."[31]

Such uses of violence were not effective in undermining the peace or in securing resources or power. In postconflict Maluku, those who threatened or used violence in such ways were usually appeased, receiving jobs or projects. In contrast, there were no efforts at cooptation in North Maluku. Instead, those who opposed the peace were increasingly marginalized as the peace process gained momentum.

Other incidents of early postconflict violence were provoked or directly committed by members of the military or police. In the early postconflict period, some in the police and military had been involved in selling the houses and property of displaced persons.[32] They feared that a return to peace would diminish such lucrative opportunities. Villagers in Mamuya, Galela, heard a series of bomb explosions throughout 2001 and 2002, which they suspected local military units had set off to try to raise tensions.[33] In Maluku, such strategies helped the military retain large numbers of troops in the province. Yet in North Maluku local elites who favored peace disciplined those within the security forces who were causing trouble. Officials and leaders were often able to get rid of military personnel who they felt were causing problems. In a number of villages including Mamuya and Duma in Galela, complaints about the behavior of local military personnel led to them being replaced by other units:

> The military were there but they were not doing a good job. . . . An example: one Sunday I was in Duma. Some people from outside the village came in a truck to have a picnic. They drank alcohol. They threw an empty bottle out of the truck and it hit the military post. The military got angry, went to the truck and started to hit people in the truck, very hard. The police were better than the military. The TNI [military] were ready to attack the people. . . . So we asked the government to send the military away, not just from Duma but from all of Galela. The village head of Duma went to the battalion commander and asked him to withdraw the military. And they did it![34]

Local officials such as Hein Namotemo, then a subdistrict head and later the North Halmahera district head, also complained to the governor about the military presence and were able to reduce the number of nonlocal BKO troops stationed in North Halmahera:

> The TNI's [military's] presence [in North Halmahera] was making the problem worse because of religious bias. Christian military members

would defend Christians. Muslims would defend Muslims. Sometimes the TNI triggered conflict by supporting people of the same religion. Not only the military but also the Brimob [military police]. . . . There were incidents between the security forces and civilians in the period of the caretaker bupati [Jidon Hangewa, 2003–5]. These incidents happened because of the negative attitude of security forces. In one particular incident, a civilian was killed. I led a demonstration to reject the presence of security forces. A military boat was due to arrive in the Tobelo port in 2000, and we refused and sent it back. For three months, there were only organic [locally-recruited] forces in the district, no external forces. Sinyo [Sarundajang, the caretaker governor in 2002] called me and told me, "You already have a bad reputation since you always reject the military. Now accept them." But I asked, "Can you guarantee to us that there will be no more disturbances?"[35]

Namotemo was successful in making the case for a reduction in troops, arguing that it was necessary to "eliminate external factors."[36] In contrast to Maluku, the military and police played a relatively small role in reconciliation and postconflict reconstruction. In North Halmahera, both sides agreed early on not to include "outsiders" in the process of reconciliation, and this included the security forces. Security forces did benefit from the declaration of civil emergency with extra budget provided for security from Jakarta. But after civil emergency status was lifted their influence became much more limited. In the words of one politician, "They got some small projects, but they were not the main player anymore."[37] The relative quickness with which stability returned to North Maluku made it difficult for the military to justify keeping large numbers, and troop levels began to fall, in particular from 2004 before Inpres funds arrived. Unlike Maluku, there are now almost no nonorganic (nonlocal) military in the province.[38]

Indeed, compared to Maluku, the police, and sometimes the military, have been more effective at dealing with incidents of violence where there is a risk of escalation, such as those where religious identity is implicated.[39] This is not to say they always perform effectively. Some interviewees saw them as being negligent in preventing brawls between youths.[40] There have been some clashes between the police and the military.[41] But beyond the early postconflict period, there is little evidence of either the military or police systematically stoking violence for their own gain or of being manipulated by members of the local elite to allow violence to occur. As in Maluku, some within the security apparatus continue to engage in illicit activities. For example, some have benefited from illegal mining around the NHM gold mine in the Kao-Malifut region of North Halmahera and manganese mining in Loloda, and from protection money guarding the Weda Bay Nickel mine in Central Halmahera and other nickel mines.[42] They also receive bribes in order to prevent corruption investigations going forward, and they are said to be involved in the illegal distribution of alcohol. Corruption of postconflict funds appears to have been as common in North Maluku as in Maluku. Yet politicians under suspicion have not used violence to prevent investigations with the provision of bribes seen as a more effective strategy. One university professor reflected on the success of such strategies: "Every time there's a case against Thaib [the provincial governor], you can be sure there will be wrongdoings in the procedure from the police or at the prosecutor's office"[43] The degree to which security forces can profit from such activities has not been contingent on perceptions of insecurity. As such, there has been little need for them to support violence.[44]

New Opportunities: *Pemekaran* and the Economy

Pemekaran [administrative splitting] helped peace . . . people became focused on their own regions.

—University lecturer in Ternate, 10 December 2010

The thoughts of the elite were channeled by pemekaran. They were kept busy.

—Political leader in Tobelo, North Halmahera, 14 December 2010

While some former conflict leaders benefited materially in the postconflict period others did not. Why did such individuals not use violence to try to secure positions or money? A key reason was the presence of an expanding set of licit channels for accumulation. This meant that it was not necessary or even optimal to employ violence to benefit.

The creation of new districts (pemekaran) across North Maluku ensured that public resources remained large even when postconflict money started to run out. The splitting of administrative provinces, districts, and subdistricts has been rife in Indonesian since the beginning of decentralization. The number of provinces rose from 26 to 33 between 1998 and 2007;[45] the number of districts had increased from 294 in 1998 to 510 by mid-2013.[46] In many parts of Indonesia, the formation of new areas has been accompanied by (sometimes violent) conflict; indeed, the escalation of the extended violence in North Maluku occurred in this context. The risks of violence are one reason why a moratorium on the establishment of new provinces and districts was put in place in 2009, followed by stricter guidelines.[47]

Yet the creation of new districts in North Maluku had a positive effect on consolidating peace. New districts were created in areas that had previously seen the highest levels of violence. When North Halmahera became a district in 2003 it led to a massive increase in public money in the area.[48] When the district became functional in 2004, it had a yearly budget of just Rp. 59 billion (around US$6 million).[49] By 2009 the annual budget had increased to Rp. 456 billion (US$46 million).[50] From 2005 to 2009, the total budget for North Halmahera district has amounted to over Rp. 1.66 trillion (US$170 million), a sizeable windfall for an area with a population of just 171,000 in 2003 that had previously received little.[51]

The formation of new districts in North Maluku led to significant economic growth and an infrastructure boom in the district that had experienced the highest toll from the violence.[52] Muslim and Christian politicians and activists noted the ways in which this helped consolidate peace:

> In 2003, North Halmahera became a district. This led to an improvement in job opportunities. Pemekaran was indeed a factor. The employment sector expanded and this prevented conflict escalation. People had no reason to complain anymore. There were many civil servant positions. The economic sector began to get going again, the private sector improved, and it helped people forget. The Christian side realized we also needed the Muslims to build North Halmahera.[53]

> Another important factor [in explaining why North Maluku has been peaceful] is pemekaran wilayah [the splitting of areas]. People have been busy developing their region and figuring out ways to turn a profit from it. . . . This has provided a distraction from the conflict. People focus on the opportunities, things like civil servant positions, that they can get in the new districts. They focus on that instead of the conflict.[54]

Pemekaran also helped reduce conceptions of elite competition as a zero-sum game. It created different realms for political competition. Elites could turn their attention away from provincial politics toward the new district administrations, reducing the relative importance of political interests in the provincial capital. Under decentralization laws, resources flowed directly from the central government to the districts, in large part bypassing provinces. This had the effect of allowing a more diverse set of patron-client networks to develop, limiting reliance on Ternate patrons.[55]

A third way in which pemekaran limited postconflict violence relates to the return of displaced people. The pemekaran project for North Halmahera started with a series of meetings between local Christian and Muslims elites from April 2000 in Manado, North Sulawesi. When the extended violence ended, the chairman of the Pemekaran Committee of the North Maluku district parliament made it a condition that before new districts could be formed, stability had to be restored and displaced people had to have returned.[56] It was rumored that North Halmahera would not get district status because displacement had reduced its population. This was a major argument used by Hein Namotemo to persuade Tobelo Christians to welcome back their Muslim neighbors.[57]

Maluku Province also saw the formation of new districts. However, these were not in the places that had experienced the highest impacts from the previous extended violence. Central Maluku, which had become a district in 1957, was split, with two new districts (East and West Seram) carved off from its territory in 2003. With central government allocations for districts determined in large part by population size and landmass, this resulted in a reduction in the revenues Central Maluku district received in 2005.[58] While resources then increased again, they remained rather static thereafter in sharp contrast to the steep increase in revenues North Halmahera received.[59] The new districts carved off from Central Maluku saw large increases in revenues of the same scale as North Halmahera.[60] However, while East and West Seram had been affected by the extended violence, it was at a lower level than in Central Maluku or Ambon.[61] In short, one of the areas of Maluku that had seen the highest levels of fighting before saw relatively stagnant resources while the epicenter of the North Maluku extended violent conflict saw a sharp rise in resources. Importantly, unlike Inpres resources, these funds were allocated through regular political processes with checks and balances in place.

Political Fluidity, Opportunities, and Nonviolent Political Competition

> **Coalitions are more fluid here [than in Ambon or Poso]. Here, it is already a melting pot. So it is less dangerous in terms of violence.**
>
> —Academic in Ternate, 17 July 2011

This increase in resources in North Halmahera and elsewhere in North Maluku could have led to problems if, as in Maluku, violence was a commonly used strategy for accessing political power and control of resources. The last chapter showed how the growth of public funds in Maluku was accompanied by an increase in violence. However, in North Maluku the new money had a positive effect. One important reason was that, in marked contrast to Maluku, political competition and alliances have been fluid in postconflict North Maluku. This has had the effect of preventing perceptions among aspiring elites of being shut out. The presence of opportunities to use peaceful strategies to achieve power and accumulate resources has lowered the motivations for elites to turn to violence.

There are multiple dimensions to this political fluidity. First, political coalitions among elites tend not to be rigid, with the membership of networks changing in response to current goals and opportunities. In contrast to Maluku, there has not been an obsession with power sharing between Christians and Muslims, and indeed, this was not a focus of either the provincial or local peace processes. In some areas, such as Central and East Halmahera districts, there have been electoral tickets made up of two Muslims despite split Christian-Muslim populations.[62] Decisions on political collaboration have been built on practical political concerns rather than on ensuring each group gets a share of power: "How the networks change always has something to do with the financial benefits that are available. This is *politik praktis*. . . . For example, in 1999 different groups aligned because they had a common enemy—the sultan and the traditions within the local government structure. But in the end, it's all about financial interests and the groups split up, joining others."[63]

Second, such practical concerns have meant that political coalitions in North Maluku have often crossed old conflict divides. Muhammad Albar, for example, had been a prominent jihadi leader on the Muslim side. He threw his lot in with the incumbent governor, Thaib Armaiyn, for his reelection campaign in 2007. Responsible for mobilizing support in Christian-majority North Halmahera, he made contact with Benny Doro, the former leader of Pasukan Merah, the Christian militia.[64] One of Benny's *anak buah* (followers), a former Pasukan Merah fighter, was sent to Ternate to join Thaib's campaign team (*tim sukses*) for the election under Albar's coordination. In 2009, Albar again asked for Benny Doro's help as he sought to run for the provincial parliament. Benny's anak buah became the coordinator of Albar's campaign team in Tobelo. Albar subsequently won, elected in large part by Christian votes from North Halmahera. In Kupa-Kupa, Doro's Christian hometown, Albar received more than 80 percent of the votes. In Leleoto, the village of Doro's protégé, Christians also voted massively for Albar. It was clear that patronage was at play. In 2010, Albar opened a patchouli plantation and factory in Leleoto, the profits of which were shared among locally recruited workers. Albar's campaign team coordinator was appointed manager of the factory. Such electoral tactics echo strategies employed in local contests across Indonesia. In North Maluku, Muslim and Christian leaders have worked together for mutual gain in the postconflict period.

More startling was the support of the sultan of Ternate for his former nemesis, Thaib Armaiyn, in the 2007 gubernatorial election.[65] Political competition between the sultan and Thaib, and others such as Bahir Andili, was a major factor in the escalation of North Maluku's extended violence which had ended with the sultan's banishment from local politics. However, the sultan realized that his ability to remain a force in the province was reliant on pragmatic compromises: the sultanate is dependent on voluntary contributions from the province and city governments, which he does not control. The sultan's support for Thaib was followed by one of his wives securing a seat in the national parliament two years later with the Democrat Party, the party of Thaib.[66] In the 2010 mayoral election in Ternate, the sultan supported an ethnic Tidorean, Burhan Abdurrahman, over the candidacy of one of his sons.[67]

Different ethnic groups have also tended to collaborate politically. Indeed, the 2010 mayoral election in Ternate city was won by a pairing of a Tidorean and with a Ternatean, ethnic groups that had been on different sides of the extended violence.

> Ethnic dynamics are fluid. Alliances and divisions between ethnic groups vary depending on the contexts and goals of the moment. Only the [ethnic] Tidore and Ternate hardly ever manage to get along. That said, the 2010 [Ternate] mayoral elections could be seen as a reconciliation between Tidore and Ternate. Burhan [the winning candidate] is Tidore, but his deputy is the sultan's man [*orang keraton*].[68]

A consequence of this political fluidity is that the costs of losing an election are lower; losing candidates, and their followers, know there may still be opportunities to benefit later. Indeed, even after the tense electoral battle for the 2007 gubernatorial elections, those who lost were not frozen out. After Thaib was declared the winner, he reportedly accommodated the team of Gafur, the losing candidate, placing them in strategic positions.[69]

Violence Specialists and the Lack of Societal Support for Violence

In Maluku, the incentives and ability of local elites to use violence for political or economic purposes was bolstered by community-level support for and tolerance of violence. In North Maluku, such societal support for violence has been largely absent in the postconflict period. There is also a relative absence of longstanding criminal preman groups. Where they do exist, they are not organizational residues of past violence and membership cuts across old conflict cleavages. This has had the dual effect of further reducing the temptations of elites to instigate violence and making it more difficult for them to do so on the rare occasions where they have tried.

Community-Level Support for Peace

The last chapter identified three factors as contributing to local support for violence in postconflict Maluku: historical patterns of conflict, ongoing segregation, and the lack of effective reconciliation. Many in North Maluku, elites and non-elites alike, emphasize the first of these as the reason why violence has been so rare in the postconflict period. They argue that North Maluku's recent peace is a natural consequence of the long history of economic, political, and cultural ties between people from different religious and ethnic groups and the common lineage (*Maluku Kieraha*) of the North Maluku people. It is these ties, it is argued, that allowed the people of North Maluku, and especially those in Halmahera, where the most vicious fighting occurred, to rapidly repair relations.

On Halmahera, at the heart of such bonds are the traditions and customs of hibualamo, or "big house," in the local language. The big house, both a physical and metaphorical entity, is a place where the different groups can solve problems together to ensure harmonious living. As we have seen, both Muslim and Christian local leaders placed these traditions at the center of North Halmahera's peace process. Those who propagated an adat-based peace process, such as Hein Namotemo, emphasize the differences between hibualamo and *pela gandong*, the traditional adat structure in Maluku.[70] Namotemo argues that hibualamo has historically created bonds between all the people of Halmahera and has mechanisms for including outsiders to a greater extent than is the case in Maluku's adat. In contrast, pela gandong sustains relationships between a limited number of villages, usually two or three. While the institution may prevent escalation of conflicts between these villages, it is powerless to affect events when other villages or people are involved.[71] Namotemo also claims that hibualamo has mechanisms for including outside migrant groups to a greater extent than is the case in Maluku's adat.

Such an explanation if true has significant implications for interpreting why violence continues in some postconflict areas. If postconflict violence is historically determined, as Namotemo and others claim, then there may be little scope for policymakers to limit violence in areas without such strong cross-cutting traditions.

Yet different traditional structures, and the strength of intergroup relations preceding the eruption of extended violence, is an unsatisfactory basis for explaining community-level support for peace in postconflict North Maluku. First, historically North Maluku has seen as much violence as Maluku.[72] Halmahera and surrounding islands were at the center of European colonial battles for control of the spice trade. This led to competition between the different sultanates, which created societal cleavages and often produced violent conflict.[73] Second, if pre–extended violence social relations were so strong in Halmahera why was violence able to erupt and escalate so easily? North Halmahera's extended violence was as brutal and sadistic as that which occurred anywhere in Indonesia. Third, it is not at all evident that the system of hibualamo, as characterized by Namotemo and other leaders, has existed in the modern era in North Maluku.

Many informants argued that hibualamo has always been only for the Tobelo people and not for other ethnic groups and, as with pela gandong, the system was largely defunct by the time of the extended violence.[74] Indeed, Duncan notes that the Tobelo people were "not well known for their concern with adat" and that people saw adat as a "sign of backwardness."[75]

It is more accurate to view the use of hibualamo in North Halmahera's peace process as being a *consequence* of the widespread desire for peace, especially among elites, in postconflict North Maluku rather than the cause of it. Local elites such as Namotemo and Samsul Bahri Umar wanted to reinvent or reinvigorate hibualamo because peace and reconciliation was in their interests. Knowledge of adat became a significant resource for Namotemo in his successful bid to become district head in 2005.[76] Muslim leaders, who felt vulnerable having been displaced from Tobelo for two years, saw adat as providing a way by which they could be reintegrated into the local economy and society.[77] Many who led such adat-based activities had formal positions in the church or mosque but were happy to emphasize historical adat ties over the tenets of their monotheistic faiths, again because it was in their interests for the violence to come to an end.[78]

Community members also bought into the hibualamo rhetoric because they wanted the violence to end. Conflict fatigue was widespread. The levels of violence experienced in North Halmahera shocked even those who had been proponents of religious cleansing. When violence subsided in June 2000, hundreds of thousands has been displaced, whole villages had been torched, and thousands had died—all in just seven months and from vicious person-to-person violence with low-tech weapons such as homemade bombs, machetes, spears, and bow and arrows. Unlike Maluku, where widespread occupation of land and property occurred, few at the community level had benefited from the violence. The escalation of violence in North Halmahera had been largely the result of a security dilemma rather than deeply entrenched socioeconomic grievances. People saw few benefits from continuing violence. Indeed, the costs of new violence could be great. An improved security condition was necessary for displaced families to return home and agricultural activity to commence again:

> Before reconciliation started, some Muslim community members who fled from Mamuya came here and asked if they could cultivate their plantations. . . . When they came here, they were guarded by the TNI [military]. Before they came, we [the Christians] had a meeting among ourselves. Hein was there and he asked us to report on conditions. We reported to him saying that the Muslims wanted to come back here to cultivate their land but that we did not want them to return. We were scared it would not just be Muslims from here who returned but also

"outsiders." Hein said to us, "Do you want to feel secure or not? If you do, then you need to ask them to come back so you can work to cultivate the plantations together."[79]

Community members were also aware that the planned creation of new districts could bolster employment opportunities but that this would be conditional on violence not reemerging. Community members thus bought into the hibualamo discourse because they wanted reconciliation; hibualamo was a handy platform to build this on.

A narrative developed on both sides that the extended violence had been driven by "outsiders": the Jakarta government, the military, outside jihadis or priests, displaced persons from Ambon, people from elsewhere in the province. Similar claims are sometimes made in Maluku but are also accompanied by accusations aimed at other Muslim or Christian locals. In Halmahera, the attribution of blame to outsiders, and the presence of traditions and myths that emphasize local commonalities, allowed for the construction of a narrative of peace and brotherhood, helping drive reconciliation. It was not that people were reconciled because of hibualamo; rather hibualamo was successfully revived because people wanted peace. This allowed people to construct a narrative that emphasized commonalties and coexistence.

The result was a peace process that tackled issues that, in Maluku, had led to continuing support for violence among many communities. In sharp contrast to Maluku, in most areas of North Maluku conflict-induced segregation was quickly dealt with. By 2003, most displaced people had returned. In some places, such as Mamuya in Galela, where Muslims returned in May–June 2001, the process of return was even quicker. The peace meetings in the early years after the extended violence involved local leaders and community members and focused on finding practical solutions to problems (such as how to ensure enough security so that people could again tend their fields) and on building cross-cutting institutional structures to take the peace dialogue forward. Lack of continuing segregation and sincere attempts to reconcile people who had been on opposite sides of the earlier extended violence were important in limiting societal support for violence in the postconflict period.

The Interaction of Societal and Elite Attitudes to Violence

There were candidates who threatened that if they were not elected there would be riots again. . . . But people didn't like that, they didn't vote for them . . . some were even roughed up.

—Former Christian militia member, Tobelo, 13 December 2010.

The previous chapter showed how ongoing community-level grievances and mistrust in Maluku were largely the result of the actions of local elites. In North Maluku, too, the attitudes and actions of local elites certainly shaped societal preferences, in particular in the early years after the extended violence ended. Their decision to build and utilize a narrative that emphasized peace and cross-cutting kinship ties, and to address problems such as displacement and segregation, bolstered community support for peace in the early period when there was still much uncertainty and trust was lacking.

However, the North Maluku case shows how the causal arrow can also point the other way, in particular later in the postconflict period when strong societal support for peace minimized any nascent temptations for elites to use violence for political or economic gain. First, it shaped the political platforms of those seeking power, especially from 2004 on. Candidates have tended to emphasize the importance of peace in their electoral strategies. Hein Namotemo, for example, in his successful bid to be North Halmahera's first elected bupati (district head), highlighted the role he had played in reconciliation efforts. Syamsir Andili, the former mayor of Ternate, gained power with a platform of "Ternate for all." In an environment of conflict fatigue, campaigns avoided incendiary appeals to religious communities. Where such tactics were used, as the Christian pastor and former conflict leader Jacob Soselisa did when seeking reelection to the North Halmahera district parliament, they have been unsuccessful. He was defeated.[80]

Second, it has meant that elites have taken actions to check violence when the potential for escalation was there. In Tobelo, North Halmahera, there were widespread allegations of fraud in the reelection of Bupati Hein in 2009.[81] Losing candidates took their complaints to the national Constitutional Court and organized a series of demonstrations. However, in the end these were called off and the candidates reluctantly accepted the election results. Frans Manery, one of the losing candidates, argued that he did this because of the potential for violence escalation.[82] The leader of Manery's campaign team noted: "People still have trauma from the conflict. We realized we had to accept [being defeated in the election] because we were afraid if we did not, it would be diverted into conflict."[83] It is questionable whether the acceptance of the disputed result by Manery and others was driven by such concerns or whether it was a function of them coming to the conclusion that they had little chance of success if they escalated protests. Yet, either way, it was clear to local challenger elites like Manery that popularity in postconflict North Maluku was contingent on appearing to be a peacemaker rather than warmonger.

Lack of local support for violence was also important in preventing the further escalation of the most serious incident of postconflict violence to take place in North Maluku. After a disputed vote count for the 2007 gubernatorial election, two candidates (the incumbent, Thaib Armaiyn, and the challenger, Abdul Gafur) claimed victory. Both sides mobilized criminal preman groups, each numbering around two thousand people, who clashed.[84] At least fifty people were injured and more than thirty buildings, including the house of Gafur, were damaged.[85] The risk of further escalation was real. In an echo of the conflict of late 1999, poskos were formed to provide logistical support to each group. The Indonesian president, Susilo Bambang Yudhoyono, told his coordinating minister for politics and security, the chairman of the National Intelligence Agency (BIN), the National Police chief, and the minister of home affairs to hold a dialogue between local leaders, but this could only be conducted in Ternate airport because the center of the town was deemed unsafe. Tensions escalated when supporters of the sultan of Ternate joined sides with Gafur. Eventually, the Constitutional Court declared Thaib the winner, and he was inaugurated in November 2008.[86] After this, tensions subsided as local elites realized that their interests would now be better served through bargaining over power and positions in the new administration rather than by using violence.

Jakarta's intervention was important through shaping the motivations of local elites. But equally key was the lack of community support for violence in Ternate. A senior leader on Thaib's side reflected: "The conflict then [2007–8] was just an elite thing. It was due to elite interests at that time. Those competing with each other had too much ambition. But the community already understood this. . . . At the time, elites tried to get people to fight. But people understood well and resisted this."[87] A local academic had similar views: "The conflict could be solved because at that time there was an awareness that conflict at the time was nothing, that no-one would benefit. The community below knew there were political interests. Because of this, they were not really influenced by the demonstrations."[88] Lack of local support for violence eventually led both sides to back down and larger-scale violence was averted.

The Relative Absence of Violence Specialists

The lack of support for violence in the postconflict period limited the temptation of the local elite to use violence for their own purposes. As important has been the relative absence of violence specialists who can be easily mobilized.

We have seen how in Maluku old conflict networks from the extended violence period continued into the postconflict period. In contrast, militia groups in North Maluku disbanded, leaving little if any organizational remnants in their wake. Both the Christian and Muslim militia who fought in North Halmahera were temporary formations. A former leader of Pasukan Merah recalled:

During the conflict, I was the kapita of the Pasukan Merah. . . . It was the people who chose me. They needed a leader. . . . We had pasukan in every village with a kapita under me. But when things were peaceful again, we used the adat [traditional culture] structure instead. There was no combatant structure anymore, no kapitas. We made them disappear. Now it is forbidden to talk about it. . . . The kapita did not become adat leaders after the conflict because of our role in the conflict. The structure was not needed after the conflict ended.[89]

The Muslim militias also disbanded. One reason why the old conflict militias did not continue to operate was because they were not provided with projects or funds in the early postconflict days. By the time more significant postconflict resources arrived in 2005, the groups had already disbanded.

The ability to keep organizational structures intact was also diminished when groups split for the 2002 gubernatorial election. Many former jihadis from Tidore backed Gafur while many others, such as Wahdah Zainal Imam, Muhammad Albar, and Muhammad Selang, supported Thaib.[90] Some former jihadis entered politics or the bureaucracy. Others, including many religious teachers from Tidore, went back to their old jobs.[91] In North Halmahera, a figure like Samsul Bahri Umar, who had led the Muslim delegation during the peace process, turned to politics, heading the district parliament. The conflict networks came together only temporarily, for reasons of immediate expediency, and soon lapsed.

Criminal preman gangs continue to operate in North Maluku as they do across Indonesia.[92] Yet they tend to be opportunistic. As with many politicians, thug leaders frequently swap who they support. Nor are such groups organizationally strong. One local leader described them as "preman *kampung* [village criminals], preman *leger* [the name for cheap hangout places for poor youth], not professional preman."[93] PAKTA (the Special Troops for Thaib Armaiyn) was only formed just before the 2007 elections. They were given uniforms. Yet after the elections PAKTA disbanded with people returning to their regular life: "orang pulang cari makan."[94]

Importantly, there is not a strong link between the old conflict networks, on either the Muslim or Christian side, and current preman groups. Brawls between rival youth gangs frequently occur in both Tobelo and Ternate. Yet they do not appear to be linked to those who were active in militia during the extended violence. New players such as Irwansyah Haris, also known as Ongen Pattimura, a preman leader of Kei (Southeast Maluku) descent, have arrived on the scene.[95] In contrast, the old militias, built on ethnic or religious solidarity, have faded away.

This chapter has shown that the theory presented in chapter 2 not only explains why large episodic violence can occur (as in Maluku) but also why and how peace can consolidate after large-scale extended violence. My explanation for the absence of frequent postconflict violence in North Maluku is rooted in an understanding of the lack of incentives for local elites to use violence strategically to secure resources and positions. This, I argue, provides a better explanation for why large episodic violence has been largely absent than rival theories such as historical cross-cutting ties between ethnic and religious groups, the absence of ex-combatant organizations, or the strength of the local state. Community support for peace has been important. However, the incentives of community members and former militia members, at least in the early postconflict period, were shaped to a large extent by the actions of local elites.

In line with the theory, signaling effects about the utility of using violence and the level of perceived opportunities for peaceful collaboration are the main mechanisms that shaped local elite incentives in ways that supported peace. Violence was rarely used in the early postconflict period by rent-seeking groups; when it was, there were sanctions, and groups who used violence were marginalized. This sent a signal that violence would not work. Further, elites have seen plentiful opportunities to use licit channels to gain power and control of resources. The creation of new districts in areas such as North Halmahera increased opportunities to accumulate through nonviolent institutional processes. The ability of elites to collaborate across old conflict divides, again a product in part of relations strengthened and legitimized through the peace processes, meant they could use these opportunities in less conflictual ways.

The comparative analysis with Maluku has pointed to the nature of the peace settlement as playing a large role in shaping incentives in the early postconflict period and of these having important, if not fully path-dependent, downstream effects. In Maluku, the peace process focused on carving up power and resources. This raised the temptation for some local elites, including criminal leaders, to use violence to access jobs and money. It also strengthened old conflict networks linking political patrons to violence specialist clients. In contrast, North Maluku's peace process did not focus on the allocation of resources or jobs, in large part because plentiful postconflict resources were not available while the peace process(es) were ongoing. Instead there was a greater focus on efforts to promote local-level reconciliation. Violent action could not strategically shape these processes, and hence it was not frequently used in the early postconflict period.

The analysis in this and the last chapter has shown how incentives for or against violence can, over time, shape norms relating to the legitimacy of using violence in the local political-economic sphere. In Maluku, violence became normalized early on, allowing it to be employed by leaders and groups at times when discretionary resources were increasing, decreasing, or when the rules of the game relating to fund use were changing. In contrast, the absence of support for violence in early postconflict North Maluku created a virtuous cycle. Elites saw benefit in being seen as champions of peace rather than perpetrators of violence. Norms against the use of violence strengthened over time. This meant that when there may have been reasons for elites to use violence strategically, such as when Inpres funds eventually arrived and when corruption investigations were instigated, elites instead used nonviolent strategies to try to achieve their goals.

SMALL EPISODIC VIOLENCE IN POSTCONFLICT ACEH

GAM leaders have not mobilized for violence because they have already received many benefits from peace.

—Academic, Banda Aceh

The big issue is "insiders" versus "outsiders"—those combatants who have access to power are less likely to be involved in criminality. . . . Most crime is related to those who do not have access to resources. Maybe they are forced to use violence because they have no other option.

—Local journalist, Banda Aceh

The postconflict experience of Aceh differs from that of the provinces examined in the previous two chapters. As in Maluku, and in contrast to North Maluku, episodes of violence have occurred frequently since the signing of a peace agreement in August 2005. Yet, unlike Maluku, violence has generally taken small-scale forms with few people killed or injured or few buildings damaged in each incident. Violent crimes account for a larger share of postconflict violence in Aceh than in either Maluku or North Maluku. This chapter explains why incidents of violence have continued to occur frequently in Aceh and why they have tended not to escalate into larger, more destructive forms of violence.[1]

Patterns of violence in postconflict Aceh can be largely explained by the differing incentives that local elites and local violence specialists, primarily lower-level former rebel combatants, have to use violence for political and economic gain. The peace settlement resulted in a vast increase in Aceh's revenues, incentivizing elite commitment to the accord. Importantly, and in contrast to Maluku, GAM elites were incorporated primarily through political participation rather than direct payoffs. Provisions to fast-track former GAM into politics, in a context where the rebel movement had the deepest and most effective patronage network, led to former combatant leaders participating in electoral competition. The interests of other elites, such as military leaders and local officials, were not threatened by the entry of GAM leaders into politics, as both sides collaborated in sharing the economic spoils of power.

In contrast, there has been a lack of opportunities for lower-ranked former combatants to get ahead using peaceful means. Flows of funds from elites to the ground have been limited and the real economy has been stagnant. Because of this, many former combatants have used violence, both to directly secure resources and to send a signal to those above.

Violence in Aceh

The Extended Violence

Extended violent conflict in late-century Indonesia did not only take intercommunal form. The fall of Suharto was also accompanied by a surge in secessionist violence at either end of Indonesia's archipelagic stretch. Separatist rebellion had engulfed Aceh, the country's westernmost province, for long periods since Indonesia's independence.[2] In the years following the demise of the New Order, conflict in Aceh morphed from sporadic episodic violence into fully-fledged civil war.

The Acehnese had been strong supporters of, and participants in, the anticolonialist nationalist movement. However, after Indonesia gained its independence discontent grew when promises from Jakarta that Aceh would become its own province and allowed to implement Islamic law were broken. This led many Acehnese to join the Darul Islam rebellion, which called for an Islamic Indonesian state.[3] The conflict was largely resolved in 1959 with Aceh given special territory status with broad powers to manage religious, educational, and customary law affairs. Over time, however, as the centralized Indonesian state gained strength, the special territory status became increasingly meaningless. In 1976, Hasan di Tiro, a descendant of an *ulama* (Muslim religious leader) who had been prominent in the war against the Dutch and who had supported Darul Islam, declared the formation of the Free Aceh Movement (or GAM, to use its Indonesian acronym) and independence from Indonesia.

The insurgency was largely wiped out by 1979, but the movement grew again from the late 1980s after fighters trained in Libya returned.[4] In response, the Indonesian military sought to destroy GAM with force, launching a decade-long military campaign in August 1989 that killed thousands and resulted in widespread human rights abuses.[5]

In the early post-Suharto days Aceh was relatively calm. Just seventy-four people were killed in the province in 1998. Yet violence rose sharply as the country's democratic transition unfolded. As in East Timor and Papua, the new political environment led to fresh demands from Acehnese civil society, leaders, and combatants. Initially in Aceh these were for an investigation of human rights abuses and for special autonomy to be introduced. However, continuing military abuses in 1999 led to a hardening of attitudes. GAM recruited from those who had lost family members or witnessed atrocities. The remarkable offer in February 1999 by Indonesia's new president, B. J. Habibie, of an independence referendum to the East Timorese led to calls for a plebiscite on Aceh's status. At least 500,000 gathered in November in Banda Aceh, the provincial capital, to call for Acehnese self-determination.

This marked the beginning of GAM's third revolt. The movement grew rapidly, moving beyond its east coast strongholds to gain a significant presence across the province. With security deteriorating—697 were killed in 1999 and a further 1,057 died the following year—the government began peace talks. A Humanitarian Pause was declared in September 2000 but had little effect as GAM used the opportunity to expand its territory to the point where it controlled 70–80 percent of the province.[6] The government turned again to using legal instruments to try to end the violence. National Law 44/1999 offered a basic special autonomy for Aceh and Law 18/2001 extended the scope to include economic issues (a large share of oil and gas revenues were to be retained by the province) and political matters (direct elections of the local government executive). However, as violence escalated, special autonomy was never fully implemented.[7]

At least 5,178 people were killed in 2001 and 2002. Fresh talks resulted in the Cessation of Hostilities Agreement (CoHA) of December 2002 but it collapsed in May 2003. The Indonesian government changed tack, declaring martial law. The province was sealed off from outside oversight with international media and aid organizations largely banned. Tens of thousands of additional troops arrived in an attempt to wipe out GAM and separatist sentiment by military means.[8] In an echo of strategies in Timor, the military recruited local antiseparatist militia to fight GAM, particularly in the ethnically heterogeneous Central Highlands.[9]

The impacts of the violence were deep. From the beginning of 1998 until August 2005, when a new peace accord was finally signed, an estimated 10,613 people lost their lives.[10] The war resulted in serious human rights abuses.[11] A representative survey conducted in 2008 found that 39 percent of all people in Aceh, more than 1.5 million people, considered themselves to be victims of conflict with the most common reasons being displacement, conflict-related mental or physical illness, and damage to people's houses.[12] Poverty levels in 2004 were higher than elsewhere in Indonesia because of the conflict.[13] In monetary terms, damages and losses from the conflict exceeded Rp. 107.4 trillion or US$10.7 billion, with over half of the province's rural infrastructure damaged.[14] The economic cost of the conflict was double that of the Indian Ocean tsunami.[15]

Aceh's extended violence differed in many ways from the violence in Maluku and North Maluku and other sites of intercommunal unrest such as Central and West Kalimantan and Central Sulawesi. The conflict cleavage was different. Whereas Christians fought Muslims in Maluku and North Maluku, war in largely religiously homogenous Aceh was between an armed insurgent movement, which had support and sympathy from large swathes of the population, and the Indonesian military. There was thus vast asymmetry in fighting technology between the two warring parties, which was not the case in the Moluccas. GAM also had a more organized and hierarchical structure than any of the Muslim or Christian militias in Maluku or North Maluku. Initial causes of the violence also differed. Analysts of the Aceh conflict have emphasized a range of factors that led to the initial rise of the insurgency. GAM built on the grievances of the many Acehnese who had failed to benefit from the discovery and development of massive natural gas fields off the east coast of the province,[16] helping shape a revitalized Acehnese nationalism[17] and lowering trust in the Indonesian state.[18] This combined with resentment of a perceived domination of Indonesian national culture by the Javanese.[19] Broken promises that Aceh would receive political and cultural autonomy compounded dissatisfaction.[20] Military abuses also fueled GAM recruitment.[21] Local political and economic competition, so key in Maluku and North Maluku, was not an important cause of the onset and initial escalation of Aceh's war.

Yet, as war continued, similarities with the intercommunal violence occurring in other parts of Indonesia became pronounced. As elsewhere, violence increasingly followed a predatory logic. The military made substantial sums from extortion at checkpoints on Aceh's main highways and raised revenue through smuggling, marijuana cultivation and trading, illegal logging, and legal businesses such as palm oil.[22] Aspinall notes that "so pervasive were these activities that many intellectuals, NGO activists, and others argued that the profit motive drove military violence because disorder provided more fundraising possibilities."[23] At the same time, GAM levied taxes (*pajak nanggroe*) on businessmen and government infrastructure contracts, were involved in the marijuana trade, and took sums for providing protection.[24] Ideology motivated many fighters, but this diminished as GAM increasingly recruited thugs to the cause.[25]

As in the Moluccas there was frequent collaboration between ostensible adversaries in rent-making activities and in ensuring that violence continued. District government heads awarded contracts to GAM contractors and officials provided GAM fighters with satellite phones. GAM also bought weapons and ammunition from the Indonesia military.[26] In the words of one senior GAM leader: "We'd make deals: for instance, the two sides would say we were having an armed clash, and both would shoot into the air, ha. Once the TNI [Indonesian military] withdrew, they'd leave their bullets behind at a spot we'd agreed before. It was usually the TNI who were about to go home who would do this."[27] The result was a war where "guerrillas and their enemies were locked not only in mortal combat but also in an intimate embrace."[28]

The Helsinki MoU and Postconflict Violence

On 15 August 2005, less than eight months on from the devastating tsunami, which killed upwards of 167,000 people in Aceh alone, a peace deal was signed in Helsinki between the Indonesian government and GAM.

The tsunami is commonly viewed as being the main catalyst for the agreement. With tens of thousands of aid workers pouring into the troubled province, all-out offensives could not take place.[29] The tsunami also created a face-saving opportunity for both sides to acknowledge that different approaches were needed. The preamble to the agreement noted that the tsunami created a moral imperative for both parties to work toward peace.

Other factors were, however, more important. The Indonesian government had been courting GAM prior to the tsunami. Vice President Kalla had used intermediaries to probe the GAM leadership's desire for a settlement.[30] Crisis Management Initiative, the NGO led by former Finnish president Ahtisaari that brokered the accord, formally invited both sides to negotiate three days *before* the Indian Ocean tsunami struck.[31] GAM realized that their goal of an independent Aceh was unattainable, at least in the short to medium term. Their forces had been decimated by martial law. GAM leaders also understood that international support for the independence of a small Muslim state astride the shipping lanes of the Straits of Malacca was unlikely in the post-9/11 world.[32] On the Indonesian side, a new president and vice president who favored a political rather than security approach to solving the Aceh problem had taken office. Yudhoyono and Kalla had both been involved in the attempts to bring peace to Maluku and Central Sulawesi. Importantly, Yudhoyono, a former military leader, commanded respect from the army's top brass. On coming to power, he replaced some senior military leaders with reformers, thereby securing a new ability to guarantee peace once an agreement was found.[33]

The resulting agreement, the Helsinki Memorandum of Understanding, or MoU, went further than previous accords. It included provisions to disarm and reintegrate rebel forces and to devolve considerable power from the national level to Aceh, while rebel leaders would recognize the sovereignty of Indonesia. More than thirty thousand Indonesian military and police left the province. An unarmed peace mission, the Aceh Monitoring Mission (AMM) was deployed by the EU and ASEAN to oversee the peace process. Presidential Instruction (Inpres)

15/2005 set out institutional responsibilities for the accord and then a national Law on Governing Aceh (LoGA, Law 11/2006) implemented many of the elements of the MoU.[34]

Unlike the Humanitarian Pause and the CoHA, the Helsinki MoU had an immediate and lasting impact. From the beginning of 1999 until July 2005, Aceh had seen an average of 133 deaths per month.[35] In contrast, just 7 people were killed in the two weeks after the signing of the MoU. The following month saw only 5 deaths and no more than 8 people died in any of the following twelve months. The reduced level of violence continued. From August 2005 until the end of 2012, there were an average of 7 violent deaths per month in Aceh. The largest number of people to die in any single month was in March 2010 when 16 people were killed following the discovery by the police of a jihadi camp in rural northeast Aceh. The establishment of the camp had little to do with the past war, and former GAM rebels were not involved in any significant way.[36]

Violence did not disappear as it largely did in North Maluku. From August 2005 until the end of 2012, there were at least 4,975 violent incidents in the province, 670 per year. Yet, in contrast to Maluku, this violence has tended to take smaller forms with less impact per incident. There have been just 29 large incidents of violence—defined as those resulting in 3 or more deaths, 10 or more injuries, or 15 or more damaged buildings—in the postconflict period. Whereas over one-third of all deaths in postconflict Maluku come from large incidents of violence, in Aceh the figure is 7 percent.[37] A greater share of violent impacts comes from crimes rather than conflicts compared to the other two provinces. Crime accounts for 66 percent of deaths in postconflict Aceh, compared with 46 percent in Maluku and 53 percent in North Maluku.[38] Beyond violent crime, a wide range of issues has led to violence, including elections and vigilante attacks in response to issues such as theft and perceived sexual indiscretion.

Very few of the violent deaths in postconflict Aceh directly relate to the old GAM-Indonesian government cleavage: only 33 of almost 5,000 postconflict violent incidents had clear separatist motivations.[39] Indeed, as I explore below, violence in Aceh has transformed from being driven by the vertical center-periphery conflict to becoming an expression of contestation between different class groups, and occasionally elites, within Aceh.

The Absence of Large Episodic Violence

Large episodic violence has been infrequent in postconflict Aceh because elites have not found it to be in their economic or political interests to use or support such violence. This has been the case for three reasons.

First, as in Maluku, the peace settlement prioritized the co-optation of former conflict elites to ensure they did not spoil the agreement. However, in contrast to Maluku, this process of incorporation was largely done by providing the rebel group with opportunities and incentives to compete for power and control of resources through formal political channels. Exceptions were made to national electoral laws to allow independents to stand for election and then for local parties to run. The willingness of GAM to enter politics was strengthened by two factors. Large volumes of special autonomy money, controlled by provincial and district governments, meant that the prizes for winning were large. Further, the strength of support for GAM, and the relative efficacy of its patronage network, meant that success was likely for former combatant leaders.

Second, other elites beyond GAM have also had incentives to compete for power and resources without resort to violence. Local government and security force leaders had developed close relations with their ostensible adversaries in GAM during the conflict. This facilitated collaboration in the postconflict period. Many in the old politico-economic elite have partnered with former GAM in areas such as contracting.

Finally, and as in North Maluku, attempts to use large-scale episodic violence in postconflict Aceh have proven costly. Effective third-party monitoring and especially in-group policing by GAM and the Indonesian government sent a signal that large episodes of violence would not be tolerated.

The Peace Settlement I: Resources for GAM Elites

Post-Helsinki Aceh was awash with money. The peace agreement promised assistance for the reintegration of former combatants and other conflict-affected groups and for postconflict reconstruction. These funds were eclipsed by vast tsunami reconstruction resources. From 2008, additional special autonomy resources became available. Beyond their role in reconstructing the province after its natural and man-made disasters, these three types of funds helped bind GAM elites into the peace settlement.

THE REINTEGRATION PROGRAM

A first source of funds for elites within GAM came from reintegration programs. In line with most internationally mediated peace accords, the Helsinki MoU mandated assistance to former combatants and other conflict-affected groups. This included economic support (clause 3.2.3), farming land, employment, or social security (clause 3.2.5), and the restoration of public and private property (clause 3.2.4). A Reintegration Fund to pay for these programs was to be established by the authorities of Aceh (clause 3.2.3). By the end of 2008, Rp. 3.7 trillion

(US$366 million) had been provided for reintegration with just over half coming from donors, NGOs, and the private sector, and the rest from the Indonesian and Acehnese governments.[40] Government funds were under the control of the newly formed Aceh Reintegration Board (Badan Reintegrasi Aceh, BRA), which was also to coordinate international assistance.[41]

These funds helped ensure the support of GAM leaders for the peace agreement. Reintegration had not been a priority for GAM negotiators in Helsinki. The impetus for including the reintegration provisions came from the international officials who were brokering the accord.[42] GAM disliked the term *reintegration* from the start as they felt it implied a division between combatants and community members that did not exist. Yet as reintegration funds arrived GAM elites found them to be useful. Some money was used to finance "gifts" for senior former rebel commanders.[43] Off-budget money from Indonesian vice president, Jusuf Kalla helped some GAM leaders establish businesses.[44]More important, rebel leaders ended up controlling the distribution of much of the money.[45] A large share of the government reintegration resources was allocated at the discretion of elites in GAM who used funds to strengthen patron-client ties with lower-level combatants. Internationally funded reintegration programs also relied on former GAM commanders to identify beneficiaries. This, as I will discuss later, contributed to grievances among lower-level former combatants, with many individuals feeling they did not receive their due share. Yet the reintegration program also helped bind elites in the movement into the peace settlement. Over time, as GAM came to political power in the province, BRA was taken over by GAM leaders, providing a source of employment and largess that could be distributed.

TSUNAMI FUNDS

GAM elites also benefited from the vast post-tsunami humanitarian and reconstruction funds. Tsunami funds were around twenty times those allocated for postconflict needs: US$8 billion, US$5.3 billion of it from outside of Indonesia, was pledged for reconstruction.[46] There were limitations to the extent to which these resources could be used in many conflict-affected areas. The vast majority of resources went to coastal areas that had usually been less affected by the conflict. Many reconstruction programs deliberately avoided targeting conflict-affected groups or regions, with agencies worried about overstepping their mandates or dealing with the complexities of the postconflict situation.[47] Nevertheless, an estimated Rp. 5.3 trillion (US$530 million) of tsunami recovery and development funds supported postconflict recovery in noncoastal areas, eclipsing reintegration funds.[48]

GAM elites were excited by the scale of such resources, both because of the potential for developing the province and the opportunities they afforded for personal gain and for consolidating their support base. Former rebels were slotted in to the tsunami reconstruction body (Badan Rehabilitasi dan Rekonstruksi, BRR), the powerful agency that controlled government tsunami funds and coordinated the international effort.[49] By November 2007, around five hundred former GAM members were employed in the BRR.[50] A former GAM negotiator, Teuku Kamaruzzaman, was appointed secretary of the executing arm of the BRR, the second most powerful position in the agency. Other senior GAM leaders such as Malik Mahmud, Muhammad Lampoh Awe, and Muzakir Manaf were given high-salaried positions with little expectation that they ever come to the office. The presence of GAM elites in the body allowed them influence on how reconstruction funds were to be spent. A new program was developed to channel around US$3 million to twenty cooperatives of former GAM fighters. GAM figures also had control over the awarding of infrastructure construction contracts.

SPECIAL AUTONOMY RESOURCES

Tsunami funds would eventually run out. By 2008, the number of international agencies working in Aceh had declined rapidly and BRR shut shop in April 2009. By this point, reintegration and postconflict money from both government and donors had also dropped steeply. This reduction in aid effected Aceh's economy, which had been driven by sectors dependent on the reconstruction effort such as construction, trade, and transport. In 2008, Aceh's economy declined by 8 percent.[51]

This could have led to problems. We saw that in Maluku that there was a rise in violence as special postconflict funds finished. However, special provisions in the LoGA (Law 11/2006), which vastly raised regular subnational government revenues for the province, ensured that the amount of money available for developmental purposes, and for satiating the needs and desires of local elites, did not fall when tsunami and postconflict funds ran out.

GAM negotiators in Helsinki had focused on ensuring that Aceh would manage the money accruing from the province's natural resources. The final MoU promised that, in contrast to arrangements in most other areas of Indonesia, 70 percent of "all current and future hydrocarbon deposits and other natural resources in the territory of Aceh as well as in the territorial sea surrounding Aceh" (clause 1.3.4) would remain in Aceh.[52] The provision had more symbolic than monetary value as most resources are expected to be exhausted soon.[53]

Far more important was the provision in the LoGA for a larger proportion of the General Allocation Fund (Dana Alokasi Umum, or DAU, the block grant from the central government to the regions aimed at equalizing the fiscal capacity of regional governments) to go to Aceh. This extra funding stream was not in the MoU and is widely viewed as being included to compensate Aceh for

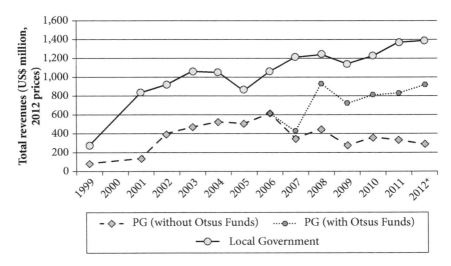

FIGURE 5.   Provincial and district revenues in Aceh, 1999–2012 (US$, 2012 prices). Note: 2012 is based on budget plans; other years use budget realization. PG = Provincial government funds. Local government includes provincial and district budgets.
Sources: 2012 Aceh Public Expenditure Analysis (unpublished document), Ministry of Finance, World Bank database

damage from the conflict.[54] It amounted to a massive injection of resources into the province, far eclipsing oil and gas revenues. The LoGA mandated that for fifteen years from 2008, Aceh would receive an additional 2 percent share of the national DAU funds then an additional 1 percent for five years after that. These revenues, renamed the Special Autonomy Fund (SAF, or *otsus*), led to an extra transfer to Aceh of Rp. 16 trillion (US$1.6 billion) in 2008–11 alone. Over the full two decades, it is estimated that the SAF will amount to Rp. 100 trillion (over US$10 billion).[55] Under Indonesia's decentralization laws, most subnational revenues are held at the district rather than provincial level. In contrast, 60 percent of special autonomy resources in Aceh go to the province, and the SAF has more than doubled provincial revenues (figure 5).

The Peace Settlement II: The Political Incorporation of GAM Elites

The comparison of Maluku's and North Maluku's peace settlements in the previous two chapters showed how providing additional resources in the early postconflict period can contribute to continuing violence. In Maluku, cash, jobs, and projects were distributed to ensure that former dissident leaders accepted the peace settlement. This lowered the risk of renewed extended violence, but it also led to some local elites using violence to capture resources and power. In contrast, fewer postconflict resources were available in the early years after the end of North Maluku's extended violent conflict. This allowed elites to focus peacebuilding activities on reconciliation rather than the distribution of spoils.

We might have expected local elites in Aceh, including former GAM leaders, to use large episodic violence in the early postconflict period to gain access to funds and positions. This did not happen because, in contrast to Maluku, the primary means of incorporating former combatant leaders was not by providing preferential access to jobs or funds but by ensuring their participation in local politics. In an environment where GAM figures had huge advantages over their competitors, including the strongest patronage network and organizational structures honed through the war, they chose to compete for power and resources through political channels rather than by using large episodic violence.

THE MOU AND THE LOGA

The peace agreement and its implementing law provided a powerful set of incentives and mechanisms that facilitated the incorporation of former rebels into the local polity. The Helsinki MoU and the LoGA gave the province significant powers. Following from the MoU, the LoGA stated that Aceh had the authority to "regulate and implement government functions in all public sectors except . . . [those] of national character, foreign affairs, defense, security, justice, monetary affairs, national fiscal affairs, and certain functions in the field of religion."[56] This went far beyond the provisions of past special autonomy arrangements for Aceh. The scope of these powers, along with the vast resources under the control of the provincial and district governments in Aceh, strengthened the incentives of former GAM leaders and others to compete in the elections.

Importantly, the MoU and LoGA also created ways for former guerrillas to access power quickly. The preamble of the MoU stated that the government of Indonesia and GAM would create conditions for "fair and democratic" government and that direct local elections would be held shortly after the peace agreement was signed. The MoU also stipulated changes to the electoral system, establishing that independent candidates could, for the first time in Indonesia's history, contest the 2006 election and that local political parties would be allowed, also for the first time, to contest legislative elections from 2009 onward.[57]

These were major concessions. There is a long history in Indonesia of seeing local parties as a potential source of national fragmentation.[58] Indeed, Indonesia is the only democracy that does not allow local parties to contest local elections.[59] Requests by GAM in the peace talks of 2001–2 for local parties to be allowed had been rejected by Jakarta.[60] The formation of local parties again turned out to be the most divisive issue during the Helsinki negotiations. After the MoU was signed, there were continued arguments over whether it allowed for independent candidates. An initial government draft of the LoGA excluded the possibility of this.[61] However, after pressure from GAM, the government relented and independent candidates were permitted.[62]

This staged approach—independent candidates first, then local parties—allowed former rebels to stand before GAM had formed a political party, a process that would require time. The MoU also granted amnesty to all persons who had participated in GAM activities and stated that they "will have all political, economic and social rights as well as the right to participate in the political process, both in Aceh and on the national level" (clause 3.2.1). This created a legal right for former GAM rebels to participate in the elections.

THE FIRST POSTCONFLICT ELECTIONS

Direct elections for the positions of provincial governor and heads of all twenty-three rural and urban districts were held in Aceh between December 2006 and January 2008. GAM-affiliated candidates participated as independents. In October 2005, GAM created a new oversight body, the National Council (Majelis Nasional), to determine GAM's political strategy. The council subsequently established the Aceh Transitional Council (Komite Peralihan Aceh, KPA) on 28 December. The KPA had the same territorial structure as GAM's armed wing, which had been formally dissolved as part of the peace process. While the goals of the KPA were initially to guide the reintegration process and to ensure that former fighters followed the terms of the MoU, it was also to become the basis of a future local GAM party.[63]

GAM did well in the elections, which were widely viewed as a success and to be "free and fair."[64] The independent GAM-affiliated ticket of Irwandi Jusuf, a former rebel leader, and Muhammad Nazar, a prominent self-determination activist, won the gubernatorial election in the first round with 38 percent of the vote, far ahead of the runner-up pair from a national Islamic party (who notably contained a GAM-affiliated vice governor candidate). GAM-linked candidates also won the district head position in ten districts. Even in those districts where GAM candidates failed to win, they often fared well. The independent GAM gubernatorial pair was the highest ranked ticket in seven of the thirteen districts where GAM failed to win at the district level.[65]

GAM thus became a mainstream and important local political player. This political incorporation of the former rebels was accomplished with a remarkably low level of political violence.[66] Over an eight-month period from July 2006, local newspapers in Aceh recorded twenty-eight election-related incidents, which included physical attacks and kidnappings, serious intimidation, as well as the physical destruction of party attributes.[67] Violent incidents accounted for just 11 percent of all election-related conflicts recorded, a similar rate to those recorded in provinces not affected by large-scale communal or separatist violence.[68]

GAM decided to compete in the elections not only because of the vast resources they would control if victorious but also because they knew their probability of winning was very high. They had a stronger grassroots network than the political parties.[69] Whereas in other regions of Indonesia party preferences have endured since the 1955 elections,[70] in Aceh the long conflict resulted in voters who lacked strong loyalties to national parties. Patronage networks, which rely on vertical connections from villagers to leaders of parties or mass organizations, were also relatively undeveloped in Aceh, even though they are common across Indonesia.[71] While war had weakened the networks of political parties and of Islamic mass movements such as Nahdlatul Ulama and Muhammadiyah, GAM's wartime structure linked its leaders to villagers. Such networks persisted after the peace agreement and were institutionalized with the formation of the KPA. This gave GAM-affiliated candidates a great advantage.

GAM candidates also benefited from a strong desire among the electorate for peace to continue and deep cynicism toward existing leaders. While no candidates campaigned against the peace process, many voted for GAM candidates because they felt they were less likely to go back to fighting if they were in power.[72] Voters also considered the track records of those candidates who had served in government positions in the past, many of whom were seen to be corrupt, nepotistic, and indifferent to the needs of the people. GAM-affiliated candidates, having never held such positions, were seen as a potentially less corrupt alternative.

DEEPER POLITICAL INCORPORATION: THE 2009 LEGISLATIVE AND 2012 EXECUTIVE ELECTIONS

GAM's incorporation into the state was completed with the April 2009 legislative elections. In July 2007, GAM established its own political party, initially called Partai GAM, later renamed Partai Aceh (Aceh Party, PA). PA stood as one of six local parties in elections for the provincial parliament and district legislatures across Aceh. PA won 33 of 69 seats in the provincial legislature and 237 of 645 seats in district elections. It emerged as the biggest party in sixteen of Aceh's twenty-three districts, with an outright majority in thirteen of those.[73] GAM's success was largely determined by the same factors that had contributed to their victory in the 2006 elections: the strength of the KPA organizational structure; concern from some voters that GAM would return to violence if they did not win; and voters rewarding the former rebel movement for its role in bringing peace to Aceh.[74]

As the elections approached, many observers worried about the potential for unrest.[75] The military ran an aggressive intimidation campaign against Partai Aceh, and there was indeed some violence in the run up to the elections with seventy-three violent election-related incidents, resulting in five deaths from the beginning of the campaign in July 2008 until the election took place.[76] However, election day was largely peaceful.[77]

Three years on, Aceh's third round of postconflict elections took place with polls for the province's district heads and governor. Since 2009, a split within GAM had emerged and the incumbent former governor, Irwandi Jusuf, stood against the GAM pairing of Zaini Abdullah and Muzakir Manaf.[78] In the run up to the 2012 contest, tensions between the two factions were extremely heated, and there was a spate of incidents of violence and intimidation. Fourteen people were killed in December 2011 including a series of shootings of Javanese transmigrants.[79] There was also intimidation on election day.[80]

However, widespread postelection violence did not come to pass: an average of six people were killed in each of the four months following the election, lower than the monthly average in the full postconflict period. Following Zaini-Muzakir's victory, Irwandi did not use violence to contest the result, instead establishing a new local party to compete in future elections.[81] Indeed, the elections served to further GAM's incorporation into both the Indonesian state and competitive electoral politics. In addition to winning the governorship, they were successful in thirteen of twenty district head contests.

THE REWARDS OF POWER: CORRUPTION, CONTRACTING, AND POLITICS AS USUAL

> **[Ex-]combatants try to access resources through development projects. . . . They follow the projects. It's like *pajak nanggroe* [the tax GAM applied during the conflict]. They take the tax, or offer security. Within projects they divide it up through subcontracting. Combatants are involved in the subcontracts. Even the big contractors from the government are affected by this. They are powerless. There is pressure from GAM to get parts of projects. Nothing is hidden.**

—Academic in Banda Aceh, 4 March 2011.

The political incorporation of GAM elites has allowed them to enjoy the spoils that come with power in Indonesia's regions. Driving down Aceh's highways, one can see the grand newly erected houses owned by senior GAM figures. Many now drive imported luxury cars. Former commanders now make visits to Singapore and Kuala Lumpur for shopping or medical checks. Upward social and economic mobility for many in the elite of the former rebel group has been rapid and extreme.

GAM elites have pursued two related strategies for purposes of accumulation. The first has been corruption. During the war, Aceh's local government institutions were plagued by massive graft. Two 2003 studies by Bank Indonesia and Padjajaran University found that Aceh was the most corrupt province in the country.[82] In the immediate aftermath of the Helsinki MoU, many in Aceh were confident that corruption would decline as the province gained more control of its affairs.[83] Yet this assurance soon diminished. A 2010 survey found that 51 percent of informants felt that corruption was worse after the tsunami than before it; only 15 percent of people said that corruption was worse when war was ongoing than now.[84] A member of the South Aceh parliament estimated that at least 30 percent of the local state budget in his district "leaks" and this was probably similar in most other districts.[85] One particularly prominent case involved the North Aceh district head, a former GAM member, corrupting such a large share of the local budget that the district was on the verge of bankruptcy.[86]

There is little evidence that GAM leaders are any more corrupt than other politicians. Yet many GAM leaders who are now elected officials have quickly learned the local political rules of the game and understand well the opportunities for theft from the state's coffers. They have benefited from a general tolerance of corruption from oversight bodies such as the State Audit Agency (BPK) and the police who have been wary about taking actions that could lead to problems. A senior state intelligence officer noted: "The only big cases [that aren't solved] relate to finance and corruption. The police don't address these because they want to keep the peace."[87]

A second strategy has been to use newfound access to power to enter the business sector. In Aceh, as elsewhere in Indonesia, good relationships to those in power are vital for aspiring entrepreneurs aiming to gain permits, win contracts, and avoid excessive taxation. Most of the senior GAM elite have become businessmen. Muzakir Manaf, the former leader of GAM's military wing and vice governor of the province from 2012 to 2017, runs a large conglomerate, PT Pulo Gadeng, which has been involved in import-export, producing steel for tsunami reconstruction, horticulture, and upgrading ports.[88] Sofyan Dawood, the former GAM commander for North Aceh, has brokered deals with large public and private companies, including from Malaysia and China.[89] Numerous other companies are run by former combatant leaders. Following his election, the non-GAM district head in Southwest Aceh allocated Rp. 12 billion (US$1.3 million) to companies run by KPA.[90]

Indeed, much "private" business is heavily reliant on state money. Throughout Indonesia, contracts are awarded based on political connections and *kontraktors* play a prominent role in politics.[91] GAM elites entered the construction sector in

a major way.[92] One mode of operations has been for GAM/KPA figures to part-
ner with existing companies. On other occasions, GAM leaders have "borrowed"
the names of preexisting contractors to win contracts. Facing the challenge that
they have few skills and little experience in contracting, they sometimes bid for
contracts and then sell them on to other contractors who have the capacity to do
the work, taking a fee of 6–15 percent.[93] GAM figures win because of their influence and potential for using violence, with their success often preordained. In
the words of one observer: "In Aceh, before projects are announced it is as if they
are owned by certain groups."[94] With the large state budgets available, the profits
that can be made are vast. Aspinall concludes that tens of millions of dollars have
made their way to GAM networks from contracting.[95]

Given the GAM elites' lack of experience and their predatory motivations,
their entry into the construction sector has unsurprisingly resulted in a reduction in the quality of infrastructure built. "Now that KPA are dominant in contracting, most projects are neglected, not finished. They withdraw money from
projects but don't finish them. This is because of a lack of experience but it is also
sometimes intentional, where they use the money for other needs. So far, there
have been no sanctions."[96] Yet the entry of GAM elites into politics and business
has also served to limit their incentives to use large-scale violence in postconflict
Aceh. It has reinforced commitment to a peace settlement from which they are
clearly benefiting. Beyond this, it has lowered their motivations to use large-scale
episodic violence. The political power of the former rebel group means that such
violent shows of strengths are not necessary to win contracts or receive projects.

Former GAM elites have entered a system, which operates across Indonesia,
where illicit deals and corruption rather than violence are the main strategies
used to achieve, exercise, and sustain power. Elites at the national and local levels
in Indonesia use shady means to access power and resources, for example, by
engaging in money politics. But violence is a rarely practiced political strategy, at
least when compared with countries like the Philippines.[97] In this regard, postconflict Aceh is unexceptional. GAM leaders have entered a local political and
economic system structured by norms and institutions that operate in a similar
way to those in other parts of the country. Aspinall convincingly argues that,
"rather than transforming the construction sector, the new GAM contractors
are being transformed by it."[98] The analysis can be extended to the involvement
of former rebel elites in Aceh's broader politics and economy: in entering the
system, GAM elites have effectively been Indonesianized.

Satisfying Other Elites

The capture by GAM of political power and the control of resources it affords could have led to violent resistance from others in the local elite such as

incumbent politicians and senior security sector personnel. That this did not occur frequently was the result of continuing opportunities for these groups to accumulate using peaceful means. This was made possible by opportunities to collaborate with GAM.

THE MILITARY

On the signing of the MoU, many observers noted the potential for the Indonesian military to wreck the peace accord.[99] Throughout the post-Suharto period, the military had resisted attempts by Indonesia's presidents to use a political and economic rather than coercive approach to bring the war to an end.[100] Spoiler actions by members of the military played a large role in the collapse of the CoHA in 2003.[101] There was also frequently expressed dissatisfaction from some in the military while the Helsinki peace talks were ongoing.[102] Reluctance to support a peace accord had its roots partly in ideological and strategic concerns: as in many postcolonial states, the Indonesian military still sees itself as the guardians of Indonesia's territorial integrity and many military leaders were inherently skeptical about the wisdom of negotiating with a group they saw as terrorists. There was also resistance because of the vast profits that Aceh's war economy generated for the underfunded organization.

The military's acceptance of the Helsinki accord, and subsequent adherence to the terms of peace, was largely a result of pressure from the Indonesian president. On assuming power, Yudhoyono removed hardliners within the military, such as TNI chief Ryamizard Ryacudu, and made it clear that the military must support the government's position. However, sweeteners were also provided to the military. The budget for the MoU-mandated troop withdrawal was set well above normal levels at Rp. 526 billion (US$58.4 million).[103] This sum was almost exactly what the military would receive in extra budget if the war had continued and the armed forces continued to receive special funding for noncombat activities in Aceh.[104] The post-tsunami aid economy also provided ample opportunities for military leaders in the province to turn a profit and many opened new businesses.[105] Military acceptance of the accord solidified as it became clear that the provisions in the MoU on human rights and retroactive justice would not be fully applied.[106] This meant there would be no serious investigation of past abuses.

Acceptance of the inviolability of the peace accord did not ensure that military elites would not use episodic violence in the postconflict period. As we saw in chapter 4, local security sector chiefs in Maluku have continued to use violence to signal their importance as a local political and economic player. Yet in Aceh, the Indonesian military by and large has chosen not to do this because they have found that it has not been necessary to use violence to ensure their place in the province's politics and economy, even with GAM in power. Old wartime patterns of collaboration, discussed above, have found new life in peacetime Aceh. GAM leaders have preferred to work with the security forces in (often illicit) business ventures rather than risk resistance. Successful GAM contractors now sometimes give donations to the local police and military, just as other business people do.[107] Common interests, and the benefits of reducing contestation and the risk that flows from it, have led to collaboration. In the words of one analyst: "KPA, GAM, and TNI [military] guys are close. They have the same interests. They like to make money, girls, and the discos in Medan [the capital of neighboring North Sumatra province]."[108] The example of Muzakir Manaf, the former rebel leader turned businessman turned politician, is illustrative. He allegedly created a company to work on wind energy with a senior member of Indonesian intelligence.[109]

The ability of the sides to work together strengthened over time. Particularly remarkable was the decision by former Aceh military commander, Lieutenant General Sunarko, to join the Partai Aceh campaign team for the 2012 elections. As late as the 2009 elections, Sunarko had taken a strongly anti-GAM position, arguing that the movement still posed a threat to Indonesian territorial integrity. Yet by 2012 he was a vocal supporter of GAM's political party. Some suggest that this support was a result of his collaboration with former GAM commanders on business projects.[110]

This is not to say that there have been no tensions between the military and former GAM. In the run up to the 2009 election, for example, a number of incidents occurred, including the abduction in late September 2008 of two Partai Aceh figures from East Aceh by the military after a solider had been kidnapped.[111] Brushes between the military and PA continued over the following months.[112] The military rounded up community members to participate in anti-PA "socialization events," roads were blocked to stop people attending PA rallies, and there was frequent harassment of PA cadres. Police investigations of the series of grenade attacks that occurred in the run up to 2009 pointed to military support for the perpetrators, although allegedly "the investigation had to stop at the gates of the military barracks."[113] However, after GAM's victory at the polls in 2009, and the new status quo of political power became clear, military tactics changed with collusion prevailing over competition.

INCUMBENT LOCAL POLITICIANS

Local politicians constituted a second group who could have violently resisted the increasing control of GAM in the political and economic realms. Their positions as incumbents gave them some control over the coercive apparatus of the state. Even though under Indonesia's decentralization, control of the security forces is a reserved power for the center, the local political elite had a long history of collaborating with local police and military commanders and had relations with security agencies in Jakarta. In postconflict Aceh, some military funding continues to come from local government budgets.[114] Some politicians have links to the antiseparatist militias, especially in the Central Highlands.

Despite this, non-GAM political elites have largely chosen not to use violence for political or economic gain in postconflict Aceh because they have been able to retain a large degree of power even as Partai Aceh increasingly dominates the local executives and legislatives. Of the sixteen mayoral contests that took place in December 2006 that did not go to a second round, for example, the victors in eight were incumbents or prominent local officer bearers.[115] In 2009, national parties won thirty-six of the sixty-nine seats in the provincial legislature, slightly more than GAM's thirty-three seats.[116] Senior local politicians standing for national parties also had a free run for national parliament seats as local parties and independents were not allowed to stand. Former rebels and incumbents thus simultaneously won strong mandates showing that competition need not be zero-sum.[117] Other long-standing local politicians, such as Abdullah Saleh of the PPP party, have continued in politics while changing their allegiance to Partai Aceh.

Collaboration between GAM and other local elites also lowered incentives for violence. In campaigning for the 2009 election, Partai Aceh worked with the Indonesian president's Partai Demokrat (Democratic Party, PD) with cadres from both parties encouraging voters to select PA for local seats and PD for national ones. PD ended up with six of the thirteen seats allocated to Aceh for the national parliament and President Yudhoyono won a massive 93 percent of Acehnese votes in the presidential poll. Governor Irwandi joined Yudhoyono's campaign as did many grassroots PA supporters.[118] Non-GAM local officials have also collaborated with newly elected GAM members on business projects.[119]

Such collaboration is less surprising than might seem, given relationships during Aceh's war. It was in the interest of local politicians and bureaucrats for the war to continue for it provided a smokescreen that masked their appropriation of state money. Officials such as Abdullah Puteh, governor of Aceh from 1999 until his arrest for corruption in late 2004, had links to GAM despite his frequent hard-line stance in advocating for a security approach to the conflict.[120] Gaining GAM's support could also be electorally useful. While campaigning to be governor, Puteh met senior GAM figures in Jakarta and gave them money in exchange for backing his campaign.[121] Other senior officials also developed close links to GAM fighters, buying them cars, giving them cuts of the government budget, and even providing them with satellite phones to aid their operations. Bonds between local officials and rebel fighters were sometimes strengthened by familial ties.[122] When the war ended, old relationships emerged from the shadows.

The High Costs of Using Large Episodic Violence

The absence of frequent large episodic violence in postconflict Aceh can thus be explained in large part by the incentives and opportunities that local elites have had to pursue power and control of resources through political channels and for former adversaries to collaborate to this end. However, as in North Maluku, the choice of local elites to use politics and pacific deal making rather than violence for purposes of accumulation was also due to the fact that it quickly became clear that using such large episodic violence was costly.

In the early post-MoU period there was effective third-party monitoring from the Aceh Monitoring Mission (AMM). Compared to many peace missions, AMM, which stayed in Aceh until after the December 2006 elections, had relatively few problems to deal with. But where violations of the accord did occur, AMM generally dealt with them in an effective manner.[123] One early incident was the destruction of the local office of SIRA, a civil society movement that had previously supported Acehnese self-determination, by a group of a hundred demonstrators, organized by the leader of a progovernment, antiseparatist front. The case was dealt with to the satisfaction of the two Helsinki signatories at a meeting of the AMM Commission on Security Arrangements (CoSA) a week later.[124] A few weeks later, AMM investigated an incident where a police officer had beaten a fish trader to death.[125] With the CoSA proving to be a useful mechanism for elites on the GAM and Indonesian government sides to settle disputes, a number of district AMM offices started to establish "mini DiCOSAs" which successfully dealt with many incidents of violence.[126]

Third-party monitoring and sanctioning was useful. Yet far more important, and, indeed, one of the reasons for the success of AMM, was the presence of what Fearon and Laitin have called in-group policing, where opposing parties each punish those in their own group who use violence.[127] Elites on both the GAM and Indonesian government sides favored the peace settlement and sent strong signals within their own organizations that large incidents of violence, that could put strains on the accord, were not acceptable.[128]

On 1 March 2008, an attack on a KPA office in Atu Lintang in Central Aceh resulted in five deaths, the largest loss of life in a single incident since the Helsinki MoU.[129] The background was a dispute between KPA and a local trade union dominated by members of former antiseparatist militias over control of the district's central bus station. The response to the incident was rapid, with the authorities, police, and the KPA hierarchy all acting to contain spillovers. Twenty-five suspects were in detention by 13 March. KPA circulated instructions for its members not to take revenge, and Malik Mahmud, the senior GAM leader, led a meeting of all seventeen KPA commanders on 4 March. Messages went down through the government and military hierarchy to antiseparatist groups that such actions would not be tolerated.[130]

Indeed, in the early years of the peace process elites on both the GAM/KPA and military sides took frequent actions to signal to their members, and to each

other, that large-scale violence was not acceptable. After two soldiers and a police officer were badly beaten in a fight with more than a dozen ex-combatants
in South Aceh in January 2007, the KPA leadership helped the local police and
military investigate the incident, resulting in the arrest of four combatants.[131]

Jakarta has also closely watched the military's behavior in the province. As
I will explore in the next chapter there have been strong directions from the Jakarta military and political leadership for the security forces not to use too much
force in performing their roles.[132] Communiqués were sent within the Aceh military structure warning that excessive use of violence would not be tolerated.[133]

Frequent Small Episodic Violence

**I don't exactly know who is doing the violence. . . . But based on my
observation, there are many among them [ex-combatants] who feel
unhappy. Some ex-combatants can access existing resources. But
there is a gap with some others.**

—Academic in Banda Aceh, 4 March 2011

While postconflict Aceh has seen few large incidents of violence, smaller episodic violence, especially violent crimes, have been common. A large proportion,
although by no means all, of this violence has been committed by lower-level
former GAM combatants.

Following the end of Aceh's war, many former combatants had great expectations for their future economic well-being. Disillusionment has risen as inequalities within the former rebel movement have grown. In this context, many have
used violence both to secure resources, for example, through violent crime, and
to send a signal to those above that they deserve a larger cut. Violence has proved
to be profitable, in large part because the costs of using it have been low. The police, wary of alienating a group who could cause trouble, have not clamped down
on violence. GAM elites, too, have largely been happy to let their former minions
"play" to keep them happy without having to distribute more rents downward.
This has created a signal that violence can be an effective strategy at the local
level, leading others to use it as well.

Ex-Combatant Expectations and Motivations
for Using Violence

Many lower-level ex-combatants have used violence because of a lack of viable
peaceful options for getting ahead economically. After the peace agreement was

signed expectations were high among former rebels. There is debate about the extent to which lower-level GAM combatants were driven by pecuniary goals. While some have highlighted the increasingly predatory motivations of many former combatants, especially those who joined after 1999,[134] others have placed more emphasis on human rights abuses as a motivating factor for joining the rebel movement.[135] However, even among those who had joined for ideological reasons, or to exact revenge, there was a concern that after years of privations in the forests and mountains they would do well out of the peace. For these reasons, expectations of economic reward were greater than among former fighters in North Maluku and, to a lesser extent, Maluku.

Six months after the signing of the Helsinki MoU, around three-quarters of ex-combatants did not have work.[136] A needs assessment for the rebel group found that many returnees were eager to take a rest after years of fighting and to spend time with their families. Others were waiting for instructions from their old commanders on what to do next: "Of the combatants who have come back, some have started working, some haven't. Whatever we can do we will do. If we ask our commander about our future, he says we must be patient."[137] Nevertheless, even at this point many former combatants were frustrated about their work situation. Prior to joining GAM, more than 96 percent of ex-combatants had been employed.[138] The vast majority of former rebels interviewed identified a lack of employment opportunities or ability to generate an income as their greatest concern.[139]

By mid-2008, the employment picture had changed. A representative survey of ex-combatants found that 85 percent were in work, a higher rate than those who had not fought before.[140] However, these new jobs often did not fit with the expectations of former fighters who felt their service entitled them to jobs with higher incomes and status. The 2006 survey had found that the vast majority of former combatants wanted jobs as traders with only a very small proportion content to farm, the residual occupation in Aceh.[141] Despite this, by 2008 former combatants were more likely than regular civilians to derive their income from rice farming or agricultural wage labor, low paying jobs, and were less likely to be employed as civil servants, traders, or teachers.[142]

DISAPPOINTMENT WITH REINTEGRATION AID

The failures of aid programs, including those aimed at supporting reintegration, to boost the welfare of lower-level ex-combatants contributed to dissatisfaction. Aceh's reintegration program has been dysfunctional with problems in both its design and implementation.[143]

One problem related to the number of former rebels who were to receive assistance. The peace agreement (clause 4.2) stated that GAM had three thousand military troops, and it was expected that this group along with the two thousand or so political prisoners, as well as victims of conflict, would receive benefits. It soon emerged that there were far more GAM than initially estimated. When retired fighters and civilian members were taken into account, GAM's strength was perhaps seven times that stated in the MoU.[144] The distinction between GAM combatant and sympathizer was a fuzzy one with the movement supported by much of Aceh's population. As GAM rose to political power, the number of individuals claiming to have been active in the rebel movement duly multiplied.[145] Two steps were taken to get around the numbers problem. First, a category of "GAM noncombatants" was added to the list of those who were to receive money from the government.[146] Second, reintegration money was distributed through former GAM commanders, who then reallocated the resources across the former combatant base as well as to other supporters. One consequence was that funds were spread widely among former rebels, with some former combatants receiving as little as Rp. 30,000, or US$3.[147] Former combatants asked why they were only being given *uang rokok* (money for cigarettes).[148]

Where former combatants did receive assistance, it often had little impact on their longer-run well-being. The government reintegration programs gave out cash with little technical assistance or monitoring to ensure money was used effectively. After initial "goodwill" payments were made, BRA developed a system whereby GAM leaders would receive funds to set up microprojects for groups of their cadres.[149] On the face of it, the development of proposals, vetted by a BRA committee, would ensure that funds were used for productive economic purposes. Yet it soon became clear that welfare impacts were less important than satisfying political pressures to disburse the money. GAM elites argued that reintegration funds were compensation for losses from the conflict and were their right under the MoU;[150] as such, there should not be rules on how they spent their money. They won the argument, the scheme was scrapped, and additional payments were made in cash to commanders with little monitoring of how money was spent. Internationally sponsored programs were generally more effective, providing training and follow-up support in addition to cash. Yet, even then, on average households who received reintegration assistance ended up faring no better than those who did not.[151]

The reintegration program served to create new demands for and expectations of assistance among former combatants and led to rising disillusionment when this was not forthcoming. Over time, it also increased suspicions from some former combatants that Jakarta and the Acehnese authorities did not care about their needs and that they were reneging on the promises of the peace deal.[152]

RISING INEQUALITIES WITHIN GAM

There is a big difference within GAM: between the high, medium, and low level. . . . The lower GAM/KPA are very angry because, first, they don't understand government administrative processes for getting access to money and, second, they don't want to be beggars to the upper level. Their position is weak in the communities.

—Activist, North Aceh, 7 March 2011

The failure of reintegration funds to meet the expectations of many former combatants were compounded by growing inequalities within the former rebel movement. As we saw earlier, the primary means by which GAM elites have got ahead has been through entry to politics and attendant opportunities in business and contracting. Access to these areas has been closed to most lower-level GAM; most of the benefits have accrued only to those in the upper echelons of the movement.

GAM had a strict hierarchical structure. Below the senior leaders, exiled in Sweden, were those with Aceh-wide responsibilities such as the *panglima negara* (state commander). Under him, Aceh was divided into 17 regions (*wilayah*) with a panglima wilayah controlling each. Within each wilayah, there were on average four area commanders (panglima *daerah*). Below the daerah level were around 270 *sagoes*, corresponding roughly in size to an Indonesian administrative subdistrict (*kecamatan*), each led by a panglima sagoe. Under these were the foot soldiers. GAM's civilian apparatus was organized similarly, and its postconflict incarnation, the KPA, largely uses the same structure.

While the war was ongoing the differences in wealth between those at higher and lower levels within GAM were relatively slight. However, after the extended violence ended, sharp disparities emerged that created jealousies and tensions:

> I went to rural Bireuen district where the ex-combatants are doing nothing. They are really bitter with KPA. They say, "Darwis [Jeunib, the former GAM commander for Bireuen], he has a big house and we have nothing."[153]

> There is differentiation in the status of higher and lower-level ex-combatants. Some ex-combatants now are not depending on their leaders. They do [what they want] by themselves. . . . This is all creating jealousy. Some have no money to pay for coffee. They see others who have luxury cars. They say, "Before we were the same."[154]

Rising inequality has been a consequence of the ways in which GAM-operated businesses, especially contractors, function. Most projects go through the panglima wilayah and occasionally through those panglima daerah who have political connections.[155] Resources are often captured at this level. "It is just the GAM elite that relies on government projects. So there are big discrepancies between the higher and lower levels."[156] GAM leaders hire locals, including many lower-level former combatants, to work on large public works projects. However, such jobs tend to last for only a short time and pay low salaries. Increasingly, local-level GAM have also found it difficult to gain work on these projects. As GAM entered politics it needed to expand its support base. GAM politicians would have been unlikely to gain sufficient support in 2009 and 2012 if they relied solely on the support of former rebel combatants. One consequence is that the patronage base for GAM political and business elites has expanded to include many who were not involved in the insurgency. Similar considerations led KPA to allow noncombatants to become members of the organization and PA to court non-GAM activists and cadres of other political parties. The loyalties of former fighters have reduced in importance. As a result, a more limited share of funds has been channeled to lower-level former combatants with more captured at higher levels or spread more widely including to non-GAM.[157]

This has led to great frustration, especially among those at the sagoe (subdistrict) level. Many ex-combatants in villages are illiterate and have lower expectations, happy to work as laborers or farmers.[158] In contrast, those at the sagoe level often have greater ambitions yet do not have the sway with higher-level GAM figures to secure projects of their own.[159] In this environment, many of these former fighters have turned to violence.

THE USES OF VIOLENCE: CAPTURING
RESOURCES AND SIGNALING

> **I interviewed an ex-combatant in Nisam [in North Aceh] called Rambo. He said his boss [a former GAM commander] gives him only a little money. If it is divided by 70 [the number of ex-combatants in the area] it's only Rp. 25,000 [US$2.5] per month. So he said, "I still have some weapons. If the situation does not change, I will do myself what needs to be done."**
>
> —Academic, Banda Aceh, 4 March 2011. Rambo, who was involved in armed robberies, was subsequently killed in a police raid.

> **There are many criminal incidents in Aceh. This is because people have big expectations. Everybody, especially on the east coast, feels they played a role in making peace. But, in reality, their expectations are not fulfilled in terms of access to the economy. There were a lot**

of promises made during the campaign for the governor and district head. This creates the foundations of grievances.

—Journalist, Banda Aceh, 3 March 2011.

In this context of frustrated expectations, less reliance on their former patrons, and a fragmenting KPA structure, former rebel combatants, especially at the sa-goe level, have increasingly used violence instrumentally. It was this level that was most factionalized and where there was the least discipline during the war.[160] For such people, violence serves two purposes.

First, violence is used to directly secure resources. This explains the rise in violent crime which has been most pronounced in GAM's old heartlands on the east coast. In 2008, the police in Aceh claimed that the number of armed crimes in the province was 22 times higher than before the Helsinki MoU.[161] A prosecutor in North Aceh, a former GAM stronghold, observed that there were cases of armed violence in her area almost every month. Cases of crime increased rapidly between 2008 and 2011 with crimes involving firearms rising most sharply. In addition to robberies, the kidnapping of children for ransom had also risen with thirty-five cases in her area in 2009 compared to just four in 2008.[162] In East Aceh, and no doubt elsewhere, kidnappings of civil servants also occur frequently.[163] Lower-level GAM also use violence to ensure they are employed on public works projects.[164] An estimated 90 percent of criminal activity in East Aceh is carried out by ex-combatants many of whom are disappointed that they did not receive their share of the postconflict spoils.[165]

Second, violence is used to signal discontent and continuing coercive capacity to elites with the aim of increasing downward patronage flows. Senior GAM leaders such as Sofyan Dawood, Ilyas Pasee, and Zakaria Saman have had grenades thrown at their houses.[166] The attacks were motivated by struggles over economic resources, in particular aid funds and illegal logging.[167] While no one was caught, it is likely that the perpetrators were disgruntled GAM members who felt their targets had not distributed a large enough share of the lucrative projects they controlled.[168] There have been other attacks aimed at politicians who have criticized former combatants' continuing practices of demanding shares of projects and imposing taxes. For example, in May 2011 a local politician was attacked while giving a public speech where he criticized continuing extortion by KPA members.[169] Such attacks have usually been intended to intimidate rather than kill. Grenades have been thrown at buildings rather than people and in almost every case no one has been injured, although there are exceptions.

Indeed, Aceh shows that local-level violence specialists are not just passive tools of elites as they are sometimes depicted in the literature. They can also use violence instrumentally to shape the decisions and actions of those above them.

Low Costs: Acceptance of Small Episodic Violence by Elites

The motivations for lower-level former combatants and others to use violence have been strengthened by the fact that the risks associated with such actions have been low. Whereas there has been little tolerance of large episodic violence that could threaten the peace process, there has been tacit acceptance by elites of smaller-scale forms of violence.

The police and military have been reluctant to investigate small-scale incidents of violence such as violent robberies and local disputes, in particular when former GAM combatants have been involved. Post-MoU, the security forces have generally used a soft approach in Aceh, preferring dialogue to more aggressive forms of investigation. Local police chiefs emphasize the nationwide policy of "Partnership with the People," or community policing.[170] Police and the military argue that such an approach is needed in an environment where they are still not widely accepted by the local population and where they need to be careful not to alienate or offend their former enemies in GAM. As one senior intelligence official noted, "They are afraid people will misinterpret police pressure."[171]

The choice of such an approach is also a function of practical concerns about the limited number of police personnel. The MoU set police numbers at 9,100 for a population of 4.4 million. While this figure has been exceeded—by 2008 there were around 13,000 police in the province[172]—per capita policing levels are still very low: "There are still few police compared to the population number. The MoU limits numbers. The police are also still unwilling to force themselves to be proactive. . . . They think the people they are facing are "crazy people." They think it would create more problems if they are more forceful."[173]

The careful, hesitant approach is also related to the widespread availability of guns in the province. The peace agreement called for GAM to surrender 840 weapons. However, this was largely of symbolic value and did not significantly deplete the former rebel group's fighting capacity. The military and others knew that GAM had more guns.[174] Indonesian intelligence is also aware that there are still some imports of guns.[175] On 7 March 2011, a factory was found producing AK47s and M16s in a rural area of Nagan Raya district. Across Aceh, 14 percent of all cases of postconflict violence have involved the use of a firearm, compared to 4 percent of incidents in postconflict Maluku and 2 percent in North Maluku. In East Aceh district, the figure is 35 percent with 171 incidents of armed violence recorded in the postconflict period.

Others highlight the extent to which the police and military have not focused on their core tasks because of other concerns. As one analyst noted: "The police and military could address the problem [of the rise in violent crime and conflict] but they are too busy working with GAM on things like illegal logging."[176]

Indeed, the failure of the police to go after Pasukan Peudeung (Long Sword Forces), a GAM splinter group that has been involved in many armed robberies and kidnappings, is likely a result of collusion between the local police and gang members.[177]

The GAM elite has also done little to sanction former combatants who engage in smaller-scale violence that is not threatening to the peace deal or to their own interests. This is the case because they do not want more pressure from those below them. Allowing violence is seen as a way of enabling ex-combatants to let off some steam while also letting them secure some resources. Coming down hard on such violence could threaten GAM leaders' interests: "They [GAM leaders] could use their channel of command to control incidents. . . . But they don't because they don't want more problems from those at the lower level. . . . Partai Aceh have the power to fix the problem. But they are not moving toward this. Some of them are educated, they understand the situation. But everyone is busy securing power, just for personal interests."[178] A World Bank report that identified extortion and intimidation from former combatants as the main barriers to growth in the province was publicly received with hostility by the then governor and former GAM leader, Irwandi Jusuf.[179] Privately, Irwandi acknowledged these issues were a problem but stated that he had to give some space to former combatants otherwise they could cause more problems for the peace process.[180]

The absence of effective sanctioning of small-scale violence that does not threaten the peace process or elite interests has shown that such violence can be a useful and relatively risk-free strategy for accumulating resources. This has resulted in postconflict violence becoming normalized among many former combatants. It has also encouraged others to use violence for instrumental purposes.

One consequence has been that many common criminals now present themselves as former GAM combatants. They do so because they feel this affords them protection with police more likely to turn a blind eye to indiscretions. It also reduces the risk of community resistance. As one local civil society figure in Peureulak, East Aceh, told me: "There is a problem here with people claiming to be GAM. They do so because of the history here. They know people are afraid of GAM."[181] Lack of effective responses to crime and local violent conflict has also led others to use violence to settle their problems. Antiseparatist militia groups in the Central Highlands have used similar tactics to former GAM to demand projects. Other community members have also increasingly resorted to violence.

Alternative Explanations for Frequent Small Episodic Violence

This chapter has developed an explanation for the frequent small-scale episodic violence in postconflict Aceh that focuses primarily on one set of actors (lower-level former combatants) and one set of motives (economic accumulation). It could be that the violence is undertaken by other actors (such as non-combatant community members or local elites) and/or that other motives (such as revenge taking) are more important. It is worth briefly considering these alternative explanations.

THE TORN SOCIAL FABRIC?

Frequent postconflict violence could be the result of destroyed social relations and diminished trust. As I discussed in chapter 2, the global literature has highlighted how wars can effect group identities, intergroup relations, and behaviors in ways that engender violence. Can this explain postconflict Aceh's frequent small-scale violence?

Most of Aceh's postconflict violence is not a result of dysfunctional intergroup relations. Unlike many civil wars, Aceh did not have multiple conflicting parties, each commanding loyalty from sections of the local population. Rather, there was strong support for GAM's goals, if not always its means, among the civilian population in most areas. As a result, there was acceptance, indeed often celebrations, when combatants returned home after the peace deal, a situation that has been observed in other postwar cases such as Timor-Leste.[182] A representative survey of 642 former combatants six months after the MoU found that 90 percent had experienced no problems on their return despite there being little reintegration money flowing at this point. In more than three-quarters of villages surveyed, traditional *peusijuk* (welcoming) ceremonies were held to celebrate the return of combatants.[183] A survey of every rural village in Aceh in 2007 found high levels of social capital and improvements in social cohesion and village solidarity since the Helsinki MoU.[184] Only 7 percent of villagers interviewed said that there were low levels of trust between "those who returned from the mountain" and other community members.[185]

As time has gone on, trust has not diminished. Of the more than one thousand former GAM members surveyed in mid-2008, only seven reported any difficulties with being accepted since they returned to their villages.[186] In some areas of the Central Highlands, where progovernment militia were strong due to the presence of non-Acehnese ethnic groups such as the Gayo and Javanese, tensions have been greater.[187] Yet even there trust has been growing, although there have been some isolated incidents of unrest. Across all the areas surveyed, 97 percent of female community members and 96 percent of civilian men reported that the presence of former combatants was not a source of division in their community. Around 90 percent of informants said they would be happy to welcome former combatants into their family through marriage and that former combatants could be among their close friends.

Revenge does not appear to be the primary motive in most incidents of violence. Certainly, there were some cases of retributive killings in the early months after the peace agreement.[188] But, by and large, instrumental uses of violence, often economically motivated, have been far more common.[189]

THE USE OF SMALL-SCALE VIOLENCE BY ELITES?

It could be that Aceh's frequent small-scale episodic violence is driven by local elites such as former GAM commanders, local politicians, or security chiefs. Such elites could feel that using large-scale episodic violence is not in their interests, because it is not necessary to achieve their goals or because it is risky, but that smaller-scale violence is a useful tool in political and economic competition.

Some analyses of postconflict violence in Aceh have emphasized elite calculations. The violence in the lead up to the 2009 and 2012 elections, which were marked by tensions between different groups in the upper echelons of GAM, may have been elite driven.[190] In July 2011, Teungku Cagee, a former GAM commander who had defied KPA orders by supporting the incumbent Irwandi in the gubernatorial elections, was assassinated.[191] In late 2011 and early 2012 there were a series of shootings, many against migrant Javanese laborers. Some saw these as being organized by Partai Aceh to send a signal to Jakarta that the planned local elections should be postponed so that they would not take place while the incumbent, Irwandi, was still governor.[192] Aceh, indeed, has seen much more electoral violence than other provinces, and the pattern of assassinations in the run up to recent elections is, within Indonesia, largely unique to Aceh.[193] Some other criminal violence is also likely condoned by local elites competing over business opportunities and extortion schemes. Indeed, some GAM elites may have an interest in attributing violence to disgruntled rank-and-file to divert attention away from themselves.[194]

However, in contrast to Maluku, there is little evidence of elites systematically organizing violence. Local elites have played a role in sponsoring some incidents of small-scale violence, particularly in the run up to elections. Yet most violence has been fragmented, involving a wide range of actors, suggesting that ground-level motivations explain more than those of local elites.

District-Level Divergence: East and South Aceh

High levels of small-scale episodic violence in Aceh can be largely explained by the incentives former combatants have to use violence instrumentally for purposes of accumulation. Further support for this argument emerges if we look at differences in levels of postconflict violence between districts within Aceh.

TABLE 13. Levels of small-scale postconflict violence in Aceh districts most affected by extended violence

DISTRICT	POPULATION	EV PERIOD DEATHS	POSTCONFLICT PERIOD INCIDENTS	DEATHS	INJ.	KIDNAP.	BUILDINGS	DEATHS PER CAPITA
Aceh Besar	307,362	838	294	73	216	13	43	32
East Aceh	313,333	1,511	494	65	275	61	41	26
Bireuen	355,989	1,443	466	66	321	18	133	25
Lhokseumawe	158,169	415	497	26	391	10	27	22
Pidie	373,234	737	377	49	244	10	21	18
North Aceh	510,494	1,989	705	66	500	33	52	17
South Aceh	209,853	903	114	15	84	4	20	10

Source: NVMS. Impacts reported are for small-scale violence (where fewer than three people die, ten are injured, or fifteen buildings are damaged in an incident). Postconflict period is August 2005 until the end of 2012. Per capita rates are per 1 million people per year. Population data are from the Indonesian Bureau of Statistics and are for 2008.

Table 13 provides data on incidents and impacts of postconflict violence in the seven districts that were most affected by the past extended violence. South Aceh is exceptional in having seen relatively little violence since the peace agreement. In contrast, east coast districts such as Aceh Besar, East Aceh, Bireuen, and Lhokseumawe have been the sites of much more postconflict violence. To tease out the reasons for such subprovincial variation, I conducted fieldwork in East Aceh (which has the second highest per capita death rate in the postconflict period) and South Aceh (which has the lowest).[195]

We might have expected South Aceh to see more postconflict violence than East Aceh. In the run up to the MoU violence was on the rise in South Aceh. From January to August 2005, there were 50 violent incidents in South Aceh resulting in 42 deaths and 23 injuries, as well as 31 kidnappings. The death toll was the second highest among Aceh's districts. In the same time period, there were 31 deaths from 44 incidents and 21 kidnappings in East Aceh. Former combatants also make up a greater share of the population in South Aceh than East Aceh. There are around 1,600 ex-combatants in East Aceh, in a population of over 300,000, compared with 1,400 in South Aceh, which has a population of close to 200,000.[196] Some have argued that ex-combatants in South Aceh are more likely to have joined GAM for economic reasons than in East Aceh. The rise in violence in South Aceh in 2002 and 2003 coincided with GAM's attempts to expand its influence from its east coast strongholds to other areas of the province that were previously less touched by violence. This involved hiring thugs and other opportunists with a taste for violence, with the result that GAM was more coercive and ill-disciplined in areas such as South Aceh where it did not have a historical presence.[197] South Aceh was also home to some of the worst human rights abuses during the extended violence. A study in fourteen districts in Aceh identified South Aceh's Kluet River valley as being a central hotspot of violations. Exposure to traumatic events in this area was double the sample average and higher than in east coast GAM strongholds.[198]

Why then has South Aceh seen so much less postconflict violence than East Aceh and many of the other east coast districts? There are two important differences between the two districts that explain divergent patterns of postconflict violence.

NETWORKS AND RESOURCE FLOWS WITHIN GAM

First, a larger share of resources is flowing down from elite-level GAM in South Aceh than in East Aceh. This is a function of differences in the ways the GAM/KPA networks are functioning in the postconflict period.

In both districts, GAM is a major player in local politics and business. Partai Aceh holds twenty-five of thirty-five seats in the East Aceh parliament and ten seats in South Aceh where it is the largest party. GAM elites are also dominant in the local economy. In East Aceh, most infrastructure projects are now run by GAM. In South Aceh, a local politician estimated that around 90 percent of projects went to KPA.[199] The process of winning such contracts is similar in both areas with a combination of political connections and sometimes intimidation used.[200] As in East Aceh, aggression is sometimes used in South Aceh. One local NGO activist noted that there have been six recent cases of GAM figures attacking the heads of local government agencies (*dinas/badan*) to put pressure on them to receive projects. There was no follow-up by the police who just replied *damai* (peace) when government officials reported the incidents to them.[201]

However, a larger proportion of the money raised at higher levels within the GAM/KPA structure reaches lower-level former combatants in South Aceh than in East Aceh. The main reason for this is that the GAM/KPA structure is less fragmented in South Aceh than in East Aceh.

In September 2004, the powerful GAM panglima of East Aceh, Ishak Daud, was killed in battle. His role was taken by Teungku Muhammad Sanusi. He was one of the older commanders, having been trained in Libya. But he had little authority with many of the young combatants who had joined in recent years.[202] He was closer to local Islamic leaders (*ulama*) than to former combatants.[203] In the absence of strong local leadership, multiple commanders at similar levels have emerged with often little coordination between them.[204]

The weak GAM leadership in East Aceh has had two effects. First, those at the pinnacle of the organization do not rely heavily on lower-level former combatants and do not always have good relations with them. Second, these district-level commanders and leaders have little ability to prevent ex-combatants from committing crimes or using violence. Ridwan, a member of the provincial parliament who had been deputy GAM commander for East Aceh during the war, was kidnapped by his former followers. The ex-combatants were unhappy that while their patron was doing well, they had seen little benefit.[205]

In contrast, KPA in South Aceh is less factionalized and the command structure functions more effectively than in East Aceh. Under the district-level leader, Abra Mudah, are four commanders, each in charge of a different geographic area: Kluet Raya, Bakongan Raya, Lhok Tapaktuan, and Labuan Haji. These four divide up contracts among themselves, but coordinate in the process.[206] The leaders who get projects tend to distribute a share to those below them. As one sagoe GAM leader noted:

> There is not a big gap between the low- and high-level [former GAM] here in terms of wealth or poverty. People below see that. It's about the distribution of resources. If someone from the high level gets a project from the government, normally they employ their followers. There's a strong instruction from above [KPA South Aceh] to not use violence or do crime.[207]

Such redistribution occurs in part for prudential reasons. A local NGO activist observed: "Here in South Aceh, if GAM get a project and don't share, then others [within GAM] will betray you, steal cement, and so on."[208] However, another factor is that there are greater norms of brotherhood and solidarity among former combatants in South Aceh than in many of GAM's east coast strongholds. There are a number of reasons for this, including the fact that most GAM in the district were recruited around the same time, meaning that differences in status between fighters are more limited than in other districts. There are also more extensive kinship relations between former combatants;[209] the district is relatively isolated, which encourages a common sense of identity, even in the face of a more diverse ethnic mix; and there is an enhanced need to ensure organizational strength in an environment where GAM do not have the same monopoly on political power as in some other districts. While some tensions have emerged between different levels of GAM, these have largely been overcome.[210]

CONTROL OF ECONOMIC ACTIVITIES

The mining really helps. If there was no mining, it would be very difficult to live. If there were no activities like this, probably there

would be conflict again. If no money, no activity, headaches. If there was no mining, well there would be problems every day.

—Village leader and former combatant, South Aceh, 20 April 2011

A second difference is the presence of local economic activities controlled by sagoe-level GAM in South Aceh. In East Aceh, lower-level former combatants rely on projects controlled by their leaders at the district level. In contrast, the discovery of gold in South Aceh, and the establishment of local cooperatives to manage mining and selling, has meant that more money-making opportunities are available for former combatants.

South Aceh is rich in natural resources and small-scale mining of resources continued through the war years. With the peace process, larger companies started to move in. By early 2011, twenty-three companies had permission for exploration, and five had been given permission for exploitation.[211] The mining companies rely on local cooperatives for labor. These are largely controlled by subdistrict-level KPA commanders and provide work for some former combatants.[212]

More important has been the growth of traditional, and illegal, mining operations in areas of the district that were previous conflict hot spots: Central Kluet, Pasir Raja, Sawang, and Sama Dua. These were set up after local leaders observed similar mining techniques being used in Aceh Jaya district and operations were expanded after they proved successful.[213] In these areas, four hundred stone-destroying machines are operating. Villages I visited in Pasi Raja were producing six kilograms of gold per day. It was estimated that across South Aceh, around twenty kilograms of gold, with a market value of around US$360,000, is being produced each day by traditional mining.[214]

These operations have many negative consequences. There have been tensions between companies and locals over the destruction of roads by trucks carrying out materials. Mercury used in traditional mining will likely have large environmental impacts in the future. The vice-district head of South Aceh also attributed recent floods in the Kluet area to mining operations, legal and illegal.[215] Mining has not led to widespread economic development in South Aceh. One local NGO member observed that since the MoU the only substantive sign of progress in Tapaktuan, South Aceh's capital, was the installation of a new set of traffic lights.[216]

However, the traditional mining operations have ensured that more money is captured by former GAM leaders at the local level than has been the case in other districts like East Aceh. Sagoe-level KPA manage the cooperatives and play a role as agents, selling their production to businessmen who then export it from Aceh. They pay no tax. There has been no effort from the police to shut down operations because they are also involved in illegal mining.[217] This has meant that there is less welfare inequality within GAM in South Aceh than in most other parts of the province and many, if not all, lower-level former combatants are doing reasonably well economically. In this environment, the incentives for local-level former combatants to use violence are minimized.

This chapter has explained why some postconflict areas experience frequent small-scale violence that does not escalate into larger conflagrations. As in Maluku and North Maluku, patterns of violence in Aceh can be understood by considering the incentives that local elites and local violence specialists have to support or use violence for purposes of accumulation.

Frequent large episodic violence has been absent in postconflict Aceh because local elites have not supported its use. In contrast to Maluku, it has not been necessary for elites, including GAM leaders, other local politicians, and security force leaders, to use large episodic violence to access political power or economic resources. It has also not been in their interest to allow others to use such violence as it could pose risks for a peace settlement from which they are benefiting. Because of this, local elites have tended not to engage in large episodic violence and have disciplined their followers on the rare occasions that such violence has occurred.

However, unlike in North Maluku, smaller-scale incidents, especially violent crimes, have been frequent. This is largely because lower-level former combatants and other violence specialists have found it to be an effective way to secure resources. In North Maluku, expectations among those who had fought in the extended violence were lower than in Aceh, in part because their participation in war was driven less by predatory motives, in part because such participation had been shorter, and because combatant organization structures quickly faded away. In contrast, expectations among lower-level former combatants in Aceh were high. In a context of limited economic opportunities at the local level, and growing inequalities within the former rebel movement, this led some to use violence to try to get ahead. Elites in Aceh have generally allowed such violence to occur where it has not impinged on their own interests. This has generated a signal for former combatants and others that engaging in small-scale violence works—that it can be profitable and is not costly. Only where lower-level combatants have had greater economic opportunities has such violence been less frequent.

Aceh provides insights on how postconflict resources can shape the incentives of different groups to use violence. In the last chapter, I argued that the absence of extensive aid in the early postconflict period in North Maluku allowed local elites to focus on reconciliation activities and that this explained why that province had not seen the same levels of violence as had Maluku, where there were far greater resources. However, Aceh's experience shows that more important than levels of resources are the mechanisms that dictate how they are allocated. In Maluku, decisions on how resources would be used were often shaped by the use or threat of violence by elites and their underlings. Aceh differed because greater efforts were made to politically incorporate former dissident leaders; their ability to benefit economically flowed from their accession to political power. As in North Maluku, informal norms of collaboration between old adversaries meant that political competition did not become zero-sum. Expansion of subnational resources vastly increased opportunities for everyone to get their slice of the cake. In this environment, and as in much of Indonesia, the use of large episodic violence to secure resources or signal strength was not necessary.

However, the Aceh case also shows how growing inequalities in a resource-rich environment can have potentially dangerous consequences. The high level of resources in Aceh served to raise the expectations of former combatants; the lack of success they had in benefiting from them increased frustrations and led some to use small-scale episodic violence strategically to capture resources. Local elites have not tolerated the escalation of violence beyond small-scale incidents. However, over the longer run local elite preferences can change, shaped in part by the attitudes of those below them. In the absence of more effective and equitable development in Aceh, which requires improvements in governance institutions, there is a risk that if elite attitudes to violence do change, the presence of disillusioned former fighters will make it very easy for elites to act on their impulses.

WHY HAS EXTENDED VIOLENT CONFLICT NOT RECURRED?

The areas of Indonesia previously affected by extended violent conflict vary in the levels and forms of episodic violence they have seen in their postconflict periods. As previous chapters explored, large clashes have frequently occurred in postconflict Maluku while Aceh has experienced high levels of small-scale violent incidents. Yet in neither province has postconflict violence escalated to the point where extended violent conflict has reemerged. Other Indonesian postconflict regions have also seen frequent deadly incidents but in all such incidents have remained sporadic.

This chapter explains why extended violent conflict has not recurred *anywhere* in post-Suharto Indonesia. In so doing, it explores the reasons for temporal variation in extended violent conflict, comparing Indonesia's initial period of democratic transition, when extended violence was present in many provinces, with more recent years, when it has been absent.[1]

To understand why there has not been renewed extended violent conflict we must turn our analytic gaze to the national level and focus on the interests of elites linked to, and battling for power within, the central state. In middle-income countries such as Indonesia, where the coercive and bureaucratic arms of the state have wide reach, the central state has the capacity to prevent the escalation of localized violence into extended violent conflict. In contrast to episodic violence, which is largely driven by local actors, I argue that escalation to extended violence in such states only occurs when members of the national state-based elite support or condone such intensification. The lack of extended violence anywhere in Indonesia today is not because of changes in the motives or incentives of local violence specialists or local elites. Rather, organized enduring violence is absent from the current landscape because there is now agreement across the national elite that such violence is not beneficial or acceptable. As a result, the central state has been able to take actions to prevent the escalation of large sporadic episodes of violence into wider unrest.

In the early years of Indonesia's transition, some security agency leaders and national politicians had an interest in allowing localized regional violence to escalate. The Indonesian military, in particular, was concerned with maintaining its power in a reforming Indonesia. The presence of escalated extended violence, especially that between warring religious and ethnic groups, amplified worries that diverse Indonesia was on the brink of disintegration. In this environment, military claims for a continuing strong role as guardians of the nation were bolstered. Some politicians, too, saw benefits from extended violent conflicts as they jostled for power and to shape the new rules of the political and economic game. There is scant evidence that the military, police, or other national elites caused violence to erupt in the Moluccas, Kalimantan, Aceh, or Central Sulawesi. Yet while violence was initially a result of local interests and grievances, these conflicts only escalated to full-scale wars because of central state inaction and sometimes active meddling.

Over time, the incentives of central state elites to support such large-scale violence have diminished as Indonesia's democracy has consolidated after the turbulent early transition years. There is now shared acceptance from national elites, including the military and police, on rules of behavior where the promotion of large-scale extended violence is not an acceptable means to bolster power or seek resources. (The use of episodic violence is still tolerated where it is not threatening to the interests of national elites.) This agreement is a product of two things: the deeper institutionalization of the Indonesian polity, which has created clearer rules of the game; and decisions by Indonesia's democracy-era presidents, and other members of the national political elite, to share power and resources in ways that allow all central elite factions to benefit. The security forces have retained a strong role, and entrenched interests from the Suharto era have not been challenged. The formation of rainbow coalitions, where parties of every political stripe have access to the spoils of government, has provided opportunities for national elites from across the political spectrum to prosper. Indonesia's growing economy has helped cement a bargain where extended violence is not countenanced even while other illiberal practices are.

Table 14 uses the book's theoretical framework to summarize the changes that have occurred and how these translate into differing levels of extended violent conflict.

TABLE 14. Incentives for central state–based actors to support violence escalation over time

FACTOR	EARLY POST-SUHARTO PERIOD (1998–2003)	LATER POST-SUHARTO PERIOD (2004–)
Benefits: Resources distributed to central state elites based on threat of/use of violence?	Yes	No
Costs: Supporting escalation shown to be costly?	No	Yes
Opportunities: Peaceful political/economic channels for accumulation by central state elites?	No	Yes
Presence of extended violence	Yes	No

National Elite Interests and Indonesia's Extended Violent Conflicts

Previous Explanations I: Local Motivations

Most accounts of Indonesia's extended violent conflicts emphasize the motivations of local actors seeking to redress grievances or achieve power in a changing Indonesia. As Suharto fell in May 1998 following massive protests in Jakarta and many regional capitals, there was uncertainty over what form a democratizing Indonesian state would take. In this environment, ethnic and religious groups in the regions, and separatist insurgents in Aceh and East Timor, turned to violence.

For Jacques Bertrand, Suharto's fall constituted a critical juncture where the rules of the game on institutional forms, and whose interests they would represent, were to be (re)defined.[2] As with the previous transitions from Dutch rule to independence in the 1940s, and the ouster of President Sukarno in the mid-1960s, violence emerged as the national model and state institutions were being renegotiated. The groups who used violence were those who had felt excluded or who disagreed with the terms of their inclusion under the New Order. "Islamists," he argues, "wanted to reopen questions relating to the role of Islam in the polity, Dayaks [in Kalimantan] refused to continue to be marginalized, East Timorese seized the moment to push for independence, and Acehnese vied to regain new terms of inclusion in Indonesia or independence."[3] The extended violent conflicts, in other words, were a consequence of the pent-up grievances and ambitions of different ethnic and religious groups (or their leaders) with violence viewed as an effective means of accessing power. National transition and associated uncertainty provided the context, but it is the largely regional elites representing these groups who are viewed by Bertrand as being the agents behind the violence.

John Sidel explicitly contrasts his argument with that of Bertrand but it shares many similarities.[4] As with Bertrand, the violence that emerged in the late Suharto and early *reformasi* days is viewed as being driven by the uncertainty groups felt over the terms of their inclusion in times of change. Focusing largely on Islamic organizations, he argues that violent action flowed from anxieties related to the boundaries of authority commanded by local religious elites. Whereas Bertrand emphasizes access to, and representation in and by, state institutions, Sidel's focus is wider, looking at social and class relations. These, he argues, determined not only when and where violence took place but also its predominant form. A similar logic drove the riots, church burnings, and electoral violence of the late New Order period, the large-scale interreligious violence in Maluku and Central Sulawesi after Suharto's fall, and the terrorist attacks that occurred from 2000 on: "Each phase of violence in Indonesia over the past ten years has been associated with one or more religious hierarchies and the problems that accompanied efforts to assert and maintain religious authority over, and identity among, one or another religious flock (*jemaah*)."[5]

Violence, Sidel argues, changed in form over time—from riots to pogroms to jihad—because different types of religious hierarchy were being challenged at different points in time. At varying points, different types of violent action were seen as being effective for preserving or extending the authority of religious groups. Yet all three types of violence are viewed as flowing from the actions of local religious leaders. As with Bertrand, the political transition, and broader structural processes of social change, are viewed as being important only in how they affected the interests and motivations of the local elites who organized violence.

Gerry van Klinken, who studies all of Indonesia's extended communal conflicts but not the separatist civil wars, differs from Sidel and Bertrand in his emphasis on the naked pursuit of power at the local level rather than the more existential struggle for the inclusion of identity groups or preservation of religious hierarchies.[6] Drawing on the theory of contentious politics, he argues that the post-Suharto extended violence was largely a product of the political-economic incentives of local elites. Fear, anomie, and uncertainty certainly contributed to violence but cannot alone explain it. Building on constructivist insights, he argues that identities were shaped and emphasized by local elites seeking to take advantage of the period of transition to pursue their own largely pecuniary goals. Escalated violence, he concludes, was "local politics by other means" and its key instigators and organizers were those "close to the levers of local power."[7]

In emphasizing the interaction between national-level changes and local motivations, the three authors each highlight important facilitating conditions for the series of extended violent conflicts that emerged in turn-of-the-century Indonesia. The transition from an authoritarian to an unknown order created uncertainty. Local leaders in different parts of the country responded by using violence to cement or extend their own control (Klinken) or to advance the position of the group and values they represented (Bertrand and Sidel). All three accounts thus emphasize the goals and agency of local elites in using violence instrumentally.

As previous chapters have shown, motivations of local elites to use violence are indeed important in understanding why initial incidents of violence occurred in the areas of Indonesia affected by extended violent conflict. However, while such motivations were necessary for extended violence to occur, taken alone they are insufficient to explain it.

The causal accounts miss an important part of the equation: Why the organizations of the Indonesian state responsible for maintaining order did not prevent violence from escalating. A fuller explanation for Indonesia's extended violent conflicts must account not only for why local individuals and groups had accentuated motivations to use violence but also why the state did not check violence escalation. One must understand why the coercive instruments of the state that could have prevented the transformation of violence into fully-fledged war did not perform such a role.

Previous Explanations II: State Institutions and the Provision of Order

To this end, Yuhki Tajima provides an important supplement to the local motivation-based arguments, developing an explanation for why the state was unable to provide order in the time of transition.[8] Given that tensions and conflict are inevitable in any society, he argues that violence only erupts when the state and/or societal institutions lose their ability to regulate these. In his view, the key violence-producing feature of Indonesia's democratic transition was not the enhanced motivations of communities or leaders to compete but a reduction in the capacity and willingness of the state's security organs to intervene in local disputes.

The late New Order period, he argues, saw a process of *keterbukaan*, or political opening, one of the features of which was a restraining of the military. As a National Human Rights Commission was established, and soldiers were court-martialed for abuses committed in East Timor, the military were less willing to intervene in communal disputes than they had been in the past. After Suharto's fall, the separation of the police from the military, who ostensibly assumed responsibility for internal security despite having little capacity to do so,[9] and increasing oversight from a civil society growing in strength and confidence, further reduced incentives for the military to repress local conflicts. Drawing on fieldwork in the province of Lampung, where frequent episodic violence emerged after Suharto's fall, Tajima argues that in places where the military had had a strong local presence, nonstate institutions to ensure order had not developed. As a result, in these areas military withdrawal led to a security vacuum with neither the state nor nonstate institutions in place to prevent small-scale incidents from occurring then escalating into regular episodic violence.

This raises the question of why escalation to larger extended violent conflict occurred in some areas (such as Maluku and Central Sulawesi) and not in others (such as Lampung). Tajima argues that such escalation happened in some locales because of the inability of local elites to coordinate to prevent out-group punishment where violence is used against other communities. This resulted in intergroup polarization that fueled spirals of violence in an environment where the coercive arms of the state were weak. Thus, while initial violence is determined by the strength of state and/or nonstate institutions to regulate conflict, escalation is determined by the ability and incentives of local elites to negotiate shared agreements to prevent this in conditions of anarchy.

The argument is theoretically innovative, linking micro and macro factors and encompassing both motivations and opportunities for violence. Drawing as it does on a battery of methods, including ethnographic process tracing, formal modeling, and econometric analysis, the theory is developed and tested with a level of sophistication rare to studies of collective violence or of political or social phenomena in Indonesia. Tajima's emphasis on the institutions that produce order (or its absence) provides an important complement to the motivation-based accounts. Tajima is right to view large-scale extended violent conflict as being an escalated version of more localized episodic clashes. His insight that the initial onset of violence in places such as Ambon and Poso, which saw escalation of large episodic violence to drawn-out extended local wars, was very similar to that in Lampung, which did not, is important. However, Tajima's argument for *why* that escalation occurred (or did not) is less convincing.

CONTINUING MILITARY STRENGTH

There is reason to question Tajima's foundational assumption that the coercive arms of the state were substantially weakened and incapacitated in the early period following the fall of Suharto. The military was one of the main means through which the power of the New Order regime was projected and maintained. Honna writes, "Political repression and ideological surveillance were the major tools in constructing and maintaining the New Order regime," and the military was the primary organ of the state to undertake these tasks.[10] Suharto, himself a former general, relied heavily on the armed forces (called ABRI during the New Order period) to put down any state-threatening unrest, with the result that much of the violence that occurred was committed by the state.[11] Under the doctrine of *dwifungsi* (dual function), which legitimated a strong role for the military in social and political affairs in addition to providing national security,

ABRI developed a hierarchical territorial command system that placed military personnel in villages across Indonesia. This allowed for extensive military surveillance even in the most remote villages and rapid interventions when communal or separatist tensions arose.[12]

Tajima argues that the military's power and confidence eroded in the late New Order period as political reforms began. Yet there is little evidence that the military was substantially weakened or that it felt subject to increased civilian oversight in the late Suharto period. Keterbukaan, which had been launched in the late 1980s, was wound back from mid-1994 when three high-circulation current affairs magazines were banned and many outspoken critics of the Suharto regime were removed from the political system. This led to greater use of violent coercion by the military in response to street protests.[13] In the final years of his presidency, there was increasing public debate about dwifungsi as Suharto sought to balance the power of the military with that of regulated civil society, and in particular the state-supported Muslim organization, ICMI, which was led by his vice president, B. J. Habibie.[14] In 1995, the national parliament, the DPR, voted to reduce military representation in the legislature from one hundred to seventy-five seats out of a total of five hundred.[15] Yet this did not lead to a significant weakening of military power, because the military's institutional power basis—which relied on the territorial security structure of its intelligence network, and a sociopolitical command line from headquarters down to villages—remained untouched.[16] The military compensated for the reduction in seats by developing a closer partnership with Golkar, Suharto's political party.[17]

Nor did the fall of Suharto in May 1998 result in a weakening of the power of the armed forces. In contrast to many other countries experiencing regime transition, Indonesian state security institutions did not collapse.[18] The territorial command structure remained in place and, as discussed later in this chapter, none of the presidents in the early post-Suharto years succeeded in reining in military behavior.

Indeed, Suharto's demise demonstrated the continuing political strength of the armed forces. His ouster was fueled by many factors, including student mobilization[19] and the desertion of his allies in the business elite in the context of the Asian financial crisis.[20] Violent protests on the streets of Jakarta and many other Indonesian cities in May called for the president's resignation. The killing of protestors by the military was followed by an orgy of violence with attacks on shops and individuals in ethnic Chinese neighborhoods leading to the loss of around eleven hundred lives. However, as Honna observes, "The military played a crucial role in facilitating and managing these developments."[21] Rather than being a sign of the diminishing power of the military to repress violence before it escalated, the riots bore the signs of military organization.[22] The final report of a Joint Fact Finding Team,[23] established by the Indonesian government to investigate the May riots, pointed to the involvement of the military. Prabowo Subianto, the head of the powerful Kostrad (the army strategic reserve command), allegedly organized the riots as well as the kidnappings of activists in a bid to undermine Wiranto, the military chief, with the aim of him assuming the commander role.[24] Indeed, "it was the regime rather than the masses that appeared to be driving the violence."[25]

With members of his cabinet deserting him, on 20 May 1998 Suharto met Wiranto who advised him to step down to avert a Tiananmen-like bloodbath. Suharto subsequently handed letters to Wiranto and his deputy that authorized them to take power.[26] That neither chose to use their letters, sticking instead to a previously agreed promise to support the ascension of Suharto's deputy, Habibie, demonstrated the confidence the military felt in their position. Two days later, Habibie dismissed Prabowo from his position. This left the Indonesian military under Wiranto less factionalized than in the past. Wiranto could present himself as a dove and reformer, having avoided the violent removal of Suharto or a military coup while allowing demands for Suharto's resignation to be fulfilled. This restrained public pressure on the military. As Mietzner notes:

> The defeat of the military hawks [Prabowo's group] created the impression within society and the political elite that reforming the armed forces in the post-Suharto era was less urgent than initially thought. The removal of those officers viewed as responsible for the kidnappings and May riots temporarily satisfied public demand for a more wide-ranging replacement of the New Order military.[27]

The result was a pact between Habibie and the military whereby the denial of absolute military power was traded off against the certainty that military interests would not be attacked. Key figures from the armed forces became part of the first postauthoritarian government.[28] The military thus entered the new era with its structures and privileges largely intact. In such an environment, its capacity to continue to use force remained. As the military concentrated on carving out a role in the post-Suharto era, it may well have focused less on intervening in small-scale disputes of the sort Tajima documents in Lampung. But there is little reason to believe that its ability to put down larger unrest in many parts of the country was diminished. Responsibility for security was not devolved to the regions under the decentralization laws. With a strong centralized command structure, and an ability to send extra troops to regions when violence erupted, the military and police should have been able to deal with escalating unrest if they so chose.

SECURITY FORCE INVOLVEMENT IN VIOLENCE

If a security vacuum was responsible for the escalation of violence in areas such as Maluku, Central Sulawesi, and Aceh, we would expect to see limited involvement by the military or other security forces in the areas where escalation occurred. Tajima does indeed provide examples of the passivity of security forces as riots broke out. Yet the fact that such submissiveness was often followed by active participation in violence by the army and police suggests limitations to the security force weakness thesis.

As I discussed in chapter 4, Christian and Muslim security forces often fought on the sides of coreligionists in Maluku. They provided financial and logistical support to Christian militia. Whereas traditional weapons such as machetes and spears had been used in the first months of the conflict, by mid-1999 standard military weapons were increasingly common with most of these originating from the security forces.[29] More startling, and with wider impacts on the escalation of violence, was the support of the military in Jakarta for the Muslim Laskar Jihad militia. In March and April 2000, several thousand Laskar Jihad members were given training by military officers in Bogor, just one hour from Jakarta. Subsequently, at least three thousand Laskar Jihad members boarded ships to Ambon where they were welcomed by military officers who provided them with guns.[30] It was the arrival of these outsider jihadis that shifted the conflict from being one of sporadic clashes to prolonged fighting.[31] Violence escalated sharply with 104 killed in May 2000 compared with an average of 25 for the three previous months. It is hard to escape the conclusion that the role of the military and police in allowing violence to escalate and endure was an active rather than a passive one. Rather than feeling hamstrung by increased civilian oversight of their behavior, as Tajima posits, the security forces acted with little constraint.

Similar although not as pronounced processes can also be observed in Indonesia's other sites of extended violent conflict. In Poso, Central Sulawesi, military and police officers took sides as partisans during the riots of May and June 2000, which killed at least 246 people.[32] As I discussed in chapter 5, in North Halmahera in North Maluku the military fueled rumors of impending attacks, heightening fears and tensions. There were also reports of locally stationed military forces abetting jihadis attacking villages in Galela and other areas of Halmahera.[33]

In Aceh, too, explanations for the escalation of violence from late 1998 that focus on military weakness and a resulting security vacuum are unconvincing. In the last four months of 1998, Indonesia's new president, B. J. Habibie, altered the old government's security policy for Aceh, ending the military occupation zone and withdrawing thousands of nonlocal military troops.[34] The military pointed to the absence of troops as being the reason why violence began to escalate in the latter half of that year. Yet in the context of a war where the state was one of the combating parties, we might expect that lower troop numbers would have led to *less* violence with GAM facing little resistance to the expansion of their territorial control.[35]

Instead, there was a rise in violence resulting from more active engagement by the Indonesian military in Aceh. The government reversed its stance in January 1999, with Aceh policy increasingly under the control of General Wiranto rather than President Habibie.[36] New military operations commenced, including Operasi Satgas Wibawa, which was supported by two thousand nonlocal military and police, in which at least forty-six civilians were killed. Riots in Lhokseumawe in late 2008 precipitated an upsurge in violence, which spread to North and East Aceh. While the police and military blamed GAM for the unrest, locals reported that soldiers had paid Acehnese youths to incite the riots. Atrocities, such as the Idi Cut massacre of February 1999, continued to be committed by the military, with none of the perpetrators brought to trial. It can be argued that such acts were organized and committed by renegades with no instructions issued from above. Yet the failure to sanction soldiers involved in the Idi Cut affair, as well as those who participated in other massacres such as that in Cot Murong,[37] suggests a high level of institutional support for the actions.

Indeed, there is ample additional evidence of the military making concerted efforts to fuel the war. As I detailed in the last chapter, security personnel repeatedly sold weapons to GAM and provided other logistical support. Military elites in Jakarta continued to apply pressure to the government for a militarized approach in Aceh; their victory was confirmed with the declaration of martial law in May 2003 after the collapse of an attempted peace agreement, in part due to the spoiler activities of the military and local militia they had armed.

If violence escalation in Aceh and elsewhere was facilitated by the actions of still-strong security forces, explanations for extended violent conflict rooted in the motivations of local elites or the weakness of security forces are at best incomplete.

The Central State and the Escalation of Violence

The missing factor in most previous explanations of Indonesia's extended violent conflicts is the role that elements of the central state, primarily although not exclusively in the military, played in supporting and facilitating violence escalation. Local desires to use violence were certainly a necessary condition for such extended violence and variations in such motivations help explain why some areas saw extended violence while others did not. However, absent central state support for or tolerance of violence escalation it is unlikely that initial intercommunal clashes in Maluku, Central Sulawesi, or elsewhere would have led to sustained violence or that violence in Aceh would have escalated so sharply from 1999. It was the confluence of the motivations of local elites to use violence and of some central state elites to allow it to escalate that explains why sporadic episodes of violence could morph into much larger, sustained deadly unrest.

An important clarification is necessary before moving on to explain why some central state actors supported violence escalation in the early reformasi period. My argument should not be taken to read that it was Jakarta alone that caused the violence. There is a long tradition in Indonesia of explaining events as the result of mysterious *dalang* (puppet masters) who are invisible when looking at the stage but who direct the actions of those occupy it.[38] Especially in the early democracy years, many commentators, and in particular Indonesian activists, explained the upsurge in violence as flowing from sinister machinations in the nation's capital.[39] Some analysts, for example, seized on the fact that police in Jakarta had repatriated over a hundred Ambonese thugs in December 1998 as evidence that Jakarta masterminded the subsequent violence in Maluku.[40]

Such conspiracy theories do not stand up to close scrutiny. Klinken, in his analysis of the Maluku conflict, rightly argues that "the view that 'Jakarta did it,' which is very popular in Ambon today is untenable . . . 'Jakarta' probably did not select Ambon for a conflagration."[41] As he documents, local elites and others had ample reason to use violence in Maluku and elsewhere, and indeed they participated in or organized much of the violence that occurred. We have little reason to believe that local leaders or their followers were but ignorant dupes, fooled by those with interests in the nation's capital.

Yet while the conspiracy theories go too far in ignoring local motivations, national-level interests *are* part of the causal story of Indonesia's extended violent conflicts. Local factors led to initial incidents of violence and initial escalation. However, the subsequent escalation to full-blown war was a result of a combination of acts of commission and of omission by the security forces. In some places, and at some times, the military and police actively abetted violence escalation; in others, the security forces were less involved but violence escalated because of decisions made not to employ coercive force. The Indonesian state could have limited the tragic explosion of localized violence into all-out wars. It was because elements of the central state, especially the military, opportunistically saw advantage in allowing such escalation to occur that it did.

Why Central State Elites Allowed Escalation to Extended Violence

In the early post-Suharto years, some members of the national elite had motivations for supporting or allowing the escalation of violence into extended violent conflict. Consistent with the book's argument, extended violence emerged at a time when the rules of the game on the allocation of power and resources were being renegotiated and when there was heightened competition between different national elites over what Indonesia's "reformed" order would look like. Violence was seen as a profitable way to protect or extend the authority of some national elites, in particular military leaders. The costs of using violence were also limited as the fragility of early post-Suharto governments meant that support from the military and other political leaders was still needed. In a context of factionalized national elites, the possibilities for using peaceful means to access or consolidate power seemed limited.

Heightened Competition, Uncertainty, and Changes to the Rules of the Game

Once Suharto had departed and the old regime had collapsed, institutional reform became inevitable. It was not a question of whether to change the rules or not but rather in which specific ways the rules were to be changed.

—Andrew J. MacIntyre, *The Power of Institutions* (2003)

The demise of Suharto was widely celebrated by national elites from across the political spectrum, but it brought with it considerable uncertainties. The lack of clarity over what the new rules of the game in democratizing Indonesia would be created fear about the potential for exclusion from new constellations of power and that economic interests, developed during three decades of authoritarian rule, would not be protected.

On the one hand, there was substantial continuity between the New Order and the early governments of the reformasi era, and this limited immediate violence. By mid-May 1998, the Jakarta riots had been brought under control, and there was no large upsurge in violence elsewhere in Indonesia during 1998.[42] Such continuity was largely a consequence of divisions within the opposition movement. Suharto had been a master of divide-and-control, supporting and then marginalizing allies within Golkar, the military, and mass movements such as the Muslim Nahdlatul Ulama (NU) and Muhammadiyah to avoid any group becoming too strong.[43] The result was a fragmented political and civil society, characterized by suspicion and contradictory impulses to collaborate or oppose the New Order regime.[44] The Islamic movements, in particular NU, oscillated between staying close to power, benefiting from the attendant patronage that this allowed, and being a force of opposition.[45] With even the keenest of observers failing to predict the end of the New Order regime a year before, forces in favor of democratization had spent little time considering what a new reformed polity would look like and building the solidarity and collective action capacity necessary to ensure they could shape the emerging post-Suharto order. This lack of cohesion and strategy in the reform movement allowed the military to engineer a transition that largely protected their interests. It also meant that the first post-Suharto government, under Habibie his old deputy, consisted largely of New Order figures. Indeed, the new "democratic" government looked very similar in makeup to those of the previous thirty years.[46]

Such regime continuity reduced national elite uncertainty and contestation. However, over time, competition, primarily between different elements of the old regime, became more marked.

THE HABIBIE PRESIDENCY

While the makeup of the first post-Suharto government differed little from those before, it soon became clear that the policies it planned to pursue were vastly different and that these would challenge entrenched interests. Indeed, the short tenure of B. J. Habibie, a stalwart of New Order politics who lasted but a-year-and-a-half in power, was more radical than that of any of the presidents who followed. Habibie was well aware that he was "the accidental president."[47] His rise to the presidency was a result of his position as vice president when Suharto unexpectedly fell. He did not have a strong political base, and the opposition movement viewed him with skepticism given his past. Understanding the fragility of his position, and the lack of legitimacy he had among the broader populace, being both unelected and a former Suharto henchman, Habibie chose a course of rapid reform.[48]

In his first few weeks after assuming power, Habibie proposed releasing political prisoners, reforming the antisubversion law, lifting press restrictions, allowing for the formation of new political parties, and holding new general elections.[49] Whereas only three political parties were permitted during the New Order period—Suharto's Golkar as well as the Indonesian Democratic Party (PDI) and the Islamic PPP—the new election law allowed for much more open competition and forty-eight parties ultimately stood in the June 1999 elections. What is more, while electoral competition had been manufactured in the New Order era, with many checks in place to make sure that the supposed opposition parties did not win too many seats, suddenly elites were subject to real political competition. Golkar was beaten by PDI-P, which had its roots in PDI, who gathered 33.8 percent of the vote, and three Muslim parties won significant vote shares. Challenges to the interests of incumbent national elites also increased with the passing of radical decentralization laws in February 1999 that turned Indonesia from one of the most centralized countries to one of the most decentralized. Together, democratization and decentralization resulted in a dispersion of power in ways that threatened old patron-client networks. As Aspinall writes on Indonesia fifteen years after these changes:

> Democracy [along with decentralization] has exacerbated the fragmentary effects of clientelism by opening up the marketplace of potential patrons and enabling them to compete with one another without being constrained by a supreme patriarch, as they were under Suharto. . . . It has also shifted power relations within patron-client relationships, tipping the balance more in favor of the clients, or at least those patron/clients and brokers who are located part way down the patronage distribution pyramids.[50]

To be sure, and as I discuss below, over time many in the national elite managed to adjust to this new institutional setting and were able to ensure they did not lose out politically or economically.[51] Yet, with the old certainties and norms of the Suharto era suddenly up for renegotiation, incumbent political elites did not know how the cards would fall and whether or not they would hold a winning hand.

The sense of uncertainty was especially great for security force leaders. Their role in leading the transition of power from Suharto to Habibie put them in a strong position as the democracy era began. However, with aggressive demands from below for military reform, and a president who seemed to be listening, the armed forces, renamed the TNI following Suharto's fall, came under significant pressure. There were ever more strident calls from activists and some political elites for the TNI to withdraw from the political arena.[52] Mietzner notes the speed at which political developments threatened to overrun the military: "Labelled as political moderates only weeks earlier for their implicit endorsement of Suharto's removal, key officers around Wiranto suddenly found themselves portrayed as opponents of further reform in the new democratic polity."[53]

Institutional changes that aimed to reduce the power of the armed forces were quick to arrive. In January 1999, the national parliament voted to further reduce the TNI's allocation to thirty-eight seats in the national parliament and 10 percent in regional parliaments. A further blow to the military was Habibie's announcement in January 1999 that he planned to hold a "popular consultation" on the future of East Timor. Since Indonesia's invasion of its neighbor following the departure of the Portuguese in 1975, Timor was effectively governed by the military rather than the civilian arms of the Indonesian government. As a result, the local economy was dominated by the armed forces who had a monopoly over the trade of coffee and who controlled many other plantations with the local population often compelled to provide slave labor to individual soldiers.[54] Many of the military's top brass had gained their stripes fighting there and felt a personal and ideological commitment to keep the restive area within Indonesia. The offer of a referendum was thus a slap in the face for senior military leaders who had not been consulted in advance by Habibie. The earlier promises made by Habibie to Wiranto started to ring hollow.

THE WAHID PRESIDENCY

Uncertainty over the new rules of the game continued in the presidency of Abdurrahman Wahid, in power from October 1999 to July 2001. In line with the constitution, Wahid was chosen as president by Indonesia's upper house, the People's Consultative Assembly (MPR), rather than by the electorate.[55] With his party winning just 13 percent of votes in the June general election he was dependent on a complicated web of support from party elites, including from the TNI, to gain power. The distribution of rent-making opportunities to parties in accord with the level of support they gave him resulted in an unwieldy cabinet of thirty-five people with most parties represented.[56] The makeup of the Wahid government did not challenge the interests of those who had done well during the New Order. Golkar was well represented as were the military with six retired or active officers in the cabinet. General Wiranto received the post of coordinating minister for political and security affairs, one of three top-ranked cabinet positions.[57]

However, Wahid's subsequent behavior in office, especially during the tenures of his second and third cabinets, threatened the interests of the military and other incumbent elites. Wahid had worked hard to obtain military support to ensure he became president, promising Wiranto that he would play an important role in government, possibly as vice president, and that military interests would be "protected."[58] This led the TNI leadership to instruct its representatives to choose Wahid in the MPR vote. However, it soon became clear that the new president planned to push for extensive military reform. He sought to marginalize officers in the palace bureaucracy and chose a member of the navy, a more liberal body than the army, as the new TNI commander.[59] He put reformers, such as Agus Wirahadikusumah, who had been active in trying to generate debate within the armed forces on military withdrawal from politics, in senior positions within the TNI.[60] Dwifungsi, which legitimated a sociopolitical role for the armed forces, was officially abolished in April 2000.[61]

Wahid also started to encourage debates about the territorial command system, a major source of off-budget resources for the military.[62] Under political pressure, the TNI initially agreed to initiate changes and a pilot project was established. However, there was immense concern from many within the armed forces about this course of action and resentment about a perceived breaking of Wahid's promise to protect military interests during his presidency.

The president also pursued other policies at odds with the views of the military leadership. He started negotiations with separatists in Aceh, which resulted in a Humanitarian Pause in May 2000, suggested federalism as a solution to the country's conflicts, and dismissed Wiranto in February 2000 from his cabinet position after the release of the commission of enquiry's report on the armed forces' behavior in East Timor. These moves created concern among the TNI leadership, in particular from those who favored a gradualist approach to military reform.

It was not only the policies pursued that caused consternation for some in the military and political elite but also the confusion and contradiction that marked Wahid's tenure. Prone to autocratic decision making, Wahid often made key policy decisions outside of cabinet. He was impulsive and inconsistent, sacking cabinet ministers frequently and often making controversial statements, which he then did not follow up on, such as suggestions that he favored a Timor-style referendum for Aceh.[63] Such erraticness and eccentricity did little to soothe the worries and uncertainties of members of the national political elite who soon lost confidence in his leadership. It also meant that the rules of the game were particularly unclear during Wahid's tenure. In July 2001, the MPR voted to impeach Wahid with the military and police factions supporting his removal.[64]

THE MEGAWATI PRESIDENCY

Uncertainty and challenges to incumbent elite interests, including those of the military, started to ebb with the accession of Megawati Sukarnoputri in July 2001 to the presidency. Compared with the first three post-Suharto years, Megawati's reign was markedly conservative. To be sure, there were some significant policy developments including constitutional changes that led to the direct election of future presidents and revisions to the electoral and regional autonomy laws. Yet these were less threatening to national elites because they were the product of long deliberations within the national parliament, where a wide range of elites were represented, rather than Megawati's government. Policymaking had changed from being "crisis-ridden," where policies were made quickly in response to rapidly emerging issues, to "politics-as-usual," where elites were able to focus more on ensuring policy change advanced their own interests.[65] National elites, united in the desire to avoid a return to the unpredictability and divides of the Wahid regime, chose to compromise, ensuring that the new legislation passed but did not affect their core interests. It was now clear, for example, that there was little taste from any part of the national elite for retroactive corruption investigations, for these could entrap the large proportion of the elite who had risen to prominence during the Suharto era.[66]

Threats to the power of the military, too, started to recede. In contrast to Habibie and Wahid, Megawati was close to the armed forces, seeing them as a guardian of the people.[67] Beyond her ideological convictions, Megawati chose to grant concessions to the military to avoid challenges to her rule. This included giving the TNI largely free rein to decide on policy in Aceh and Papua, allowing for resistance to, and ensuring the ultimate failure of, autonomy deals.[68] Megawati also approved a reshuffle of the TNI leadership that marginalized reformers and reduced civilian oversight of the armed forces. When her defense minister, Matori Abdul Djalil, resigned in August 2003 after suffering a stroke, she chose not to replace him before the expiry of her term more than a year later, leaving the military free to pursue security policies of its own choosing. Reform issues, such as changing the territorial command structure and military financing, disappeared from the mainstream political agenda.[69]

Megawati's tenure did see an end to the extended intercommunal violence in Poso and Maluku, with government-led peace agreements signed in both areas. However, these were driven not by Megawati but by members of her cabinet, in particular Susilo Bambang Yudhoyono, her coordinating minister for political and security affairs and a former military general. The agreements did not negatively impact on the interests of the security forces in those provinces. They continued to have large number of troops stationed there, and they also benefited from the arrival of postconflict funds.

Expected Benefits of Allowing Violence Escalation

The initial years of the post-Suharto era were thus characterized by significant uncertainty over what a newly democratic Indonesia would look like and whose interests would be represented in the changing order. In this environment, the military, supported by some members of the national elite, allowed violence to escalate because it proved to be politically and economically profitable.

HIGH BENEFITS OF ALLOWING VIOLENCE ESCALATION

Elements of the military supported and sometimes facilitated the escalation of violence because they believed it was an effective way to retain a place at the center of the Indonesian polity and to ensure that privileges and funding sources, built up during the New Order era, were not undermined. Over time, as violence in Maluku, North Maluku, and Central Sulawesi endured and intensified, it became clear that such violence was beneficial for the military and other national political elites.

The violence that appeared to be sweeping across the country from 1999 on provided support for the stance that a strong military was still (or especially) needed in a democratizing Indonesia. The destruction in Kalimantan, the Moluccas, and Central Sulawesi shocked politicians and civil society alike in the nation's capital, with stories of the interethnic and interreligious brutality published in newspapers on a daily basis.[70] During the New Order, discussion of ethnic and religious divides had been forcefully censored, yet primordialist views of identity groups being essentially different in character and nature remained common. The emergence of intense and savage intercommunal violence only served to accentuate worries that violent fragmentation of the nation, as had occurred in the Balkans, was likely.[71] While calls for a return to the autocratic days of Suharto, when order had been ensured at the barrels of the military's guns, were lacking, support for a stronger projection of state power to hold Indonesia together started to emerge.[72]

This worked to the military's advantage. Mietzner argues that, "like in previous periods of Indonesia's modern history, the high levels of political conflict among the civilian elite in 2000 and 2001 allowed the TNI to depict itself as an apolitical institution above partisan interests, a mediator between divided parties, and a defender of national (and now even democratic) interests."[73] As violence swirled across the country, perceptions of the military became more positive. The proportion of opinion poll respondents with a favorable view of the armed forces increased from 28 percent to 58 percent between September 2000 and October 2001, while the share with an unfavorable view declined from 61 percent to 31 percent.[74]

Increased support from civilians and many in the political elite strengthened the military's hand in resisting pressures for security sector reform. As we have seen, while some changes were made, for example reducing the military's formal political role and abandoning the ideological framework of dwifungsi, more substantive reform soon stalled. Indeed, it is no coincidence that the period of most extensive intercommunal extended violence, and of high levels of violence in Aceh, was the tenure of Wahid, the one post-Suharto president who made concerted efforts to push forward military reform and who notably sacked General Wiranto.[75] Allowing such violence to occur strengthened the military's position in resisting such reforms. As Mietzner notes, "Fearing that further experiments with TNI reform could reduce the ability of the armed forces to crack down on separatist rebels, the majority of politicians agreed to suspend their reform efforts until the security situation had stabilized."[76]

Supporting the escalation of violence in Maluku and elsewhere was also in the interests of other members of the national political elite who wanted to force an end to Wahid's presidency. Fuad Bawazier, the minister of finance in Suharto's last cabinet and a sharp critic of Wahid, was among those in the elite who provided financial support to Laskar Jihad.[77] Others such as Amien Rais, a university professor who had been at the forefront of the reformasi movement and who led the modernist and largely moderate Islamic PAN party, also generated political capital from the violence in his effort to get rid of Wahid. Addressing a crowd of thousands of Muslim demonstrators in Jakarta in January 2000, he called for a jihad against Christians in Maluku.[78] For such politicians, and for military leaders, the violence in Maluku and elsewhere supported efforts to impeach Wahid as it seemingly demonstrated his incapability as a leader.[79]

LOW COSTS OF VIOLENCE

Not only did the escalated extended violence prove beneficial for the military, but it also became clear that the risks of supporting violence escalation were minimal. Institutionally, the military experienced no negative consequences from their role in facilitating violence escalation, and this sent a strong signal that such actions were permissible. Similarly, almost without exception, individual officers and foot soldiers who allowed escalation, either through active engagement or through their inactivity, were not punished.

The response to the military's performance in Maluku was typical. President Wahid was extremely angry after the TNI chose not only to ignore his order to prevent Laskar Jihad departing for Maluku but to aid the militants' passage.[80] Despite this, politically weak Wahid was in no position to discipline military commanders. Indeed, as conflict escalated he was forced to declare a state of civil emergency in June 2000. While this did not afford the military the absolute control they would have had in the case of a military emergency, it did bolster their power in the province and allowed them a large say in the allocation of special funds.[81]

Similarly, reports of the violent conflicts in Central Kalimantan and West Kalimantan describe the military and police standing idly by while massacres took place, even extorting fleeing Madurese before letting them board ships to leave the island.[82] Despite this, no senior figures from the security forces were reprimanded.

In Aceh, the use of violence by the military also bore little risk. Soldiers involved in massacres such as those that occurred in Habibie's tenure in Idi Cut and Simpang KKA were not brought to trial.[83] An Independent Commission for the Investigation of Violence in Aceh, established by Habibie in July 1999, documented five thousand rights violations. But when the report was presented to the new president Wahid in November of that year, he did not follow up on the results.[84] In May 2000, twenty-four soldiers were convicted of killing a mystic cleric, Teuku Bantaqiah, and fifty-six of his followers the previous year. Sentences were substantial, ranging from 8.5 to 10 years. But the highest-ranking sentenced officer was only a captain and their commanding officer was never tried.[85] In November 1999, six senior generals were summoned to testify before a parliamentary committee on abuses committed during the martial law period.[86] However, none were prosecuted, and the military continued to commit abuses until the signing of the peace deal almost six years later.

In East Timor, too, the military's role in supporting violence escalation had few negative consequences for them. When militias went on a wild rampage following the overwhelming vote for independence in the August 1999 referendum, it was clear that the Indonesian military was responsible.[87] Under strong international pressure, the Indonesian parliament first established a special human rights court and then an ad hoc human rights court to deal with East Timor cases. However, the former court applied the principle of "nonretroactivity," meaning that only cases that occurred after the law was passed could be considered, and Wahid, under strong pressure from the military, also agreed to a similar principle for the East Timor court. In the end, eighteen men including ten military officers were brought to trial. However, of the eighteen, only six were found guilty and the appeals of all but two, both East Timorese civilians, were successful.[88] Even with strong international condemnation of the Indonesian military's postreferendum behavior, there was limited pressure for its leaders to be brought to trial. With the United States and its allies looking for support in the war on terror, foreign powers were concerned with finding ways to reestablish military-to-military ties, which had been suspended in the Suharto years, rather than ensuring that rights violations perpetrated by the military were investigated.[89]

Other Opportunities for Peaceful Accumulation

In the early post-Suharto years, allowing violence escalation thus served the interests of the TNI leadership who were working to protect the privileges and status they had built up since Indonesia's independence. Violence was chosen as a political strategy not only because it proved beneficial and noncostly but also because few peaceful options existed to achieve these goals.

The political transition did mean that the armed forces remained at the center of Indonesia's polity but over time their formal political role declined. As discussed earlier, reforms beginning in the year 2000 forced the armed forces to abandon the ideology of dwifungsi, which had legitimated their role in nonsecurity affairs. Not only was military representation in the Indonesian parliament cut in half in 1999, constitutional amendments passed in 2002 removed them from the parliament completely beginning with the 2004 elections.[90] National Law on the TNI 34/2004 included provisions that prohibited the TNI from using its territorial network for political organizing purposes.[91] As Golkar's parliamentary representation declined, and as it sought to recover its legitimacy among the electorate, the opportunity to use Suharto's old party as a vehicle for their interests also diminished. With active armed forces officers banned from standing in elections, few formal institutionalized political channels existed to ensure that the TNI's interests were protected.

As a result, continuing influence on policy was a product of informal relations between TNI leaders and Indonesia's president and parliamentarians. In the context of demands from below for reform, using violence—ostensibly in the interests of the nation—proved to be the most effective means to push for continuing influence in a reforming Indonesia.

Changing National Elite Motivations and the Nonrecurrence of Extended Violence

By February 2002, all of Indonesia's intercommunal extended violent conflicts had come to an end, although significant unrest continued in Central Sulawesi and Maluku for the first few postconflict years. The signing of the Helsinki MoU for Aceh in August 2005 ended the province's civil war. Since then, deaths from violence in Indonesia have been the result of sporadic episodic violence.[92]

There have not been renewed bouts of extended violence in recent years because of changes in the incentives of national elites with regards to the utility of violence. The initial post-Suharto period (roughly May 1998 to the accession of Megawati and, to a lesser extent, during her presidency) was one of uncertainty, with the expected benefits of violence escalation high for some in the national elite and a lack of available opportunities for military elites to protect their interests using licit political channels. In contrast, since 2004 the Indonesian polity has become increasingly institutionalized as agreed rules of the game have been forged where support for escalated extended violence is not deemed acceptable.

The Yudhoyono Presidency: Reduced Uncertainty and More Established Rules of the Game

Whereas the early years of the post-Suharto era were marked by deep and messy contestation over the rules of the game, the two-term presidency of Susilo Bambang Yudhoyono saw a stabilization of Indonesia's polity. As the legal framework of Indonesia's democratic order was fleshed out, uncertainty amongst national elites over the acceptability of the use of large-scale extended violence declined.

The year 2004, when Yudhoyono rose to the presidency, is commonly viewed as the end of the period of turbulent transition.[93] That year saw the first direct popular election of an Indonesian president. This reduced, although did not completely remove, the scope for political deals between parties to determine who would reach the summit of Indonesian state power.[94] Whereas the presidencies of Wahid and Megawati were an outcome of inter-elite bargaining, new and inflexible procedural rules were now in place to determine who the Indonesian president would be. Other institutional reforms, some of which predated 2004, also mattered. Particularly important was the establishment in August 2003 of a Constitutional Court with authority to decide conflicts between state institutions, rule on contested election results, and determine the constitutionality of legislation.[95] The court soon established itself as a respected referee in state affairs, and its rulings have almost universally been accepted and enforced. Whereas previously decisions on whether the behavior of the president or vice president warranted their dismissal were made by the politicized MPR, this decision now lay in the hands of the more apolitical court.[96]

Together, these and other institutional reforms have served to move the Indonesian central state in the direction of North, Wallis and Weingast's "open access orders" where the state is an autonomous impersonal body with perpetual legal personality and where legal institutions protect the rights of those who do not have direct connections to power. The "normalization of politics,"[97] with open elections the accepted means to access power, has meant that struggles for power are now largely expressed through formal institutional channels.[98]

In addition to changes to formal institutions, political decisions and strategies played a role in reducing uncertainty. Yudhoyono, following the practices of his predecessors, chose to disburse power widely across the political elite. His cabinets included representation from all major political parties except PDI-P. Indeed, of the thirty-five members of his first cabinet in 2004, only two came from the Democrat Party, his political vehicle, with three representatives from the Islamic PKS party and four retired military officers.[99] Ministries were also divvied up between political parties ensuring that within-party patronage flows could be maintained.[100] As a result, the prediction of Linz that "presidentialism is ineluctably problematic because it operates according to the rule of 'winner-takes-all'— an arrangement that tends to make democratic politics a zero-sum game, with all the potential for conflict such games portend,"[101] has not come to pass. A deep fear of political conflict and instability in Yudhoyono's thinking, with the president preferring to act as a mediator rather than a leader, led to political decisions that kept people on board, often at the expense of more substantive reforms.[102]

Yudhoyono, to a greater extent than any of his predecessors since Suharto, was also successful in restraining the impulses of the military to use violence for their own purposes. This involved a combination of the provision of carrots and the use of sticks. On the one hand, military acquiescence to the new rules of the game was effectively bought by ensuring there was little effort to push for deeper "second generation" military reforms that might affect the TNI's interests.[103] There was no renewed move to force an abandonment of the territorial command structure and very limited progress in ensuring the military hand over control of the businesses that provide a major source of institutional funding and personal profit.[104] The state's defense budget almost tripled between 2003 and 2009.[105]

On the other hand, Yudhoyono, a former general, was able to sideline conservatives within the military such as Ryamizard Ryacudu, the army chief of staff and Megawati's choice for TNI leader. The leaders Yudhoyono installed were loyal to him and accepted that they were under the authority of Indonesia's constitutionally elected leaders, realizing that if they did not endorse the new political reality they would be swept away by it.[106] As a result, the military increasingly pulled back from direct engagement or manipulation of national politics. The more highly institutionalized polity meant that, in contrast to the tenures of Habibie, Wahid, and Megawati, political elites did not turn to the military for support to maintain or access power.

This is not to say that Indonesia became a fully institutionalized liberal democracy. Two decades on from Suharto's fall, old oligarchic elites have survived and prospered, money politics is rife, and Indonesia lags on most global measures of the rule of law.[107] While national-level institutions have strengthened, new subnational governments, empowered by decentralization, often exhibit even more illiberal tendencies;[108] as previous chapters have shown, lack of institutionalization of the polity at these levels provides space for elites to use violence for their own purposes. Yet the very compromises that negatively impacted on the *quality* of democracy also led to democratic *stability*:

> The country has dealt with key challenges in ways that have come with costs. Spoilers have been accommodated and absorbed into the system rather than excluded from it, producing a trade-off between democratic success and democratic quality. This trade-off has not been an unfortunate side-effect of Indonesia's democratic transition; rather, it has been central to its dynamics, and even an important ingredient in its success.[109]

As Sukma in his analysis of the 2009 elections terms it, Indonesia is a "defective system, resilient democracy," where there is a "high degree of stability and resilience in Indonesia's new democracy, despite the problems."[110] Democracy may be "collusive,"[111] but this collusion provides stability.

Expected Benefits of Allowing Violence Escalation

The protection of old privileges ensured that national elites, including military leaders, found diminishing relative benefit in allowing large-scale violence to occur. The perceived costs of supporting large-scale violence also increased.

Whereas both the extended intercommunal conflicts and the ongoing civil war in Aceh strengthened the military's position in the early post-Suharto period, supporting such violence was not necessary during the Yudhoyono years. As it became clear that their position was not under threat, military leaders did not have the same incentives to use unrest in the regions for their own purposes.

The costs of supporting the escalation of violence also increased. In the early years of the transition, government leaders were unable or unwilling to impose sanctions on military officials and others who contributed to unrest in the regions. In contrast, clear signals were sent that while localized episodic violence was acceptable, support for larger conflagrations of unrest was not.

On assuming power Yudhoyono moved to sanction some of those who had been responsible for violence escalation in the past. The removal of Ryamizard, who had played a large role in undermining the 2002–3 peace agreement in Aceh, sent a strong signal that the new president was prepared to sack generals who did not support government policies.[112] This helped ensure compliance from the military when the prospect of renewed extended violence loomed large. On 7 September 2005, less than a month after the signing of the Helsinki peace deal, Yudhoyono called a meeting of senior generals where he made it clear that they must support the peace process.[113] Following this, Endriartono Sutarto, Yudhoyono's TNI chief, "told the TNI leadership that I don't want any senior officers talking out against government policies. If you want to oppose government policies, then you must leave the TNI."[114] Detractors of the Helsinki MoU within the military were increasing marginalized.

Similar signals were also sent that supporting a renewal of extended intercommunal violence was not acceptable. Following the September 2011 riots in Ambon and a series of bombing in the following months, which threatened to escalate into larger enduring violence, the regional and district police chiefs were transferred to dead-end jobs.[115] While there is no evidence to show that national-level elites conspired to cause the violence, such responses did send a message that any such support would not be tolerated.

Other Opportunities for Peaceful Accumulation

As important as changes in the expected benefits of using violence was the expansion of opportunities to use peaceful means for purposes of accumulation. As I discussed earlier, the Yudhoyono governments chose to distribute rent-making opportunities to fend off potential challenges. Cabinets and parliamentary commissions included representation of all of Indonesia's major parties. This meant that national political elites from across the party spectrum had an interest in supporting the current order from which they were benefiting. The disbursal of power and rent-making opportunities generated buy in to a status quo that appeared beneficial across the political elite. Accelerated economic growth, which reached more than 6 percent in 2011 and 2012,[116] with Indonesia outperforming every major Asian economy but China, also reduced the impetus of national elites to support escalated violence that could have reduced levels of foreign direct investment.[117]

Similarly, the failure of the Yudhoyono governments to pursue deeper reforms of the military prevented challenges to Indonesia's democracy. The continuing presence of the territorial command structure, combined with tolerance of illicit business activities, ensured that senior military and police officials continue to prosper economically in post-Suharto Indonesia. Under such conditions, support for escalated violence was no longer necessary.

Mechanisms for Preventing Violence Escalation: Co-Optation of Belligerents and More Effective Security Responses

Changes to the expected benefits and costs of supporting violence escalation, and to the degree to which peaceful opportunities for accumulation were present, thus explain why military leaders and other national political elites no longer supported extended violent conflict. This has led to the absence of recurring or new extended violent conflicts in Indonesia through two mechanisms: an increased ability of the state to co-opt dissidents at the local level through peace processes; and more effective state security responses to incidents of violence, which has ensured that they have not escalated into broader enduring unrest (figure 6).

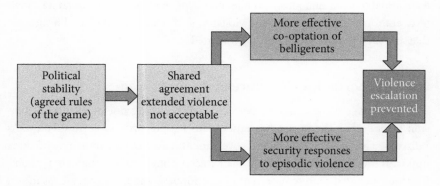

FIGURE 6.   Mechanisms for preventing violence escalation.

CO-OPTATION OF BELLIGERENTS

The first mechanism is the increased ability of the central state to formulate and implement peace agreements that have allowed for the co-optation of conflict elites at the local level. By early 2002, the central government, less divided with Megawati's accession, could bring extended violent conflict to an end in Central Sulawesi and Maluku after the signing of two government-sponsored peace agreements. As I discussed in chapter 4, the Malino accord for Maluku succeeded in ending the extended violence not by addressing the rhetorical underlying causes of conflict as expressed by belligerents but by using postconflict funds to buy off conflict leaders and their followers as well as satisfying the interests of security force leaders. The Central Sulawesi peace process served a similar function.[118] For both peace settlements, reduced incentives by national elites to stoke intercommunal violence allowed for the deployment of state funds to co-opt local elites.

While the Megawati government was less fragile than those of her two predecessors, allowing for progress to be made in ending the intercommunal extended violent conflicts, the military was still able to resist pressures for a peaceful settlement in Aceh where they had more entrenched interests. This changed with the presidency of Yudhoyono who, with strong control over the military, could ensure a peace process was forged and then implemented despite the resistance of some national elites.

IMPROVED SECURITY RESPONSES

While the increased ability of the central state to co-opt elites explains why extended violence in Maluku, Poso, and Aceh came to an end, it is improved security responses to violence that explains why episodic violence has not reescalated after the peace settlements. Such improved security responses are apparent if we examine the state's reaction to recent large episodes of violence that appeared to have the potential to escalate into much broader and deadly infernos.

The 2011 riots in Ambon, Maluku, were one such episode. Ineffective local police and military responses to the suspicious death of a Muslim motorcycle taxi driver led to riots and group clashes that resulted in the deaths of seven more people and the displacement of three thousand people. As radical Muslim websites called for renewed jihad and local residents began to arm themselves and set up security patrols, the prospect of renewed extended violence loomed large. However, in contrast to earlier years, there was relatively rapid intervention by the central state to prevent further escalation. On the evening of the first day of rioting, President Yudhoyono ordered the national police chief to beef up security in Ambon. Four hundred additional police officers, including two hundred Brimob (mobile paramilitary police) were quickly deployed to Ambon from Makassar (on Sulawesi island) and Surabaya (Java). Yudhoyono also ordered the coordinating minister for political, legal, and security affairs to meet with the national police and military chiefs and Maluku's governor to coordinate preventive actions. The police began to search all passengers bound for Ambon as a precaution against an inflow of provocateurs and sent text messages to Ambon's residents appealing for calm. With the clear signal of the seriousness of the incident coming from above, the performance of locally stationed police and military improved and by the end of the second day of clashes violence had largely come to an end.[119] The seriousness and effectiveness of the response contrasted not only with those in the extended violence period but also the response to the 2004 RMS riots, where the central government only intervened after five days of violence, which had led to thirty-four deaths and the displacement of fifteen thousand people.

The effectiveness of security force responses to incidents of large-scale violence has also improved in other postconflict provinces. In Central Sulawesi, ineffective security responses allowed for frequent incidents of violence in the early years following the signing of the Malino agreement. However, after the beheading of three Christian schoolgirls in October 2005, central government security responses started to improve and as a result the death toll in Poso in 2006 was well below that of previous years.[120]

Security force responses to incidents that threatened to escalate in Aceh also improved significantly after the Helsinki peace agreement was signed. A 2008 attack on an office of KPA (the organization for ex-GAM combatants) in Atu Lintang in Central Aceh led to five deaths and was the biggest threat yet to the peace process. Militia attacks on peace monitors in the same region had derailed the 2002–3 peace process. In contrast to the past, the response of the security forces was rapid and effective. Within two weeks, twenty-five suspects were detained and the government sent strong messages to militia through the military structure that any future such actions would lead to harsh security responses.

Beyond Indonesia's postconflict areas, there have also been rapid and effective deployments of security forces when unrest has threatened to spin out of control. In September 2010, interethnic clashes in Tarakan, East Kalimantan, killed at least five with forty thousand displaced.[121] Local security forces were unable or unwilling to prevent the violence; a video recording of the riot showed both the military and police standing by merely observing the fighting. Yet violence did not escalate further because of the intervention of the central state. Within two days, the national police and military chiefs had arrived in Tarakan and took to the streets to call for calm. A Brimob unit arrived on the second day of fighting to assist local security forces and prevented speedboats from bringing in reinforcements for the combatants from surrounding islands. The will of the center to prevent escalation was demonstrated by a statement from President Yudhoyono who said that the security forces must learn from the past extended violence in Central Kalimantan where the response had been ineffective and too late.

QUANTITATIVE EVIDENCE OF IMPROVED SECURITY RESPONSES

The incidents discussed above provide suggestive evidence of improved security responses whenever incidents of violence threaten to escalate significantly. The findings are strengthened further if we consider quantitative evidence on changes in responses to violence by the military and police over time.

Figure 7 shows the number of incidents of highly mobilized violence (riots and group clashes) in provinces that have seen high levels of violence over time.[122] The number of incidents rose sharply from 1998 to 2004, then fell in 2005 when the extended violence in Aceh came to an end. Since 2006, the number of such incidents has been on the rise again, increasing 300 percent between then and 2012. This appears to show the ineffectiveness of the security forces in preventing riots and group clashes from occurring.

However, the figure also shows how security forces have increasingly intervened in mobilized incidents of violence and how such intervention has increasingly been effective in bringing violence to a halt. There has been a sharp increase

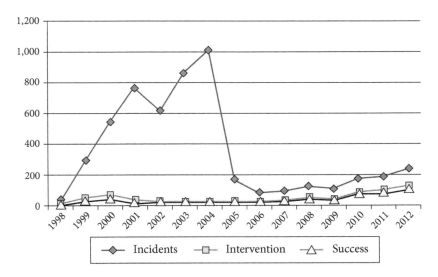

FIGURE 7.   Incidents of mobilized violence, security force intervention, and successful intervention.
Source: NVMS.

in both the proportion of cases where intervention has occurred and the percentage of incidents where interventions have been successful, that is where violence stopped after the intervention.[123] Whereas security forces intervened in less than 3 percent of riots and group clashes in 2004 and 17 percent in 2005, this rose to over 50 percent in 2010, 2011, and 2012. Similarly, while there were successful interventions by the security forces in only 2 percent of such incidents in 2004 and 12 percent in 2005, the proportion of incidents where there was successful security force intervention increased to over 42 percent between 2010 and 2012. Over time, the likelihood that a security force intervention where it occurs was successful also increased. In 2006, 63 percent of security force interventions in riots or group clashes were successful in halting violence. By 2012, this figure had risen to 83 percent.

Security force interventions in mobilized incidents of violence thus increased and became more successful in limiting further violence escalation. This can be seen in the reduction in the average number of people killed in each incident. In 2004, 1.2 people were killed for every riot or group clash that occurred. By 2008, it took five riots or group clashes to kill one person and this figure has stayed fairly constant since then.

If security interventions are becoming more effective, why is it that the number of riots and group clashes have increased over time? This is because local-level actors continue to have incentives to use episodic violence, and the central state, as well as its government and security representatives at the local level, by and large tolerate this. As shown in previous chapters, the continuing use of episodic violence is profitable and noncostly in some postconflict areas. The resulting high expected benefits of using violence leads to repeat use by some and others also employing it. Toleration of the poor performance of security agencies in preventing such episodic violence, and the lack of follow-up in arresting and prosecuting those involved, has created an environment where local leaders and citizens can use episodic violence instrumentally.[124] Except in cases of strategic importance to central state elites, such as terror attacks, or where there is a large outcry from the media for follow-up,[125] the central state rarely puts pressure on local police and military officers to pursue cases or to act effectively.

However, while episodic violence is still often tolerated by the central state, escalation into larger state-threatening extended violence is not. This has led to more effective responses to large incidents of violence that threaten to spiral into extended violence but not to incidents of violence that appear to have a limited time span or that have little national significance.

This chapter has provided an explanation for changes over time in extended violent conflict in Indonesia. Changes in the incentives of national-level elites, in particular security force leaders, explain why extended violence occurred in the early transition period and why it is now absent in Indonesia.

The analysis has implications for our understanding of why extended violent conflicts, including subnational civil wars and enduring intercommunal conflicts, can occur in middle-income states. First, the chapter has highlighted that theories of extended violence must consider not only the motivations of rebel groups and local belligerents but also the functioning of the state. The dominant focus of much of the civil war literature has been on explaining why rebel groups form and use violence with either greed- or grievance-based motivations. At least as important in explaining such conflicts is the role the state can play in allowing for, or facilitating, violence escalation. In this respect, my analysis shares some similarities with more recent work on civil wars that emphasizes the importance of opportunities for rebellion. However, I see such opportunities not as a function of rough geographic terrain or the presence of lootable resources to finance rebellion, factors that allow rebel groups to flourish.[126] Rather, I place my emphasis on the role the state plays in allowing violence to escalate. For both seemingly horizontal intercommunal conflicts, where the state is not an active party, and separatist insurgencies, understanding state behavior is key to understanding why violence escalates to the level of war or why it does not.

Second, my emphasis on the role of the state is different than those who see civil wars and other extended violent conflicts as being the product of weak states. Focusing on (a lack of) capacity raises the question of why extended subnational conflicts can occur in states that have strong bureaucratic and coercive capacity. I argue instead that we need to look at why states with the potential ability to control unrest—capabilities that are present not only in developed countries but also in many middle income states—choose not to do so. This is a product not of technocratic capacity but of the incentives of those in the central state-based elite. We need to disaggregate the state to understand the interests of those who occupy it. Extended violence broke out in a number of provinces of Indonesia following the fall of Suharto not because the state was temporarily incapacitated but because key figures within the state saw such violence to be in their political and economic interests.

Finally, the chapter has shown how efforts to end extended violent conflicts can sow the seeds for continuing episodic violence. Peace settlements were achieved in Indonesia in large part through the co-optation of local elites. Bargains were forged whereby rent-making opportunities were created for local elites, including local security officials, on condition that groups refrained from the use of extended violent conflict. These bargains allowed for the continuation of illiberal practices, including money politics and the use or threats of localized episodic violence. Such practices, through their impact on intercommunal and interelite relations, have meant that tensions remain in some of Indonesia's postconflict provinces such as Maluku and Aceh. Ignoring the illiberal practices of the police and military, which sometimes allow for localized violence to occur, has helped secure their commitment to the state, hence ensuring that extended violent conflict has not recurred.

This raises the question of whether Indonesia can be viewed as a success. I have not yet made a normative judgment about whether the continuation of episodic violence and illiberal practices is a price worth paying to secure the stability that was so lacking in the early years of the postauthoritarian transition. In many respects, it is: stability has provided freedom from fear for many Indonesians and the economic growth it has facilitated has had positive effects on the lives of many, even as inequality has risen. However, the question remains as to how strong these new institutional rules of the game are and whether the ongoing presence of violence in Indonesian society, along with old practices such as corruption, collusion, and nepotism, may eventually undermine them. As Aspinall reminds us, "Poor governance is often the midwife of authoritarian reversals . . . and Indonesian democracy is not yet out of the danger zone."[127]

CONCLUSIONS

What causes postconflict violence to occur frequently in some places emerging from extended violent conflict and not in others? Why does episodic postconflict violence take different forms in different areas? And what causes episodic violence to escalate into larger renewed extended violent conflict? This concluding chapter seeks to contribute answers to these questions by summarizing the findings, arguments, and theory developed in the book. It then points to implications for how we can best understand and study postconflict violence. The chapter ends with suggestions for how this new understanding should shape the policies and practices of those aiming to consolidate peace in postconflict areas across the globe.

When Violence Works

Postconflict violence is best understood not as the result of dysfunctional intergroup relations, unaddressed grievances, or of low state capacity. These issues can make violence more likely but they do not alone cause it. Rather, we can better comprehend why postconflict violence occurs, or why it does not, by focusing on when violence works—on the conditions under which different sets of actors have incentives use violence for purposes of economic or political advancement. Examining the political economy of violence—the reasons why violence is profitable in some places at some times, and not in others—illuminates why postconflict violence occurs or does not. Differing incentives for different sets of actors explains why postconflict violence takes varying forms, for combinations of support for violence from different groups determines the forms postconflict violence will take.

Why Postconflict Violence Occurs

Postconflict violence usually, if not always, occurs because it serves instrumental functions for those who employ it. These include to directly secure resources or power, to signal strength to those in positions of authority (so they distribute resources or power), and to shape the rules of the game on acceptable behavior. Three sets of factors determine whether and when individuals have incentives to use violence for these purposes and hence why it occurs.

First, *the ways in which resources are distributed and power is divided* in the early postconflict period is key. Violence will occur when it works. In areas emerging from extended violent conflict, individuals and groups do not know whether or not the rules of the game that defined acceptable and unacceptable behavior during times of war are still in operation. While war rages, violence is an everyday means of pursuing goals. As Kalyvas has shown, such violence not only serves the ostensible master narrative goal of the conflict, for example, to forcibly ensure that an area receives independence or autonomy, or for a group to gain power in the local political arena, but also occurs because extended violent conflict creates space for individuals to achieve often more mundane personal goals.[1] Indeed, success in war requires leaders of conflicting groups to allow such violence to occur. As the rebel recruitment and war economy literatures emphasize, allowing such personal goals to be achieved is an important way to overcome the collective action dilemma whereby individuals risk life and limb to achieve group goals and goods from which free riders—those who chose not to fight—can also benefit. For this reason, acts of violence based on personal pecuniary motivations are tolerated and, indeed, often encouraged.

Peace settlements, whether peace accords or military victories, are critical junctures in that the rules of the game that govern the role of violence in political and economic competition are up for redefinition. Leaders and (former) foot soldiers do not know whether peace will hold, whether the terms of peace will be applied, and whether violence will continue to be profitable for those who use it. In deciding whether to continue to use violence in such uncertain conditions, individuals will look to the signals created by the success, or lack of, of acts of violence in the early postconflict period. Where such violence continues to be profitable for those who use it, recurring incidents of violence are more likely.

The ways in which postconflict resources are deployed are key to this. Rewarding those who use or threaten violence in the early postconflict period with money, jobs, or projects creates a signal that violence continues to be a useful strategy for accumulation. This leads to repeated use of violence by some and others to also employ it.

Second, and related, individuals factor in the *expected costs of using violence* in the postconflict period. Where the risks of using violence are high, individuals will be less likely to use it. Again, the signal sent by those with authority is extremely important. Where those who use or threaten violence face arrest or other sanctions, people will be more likely to use other nonviolent means to try to achieve their goals.

Third, and finally, the *degree to which peaceful opportunities exist* is important in determining whether or not postconflict violence will occur. Violence may be beneficial and usually noncostly; but it is still inherently a risky endeavor. Most if not all people in postconflict societies will prefer to achieve their goals through channels that do not involve this risk. Where political institutions and economic opportunities exist that allow individuals and groups to get ahead without resort to violence, people will be less likely to use violence as a strategy for accumulation. This points to the importance of ensuring that barriers to political power and to economic achievement are limited.

Variation in such factors explains not only where frequent postconflict violence occurs (and, conversely, where it does not) but also temporal variation in such violence. Violence tends to rise at times when there are changes to the expected benefits and costs of using violence and to the extent to which peaceful opportunities for accumulation are unavailable.

Why Postconflict Violence Takes Different Forms

Violence can be of varying types with each resulting in different destructive impacts. It may take episodic form, with smaller or larger per incident impacts, or may take the form of extended enduring large-scale violent conflict. Rather than treating, and studying, each in isolation, it is fruitful to conceptualize each as being escalated versions of the same class of events. In other words: to understand why large episodic violence occurs, we need to consider what causes small-scale incidents to grow in size; to understand why extended violent conflict happens, we need to consider the factors and processes that lead to large-scale episodic incidents growing in scale and frequency to the point where intercommunal or civil war takes hold.

The types of violence that will occur in an area depend on combinations of support for the use of violence by different sets of actors. The book has identified two key sets of actors who, collectively, determine whether episodic postconflict violence occurs and the forms it takes: local violence specialists (including, but not limited to, former combatants) and local elites (defined as those with formal or informal authority in postconflict areas but subject to the authority of the central state). Where only local violence specialists support the use of violence, postconflict violence will tend to be small in scale. In contrast, where local elites also support the use of violence, large-scale episodes, such as deadly riots or group clashes, will also occur. Such incidents require the organization and/or tolerance of violence by local elites; as such, without their support for violence escalation, episodes of postconflict violence will remain small or will be absent if local violence specialists are not present or face sanction when they use violence. In determining levels of episodic postconflict violence, the attitudes and actions of national elites outside of the areas where extended violence took place only matter in as much as they shape the incentives and hence actions of local players.

The book has used comparative analysis of districts within three Indonesian provinces, which differ in both the presence and scale of postconflict violence, to show how variation in the three factors identified above lead to different postconflict outcomes (tables 15 and 16).

TABLE 15. Incentives for local elites to support violence and the presence of large episodic violence

	MALUKU	ACEH	NORTH MALUKU
Benefits: Resources distributed to local elites based on threat of/use of violence?	Yes	No	No
Costs: Supporting escalation shown to be costly?	No	Yes	Yes
Opportunities: Peaceful political/economic channels for accumulation by local elites?	No	Yes	Yes
Level of large episodic postconflict violence	High	Low	Low

TABLE 16. Incentives for local violence specialists to support violence and the presence of small episodic violence

	MALUKU	ACEH		NORTH MALUKU
		EAST ACEH	SOUTH ACEH	
Benefits: Resources distributed to local violence specialists based on threat of/use of violence?	Yes	Yes	No	No
Costs: Use of violence shown to be costly?	No	No	Mixed[a]	Yes
Opportunities: Peaceful political/economic channels for accumulation by local violence specialists?	No	No	Yes	Yes
Level of small episodic postconflict violence	High	High	Low	Low

a There has been little tolerance by local elites, but the security sector tolerates such violence.

In Maluku, which has seen both frequent small and large episodic postconflict violence, violence has proven to be beneficial and noncostly for local elites and local violence specialists alike, and both sets of actors have faced barriers to using peaceful means to get ahead. In this environment, local elites and local violence specialists have used violence for purposes of accumulation.

In contrast, in largely peaceful postconflict North Maluku, the costs of using or supporting violence have been high for both sets of actors and the benefits have been low; there have also been more opportunities for accumulation through nonviolent means for both groups. This has led local elites and community members to choose not to use violent means to get ahead.

In Aceh, large-scale episodic violence has been largely absent because local elites have seen few benefits from using such violence, they have faced high costs when they have tried to do so, and because the peace settlement has provided many opportunities for accumulation through nonviolent institutional means. Levels of small-scale episodic violence vary between districts within postconflict Aceh because of differing incentives for local violence specialists, primarily former rebel combatants, to use violence.

Why Extended Violence (Re)occurs or Does Not

Extended violent conflict, whether civil war or enduring intercommunal violence, can usefully be viewed as an escalated version of large episodic violence. Drawing on an analysis of the conditions present in the early years after the fall of the authoritarian New Order regime, and how these have changed as Indonesia's democracy has consolidated, I have developed a theory of why extended violence can occur even in stronger states. My emphasis is on the role of a third set of actors: national elites linked to, and battling for power within, the central state. Support for violence by local elites and local violence specialists, a primary focus of many analyses of Indonesia's extended violent conflicts, are necessary conditions for such violence to occur. But, taken alone, they are insufficient to explain why episodic violence escalated to fully blown wars. National elite complicity was also necessary.

In states with broad bureaucratic and coercive reach, conditions that characterize most middle-income countries, extended violence only occurs when support for further escalation from members of the national elite is present. In the early democracy years, members of the central state elite in Indonesia, in particular military leaders, saw high benefits and low costs from supporting such escalation. With pressure to reform the military, and to kick out Suharto-era leaders, some national elites perceived there to be few peaceful means to ensure that old rights and privileges would continue to be protected. In this environment, supporting the escalation of episodic violence into much larger enduring confla-grations proved to be an effective strategy. Only as threats to elite interests have declined, and as more impersonal institutions that provide checks on national elite behavior have taken form and grown in strength, have incentives to support extended violence diminished.

Implications for Understanding Postconflict Violence

The theory developed in this book is deliberately and consciously parsimonious. Iteratively skipping back and forward between deductive and inductive reason-ing, I developed a theory of postconflict violence that focuses on a limited set of factors and mechanisms. Case materials demonstrate that the theory does a good job in explaining differing patterns of postconflict violence in Indonesia. There are some disadvantages to such parsimony, in particular in explaining specific events rather than patterns of events. The case chapters, in applying and develop-ing the theory, have shown that in some cases other factors such as preexisting norms and preferences are important.[2] As with all social phenomena, contin-gency and chance, which cannot be easily modeled by social scientists, also play a role. However, a major advantage of developing a simple, focused theory is that it allows for portability to other contexts beyond Indonesia. The theory should ultimately be judged by the extent to which it can explain patterns of violence in a range of postconflict areas.

If the theory is right, it has a number of implications for how we should un-derstand and study postconflict violence. Many of these insights also apply to the study of violence outside zones of past extended violence.

Focusing on Incentives to Use Violence

First, the book has shown that focusing on the political economy of violence, on the incentives that individuals and groups have to use violence (or not) in the postconflict period, can be a fruitful strategy. Enduring grievances or "root causes" can motivate individuals and groups to take actions to achieve redress. But theories based on such factors need to explain why the aggrieved choose to use *violence*, one of but a number of possible strategies, as a means for this. Similarly, the nature of intergroup relations can explain levels of tensions in each society. But our theories need to specify why such conflict takes *violent* form. This requires us to zoom in on the factors that shape the decision-making processes and ultimate choices of individuals to use violence or not. In explaining complex social phenomena such as postconflict violence, researchers need to provide more deeply specified, and empirically grounded, explanations that show how macrolevel conditions shape individual decisions (and vice versa).

Methodological implications follow. Econometric analyses, which examine how structural factors co-vary with different levels of violence, have limited promise in building theories that demonstrate how differences in environmental factors shape human decision making. To be sure, many researchers are aware of these limitations and have increasingly collected and employed data that allow for consideration of variation at much lower levels (e.g., villages and even households). This is helpful. Yet most quantitative studies of violence, and even more so of postconflict violence, have still focused on assessing the extent to which X increases the risk of Y; data, rather than deductively generated theory, often bolstered by just anecdotal examples, have infrequently been used to show *how* and *why* the independent and dependent variables are connected. Qualitative analyses provide opportunities to explore in greater depth the links between purported causes and effects. Unfortunately, many such studies have also failed to build rigorous arguments and theories that show the *mechanisms* through which the two are linked. This book has shown the usefulness of mixed methods approaches that involve the deployment of finely grained quantitative violence data and comparative microlevel case study work, involving fieldwork and the use of process tracing.

Second, in unpacking such incentives it is useful to look at the instrumental functions violence can serve in postconflict areas. There is a long tradition of viewing violence in pathological terms. But there is much to be gained by treating individuals and groups as largely rational. To adapt the title of Christopher Cramer's book, "violence is not a stupid thing,"[3] a logic exists. In the Indonesian cases, most of the time, individuals who use violence do so because they feel it works in that it is an effective way for them to achieve their goals. To understand why postconflict violence occurs, it is necessary to determine what these goals are and why people believe violence may be a useful way to achieve them. Again, rigorous fieldwork is necessary for this.

Focusing on how violence is used to achieve political or economic power explains much, if not all, postconflict violence. This is not to say that all individuals in postconflict areas are cold-hearted chasers of riches. Rather, seemingly pecuniary goals are important not only for personal or group enrichment but also to ensure people's wider interests are protected. Where impersonal institutions that protect basic rights and check the actions of those in power are weak or not present—and this is the case in many postconflict areas across the world—economic and political achievement can prevent exploitation by others. Because getting ahead economically and politically can simultaneously be a goal *and* a means to achieve other goals, there is little to be gained from labeling people's motives for using violence as being driven by greed or grievance. However, focusing on issues normally explored under research agendas that are focused on greed-type issues (such as the use of violence to capture resources or power) can take us far in also understanding violence where there is a prominent backdrop of grievances.

The Links between Different Forms of Violence

The book has shown the usefulness of considering different types of violence within one study. The vast majority of studies of postconflict violence have focused on why civil wars recur or not; such research strategies—where violence is measured in binary terms, either present or absent—do not allow for consideration of why episodic forms of postconflict violence occur. Studies have also tended to consider the two types of extended violent conflict—civil war and intercommunal extended violence—separately, treating the two as phenomenologically distinct. My research approach, which includes areas (and time periods) that vary in the presence of three different forms of violence (extended, large episodic, small episodic) has allowed me to do a few things.

First, it has enabled me to consider what is similar and what is different about different forms of violence. There are common causal factors for all three types of violence—and for the intercommunal and civil war subtypes of extended violent conflict. For each type of violence, issues related to the ways in which resources and power are distributed are key. Each type of violence becomes more likely when those who use violence are rewarded; each type of violence is more likely when few channels exist to allow individuals to get ahead economically and politically using peaceful means.

At the same time, there is a key difference between each type of violence: what makes extended violence different from episodic violence, and what makes large episodic violence different from small-scale episodic violence, is who is organizing or facilitating violence. Small-scale violence, is largely a product of nonelites at the local level. Larger-scale episodic violence requires the support of local elites. Extended violent conflict, in turn, requires support from national-level actors. Considering all three forms of violence together has thus allowed me to develop a theory of violence escalation, which sets out the conditions under which violent acts become more destructive, sometimes ending up as fresh extended violent conflict. Studying any one form alone would not have made this possible.

Implications for Policymakers

The book's arguments have a number of implications for the formulation of policies and programs to prevent postconflict violence.

The Use of Postconflict Funds

Postconflict violence can be the result of postconflict resources inadvertently creating incentives for continued violence. Globally, practitioners and academics alike have highlighted the need for special postconflict programs to co-opt potential spoilers of the peace. To this end, DDR (disarmament, demobilization, and reintegration) programs are a now almost universally employed tactic to buy the allegiance of those who fought before. Paying off elites and former combatants who could derail peace processes is deemed important with the corruption and the lack of justice this entails a price worth paying in the early postconflict years.[4] I do not argue against such programs. Providing funds to former combatant leaders and foot soldiers may be an effective way to ensure they abide by peace accords. The analysis of Aceh, in particular, showed the utility of using resources for purposes of incorporation to ensure that the nascent peace gained strength.

However, the book argues against using funds to satiate the desires of belligerents who use violence *after extended violent conflict has come to an end*. Those with the capacity or taste for violence will look to responses to violence that is committed after peace accords are signed, or extended violent conflicts otherwise end, to determine whether violent action is still a legitimate and profitable strategy. Policymakers need to send a clear signal that the rules on the acceptability of violence in the postconflict era are different to those that were in operation during the extended violent conflict. Distributing resources to those who use or threaten to use violence in the early postconflict period can send out a signal that violence remains tolerable. As occurred in Maluku, this can lead to violence continuing to be a modus operandi in political and economic competition.

Security Responses and Legal Institutions

How then to deal with the acts of violence that will almost inevitably occur in the early postconflict period? My argument points to the importance of ensuring that those who commit such violent acts face sanction. Arresting and prosecuting such people is of vital importance to send out a clear signal that the continuing use of violence no longer works.

In most postconflict areas this implies three things. First, there is a need to build the capacity and professionalism of the security agencies, primarily the police, in responding effectively to postconflict violence. The police in areas emerging from extended violence will often be dysfunctional, with past violence having distorted the incentives for them to do their job properly. While supporting deeper institutional security sector reform will often take years, in large part because it will often be resisted, in the short to medium term it may be useful to consider developing an elite branch within the police to investigate and respond to large incidents of postconflict violence.

Second, there is a need to build up justice institutions to ensure that those who use violence face appropriate sanctions. My concern is not with developing institutions such as truth and reconciliation commissions that deal with past abuses, the predominant focus of law-related postconflict programs, but on building systems to prosecute those who use violence after the peace settlement. Legal institutions will also often be weak and dysfunctional in areas emerging from extended violent conflict. Again, while longer-term work on building judicial functioning is required, a short to medium term strategy may be to use nationally appointed special courts, as has been used in Indonesia and elsewhere to address corruption cases, to deal with incidents of postconflict violence.

In-group policing can also be an effective strategy for limiting the use of postconflict violence. Providing incentives to leaders of formerly conflicting groups to discipline those under their authority who use violence is potentially a powerful means to limit such acts while state security and justice institutions are being built.

Expanding Opportunities in Postconflict Areas

There is also a need to increase the economic and political opportunities for elites and local-level violence specialists in postconflict areas. Where such opportunities exist, individuals within each group may be less tempted to use violence for profit.

There is a need to take actions to boost job-creating growth. High levels of unemployment raise the risk of individuals turning to violence. Ensuring there are economic opportunities for local elites, for example, to develop and grow businesses, is also important. The challenge—and not an easy one to overcome—is to ensure those with the capacity to spoil the peace have opportunities, while also ensuring that providing access to economic opportunities is not a response to threats or acts of coercion. Providing additional state resources to support economic development has a role. However, it is important that such resources are channeled through formal institutional channels, where checks and balances and accountability mechanisms are in place, to prevent funds being captured and used to cement old patron-client networks that can be mobilized again for violence.

Ensuring that former conflict elites are not excluded from achieving political power is also important. In Aceh, provisions in the peace accord that facilitated GAM's entry to local governments and parliaments played a vital role in limiting former rebel leaders' incentives to use violence. In preventing the exclusion of particular groups, the Indonesia cases highlight the limitations in some places of formal power-sharing rules. These can lock in conflict-era identities and ensure that political divides continue to be structured by conflict cleavages. In many places, rather than dividing power between groups, it may be more effective to focus on ensuring there is a level playing field for leaders of different stripes to compete for power through political channels. Approaches that distribute power and control of resources across more institutions (for example, by allowing for the formation of new subnational administrative regions in postconflict areas) can expand the set of opportunities, thereby reducing the costs to elites who fail to achieve power in some areas.

Building the National State

Finally, policymakers and practitioners focused on consolidating peace in post-conflict areas need to also develop strategies to support the development of central state institutions. The risks of extended violence are higher where national elites support such subnational violence. The incentives of leaders and civilians in postconflict areas are important determinants of postconflict violence. But, in middle-income states, it is only where groups linked to the central state condone or facilitate violence escalation that episodic violence can morph into renewed extended violent conflict.

Efforts to support national states in countries that have experienced past large-scale violence have tended to focus on building capacity in areas such as the security sector, public revenue collection, and budgetary planning. These are certainly important endeavors. Yet the actions of central state elites are driven at least as much by the incentives they have to use violence as a strategy for accumulation as by capacity issues.

Lowering incentives for national elites to support violence requires dual strategies that ensure that national elites have opportunities to access power and resources using peaceful means while building impersonal institutions that provide checks and balances on those in power. In countries in the early stages of political transition, a situation common to many areas affected by or emerging from extended violent conflicts, the former may mean limiting reform pressures that can undermine the interests of those previously in power. Yet such co-optation-focused strategies alone provide a shaky platform for preventing the reemergence of extended violence. By protecting incumbent interests, they limit opportunities for others. Providing preferential access to those who have the capacity to organize or allow violence to occur can also send out a dangerous signal that coercive pressure can be a fruitful strategy for aspiring national elites.

Those seeking to prevent the reemergence of extended violent conflict need to focus on building strong state institutions that limit the ability of national elites to use violence for their own purposes. In short, this requires building the rule of law. Efforts focused on this will, when successful, have a larger positive impact in consolidating peace than the more traditional peace-building programs often favored by both donors and governments in postconflict areas.

Glossary

ABRI Angkatan Bersenjata Republik Indonesia (Armed Forces of the Republic of Indonesia), the name for the armed forces during the Suharto era

ACD Uppsala Armed Conflict Dataset

ACLED Armed Conflict Location and Event Dataset

Adat Traditional/customary law

Agas Christian gang (Maluku)

Akar rumput Literally grassroots, synonym for Christian militia groups (Maluku)

Aktor lapangan Field-level actors

AMM Aceh Monitoring Mission, an unarmed peace mission deployed by the EU and ASEAN to oversee the implementation of the Helsinki MoU in Aceh

Anak bua Followers

Angkot Public bus

APKLI Asosiasi Pedagang Kaki Lima Indonesia (Association of Street Vendors Indonesia)

ASEAN Association of Southeast Asian Nations

Bappeda Provincial planning ministry

BIN Badan Intelijen Negara (National Intelligence Agency)

BKO Bawah Kendali Operasi (Extra nonlocal security forces)

BKPMD Badan Koordinasi Penanaman Modal Daerah (Indonesian Regional Investment Coordination Board)

BKPRM Badan Komunikasi Pemuda Remaja Masjid Indonesia (Coordinating Body of Youth Activists of the Mosque)

BPK Badan Pemeriksa Keuangan Republik Indonesia (Audit Board of the Republic of Indonesia)

BPS Badan Pusat Statistik (National Statistics Agency)

BRA Badan Reintegrasi Aceh (Aceh Reintegration Agency), a government agency that oversaw the implementation of reintegration programs in Aceh

Brigade Hizbullah Muslim militia group under the Laskar Mujahidin umbrella (Maluku)

Brimob Brigade Mobil (mobile brigades), special forces unit of the police

BRR Badan Rehabilitasi dan Rekonstruksi (Rehabilitation and Reconstruction Agency), government agency that oversaw the tsunami reconstruction program in Aceh

Bupati Head of rural district

CAVR Comissão de Acolhimento, Verdade e Reconciliação de Timor-Leste (Timor-Leste Commission for Reception, Truth, and Reconciliation), independent truth commission established under the UN Transitional Administration in East Timor

CoHA Cessation of Hostilities Agreement, unsuccessful December 2002 peace accord (Aceh)

Coker Christian gang (Maluku)

CoSA Commission on Security Arrangements under the Aceh Monitoring Mission

COW Correlates of War dataset

Daerah GAM administrative area (there are four Daerah within each Wilayah in Aceh)

Dalang Puppet master

Darul Islam House of Islam, Islamist group that aimed to establish an Islamic state of Indonesia

DAU Dana Alokasi Umum (General Allocation Fund), unconditional cash transfer from central government to local governments

DDR Disarmament, Demobilization, and Reintegration

Desentralisasi Decentralization

Detachment 88 Indonesian special forces counterterrorism squad

DiCoSA District-level Commission on Security Arrangements under the Aceh Monitoring Mission

DPR Dewan Perwakilan Daerah (House of Representatives), Indonesia's national parliament

Dwifungsi Dual function, doctrine that legitimized a sociopolitical role for the armed forces, officially abolished in April 2000

EU European Union

FDI Foreign direct investment

FKK Forum Koordinasi dan Komunikasi (Forum for Coordination and Communication), government oversight body of the peace process (Aceh)

FKM Front Kedaulatan Maluku (Front for Moluccan Sovereignty), Christian militia group that aimed to continue the struggle for the RMS for independence (Maluku)

FKUB Forum Kerukunan Umat Beragama (Inter-Religious Harmony Forum)

FPI Front Pembela Islam (Islamic Defenders Front), hard-line Islamist group

FPMB Forum Pemuda Muslim Baguala (Baguala Muslim Youth Forum (Maluku)

FSUI Forum Silaturahmi Umat Islam (Coordinating Forum of Muslim Society (Maluku)

GAM Gerakan Aceh Merdeka (Free Aceh Movement), former separatist movement fighting for independence of Aceh

GDP Gross domestic product

Gerindra Indonesian political party

Golkar Golongan Karya (functional groups), government's party under the New Order

Halmahera Baku Dapa 1 Eleven-day meeting of Christian community leaders (North Maluku)

Helsinki MoU Helsinki Memorandum of Understanding, Aceh peace accord signed 15 August 2005

Hibualamo Big house, system of adat from Tobelo, North Halmahera (North Maluku)

Humanitarian Pause Failed cease-fire in Aceh, September 2000

ICG International Crisis Group

ICMI Ikatan Cendekiawan Muslim Indonesia (Indonesian Muslim Intellectuals Association)

Inpres Instruksi Presiden (Presidential Instruction)

ITP Institut Titian Perdamaian (Peace Building Institute)

JI Jama'ah Islamaiyah, terrorist group

Jihad Holy war

Kabupaten Rural district

Kaki lima Street food sellers

Kapita Militia commander (North Maluku)

Keppres Keputusan Presiden (Presidential Instruction)

Komnas HAM Komisi Nasional Hak Asasi Manusia (National Commission on Human Rights)

KOMPAK Muslim militia group under the Laskar Mujahidin umbrella (Maluku)

Kopassus Komando Pasukan Khusus (military special forces)

Kost Boarding house

Kostrad Komando Cadangan Strategis Angkatan Darat (Army Strategic Reserve Command)

Kotamadya Urban district

KPA Komite Peralihan Aceh (Aceh Traditional Council), political structure of GAM after it transformed from an armed organization

KPK Komisi Pemberantasan Korupsi (Corruption Eradication Commission)

KPU Komisi Pemilihan Umum (elections commission)

Krismon Krisis moneter (Asian financial crisis)

Laskar Jihad Jihad Warriors, Islamist militia group (Maluku)

Laksar Kristus Christian Warriors, Christian gang (Maluku)

Laskar Mujahidin Mujahidin Warriors, umbrella group for Islamist militias (Maluku)

LoGA Law on Governing Aceh (Law 11/2006), national law that implemented the Helsinki MoU

Majelis Latupati Latupati Council, network of local traditional leaders (Maluku)

Majelis Nasional National Council, GAM oversight body created in October 2006

Malino accord Peace agreement for Central Sulawesi, December 2000

Malino II accord Peace agreement for Maluku, February 2002

Maluku Jieraha Idea of common lineage of North Maluku people

MPR Majelis Permusyawaratan Rakyat (People's Consultative Assembly), Indonesia's upper house

Muhhamadiyah Large Muslim organization

MUI Majelis Ulama Indonesia (Indonesia Ulama Council)

Negeri Traditional community (Maluku)

New Order Suharto's regime (1966–98)

NHM Nusa Halmahera Minerals, Indonesian company that operates the Gosowong gold mine in North Halmahera (North Maluku)

NGO Nongovernmental organization

NU Nahdlatul Ulama (Association of Muslim Scholars), large Muslim organization

NVMS National Violence Monitoring System

Otsus Dana otonomi khusus (special autonomy funds), additional resources given to Aceh under the peace agreement—also called SAF

PA Partai Aceh (Aceh Party), political party of former GAM movement

Pajak Nanggroe State tax, tax levied by GAM (Aceh)

PAKTA Pelangi Khusus Thaib Armaiyn (Special Troops for Thaib Armaiyn) (North Maluku)

PAN Partai Amanat Nasional (National Mandate Party)

Panas pela Heating of the pela, an adat ceremony to reinforce binds between people (Maluku)

Panglima Commander, can be of military or militia group

Panglima Daerah GAM commander for Daerah region (Aceh)

Panglima Sagoe GAM commander for Sagoe region (Aceh)

Panglima Wilayah GAM commander for Wilayah region (Aceh)

Partai Demokrat Democrat Party (PD)

Pasukan Jihad Jihad Forces, Muslim militia (North Maluku)

Pasukan Kuning Yellow Forces, Militia group supporting the sultan of Ternate (North Maluku)

Pasukan Merah Red Forces, Christian militia (North Maluku)

Pasukan Pedudeung Long Sword Forces, GAM splinter group (Aceh)

Pasukan Putih White Forces, Muslim militia (North Maluku)

Pasukan Siluman Phantom Forces (Maluku)

PBB Partai Bulan Bintang (Crescent Star Party)

PDI Partai Demokrasi Indonesia (Democratic Party of Indonesia)

PDI-P Partai Demokrasi Indonesia-Perjuangan (Indonesian Democratic Party of Struggle)

Pela gandong Form of adat emphasizing traditional village alliances based on common ancestry (Maluku)

Pemekaran Flourishing, the splitting of government administrative areas

Peusijuk Traditional welcoming reconciliation ceremony held when fighters return home (Aceh)

PKS Partai Keadilan Sejahtera (Justice and Prosperity Party)

PODES Potensi Desa survey (Village Potential survey)

Pokja Working group

Polres Kepolisian Resor, district-level police

Posko Jihadi coordination post (North Maluku)

PPATK Pusat Pelaporan dan Analisis Transaksi Keuangan (Financial Transactions Reporting and Analysis Center)

PPP Partai Persatuan Pembangunan (United Development Party)

Preman Thugs

PRIO Peace Research Institute Oslo

Reformasi Reform

Renstra Five-year strategic plan

RMS Republik Maluku Seletan (Republic of South Moluccas), group seeking independence for Maluku

Rp. Rupiah, the Indonesian currency

SAF Special Autonomy Fund (also called Otsus)

Sagoe GAM administrative area, roughly equivalent to an Indonesian subdistrict (Aceh)

SARA Suku, Agama, Ras, Antar golongan (Ethnicity, Religion, Race, Inter-Group), a policy under Suharto that differences between these matters should not be discussed

Satpol PP Public order officers/municipal police

SMS Text message

STAIN Sekolah Tinggi Agama Islam Negeri (Islamic College in Maluku)

Tim sukses Campaign team

TNI Tentara Nasional Indonesia (Indonesian National Army), formerly called ABRI

Uang rokok Smoking money

UCDP Uppsala Conflict Data Program

Ulama Muslim religious leader

UNODC United Nations Office on Drugs and Crime

Unpatti Universitas Pattimura (Pattimura University) (Maluku)

UNSFIR United Nations Support Facility for Indonesian Recovery

US$ United States dollars

Wali kota Head of urban district

Warung Food stall

Wilayah GAM administrative area, roughly equivalent to an Indonesian district (Aceh)

THE NATIONAL VIOLENCE MONITORING SYSTEM DATASET

This book draws on the new National Violence Monitoring System (NVMS) dataset, which includes more than 158,000 incidents of violence in Indonesia since 1998. This appendix provides details on the motivation for building the NVMS, what it contains, and how it was developed.

Why Build a New Dataset of Violence for Indonesia?

Prior to the NVMS, three main types of quantitative data on violence existed: Indonesian government statistics, both police records and from the periodic Village Potential (PODES) survey; NGO and state-mandated watchdog reports on rights violations and violence; and a large newspaper-based dataset put together by the United Nations Support Facility for Indonesian Recovery (UNSFIR). None of these data sources is adequate for assessing patterns of postconflict violence in Indonesia. To varying extents, they suffer from a number of problems: violence is underreported; incidents are not classified in standardized ways that allow for temporal and spatial analysis; smaller-scale incidents are excluded; and information for recent years is not included. It was thus necessary to put together a new dataset.

While Indonesian police statistics are used in global assessments of homicide rates the data have significant weaknesses.[1] One issue is that Indonesian police data substantially underreport violence and its impacts. A study conducted as part of the preparation of the NVMS compared police data with that obtained through a reading of local newspapers for a six-month period in 2005 in Maluku. While police data showed 12 violent incidents leading to 12 fatalities, newspapers reported 67 violent incidents resulting in 24 deaths. The police only recorded cases that were written up for formal processing; this meant that incidents where charges were not pressed, or where perpetrators escaped, were not captured.[2] A more recent comparison of police statistics in the Greater Jakarta area with incidents reported in local newspapers found that the police data underestimated murders by 80 percent and rapes by 65 percent.[3] Where police capacity is lower than in Indonesia's capital, police data are likely to miss even more violent incidents.

A second problem with Indonesian police data is that they are not standardized across areas. An assessment of Maluku and North Maluku police data, for example, found that different categories were used to assign incidents to types in different places.[4] There is no central body within the national police force that systematically gathers and collates violence or crime data collected at more local levels. Hospital records on fatalities, used elsewhere to estimate homicide rates, also tend to be incomplete in Indonesia and do not adequately record information on the cause of death.

Since 2003, the government of Indonesia's Bureau of Statistics has collected data on violence through its Village Potential (*Potensi Desa*, or PODES) survey, which is conducted every three years. The nationwide survey asks village heads about violence that has occurred in the past year and the impacts it has had. While providing more comprehensive and standardized information than the police data, PODES still has weaknesses.

First, the accuracy of the violence data is questionable. In areas with large-scale extended violence, PODES appears to overreport fatalities. The 2003 survey—which provides data on violence between September 2001 and August 2002[5]—reported that of 4,849 people who died from conflict across Indonesia, 4,106 lost their lives in the extended violence provinces of West and Central Kalimantan, Central Sulawesi, Maluku, North Maluku, and Aceh.[6] NVMS data for the same provinces record 3,415 deaths from violence. In contrast, it appears that in "lower conflict" areas PODES underreports violence. Barron and Sharpe's study of two Indonesian provinces that were not affected by large-scale extended violence compared violence reported in local newspapers with that recorded in PODES for the 2001–3 period. In twelve districts in the two provinces, they found that local newspapers picked up 2.6 times as many deaths as did PODES.[7] More strikingly, the 2005 PODES reported that just 276 people were killed from violent conflict nationwide.[8] NVMS data for the same period for sixteen Indonesian provinces, half the Indonesian total, found 1,207 deaths from conflict.[9]

These inaccuracies flow in part from the perverse incentives informants face in responding to survey questions, which can lead to under- or overreporting of violence. Responses may depend on expectations about how the survey will influence policy decisions.[10] Indonesia's high conflict areas received special sources of assistance; local leaders may feel that exaggerating the number of deaths in their area could lead to more funds arriving. In contrast, respondents in areas that are not experiencing extended violence may want to underplay the local violence that is present in their area given the stigma associated with it.

A second reason for data discrepancies is a result of an inherent problem of most surveys—they rely on recall and on common understanding of the questions asked.[11] Village heads interviewed for PODES may find it difficult to remember what violence occurred in the past year and what in the year that preceded it. (The year 2000 and early 2001 saw particularly high fatality rates in the areas of Indonesia affected by extended violent conflicts. It may be that village heads reported some of these earlier deaths in the 2003 survey.) Further, the types of incidents that occurred in the areas of extended violent conflict may be more likely to be reported to PODES enumerators than those that occurred in lower conflict areas. Village heads may associate the term "conflict" with only large-scale outbursts of collective violence. If this is the case, smaller-scale violent incidents will likely go unreported, perhaps explaining underreporting of violence in provinces that were not affected by extended violence.

A final limitation of using PODES to assess patterns of postconflict violence is that the dataset does not provide full time series data. It contains information on violence that has occurred in the year preceding each enumeration. This means we only have data for one year in every three and we do not have information on when exactly the violence occurred.

A third source of data is that collected and collated by NGOs and state-mandated bodies. The Setara Institute publishes information on human rights violations and the National Commission on Violence Against Women records incidents of sexual abuse. The Peace Building Institute (ITP), a local NGO, tracks incidents of violence. Yet the methodology used is unclear and data collection protocols do not appear to be uniformly followed. The ITP data, which have been used by Indonesian policymakers and often makes headlines, records just 600 incidents of "conflict or violence" in 2009 across all of Indonesia, resulting in 70 deaths, 395 injuries, and 421 damaged buildings.[12] In contrast, the NVMS dataset for sixteen provinces, found 4,138 incidents of violent conflict in the same period, resulting in 267 deaths, 4,442 injuries, and 828 damaged buildings.[13]

UNSFIR-2

The weaknesses of existing data motivated an important effort by Ashutosh Varshney and the United Nations Support Facility for Indonesian Recovery (UNSFIR) to build a new dataset on Indonesian violence. In doing so, they turned to newspaper reports of violence. Varshney had previously built a dataset on riots in India using newspaper accounts and aimed to do the same for collective violence in Indonesia.[14] After an initial failed attempt using national-level sources, a second database (UNSFIR-2) turned to provincial-level newspapers.[15] The resulting database, which includes data for 1990–2003, is the best record of violence in Indonesia's early transition period.

However, there are a number of limitations to UNSFIR-2 for our purposes. First, it does not include Aceh, the site of Indonesia's most deadly extended violence. Second, the data do not go beyond 2003. As such, the dataset tells us next to nothing on how violence has evolved after the large-scale extended violent conflicts in Indonesia's regions ended. Third, the dataset does not include most smaller-scale incidents of violence. UNSFIR's focus was on collective violence with incidents between individuals not included. This made sense given the goal was to assess levels of violence in the early post-Suharto period, when most deaths were likely the result of the large-scale extended violence that hit a number of provinces. However, the exclusion of smaller incidents means that much of the violence that has occurred since the large-scale extended conflicts have come to an end is missed.[16]

Previous studies have also shown that provincial newspapers, while providing a more accurate picture than national ones, still significantly underreport levels of violence. Barron and Sharpe compared death tolls from UNSFIR-2 with those from a violence dataset using subprovincial papers for twelve districts in two Indonesian provinces for 2001–3. Employing the same definition as UNSFIR, they found three times more deaths from collective violence.[17] Other research, such as Welsh's study of lynching, also suggests that UNSFIR underestimates deaths from smaller-scale violence.[18]

A New Dataset: The National Violence Monitoring System (NVMS)

The new National Violence Monitoring System (NVMS) dataset addresses many of the weaknesses of existing data. It contains information on incidents of violence in sixteen Indonesian provinces, which include all of those that experienced extended violent conflict.[19] It uses subprovincial as well as provincial sources to ensure that small-scale violent incidents are captured and uses multiple news sources for each area to minimize inaccuracies. The full dataset, which covers the 1998–2012 period,[20] contains 158,363 discreet incidents of violence: 40,176 incidents of violent conflict, 96,378 incidents of violent crime, 14,299 incidents of domestic violence, and 7,510 incidents of violence used by security forces. Collectively, these incidents resulted in 35,594 deaths, 128,534 injuries, 75,364 damaged buildings, 4,298 kidnappings, and 21,844 sexual assaults. Almost 50,000 of these incidents occurred in the six provinces that experienced extended violence that are the focus of this book.

Putting the dataset together involved four main steps.[21] The first was deciding which provinces to cover. Two principles guided this. All the provinces that experienced large-scale extended violence were included: Maluku, North Maluku, Central Sulawesi, Central Kalimantan, West Kalimantan, and Aceh. Further provinces were then selected to cover all of Indonesia's main islands: Java, Sumatra, Sulawesi, Kalimantan, Papua, and the group of smaller islands that stretches from Bali to East Nusa Tenggara. This ensured that the data included areas with high, medium, and lower levels of violence. While the data are not formally representative of all of Indonesia, the large coverage (57 percent of the Indonesian population live in areas surveyed), wide geographic spread, and inclusion of areas with a range of violence levels gives us confidence that patterns observed extend to other parts of the country.

The second step was to decide which sources to use in each province. Media assessments were conducted in the selected provinces, aimed at determining coverage (what papers are published, what districts within the province they cover, the availability of archives) and the accuracy of reporting. Newspapers with narrow coverage, weak archives, overt political biases, and those that did not employ fact-checking of stories were excluded. The assessments involved extensive interviews with newspaper staff.

After deciding on which papers to use, researchers were sent to each province to collect newspaper articles on violence. Every page of the archives of the selected newspapers was photographed, generating more than 2 million images. Teams in Jakarta then combed through the images and "clipped" articles related to incidents of violence, including both conflict and crime. A standardized coding template was completed for each article. For each incident over thirty variables were coded, including when and where the incident took place; whether it was a crime, a conflict, domestic violence, or security force violence; its physical impacts (deaths, injuries, people sexually assaulted, and kidnapped, all gender disaggregated, and buildings damaged); the actors involved; the issue that appeared to drive the violence; the form violence took; the weapons used; and what interventions were taken to try to stop escalation and whether they were successful. Where articles reported different impacts the more conservative figures were used. Rigorous quality control measures were employed to try to pick up any mistakes.[22]

Data gaps were filled using reports of violence from other sources. This involved systematically going through academic articles and books on violence in Indonesia. We also reviewed policy papers, including those from the International Crisis Group and Human Rights Watch. Events recorded in other datasets (UNSFIR-2, ITP, and Barron and Sharpe's two-province database) were incorporated where there were archival gaps. Comparing such data sources also resulted in the recoding of some incidents, for example where the initial type of violence was unclear from the newspaper article or where the death toll from an incident rose over time. Finally, we asked experts on particular conflicts to look at the data on their provinces to assess plausibility and to try to identify any inaccuracies. The process of putting the dataset together took four years.

Prior use of the newspaper method in a number of Indonesian provinces shows that it provides a reasonable picture of violence patterns and trends.[23] Indonesia's newspapers operated during periods of large-scale violence—the dataset, for example, includes almost twelve thousand incidents reported during Aceh's war. The post–New Order press has also been largely free; indeed, it is perhaps the most vibrant and open in Southeast Asia.[24] The emerging consensus is that using subprovincial newspapers is the best means of tracking levels of violent conflict and its impacts in Indonesia in ways that allow for temporal and spatial disaggregation.[25] The Indonesian government has adopted the National Violence Monitoring System to track violence in real time.

This is not to say that the NVMS dataset is without weaknesses. Reporting in Indonesian newspapers, as elsewhere, can at times be inaccurate, and there may be biases in some articles. The coding of an incident's type, that is what the incident was about, sometimes involves a degree of subjectivity. Some information will be missing from reports and may need to be inferred by the coders. Undoubtedly errors crept into the coding of some incidents. But the level of effort put into training for coders, developing manuals, implementing extensive quality control procedures, and triangulating data with other available sources minimized these problems.

Notes

INTRODUCTION

1. The following chronology draws on ICG (2011b, 2012a), communication with my research team in Ambon, September 2011, and local newspaper accounts.

2. Unless otherwise stated, violence incidence and impact figures used throughout the book are from the National Violence Monitoring System (NVMS) dataset. More information on the dataset is provided in the appendix. The displacement figure is from ICG 2002.

3. Brown, Wilson, and Hadi 2005.

4. I define large episodic incidents as those that resulted in three or more deaths, ten or more injuries, or fifteen or more damaged buildings.

5. The postconflict period is that after the end of large-scale hostilities (extended violence). The term is, of course, not without conceptual problems: in many cases neither the underlying conflict, nor indeed violence, has ceased. Nevertheless, the term is commonly used in both academic writing and policy discourse and, as such, I use it here. I discuss my use of the term, and other key concepts employed, in the next chapter.

6. This figure excludes deaths in East Timor, now Timor-Leste. Timor is not covered in this study, because it gained independence after two decades of illegal Indonesian occupation. A further 693 people were killed in ethnic violence in West Kalimantan in 1997 in the final year of the Suharto regime. Papua and West Papua provinces in eastern Indonesia are also commonly thought of as having experienced extended violent conflicts but violence there has been more sporadic.

7. Collier, Hoeffler, and Soderbom 2008. Walter (2004) and Suhrke and Samset (2007) question the figures of Collier and his colleagues, but they concur that a past history of civil war is a robust predictor of further civil war onset.

8. Ross 2004; Humphreys 2005.

9. Blattman and Miguel 2010.

10. Besley and Persson 2011; Walter 2009b.

11. Fearon and Laitin 2003.

12. Hegre et al. 2001.

13. Where renewed wars occur, GDP contracts by 2–2.2 percent per year (Collier 1999; Hoeffler and Reynal-Querol 2003; Restrepo et al. 2008) with a typical civil war resulting in damages and losses of between US$60 billion and US$250 billion (Chauvet, Collier, and Hegre 2008). In such places, incomes are reduced by around 15 percent and the proportion of people living in absolute poverty increases by almost one-third (Moser 2006).

14. Geneva Declaration Secretariat 2008, 51; McNeish and Lopez Rivera 2012. Between 2004 and 2009, El Salvador, a country previously scarred by civil war, had the highest homicide rate in the world (Geneva Declaration 2011). Not all of this violence has its roots in the extended violence from before. Much of the recent violence is a result of gang and drug wars, with ambiguous links to the past civil wars. For discussions, see Demombynes 2011; and World Bank 2011a.

15. Geneva Declaration Secretariat 2008, 1.

16. Muggah 2009b; Ghobarah, Huth, and Russett 2003.

17. Dominguez 2008, 13–14.

18. This estimate is for just ninety countries (Geneva Declaration Secretariat 2008).

19. The sole exception is Daly (2016) who focuses on why some armed militia groups within Colombia have remilitarized while others have not. However, the focus is on variation in remilitarization rather than violence per se.

20. The dataset is the Indonesian National Violence Monitoring System (NVMS). This was a joint endeavor with the World Bank, who paid for much of the work. Those involved in the creation of the NVMS are noted in the preface to this book. The book uses the data for the 1998–2012 period. Since then, additional incidents that occurred between 2013 and March 2015 have been added, bringing the total number of incidents to 237,885. The largest other single country violence dataset is the ESOC Princeton Iraq Civil War Dataset which, as of October 2015, contained information on 193,264 "significant activities."

CHAPTER 1. STUDYING POSTCONFLICT VIOLENCE

1. Important work includes Hartzell, Hoddie, and Rothchild 2001; Walter 2004, 2010; Doyle and Sambanis 2000, 2006; Collier, Hoeffler, and Soderbom 2008; Fortna 2008; and Toft 2010. Boyle 2014 also uses a large-n dataset, but he focuses not only on war resumption but also on other kinds of strategic postconflict violence. Licklider's 1995a pioneering book is also within this large-n tradition, although he does not use sophisticated statistical analysis.

2. Edited volumes include Licklider 1995b; Zartman 1995; Forman and Patrick 2000a; Stedman, Rothchild, and Cousens 2002; Call with Wyeth 2008; Chesterman, Ignatieff, and Thakur 2005; Hoddie and Hartzell 2010; and Suhrke and Berdal 2012. Other single-authored works include Hampson 1996; Paris 2004; Spector 2011; and Call 2012. Boyle 2014 uses both qualitative and quantitative methods.

3. Berdal 2012, 312. Emphasis added.

4. Przeworski and Teune 1970, 36.

5. Snyder 2001, 93.

6. Blattman and Miguel 2010, 8.

7. Varshney 2002; Wilkinson 2004; Straus 2006.

8. Kalyvas 2008a. Papers on Indonesian violence using subnational data include Barron, Kaiser, and Pradhan 2004, 2009; and Tajima 2012, who use the village as the unit of analysis; and Tadjoeddin and Murshed 2007; Mancini 2008; Murshed, Tadjoeddin, and Chowdhury 2009; Tadjoeddin, Chowdhury, and Murshed 2011; Østby et al. 2011; and Pierskalla and Sacks 2017, who use the district. See also Tadjoeddin 2014.

9. Peou 2012.

10. Collier, Hoeffler, and Soderbom 2008.

11. Stewart 2011.

12. Kalyvas 2006.

13. Weinstein 2007, 17. This is because civil war datasets typically use overly restrictive death thresholds for ascertaining when a civil war is taking place and because civil war datasets only include cases of extended violence where the central state is an active player. I discuss these issues further below.

14. Parks, Colletta, and Oppenheim 2013. This figure only includes subnational conflicts where the state is one of the fighting parties and not extended intercommunal conflicts where the state does not actively participate.

15. Raleigh and Hegre 2005.

16. Parks, Colletta, and Oppenheim 2013.

17. Ibid.

18. Barron, Arthur, and Bartu 2012.

19. Varshney, Tadjoeddin, and Panggabean 2010, 42. Their data exclude the locations of separatist violence (Aceh and Papua) and do not include episodes of violence between individuals that can have significant cumulative impacts.

20. Berdal, Collante-Celador, and Buzadzic 2012, 75.

21. See, for example, the crime statistics reported in Boyle 2014, 118–122.

22. Raleigh and Hegre 2009.

23. Daly 2012.

24. The two most prominent international databases on political violence, the Armed Conflict Location and Event Dataset (ACLED) and the UCDP/PRIO Georeferenced Events Dataset (UCDP), now geo-code the location of incidents.

25. National factors may have more utility in explaining temporal variation in violence. I argue in the book's penultimate chapter that large-scale extended violence has not recurred anywhere in Indonesia because of changes in national institutions.

26. Extended communal violence usually, although not necessarily, takes the form of conflicts between ethnic or religious groups. This is because, as Horowitz (1985, 2001) along with many others has noted, such ascriptive identities provide a particularly clear basis for mobilization and the determination of insider-outsider status. However, they may also take place between other identity groups, such as those with different political or ideological affiliations (such as class groups). Because of this, I use the signifier extended communal violence rather than collective ethnic or religious violence.

27. Cramer 2006, 72–74.

28. Scacco 2009, 6.

29. Weinstein 2007.

30. Gurr 1986; Varshney 2007.

31. This has stymied theory generation. Kalyvas (2008c), for example, bemoans the fact that constructivist insights from the ethnic violence literature that emphasize the fluidity of identities have not been incorporated into the mainstream theoretical or empirical civil war literature, at least in economics or political science.

32. Blattman and Miguel 2010, 6.

33. Horowitz 2001.

34. Tilly 2003.

35. Isaac 2012.

36. Kalyvas 2004.

37. Kalyvas 2008b.

38. Under Kalyvas's typology, Aceh and East Timor are examples of "asymmetrical non-conventional civil wars," with guerrilla warfare employed by insurgents against the standing Indonesian army. Maluku, North Maluku, West and Central Kalimantan, and Central Sulawesi experienced "symmetrical" wars, where parties were relatively evenly matched in strength and the state was not a warring party.

39. Civil wars are classically defined as intrastate armed conflicts between two parties, one of whom must be the central state, resulting in a thousand or more deaths per annum, where the strongest side experienced at least 5 percent of those deaths. This is the definition employed by the Correlates of War (COW) dataset (Singer and Small 1972, 1994; Sarkees 2000). COW records whether a country experienced civil war for each year. Cases where annual deaths are lower than a thousand, where the state is not a direct party to the conflict, or where deaths are one-sided are not included in the dataset. Other datasets, such as the Uppsala Armed Conflict Dataset (ACD) do not use a single threshold. ACD differentiates between "wars" (where there are more than a thousand battle deaths in a single year—as with COW), "intermediate armed conflicts" (where there are more than twenty-five, but less than a thousand battle deaths per year, and a total conflict history of more than a thousand deaths), and "minor conflicts" (where there are more than twenty-five battle deaths per year but less than a thousand in total). Armed conflicts still need to be between governments and a rebel group. See Erikson and Wallensteen 2004. However, the Uppsala dataset has generally not been used to examine the recurrence of civil war.

Elbadawi, Hegre, and Milante 2008 is a rare exception, coding a civil war as having "restarted" where a given conflict resulted in less than twenty-five deaths in one year and then twenty-five or more in the next year (ibid., 452). This is clearly problematic for a number of reasons, including (a) the fact that these are minor conflicts not civil wars according to dataset rules, and (b) a temporary fall in violence below the threshold of twenty-five deaths is counted as a conflict termination, even though it may just be a reduction in intensity in an ongoing conflict. This second issue probably explains their finding that an "increasing proportion of onsets were recurrences" (ibid., 453). Some other analyses of civil war have employed different thresholds. Fearon and Laitin 2003, for example, require a hundred deaths per year to code a civil war as ongoing. Doyle and Sambanis 2006 add additional criteria that a conflict must fulfill to be counted as a civil war.

40. Barron, Engvall, and Morel 2016.
41. Sambanis 2002.
42. Sambanis 2004, 821.
43. Barron, Engvall, and Morel 2016, 27–29.
44. Sambanis 2004.
45. Suhrke and Berdal 2012; Nordstrom 2004.
46. Boyle 2012.
47. Samset 2012.
48. Rodgers 2003, 2006.
49. Andreas 2004.
50. King, Keohane, and Verba 1994. See also Geddes 2003, chapter 3, who strongly warns against selecting on the dependent variable, showing how numerous studies of democratization have reached inaccurate conclusions because of bias in case selection. King, Keohane, and Verba's arguments build on Mill's (1872) method of difference. Van Evera 1997 and Brady and Collier 2004 provide critical discussions.
51. Factors (a), (b), and (c) may still contribute toward causing X, but they cannot alone cause X.
52. Coser 1956.
53. Galtung 1969. Structural violence occurs where a society is characterized by underlying conditions of dominance and exploitation, meaning that "positive peace," where such inequality is addressed, cannot take hold. Structural violence, however, is only indirectly physically violent. It may be a cause of physical violence but it does not necessarily lead to physical destruction. Extending the use of the term *violence* to include structural violence prevents us from assessing why in some cases such underlying conditions lead to physical violence while in others they do not.
54. Suhrke 2012, 6.
55. Kalyvas (2006) has shown that much of the violence within civil wars is often episodic, with violence taking place between neighbors driven by motivations that may be divorced from those of the broader parties organizing violence. However, such violence occurs within the context of war, making it fundamentally different from the episodic violence that occurs during times of "peace" or postconflict periods.
56. Across the world, development has been driven by the use of violence; states have been forged in large part through war, often between states (Tilly 1975, 1992; Acemoglu and Robinson 2006; Fukuyama 2011) and sometimes within countries (Slater 2010a), and development and violence have tended to go hand in hand (Bates 2001).
57. Collier and Hoeffler 2004.
58. Muggah 2009a, 228.
59. World Bank 2011a, 54.
60. Horowitz 1985; Sambanis 2001.
61. Tilly 2003.

62. These cutoff points were defined after I conducted initial fieldwork. In that fieldwork, I looked at a number of cases with different physical impacts (in terms of deaths, injuries, and properties damaged) and tried to establish whether there were patterns in levels of organization across cases with different levels of impact. I then asked a range of informants about which cases they perceived to have been "large" and which were smaller. Clearly this was a rather subjective exercise. As with attempts to measure civil war, there is no first principles basis that leads us to use any particular cutoff point for determining whether an incident is large or small. I ran analyses with slightly different parameters, including two or four deaths rather than three, but findings on spatial variation did not significantly change.

63. Mahoney and Goertz 2006.

64. Kalyvas 2008a, 402.

65. As Elster (1989, 3–4) puts it: "To explain an event is to give an account of why it happened. Usually . . . this takes the form of citing an earlier event as the cause of the event we want to explain . . . [But] to cite the cause is not enough: the causal mechanism must be provided, or at least suggested." On the utility of approaches to social science that focus on causal mechanisms rather than causal effects, see also Hedstrom and Swedberg 1996; and Elster 2007, in particular chapter 2.

66. Tilly (1997a, 48) argues that theoretical propositions should not be based on "large-N statistical analysis" but on "relevant, verifiable causal stories resting in differing chains of cause-effect relations whose efficacy can be demonstrated independently of those stories."

67. King 2004; Kalyvas 2003, 2007; Petersen 2002.

68. Such a philosophy of social science leads to a degree of methodological individualism in that it sees individual actors rather than structures per se as being the "causal agents"; explanations and theories are built on the "causes and consequences of their actions" (Hedstrom and Swedberg 1998, 10). This approach provides a means to identify how macro factors or structures drive microlevel behavior and how this in turn shapes the macro environment (Hedstrom and Udehn 2009, 32–37; Gambetta 1998).

69. Tilly 1995.

70. The appendix provides details on why a new dataset of violence in Indonesia was needed and how the NVMS was put together. The dataset is introduced in Barron, Jaffrey, and Varshney 2016.

71. The version of the dataset used in this book has forty-four times as many incidents as are included in the UNSFIR-2 dataset, which has a similar time span. The ACLED dataset is probably the largest violence dataset containing events data at the subnational level for multiple countries (see Raleigh et al. 2010). It records 57,000 violent incidents between 1997 and 2012, less than 40 percent of those in the NVMS, but this is for fifty countries. Indonesia is not covered by ACLED. The number of incidents in ACLED for individual countries is often small. In Cambodia, for example, the dataset contains 357 incidents between 1997 and 2010. The Colombia dataset used by Daly (2016) includes 29,000 violent events. Weinstein's newspaper events dataset contains 1,400 violent incidents in Mozambique (1976–2004), 800 in Uganda, and more than 4,000 in Peru (Weinstein 2007, 368). The NVMS has subsequently been expanded to cover all of Indonesia. The latest version includes 237,885 incidents between 1998 and March 2015.

72. I chose the district as the unit of analysis because variance in violence is most marked at that level and because the district is so politically and economically important in postdecentralization Indonesia. The province is the highest level of subnational government in Indonesia. As of 2010, there were thirty-three provinces in the country. Urban and rural districts (*kotamadya* and *kabupaten*) are the next tier of government. There are around four hundred districts in Indonesia, with populations typically ranging from 100,000 to 600,000 people.

73. Bates et al. 1998, 10, note that such an approach "combines analytic tools that are commonly employed in economics and political science with the narrative form which is more commonly employed in history." As such, the approach is a manifestation of the "historical turn in the social sciences" (McDonald 1996) and is a response to Stone's (1979) call to return to the narrative tradition. My approach shares many similarities to that of Bates and his colleagues (for example, by generating historical accounts, using process tracing, focusing on the incentives of different actors, and employing microlevel reasoning), but there are also some differences (such as my use of field research rather than archival methods, attention to case selection, and the use of structured comparative analysis).

74. Geertz 1973.

75. Fenno 1990.

CHAPTER 2. EXPLAINING POSTCONFLICT VIOLENCE

1. Fearon (1995, 409), in his influential discussion of rationalist explanations for interstate wars writes, "Under broad conditions the fact that fighting is costly and risky implies that there should exist negotiated agreements that rationally led states in dispute would prefer to war." The central puzzle, he adds, is to "explain adequately what prevents leaders from reaching *ex ante* (prewar) bargains that would avoid the costs and risks of fighting" (ibid., 380). This puzzle, as Walter (2009a) has shown, is also salient to understanding why civil wars occur, why they last so long, and why they sometimes recur.

2. A third factor is issue indivisibility where some things cannot be compromised over. Toft (2003), for example, argues that wars over territory that is seen as indivisible because of its importance to the identity of an ethnic group are harder to solve and more likely to recur. Powell (2006) argues that issue indivisibility is actually a form of the commitment problem.

3. Mason, Weingarton, and Fett 1999; Smith and Stam 2004.

4. See, for example, Mason and Fett 1996; Hartzell, Hoddie, and Rothchild 2001; Walter 2004; and Fortna 2008. There are other observationally equivalent mechanisms, such as conflict fatigue and trauma, by which longer extended violence could result in more robust postconflict peace.

5. Posen 1993.

6. Fearon 2004; Walter 2002. Hartzell, Hoddie, and Rothchild (2001) find that, along with the provision of territorial autonomy, the presence of "third party enforcers" is the most important factor in explaining why negotiated agreements stick. Others have highlighted the importance of third-party guarantees, including the presence of peacekeepers (Fortna 2008), security guarantees from foreign nations (Collier 2008), well-equipped United Nations missions (Doyle and Sambanis 2006), and constitutional checks and balances (Walter 2010).

7. Victors can take full control of the coercive arms of the state, limiting the ability of losers to use violence. This means a victor can credibly commit not to use force excessively because such a commitment does not make him vulnerable to renewed attack. In contrast, negotiated settlements may be more prone to breakdown. Postconflict power-sharing arrangements are likely to be required as no party has a full monopoly on the means of violence. This may make future challenges more likely (Wagner 1994). Indeed, the cross-country evidence shows that peace that results from civil wars that end in military victory is more secure than that following a negotiated agreement. Licklider (1995b) observes that whereas 15 percent of the former see a renewal of war, the figure is 50 percent for those finished by negotiations; Fortna (2008) and Toft (2010) reach similar conclusions.

8. Daly (2016) discusses these issues in the context of postconflict areas of Colombia.

9. For example, Berdal and Malone 2000.

10. Kaldor 1999; Berkeley 2001; and Mueller 2004, for example, argue that civil war violence is now often fueled by criminal motives and actions.

11. Keen 1998, 43.

12. Wilkinson 2004, 1.

13. Brass 1997, 2003.

14. Gagnon (1994, 134), for example, in his analysis of violence in Serbia, concludes that "violent conflict along ethnic cleavages is provoked by elites to create a domestic political context where ethnicity is the only politically relevant identity."

15. Staniland 2012, 243. He identifies six wartime orders involving differing degrees of state-insurgent cooperation and distribution of control. In four of these, there is some degree of collaboration between sides. "Bargains, deals and tacit understandings between states and insurgents," he emphasizes, "are common in civil war."

16. Andreas 2008, 8.

17. Ibid., 42.

18. Kalyvas 2003, 2008c; Bates 2008a, 9–10.

19. This is because ascriptive identities, solidified through past violence, may provide an easier channel for elites to mobilize others for violence than do other identities (e.g., Kaufman 2001). The evidence is mixed on whether extended ethnic violent conflicts recur more often than other extended conflicts. Doyle and Sambanis (2006) argue this is the case, whereas Hartzell, Hoddie and Rothchild (2001) and Walter (2004) find no relationship between what is at stake in the conflict and rates of recidivism. Licklider (1995b) argues that negotiated settlements for identity conflicts are less stable.

20. Varshney 2002.

21. Bräuchler 2015, 11.

22. For example, Gurr 1970.

23. Cederman, Weidmann, and Gleditsch 2011.

24. Stewart 2008.

25. Colson 2000; Clark and Kaufman 2008.

26. OECD DAC 2010.

27. Horowitz 1985, 140.

28. Varshney and Gubler 2012, 198.

29. Wolf (1964, 1999), for example, has argued that cultures are in part derivative of the power relations that prevail within a society. Brass (1991) extends the point to show how these cultures are then used as resources to be mobilized for the acquisition of further political power, economic benefit, or social status.

30. Brass 2003; and Tambiah 1996.

31. Scacco 2009, 5.

32. Petersen 2002, 5.

33. Olson 1965.

34. Popkin 1979; Gates 2002; Weinstein 2005.

35. Wood (2003, 2) in her study of Salvadorian rebels, argues that their participation in violence came from a "pleasure in agency," where the very assertion of interests and identity through violence created individual-level utility.

36. Tambiah 1996.

37. Petersen 2002, 19.

38. Ibid., 20.

39. Daly (2016) argues that whether groups recruited locally or not determines the extent to which they maintain their networks postwar and that this shapes the strategic interactions they have with other armed groups and hence the likelihood of them remilitarizing.

40. Boyle (2014) emphasizes two pathways by which armed groups may use violence again. The second indirect pathway is a result of the factionalization of armed groups.

41. For example, much of the postconflict violence in Central American countries involves different actors to those from the conflict period.

42. Tilly 2003, 35–41.

43. Hobbes [1651] 2008; Weber 1946. Premodern societies have means of retaining order in the absence of a state (e.g. Bates 2001; Fukuyama 2011), and these can be effective in limiting violence (Taylor 1982). However, in almost every postconflict area, and certainly those in Indonesia, the state pervades most areas of life and hence order will likely be contingent on it.

44. A partial list of recent volumes on internationally supported state building includes Milliken 2003; Rotberg 2003; Chesterman 2004; Fukuyama 2004; Caplan 2005; Chesterman, Ignatieff, and Thakur 2005; Chandler 2006; Call with Wyeth 2008; Ghani and Lockhart 2008; Belloni 2008; Paris and Sisk 2009; Newman, Paris, and Richmond 2009; and Berdal and Zaum 2012.

45. Besley and Persson 2011, xi.

46. World Bank 2011a. Another study found that in 60 percent of the country years in which there were failed states in Africa between 1970 and 1995, there were also civil wars (Ndulu et al. 2007, cited in Bates 2008b, 3).

47. Collier, Hoeffler, and Rohner (2009) argue that the feasibility of rebellion is more important than the motivations of groups to rebel.

48. Jutersonke, Muggah, and Rodgers 2009.

49. The distinction here fits with that of Bates (2008b, 2) who defines state failure as having two constituent elements: (a) loss of monopoly on the means of coercion; and (b) the transformation of a state into an instrument for predation.

50. This is consistent with other work that finds strong correlations between income and the outbreak of civil war. See Sambanis and Hegre's 2006 review.

51. Woodward 2002.

52. Case studies of postconflict violence in Kosovo, Lebanon, and Guatemala are provided in Suhrke and Berdal 2012. On violence in postconflict areas of the Philippines, see Jubair 2007; and McKenna 2008. On recent violence in Northern Ireland, see Walsh 2013.

53. On hybrid regimes and civil war, see Gates et al. 2006; and Goldstone et al. 2010; on links with social violence and crime, see LaFree and Tseloni 2006; and Fox and Hoelscher 2012.

54. Paris (2004), following Snyder (2000), emphasizes how the transition to democracy can be dangerous in postconflict areas and argues that institution building should come before democratization or market expansion.

55. Collier, Hoeffler, and Soderbom's cross-country analysis (2008, 470) finds that the net effect of an election is to increase the risk of war resumption. See also Caplan 2005, 120–121, who argues that "elections have been used as an exit strategy [for internationals] . . . elections have thus sometime been arranged too soon from the standpoint of a fragile place to withstand the competitive pressures of the electoral process.

56. Jaffrey and Slater 2017.

57. Saideman et al. 2002. Collier, Hoeffler, and Soderbom (2008, 471) find that the risk of war resumption drops from 46.2 percent (without autonomy) to 12.2 percent (with autonomy), although the small sample sizes mean that results are not statistically significant.

58. Barron and Clark (2006). Brancati (2009) argues that the impacts of decentralization on the likelihood of postconflict violence are mixed, dependent on part on whether decentralization leads to the formation of regional parties (which can lead to more violence) or not (where it can bolster peace). Yet in areas where extended violence took the form of communal violence rather than conflict against the central state, it is unclear why regional parties should matter.

59. Call 2012.

60. The Asia Foundation 2016.

61. Lijphart 1968, 1977.

62. Ignatieff 2017, 95–96.

63. Horowitz 1985; Sisk 1996.

64. Jarstad 2008.

65. For example, Bueno de Mesquita et al. 2003; Bates, Grieff, and Singh 2002.

66. North, Wallis, and Weingast 2009, 17.

67. Ibid., 18.

68. Tambiah 1996, 214.

69. See, for example, Brass 2003; Tambiah 1996; Horowitz 2001; Kakar 1996; and Berenschot 2011.

70. Wilkinson 2004, 5.

71. Wilson 2011.

72. Central states in most countries will tolerate a certain level of episodic violence that is not challenging to national elites' status or wealth or to the ability of the state to collect tax revenues. Slater (2010a) argues that when such violence is concentrated in remote, less urbanized regions, developing effective responses is unlikely to be a priority for central state elites.

73. This hypothesis only applies to states with a reasonable level of capacity. As such, the theory is likely to have more applicability to at least moderately strong states than to weak or failing states.

74. Petersen 2002.

75. Chandra 2007, 86.

76. Joseph 1987.

77. North, Wallis, and Weingast 2009, 2.

78. Forman and Patrick 2000b, 1.

79. Muggah 2009b, 7. On the functions of such "DDR" programs, see UNDDR 2006 and Swedish Ministry of Foreign Affairs 2006.

80. Stedman 1997.

81. Reno 2008; Zaum and Cheng 2011.

82. Bermeo 1992, 277.

83. Ibid., 281.

84. Pinker 2011.

85. As I show in subsequent chapters, the fact that there is variation in the support of local elites for violence across areas with the same electoral framework demonstrates that these formal rules of the game alone do not determine such support.

86. See Mahoney 2000; Pierson 2000; and Thelen 2003 on path dependence.

87. Axelrod 1986, 1097.

88. On tipping points and norms, see Schelling 1960.

89. Varshney 2003.

CHAPTER 3. VIOLENCE AND INDONESIA'S DEMOCRATIC TRANSITION

1. Cribb 1990; Robinson 1995; Heryanto 2006.

2. See, in particular, the articles in Anderson 2001; and Colombijn and Lindblad 2002.

3. Bourchier 1990; Barker 2001; Siegel 1998.

4. Sidel 2006.

5. Data are for Central Kalimantan, West Kalimantan, Maluku, North Maluku, Aceh, Central Sulawesi, NTT, Papua, and West Papua (from NVMS); and Banten, Jakarta, West Java, East Java, Central Java, Riau, West Nusa Tenggara, and South Sulawesi (from the UNSFIR-2 dataset, discussed in appendix A). This figure does not include deaths from

East Timor. The figure is an underestimate as UNSFIR-2 does not record most smaller incidents of violence.

6. On violence during authoritarian breakdowns, see Mansfield and Snyder 1995; Snyder 2000; Hegre et al. 2001; and Huntingdon 1991. For violence during economic changes, see Chua 2003; Paris 2004; and Cramer 2006. Uvin 1998 provides a tragic case study of these processes in Rwanda.

7. Chapter 7 provides a discussion.

8. CAVR 2005a.

9. Papua is sometimes also thought of as experiencing civil war. However, separatist violence there has tended to be episodic rather than enduring. Impacts—in terms of deaths, injuries, and damaged buildings—have also been much lower than for any of the extended violent conflicts.

10. Useful studies include Acciaioli 2001; Aragon 2001; McRae 2013; and Tajima 2014 on Central Sulawesi; Peluso and Harwell 2001; and Davidson 2008 on West Kalimantan; and Klinken 2000; and Smith 2005 on Central Kalimantan. References on Maluku and North Maluku are provided in chapters 4 and 5. Klinken (2007) covers all five extended communal violent conflicts. Sidel 2006 analyzes Maluku, North Maluku, and Central Sulawesi, as well as riots and terror attacks elsewhere. Bertrand 2004 includes analysis of Maluku, North Maluku, West Kalimantan, and Central Kalimantan. Anwar et al. 2005; Kingsbury 2005a; and Coppel 2006 gather articles on the extended violent conflicts.

11. ICG 2001c.

12. Purdey 2006.

13. Data from UNSFIR-2.

14. Panggabean and Smith 2010.

15. Welsh 2008. Data are for West Java, Bali, Bengkulu, and South Kalimantan. Welsh chose these provinces because they were thought of as less violent than other Indonesian provinces. Other work on lynching concludes that it was widespread in the early transition period, in particular on Java, but finds victim numbers lower than Welsh's estimates. See, for example, Barron and Sharpe 2005.

16. See, for example, Barron and Madden 2004; and Tajima 2004, 2008, on routine violence in Lampung Province; Barron and Sharpe 2008 on East Java; Vel 2001 on Sumba, East Nusa Tenggara; and Herriman 2007; and Siegel 2006 on "witchdoctor" killings in East Java.

17. Data are for the provinces mentioned in note 5 of this chapter, with the exception of Riau, which is not included because we do not have recent data. Data from the year 2004 are missing for the four provinces on Java, South Sulawesi, and West Nusa Tenggara. Smaller-scale episodic violence is likely underreported for the earlier years given that we rely on UNSFIR-2 for some provinces for the pre-2005 period.

18. The Habibie Center 2012, 2013.

19. It was also necessary to define the starting point for the extended violence period for each province. A similar approach was used. Accounts of each extended violent conflict generally identify a triggering incident (or incidents) that led to violence escalation. The date of the trigger was used as the beginning of the extended violence period if (a) there appeared to be a direct link between the incident and the larger violence that came after; and (b) NVMS data showed an upsurge in violence following the trigger.

20. The end dates are a function of when I have data until and, conceptually, do not indicate any change in patterns of conflict or violence for a given province.

21. West Kalimantan's population was 4,178,498 in 2008. Only Aceh has a larger population.

22. The share is highest in Aceh, where 35 percent of deaths from small episodic violence were the result of violent crimes.

23. I do not present the number of incidents of small-scale violence because this measure is vulnerable to differences in reporting coverage within provinces. The newspaper assessments, conducted as part of the NVMS database construction, found that in some areas fewer incidents of violence make it into local newspapers because there are fewer local journalists (e.g., in very remote areas) or because there is a lack of space in the papers (this particularly affects more urbanized areas where there are more stories to report). However, the assessment also found that even in areas where some violent incidents do not get reported in papers, the vast majority of incidents that resulted in a death do make it. As such, deaths are a better indicator of levels of small-scale episodic violence than is the number of incidents. In contrast, large incidents with large impacts always get reported. As such, we can use the number of incidents as an indicator of levels of large episodic violence.

24. Large episodic violence in postconflict Maluku injured 1,148 people, almost triple that in any of the other postconflict provinces. These incidents also damaged over 1,500 buildings in Maluku.

25. I use 2008 administrative boundaries for the district-level breakdowns throughout the book. In Central Kalimantan, which had fourteen districts in 2008, 857 deaths (or 83 percent of the provincial total during the extended violence) occurred in just one district: East Kotawaringan. No other district experienced more than 82 deaths (Kapuas) although there were 584 damaged properties in that district and 119 in Palangkaraya District. In the 1997 extended violence in West Kalimantan, deaths were concentrated in Landak District, which saw 449 of the 669 deaths (67 percent of all provincial deaths). Two other districts (Pontianak and Sanggau) saw more than 50 deaths. The 1999 violence was more concentrated, with 381 of 434 deaths (89 percent) occurring in Sambas District. In Central Sulawesi, 438 deaths (85 percent) were in Poso District. Other districts saw relatively large numbers of buildings damaged (459 in Tojo Una-Una and 354 in Palu, although this is much smaller than the 4,930 damaged buildings in Poso) but deaths in these districts were relatively low: three and 17, respectively.

26. The impacts of violence in Maluku Province were spread out with five districts (out of eleven) seeing more than 200 deaths. However, almost three-quarters of all deaths occurred in Ambon and Central Maluku districts. Likewise, the extended violence in North Maluku spread across the province with four districts (out of eight) experiencing more than 200 deaths. Many other districts, while seeing fewer deaths, also saw significant impacts. Almost 1,000 properties were damaged, for example, in each of Morotai and Ternate districts. Yet, again, the largest share of violence was concentrated in a limited area. North Halmahera district saw 2,016 deaths, the highest of any district in Indonesia. Aceh's civil war also affected almost every corner of the province: sixteen of twenty-three districts experienced more than 200 deaths during the extended violence. However, a more limited number of districts saw extremely high impacts: six districts saw more than 500 deaths, and three more than 1,000 deaths.

27. The relevant laws are the Law on Regional Government (22/1999) and the Law on Fiscal Balance between the Central Government and the Regions (25/1999). The former was revised by a new Law on Regional Government (32/2004), which strengthened the powers of central and provincial governments. Crouch 2010, chapter 4, provides a useful discussion. See also Erb and Sulistiyanto 2009. Aceh and Papua provinces are exceptions. In both, special autonomy agreements have meant that more powers and resources are held at the provincial level.

28. Hoffman and Kaiser 2002; World Bank 2003.

29. E-mail correspondence with World Bank expert on public finance, May 2012.

30. Shah, Qibthiyyah, and Dita 2012.

31. In 2005, Ambon was 51 percent Protestant, 45 percent Muslim, and 4 percent Catholic. Central Maluku was 56 percent Muslim, 43 percent Protestant, and 1 percent Catholic (BPS Maluku 2005).

32. Ternate is slightly smaller than Ambon with a population of 162,247. Both districts have a similar level of urbanization: 84.9 percent (Ternate) and 87.3 percent (Ambon). One important difference is that Ternate is now predominantly Muslim (96 percent) while Ambon is religiously balanced (BPS Maluku Utara 2005; BPS Ambon 2000).

CHAPTER 4. LARGE EPISODIC VIOLENCE IN POSTCONFLICT MALUKU

1. In annual per capita terms, there have still been 2.5 times as many large postconflict violent incidents in Maluku as in Central Sulawesi.

2. ICG 2000; Klinken 2001, 2007; Crouch 2010; and Al Qurtuby 2016 provide background and chronological details.

3. Crouch 2010, 245, cites Sinansari Ecip 1999, 69–70, in noting that in the late 1990s, twenty-five of twenty-nine senior posts in the city bureaucracy were held by Christians.

4. Hefner 2000.

5. Bertrand 2002.

6. "Nonindigenous" inhabitants—those born outside Maluku—increased from 5.2 percent in 1971 to 14.1 percent in 1995. Most incomers were Muslims, primarily from Sulawesi, and this altered the province's religious composition. The Muslim population in Maluku increased from 49.9 percent in 1971 to 54.8 percent in 1985 (Trijono 2001, 14–15). By 1990, this figure had reached 58.6 percent (Klinken 2001, 12). In Ambon city, Protestants were a slight majority in 1998 making up 53.6 percent of the population compared with 41.0 percent Muslims, 5.3 percent Catholics, and 0.2 percent others (BPS Ambon 2000, 127). In 2008, Protestants constituted 50.3 percent of the local population, Muslims 43.0 percent, Catholics 6.3 percent, and others 0.4 percent (BPS Maluku 2010, 185).

7. Klinken 2007, 90.

8. Bertrand 2004.

9. Crouch 2010, 91.

10. Husain 2007, 161.

11. Spyer 2002, 25.

12. On Laskar Jihad, see Hasan 2006. The groups under the Laskar Mujahidin umbrella included KOMPAK, Jama'ah Islamaiyah (JI), Brigade Hizbullah, and the Islamic Defenders Front (FPI). See Azca 2011; and ICG 2005c.

13. Interviews with Muslims and Christians in Ambon, December 2010.

14. Laskar Kristus (or the Christian Warriors), which had particularly strong links with the Church, was led by Agus Wattimena who was mysteriously killed on 20 March 2001. Schulze (2002, 63) describes him as having controlled a Christian self-defense militia, which incorporated twenty-five small groups totaling one hundred to two hundred members in Ambon city as well as groups on other islands. His funeral was attended by the chief police and military officers in the province (Bohm 2005, 152).

15. Adam 2010.

16. Adam 2009.

17. Sidel 2008, 47.

18. Azca 2006.

19. Crouch 2010, 256.

20. Azca 2004.

21. Crouch 2010, 255.

22. Aditjondro 2001.

23. In 2008, Ambon and Central Maluku accounted for 47 percent of the province's population (BPS Maluku 2010).

24. Crouch 2010, 263.

25. ICG 2005c.

26. The RMS was formed by Protestant Ambonese who had worked for the colonial Dutch government and, particularly, the colonial military. This group had lived a relatively privileged existence vis-à-vis the local Muslim population. When the Japanese occupied Ambon they began to promote Muslims and those from the nascent Indonesian national-ist movement. In response, there were attempts to establish a state independent from the new Indonesia, initially for eastern Indonesia, then for southern Maluku. The establish-ment of a Republic of South Moluccas was declared on 25 April 1950, but the RMS was defeated by the Indonesian military in November of that year. Sporadic fighting continued to occur on Seram Island, now in Central Maluku district, until 1962, but in 1963 around twelve thousand Moluccan soldiers left Indonesia to resettle in the Netherlands where a government-in-exile was formed. Support for an independent Maluku diminished rapidly in Ambon and surrounding islands. Chauvel (1990) provides a history of the movement.

27. The unfurling of a RMS flag in front of the Indonesian president during a visit to Maluku in 2007 resulted in a police clampdown. There have been accusations that the police in Maluku have routinely tortured FKM/RMS activists. In September 2010, a Moluccan separatist, Yusuf Sipakoly, who had been arrested in 2007 after the flag incident, died in custody from injuries that his family claim were sustained during torture (The Age 2010).

28. These and the other Malino clauses were rather vague with parties committing to end all conflicts and disputes (clause 1), abide by the process of law enforcement (2), reject separatist movements (3), respect local culture (4), ban illegal organizations (5), establish an investigation team (6), allow for the displaced to return home (7), reequip the security forces (9), and uphold good relationships (10).

29. Christian Malino delegate, Ambon, 11 December 2010.

30. Klinken 2007, 89.

31. Interviews, elites and villagers in Central Maluku, December 2010.

32. Bohm (2005, 216–217) provides a translation of an article by the central board of Laskar Jihad in their bulletin (original version no longer accessible). It is worth quoting a short section: "It is too early to talk about reconciliation whilst one community is still traumatized with this expression. Those delegates that convened [in Malino] are not suf-ficiently representative to talk in the name of the people. This reconciliation even turns upside down the Muslim ranks. One by one, those who used to be public figures have been trapped associating with the Christians and now have become people that are good for nothing. Trash. The Muslims also experience filthiness from inside. Day by day those who should lead the community are renouncing their duties. Therefore, be not appalled if the Muslims grow in determination to reject any compromise, let alone reconciliation." On 24 April, Laskar Jihad's leader, Ja'far Umar Thalib, arrived in Ambon and made a speech on the Muslim SPMM radio station urging Muslims to make war on Christians. In a speech at a public religious meeting (*tabligh akbar*) on 26 April, Ja'far again told his audience to wage war on Christians and denounced the Malino agreement as "treason" (ibid., 237).

33. These included Ustadz Mohammad Attamimi, a lecturer at the Ambon Islamic College in Maluku (STAIN), Djamu Tuani (the local secretary of the Indonesia Ulama Council, MUI), Luqman Ba'abduh (of Laskar Jihad), and retired brigadier general Rustam Kastor.

34. See Crouch 2010, 260–261; Bohm 2005, 221. This continued when Yudhoyono and Kalla subsequently became president and vice president in 2004.

35. Jakarta, 2 December 2010.

36. Central Maluku, 12 December 2010.

37. Crouch 2010, 267.

38. ICG 2005c.

39. Muslim delegate to Malino, Central Maluku, 12 December 2010.

40. Husni Putuhena continued his career in the provincial religious affairs ministry under Attamimi and became a close ally of the West Seram district head. Azis Fidmatan, another member of the team and an ex-official in the provincial ministry of trade, became the subdistrict head of the Kur Islands in Southeast Maluku. Phone discussions with Muslim activist and a journalist, August 2012.

41. Ambon, 13 July 2011.

42. Smith 2009, 158.

43. Crouch 2010, 267.

44. Both were signatories to the Malino peace agreement as representatives of the so-called *akar rumput* (grassroots, a synonym for Christian criminal preman or militia groups).

45. Interviews in Ambon and Central Maluku, July 2011.

46. Muslim delegate to Malino, Jakarta, 2 December 2010.

47. See Klinken and Aspinall 2011 on opportunities for corruption in Indonesia's construction sector.

48. Some informants in Maluku reported a higher figure of Rp. 4.2 trillion (US$420 million). However, it appears that Rp. 2.2 trillion was disbursed from Jakarta (World Bank 2010). Inpres funds were Rp. 663 billion (2005), Rp. 741 billion (2006), and Rp. 817 billion (2007). Each year, the Maluku local government proposed more than 1 trillion rupiah in assistance (hence perhaps the higher estimates) but not all proposed projects were funded.

49. Inpres funds constituted a smaller share of provincial funds in 2006 and 2007, in large part because national-level reductions in fuel subsidies led to large increases in subnational transfers. However, Inpres funds were still substantial. Figures are from the World Bank's (2010) public expenditure analysis for Maluku. Inpres funds are not counted in reports of subnational expenditures, because they are central government funds executed through line ministries.

50. Anticorruption activist, Ambon, 19 December 2010; Muslim delegate to Malino, Central Maluku, 12 December 2010.

51. Interviews in Central Maluku, December 2010.

52. Interviews in Ambon and Central Maluku, December 2010.

53. Ambon, 19 July 2011.

54. Ibid.

55. Parliamentarians, Central Maluku, 14 July 2011; interview, local NGO worker, Ambon, 21 July 2011.

56. Sulaiman Latupono, Ambon, 10 July 2011. APKLI were allegedly involved in the 2006 clash between street sellers that led to the damage of more than two hundred buildings. FPMB may also have played a role in the 2004 RMS unrest. On the eve of the outbreak of violence, Latupono, along with the head of PRM (Youth Reform Movement for Maluku), Muhammad Saleh B. Nurlete, announced the establishment of a "militia to rescue the nation," which would use physical power to combat RMS and FKM (Bohm 2005, 334).

57. He was appointed a member of the Ambon parliament for the 2007–9 period, replacing Franky Hewat (of the Islamic PBB Party) who had passed away. Latupono then joined the Gerindra Party, which is led by the retired army general, Prabowo Subianto, and was appointed deputy chairman of Gerindra Maluku. Muslim youth leader, Ambon, 10 July 2011.

58. Ambon, 13 July 2011.

59. Interviews with Ambon police chief (Ambon, 11 July 2011) and Maluku police chief (Ambon, 12 July 2011).

60. See chapter 7.

61. The two battalions are Yonif 133 Yudha Bhakti and Armed Bukit Barisan. In total, around nine thousand military personnel, including civilians, are stationed in Maluku province. Interviews with the military in Ambon, July 2011.

62. BKO military also allegedly extort traders bringing fish from Seram Island to Ambon. Interviews with a range of informants in Ambon and Central Maluku, December 2010 and July 2011.

63. Interviews with journalists, activists, and community members, Ambon, 11 July 2011.

64. Ambon, 13 July 2011.

65. Jacky Manuputty, Ambon, July 2011.

66. Human rights activist, Ambon, 11 July 2011.

67. Journalist and peace-building activist, Ambon, 10 July 2011.

68. Interviews in Ambon, December 2010 and July 2011, including with the National Commission for Human Rights.

69. Interviews with senior police by Najib Azca in August 2002.

70. Aspinall 2011a, 291.

71. Tomsa 2009a, 2009b.

72. Data are until the end of 2012. District elections account for 71 incidents, four deaths, 73 injuries, and 33 of the damaged buildings. Ten such incidents occurred in 2008 (4 injured, 13 buildings damaged), 14 in 2009 (1 dead, 10 injuries, 1 building), and 17 in 2010 (36 injuries, 15 buildings). Provincial-level contests resulted in 5 incidents, injuring 6 people and damaging 2 buildings. Three of these incidents related to the reelection of Governor Ralahalu in July 2008.

73. Of the sixteen provinces in the NVMS dataset, eight show a higher number of violent incidents related to national, provincial, or district elections from 2002 until the end of 2011. These include other provinces that experienced extended violence: Aceh, for example, saw 159 incidents of electoral violence which resulted in 11 deaths; North Maluku and Central Sulawesi saw 103 and 85 incidents, respectively. Other provinces not affected by extended violence also recorded higher levels of electoral violence than did Maluku. South Sulawesi and North Sumatra, for example, had 104 and 90 incidents, respectively. Papua saw the greatest number of deaths from electoral violence with 28 killed.

74. This dynamic has been observed elsewhere in Indonesia. See Tomsa 2015.

75. Christian Malino delegate, Ambon, 9 December 2010.

76. Lijphart 1977.

77. Information is primarily from interviews in Ambon, December 2010 and July 2011.

78. Article 11 reads: "To support the rehabilitation of Pattimura University for common progress, as such, the recruitment system and other policies will be transparently implemented based on the principle of fairness while upholding the necessary standard."

79. In fact, data released by the Unpatti rector showed that Muslims made up 528 of 1,804 (or around 29 percent) of those admitted. This is still a far smaller proportion than the 1,196 Protestants admitted (66 percent). However, Muslims who did apply were more likely than Protestants to be admitted; 48 percent of Muslim applicants were admitted compared to 41 percent of Protestants and 38 percent of Catholics.

80. Interviews in Ambon and Central Maluku, December 2010 and July 2011.

81. Yayasan Abu Bakar Ash-Shiddiq, a foundation established by an ex-Laskar Jihad member who remained in Maluku, has close links to many political players in the province. Its present chairman, Abdul Wahab Lumaelan, is active in other Muslim organizations in the province, chairing the Coordinating Body of Youth Activists of the Mosque (BKPRM) and acting as provincial secretary of the Coordinating Forum of Muslim Society (FSUI). Another leading figure in the foundation is Nasir Kilkoda, a senior official

of the state Coordinating Body for Local Investment (BKPMD). Two businessmen, Haji Nurdin Fata and Pak Erwin, are also involved in its leadership, reflecting the wide network that has been developed by ex–Laskar Jihad members in the province. Interviews in Maluku, July 2011.

82. Interviews in Ambon and Central Maluku, December 2010.

83. The choice of PKS was an interesting one given that the party is known as having a nonviolent platform and was not seen as legitimate among most jihadi activists. In an interview with Najib Azca in prison in 2008, a jihadi activist called PKS the most dangerous enemy of Islam because it mixes Islamic identity with an acceptance of the democratic system and an "accommodating" character. He said that PKS actually stood for "partai kafir sejati" (the true infidel party).

84. Tunny 2006.

85. Muslim driver, Ambon, 11 December 2010.

86. Some of the militia from the extended violence period have disappeared. Coker, as an organization, has not been active since the arrest of Berty and his lieutenants in mid- to late 2002. Many of those who were not jailed moved to Jakarta. Agas, a militia group made up of Christian child soldiers, also no longer exists. Agas was an ad hoc militia group that was established in the midst of communal war, and it declined once violence waned after several of its leaders were killed and others left Maluku. Some members joined Coker after Malino while many others drifted away.

87. Bartels 1977.

88. Space does not allow for an extensive discussion of the role of traditional institutions and adat. Bräuchler 2005, chapters 4 and 5, provides a useful discussion.

89. On these processes across Indonesia, see Davidson and Henley 2007. Adam 2008 discusses the revitalization of adat in Maluku. On land conflicts resulting from incompatibilities between adat and national law, see Clark 2004.

90. These cases have been particularly prominent in rural areas of Ambon Island and Seram Island, both in Central Maluku. Across Maluku, and including both large and small incidents of violence, there have been 194 land conflicts in the postconflict period (until the end of 2012), leading to 50 deaths, 388 injuries, and 394 damaged buildings.

91. IDMC 2011.

92. This includes fights over loss of face (the majority of incidents), violent responses to issues such as accidents, theft, sexual indiscretion, and responses to a range of other moral issues. Central Maluku district saw 36 such incidents leading to 11 deaths, 87 injuries, and 141 damaged buildings in the same period.

93. Brown, Wilson, and Hadi 2005, 56–60; Indonesian Institute of Sciences et al. 2011.

94. Bräuchler 2015, 120. Bräuchler provides an extensive and useful discussion of the reconciliation initiatives and the ways in which many of them built on traditional practices. She argues that any sustainable reconciliation must be built on the resources of traditional practices but also notes the immense challenges of doing so.

95. Ambon, 19 December 2010.

96. For more details on the functioning of these organizations, see Barron, Azca, and Susdinarjanti (2012, 87–90). See also Tomsa (2009b) who discusses how Majelis Latupati was used by the incumbent governor, Ralahalu, to spread patronage to bolster his reelection chances in 2008.

97. The proportion of damaged buildings is lower because of one incident in August 2006, a riot involving street sellers that led to the damage of 200 buildings, and because of 324 buildings damaged in five incidents in 2012.

98. Delays from the Presidential Secretariat led to discrepancies between ministerial and departmental planning cycles so funds did not become available that year (Smith 2009, 160). In 2004, the provincial government released a new five-year strategic plan (renstra) that focused on development and postconflict peace building (Brown, Wilson,

and Hadi 2005, 51), and Bappeda, the provincial planning ministry, prepared an action plan for fund use.

99. Ambon, 13 July 2011.

100. Butt 2011.

101. Schütte 2012.

102. See also, ICW 2009.

103. Information primarily from interviews in Ambon and Central Maluku, December 2011 and July 2012.

104. Another case is that of the Aru district head, Theddy Tengko. The case is discussed in Barron 2014.

105. Anticorruption activist, Ambon, 11 July 2011.

106. Ibid.

107. Some informants also reported that the teacher criticized the prophet Mohammed for having many affairs and said Muslims prayed like animals. This case study is based on interviews in Masohi in December 2010 and July 2011.

108. Senior policeman, Masohi, Central Maluku, 15 July 2011.

109. Interviews in Masohi, July 2011.

110. Senior policeman, Masohi, Central Maluku, 13 December 2010; senior policeman, Ambon, 17 December 2010.

111. Multiple interviews in Ambon and Central Maluku, December 2010 and July 2011.

112. A former KPK commissioner, interviewed in Jakarta, was not familiar with the case. He did confirm, however, that during his period with the commission, KPK trips to Papua province had been called off after reports of rising tensions.

113. Local NGO staff, Ambon, 21 July 2011.

114. Central Maluku, 16 July 2011.

115. One informant reported the chronology as follows: "On 25 November, a passenger on an *angkot* [public bus] read out an SMS that said that there would be a riot in the city of Ambon. That person then got down from the *angkot*. After he was asked to go to the police station to prove whether there was an issue or not he disappeared. That evening, there was another SMS saying that two Muslim villages had been burned. When I tried to confirm this by phoning the area in question, I found that nothing had happened." Muslim driver, Ambon, 11 December 2010.

116. Anticorruption activist, Ambon, 17 December 2010.

117. NGO member, Ambon, 18 July 2011.

118. Anticorruption activist, Ambon, 18 July 2011.

119. Spyer 2002, 26.

120. Al Qurtuby 2016.

121. See ICG 2011b, 2012a, for discussions of different theories.

122. E-mail correspondence with Sidney Jones, September 2011.

123. Tempo 2011.

124. Interviews with a journalist and women peace-building activist, Ambon, 10 July 2011.

125. Discussions with local sources in Ambon, September 2011.

126. According to the Maluku police chief (11 July 2011, Ambon), police in Papua are given an extra living allowance but living costs are higher in Maluku. He also complained that the police did not have the helicopters or speedboats they need. There are 7,000 police personnel in Maluku, distributed across eight polres. The polres covering Ambon Island and the neighboring Lease islands (Central Maluku) has 993 personnel.

127. In contrast, we should not see support for violence in Maluku from the central state. If such support were present, then we would expect incidents of large episodic violence to escalate into extended violence. I examine the attitudes and actions of the central state to violence in Maluku in chapter 7.

CHAPTER 5. NORTH MALUKU'S PEACE

1. Wilson (2008) provides the best overview and analysis of the North Maluku conflict. See also Duncan 2014; and Bubandt 2001. Tomagola 2000, and the articles in Nanere 2000, present vastly different interpretations of the extended violence.

2. Smith 2009.

3. Wilson 2005. Bubandt (2000) explores further how the violence in North Maluku and in Maluku became understood as "religious," arguing that on both sides a millenarian narrative that equated the violence with a divine transformation of the world created a grand narrative for the conflict.

4. Bubandt 2008.

5. Duncan 2005.

6. Wilson 2008, chapter 5.

7. Interviewees, Christian and Muslim alike, noted that the military often took sides or were ineffective because of material interests. A Muslim community leader in Mamuya, Galela, argued: "The military didn't help. Satgas 342 were from West Nusa Tenggara Province. When the conflict happened, they were here and they should have tackled it soon. But why did the conflict last so long? It's an indication that the TNI [military] had interests. The central leaders of the TNI had interests. You could see this from the behavior of Satgas 342" (Mamuya, 13 July 2011). A Christian leader in the nearby village of Duma recounted his experience: "I saw myself that in 1999 the military backed up the Muslim troops. They gave them weapons. It was the military who shot Christians here, not the Pasukan Jihad. The ones shooting guns, they were not Muslims [meaning jihadis], they were military. I saw it with my own eyes" (Tobelo, 9 July 2011).

8. Tobelo, 11 July 2011.

9. Norwegian Refugee Council 2002.

10. Wilson 2008, 167.

11. It was unlikely that the Christian family had left the bomb behind. During the extended violence, the house was owned by a Muslim who had fled Tobelo. The owner had returned to the house after it was vacated by the Christian family in order to carry out some repairs. It is likely that the Muslim owner would have discovered the bomb if it had been there at that time. Instead, it emerged that a Brimob (police special forces) unit was behind the bomb. After protests from the community about frequent suspicious bombings, the Brimob unit was replaced and the bombings stopped. Correspondence with Chris Wilson, November 2012.

12. ICG 2009a.

13. These impacts were spread over forty-two different incidents from October 2007 to October 2008. Many of these incidents were "small," but cumulative impacts were large.

14. Megawati gave a speech calling for reconciliation. However, neither she nor other central government officials played any further substantive role in ongoing peace and reconciliation meetings (village leader, Mamuya, 13 July 2011).

15. Information from Tindage 2006 and interviews in Tobelo and Galela, December 2010 and July 2011.

16. These were held on 30 December 2000 (Gura village, Tobelo), 2 January 2001 (Gamsungi, Tobelo), 11 January 2001 (Togawa, Galela), 26 January 2001 (Togawa, Galela), 19 February 2001 (Tobelo), 10 March 2001 (Gura, Tobelo), and 7 April 2001 (Gamsungi, Tobelo).

17. The full declaration can be found in appendix B of Duncan 2014.

18. Jidon Hangewa, former acting district head North Halmahera, Tobelo, 8 July 2011.

19. Smith 2009.

20. Muslim militia leader, Ternate, 11 December 2010.

21. Ibid.

22. Smith (2009, 292) estimates all government postconflict funds prior to Inpres 6/2003 as being around Rp. 260 billion (US$26 million).

23. Ibid.

24. Muslim politician and businessman, Ternate, 5 July 2011.

25. Muslim politician and activist, Ternate, 5 July 2011.

26. I consider the impact on motivations for members of society below.

27. Former Pasukan Jihad leader, Ternate, 11 December 2010.

28. Ternate, 9 December 2010.

29. Christian former senior civil servant, Tobelo, 12 July 2011; journalist and peace activist, Tobelo, 13 December 2010.

30. Tobelo, 9 July 2011.

31. Tobelo, 13 July 2011.

32. Former Christian militia leader, Tobelo, 13 December 2011.

33. Interviews with Muslim and Christian village leaders, 13 July 2011.

34. Christian leader from Duma, Tobelo, 13 July 2011. This account was verified by other interviewees.

35. Hein Namotemo, Tobelo, 11 July 2011.

36. Namotemo's claims were substantiated by both Muslims and Christians interviewed in Tobelo in July 2011. However, some claimed that it was not only Namotemo who had stood up to the police and military but also other local leaders.

37. Ternate, 6 July 2011. The acting governor at the time, Effendi, was a former military man.

38. There are 100 nonorganic (nonlocal) troops in the province compared to 2,154 organic troops. The nonorganic troops are rotated every year (military official, Ternate, 18 July 2011). In contrast, there are still 1,100 nonorganic troops in Maluku and many have been in Maluku for long periods of time, allowing them to develop rackets and other side businesses.

39. University lecturer, Ternate, 8 December 2010.

40. Former Muslim militia member, Ternate, 16 December 2010; interview, NGO worker, Ternate, 8 December 2010.

41. North Maluku police chief, Ternate, 14 July 2011.

42. Interviews, Kao-Malifut, 14–15 July 2011. See also D'Hondt and Sangaji 2010.

43. Ternate, 5 July 2011.

44. Interviews, Tobelo, July 2011.

45. ICG 2007b.

46. Hill and Vidyattama 2014, 70.

47. The International Crisis Group has produced useful case studies of the link between administrative splitting and conflict in South Sulawesi (ICG 2003), West Sulawesi (ICG 2005a), and Southeast Maluku (ICG 2007b). See also Tomsa 2015.

48. It was created under national Law 1/2003, which also established the districts of South Halmahera, West Halmahera, East Halmahera, the Sula Islands, and Tidore city.

49. Former district parliamentarian, Tobelo, 13 July 2011.

50. Data from World Bank's subnational database (2012). Values until 2007 are actual revenues; values for 2008–9 are predicted revenues. Population data are from the Bureau of Statistics' annual statistical yearbooks.

51. In 2001, the provincial budget for North Maluku (population 781,239) was Rp. 151 billion. By 2003, this had risen to Rp. 249 billion. This is less than the total amount North Halmahera district has received in any year apart from 2004 and 2005.

52. Barron et al. 2010.

53. Christian politician and activist, North Halmahera, 10 July 2011.

54. Muslim politician and activist, Ternate, 5 July 2011.

55. Lecturer, Ternate, 10 December 2010.

56. Tindage 2006.

57. Christian traditional leader and politician, Tobelo, 12 December 2010.

58. The largest share of district revenues, around 56 percent in 2005 (World Bank 2008f), came from the General Allocation Fund (DAU), an unconditional transfer of funds from the central government to all local governments aimed at achieving fiscal balance. The DAU allocation is calculated using a formula based on population, area, regional per capita income, human development indices, salary expenditures, and the level of local revenues.

59. Central Maluku's revenues in 2004 were around Rp. 401 billion. This reduced to Rp. 362 billion in 2005. Thereafter revenues stabilized at between Rp. 553 billion (2006) and Rp. 668 billion (2008). In contrast, revenues in North Halmahera almost quadrupled between 2005 and 2009.

60. The new East Seram District saw revenues rise from Rp. 100 billion in 2005 to Rp. 412 billion (2008); West Seram saw a similar increase from Rp. 94 billion (2005) to Rp. 342 billion (2009).

61. During the extended violence in West Seram 205 people were killed, and 39 were killed in East Seram.

62. University professor and activist, Ternate, 8 December 2010.

63. Activist, Ternate, 28 June 2011.

64. Albar's networks cut broadly across ethnic and religious lines before the extended violent conflict, and he and Benny had been friends before they ended up on opposite sides of the conflict. This existence of fluid crosscutting networks before the extended violence facilitated the quick return to business-as-usual after mid-2000. The conflict was a disruption in the web of relationships that were able to reform afterward. This contrasts sharply with Ambon and Central Maluku, where the extended violent conflict reinforced preexisting cleavages.

65. Although the two had been allies in early 1999 before the violence in Malifut. Thanks to Chris Wilson for this point.

66. Sultan of Ternate, Ternate, 16 December 2010.

67. NGO and political activist, Ternate, 16 July 2011.

68. Politician and activist, Ternate, 5 July 2011.

69. Former head of the North Maluku electoral commission, Ternate, 17 July 2011. He also noted that many of Gafur supporters had been placed in lower-level (echelon III and IV) bureaucratic positions. Abdul Gani Kasuba, the deputy governor, confirmed this: "We didn't make a deal with the Gafur side. But Pak Thaib [the governor] has a right, the authority, to put people in positions. He put some of Gafur's people in positions" (Ternate, 17 July 2011).

70. Pela gandong involves relationships of civil reciprocity. Communities support other communities, for example in offering their labor when public works are being built. This reciprocal exchange cements intervillage relationships, including between Christian and Muslim villages. Ceremonies to reinforce these binds (*panas pela,* or heating up the *pela*) remind community members of their obligations to each other. Information from fieldwork in Central Maluku, December 2010. See also Adam 2008; Dassen 2010; Bartels 1977; and Bräuchler 2015.

71. Muslim NGO head, Ambon, 11 December 2010; Christian delegate to Malino, Ambon, 19 December 2010.

72. See Duncan 2014, chapter 2.

73. See Andaya 1993; Ellen 1993; and more generally, Ricklefs 2008, chapter 6. This was emphasized by some interviewees: politician and activist, Ternate, 5 July 2011; district head North Halmahera, 11 July 2011.

74. Interviews in North Halmahera, July 2011.

75. Duncan 2009, 1078.

76. Ibid., 1092.

77. Ibid., 1096.

78. One priest argued that "when you talk about adat, people put religion aside." Ternate, 9 December 2010.

79. Staff of village government, Mamuya, Galela, 13 July 2011.

80. Soselisa was a firebrand pastor from Kupa-Kupa, Tobelo, who actively supported the Pasukan Merah crusade, blessing weapons and militia members before battle. He ran successfully for election to the district parliament in 2004 but was voted out in 2009. A number of informants argued that this was because locals did not like his anti-Muslim rhetoric. Interviews with former Pasukan Merah fighters, 13 December 2010 and 15 December 2010, North Halmahera.

81. Benjamin Wagono, the chairman of the local electoral commission (district KPU), was subsequently jailed. Namotemo allegedly gave a Rp. 100 million (US$10,000) bribe to Wagono, but no action was taken against the district head. There is some evidence that other candidates also provided bribes to the KPU. Journalist, Tobelo, 12 July 2011.

82. Tobelo, 12 July 2011.

83. Ibid.

84. Interviews in Ternate, July 2011.

85. ICG 2009a.

86. Interviews in Ternate with various officials and community leaders, July 2011.

87. Ternate, 17 July 2011.

88. Ibid.

89. North Halmahera, 11 July 2011.

90. Politician and activist, Ternate, 5 July 2011.

91. Politician, Ternate, 6 July 2011.

92. Wilson 2010.

93. Politician and activist, Ternate, 5 July 2011.

94. Politician, Ternate, 5 July 2011. It is worth noting that PAKTA was led by Selang, one of the former jihadi organizers. However, it did not draw extensively on old conflict networks.

95. Ongen should not be confused with the figure of the same name who has been active in Ambon and who is from Seram Island.

CHAPTER 6. SMALL EPISODIC VIOLENCE IN POSTCONFLICT ACEH

1. Fieldwork for this chapter was conducted in 2011 and focused primarily on developments from 2009 on. For information on the 2005–9 period, the chapter draws heavily on studies I conducted with the World Bank when working in Aceh during those years, cited throughout the chapter.

2. The articles in Reid 2006 provide a useful review of the historical background to "the Aceh problem." Reid (2010) notes that since the first Dutch invasion of the independent sultanate of Aceh in 1873, peace has been the exception rather than the norm; Aceh spent 86 of the subsequent 132 years in armed resistance against Jakarta.

3. Sulaiman 1997.

4. Barber 2000.

5. HRW 2001.

6. Schulze 2004.

7. McGibbon 2004; Miller 2006.

8. Sukma 2004.

9. Schulze 2004, 42–43; Miller 2009, 109–110.

10. It is unclear how many people died before 1998. Aspinall (2009a, 112) notes that one thousand to three thousand people died from military violence from mid-1990 until 1998, although many Acehnese say these figures are too low. An unknown number of people died at the hands of GAM. Killings before 1990 were less common.

11. HRW 2003; AI 2004; Good et al. 2006, 2007.

12. MSR 2009, 22.

13. World Bank 2008a.

14. MSR 2009, 32.

15. Ibid., 36.

16. Kell 1995; Ross 2005.

17. Aspinall 2007.

18. McCarthy 2007.

19. Sulaiman 2006.

20. Miller 2009.

21. Robinson 1998.

22. Olken and Barron 2009; ICG 2001b; Eye on Aceh 2004; McCulloch 2005; Kingsbury and McCulloch 2006.

23. Aspinall 2009a, 183.

24. Robinson 1998.

25. Schulze 2004.

26. Miller 2009, 76.

27. Aspinall 2009a, 189.

28. Ibid.,152. The degree of collusion between the two sides is emphasized most by Drexler (2008), who argues that the Indonesian military armed and largely controlled GAM.

29. Awaluddin 2008.

30. ICG 2005b; Husain 2007; Awaluddin 2009.

31. Aspinall 2005a, 2; Morfit 2007, 117–118.

32. Barron and Burke 2008, 10–11.

33. Morfit 2007. The next chapter explores the evolution of executive-military relations in post-Suharto Indonesia.

34. Aspinall (2005a) provides an initial analysis of the MoU, and Barron and Clark (2006, 7–9) examine the clauses of the MoU and the LoGA. See also the articles in Aguswandi and Large 2008, especially May 2008, as well as Aspinall 2007; and ICG 2005d, 2006a. MSR 2009, 133–136, discusses the Presidential Instruction.

35. Violence reduced sharply after the tsunami. In December 2004, 167 people were killed in 121 incidents. In January this fell to 12 deaths (24 incidents). Violence, however, rose again between April and July, with an average of 48 people dying per month in this period.

36. ICG 2010, 1.

37. Similarly, 25 percent of deaths in postconflict North Maluku have come from large incidents. In postconflict Maluku, 69 percent of damaged buildings are from large incidents of violence while in Aceh the figure is 33 percent.

38. Incidents are defined as crimes rather than conflicts when a preexisting cleavage between disputing parties could not be identified. See the discussion in chapter 1 of the conceptual and methodological difficulties of distinguishing crime and conflict.

39. These incidents resulted in 12 deaths (of a total of 597 in the postconflict period), 21 injuries (of 3,345), and 78 damaged buildings (of 704). Six of these incidents occurred in the two weeks before the signing of the MoU, 5 in the two weeks after the MoU, and another 4 occurred in September or October. After this, these types of incidents largely faded away with just 2 incidents in 2006, 4 in 2007, 8 in 2008, and 2 in 2010.

40. MSR 2009, 51. The largest contributor by far was the government of Indonesia (Rp. 1.5 trillion, or over US$150 million).

41. Reintegration funds decreased after 2008. From 2005 to 2008, an average of US$78 million was provided per year in reintegration assistance from all sources. From 2011–12, the annual total was US$14 million. Almost all the post-2008 reintegration funding came from the national and provincial governments, channeled through the BRA (Barron, Rahman, and Nugroho 2013).

42. Kingsbury 2006, 41.

43. An anecdote illustrates. One evening in late 2005, I was dining at the house of the acting governor of Aceh. Our discussions were interrupted by the arrival of Darwis Jeunib, the former guerrilla commander for Bireuen District. Darwis had come to pick up the keys to a new car, which the governor told us was a personal gift from himself using special off-budget resources provided by Jakarta to help address the "needs" of ex-combatant leaders.

44. Crouch 2010, 318.

45. ICG 2005d.

46. Masyrafah and McKeon 2008, 6.

47. Burke and Afnan 2005.

48. MSR 2009, 51.

49. Clause 1.3.9 of the Helsinki agreement provided the mandate for this.

50. Aspinall 2009b, 14.

51. World Bank 2009a.

52. Law 25/1999, which applies to most other Indonesian provinces, states that 15.5 percent of oil and 30.5 percent of gas revenues remain in the province.

53. While the implementation of the 2001 special autonomy agreement boosted natural resource revenues kept within Aceh by more than 150 times, from Rp. 26 billion (US$2.6 million) in 1999 (or 1.4 percent of total revenue) to Rp. 4 trillion (US$400 million) in 2004 (40 percent), it is projected that these revenues will drop significantly as oil and gas resources are exhausted. This is largely due to the decline in output at the Arun natural gas plant in North Aceh. Since production began in 1978, more than 90 percent of natural gas resources have been exploited. Production, which reached 2,200 million cubic feet per day (MCFD) in 1994, fell to 900 MCFD in 2005 (World Bank 2006b). This declined to 111 MCFD for the first six months of 2008 (World Bank 2008b).

54. Rachmadi and Swamurti (2006).

55. World Bank (2011c).

56. LoGA, article 7. This differs from the text of the Helsinki MoU, which can be interpreted as only reserving powers in six areas for Jakarta. The subclause on areas of "national character" was added for three reasons: (a) some areas are constitutional obligations for the central government, for example in areas of service provision; (b) some are related to international conventions; and (c) the implementation of some areas by the government of Aceh would affect other areas of Indonesia (May 2008).

57. Helsinki MoU clauses 1.2.1–1.2.3.

58. Hillman 2012a.

59. Hillman 2012b, 151.

60. Miller 2009, 158.

61. ICG 2006b.

62. Local parties were only allowed to contest provincial and district seats and not national ones. However, this was not a problem for GAM who were primarily interested in gaining power in Aceh rather than representing Aceh in Jakarta (Palmer 2010, 289–290). In July 2007, the Indonesian Constitutional Court amended national Law 32/2004 on Regional Government to allow independent candidates to stand in local elections elsewhere in Indonesia (ICG 2011a, 1–2).

63. ICG 2006b, 2–3.

64. EUEOM 2007.

65. Clark and Palmer 2008.

66. Forbes Damai/DSF 2006.

67. Data are from a World Bank dataset, which records incidents of conflict (violent and not) related to the elections. See Clark and Palmer 2008.

68. A study of the 2004 legislative elections in four other provinces found a similar number of cases of electoral conflict with approximately 11 percent resulting in violence. In the sole postconflict province in that study, Maluku, 20 percent of electoral conflict incidents were violent, a higher rate than in Aceh (Barron, Nathan, and Welsh 2005).

69. ICG 2007a.

70. Bunte and Ufen 2008.

71. Klinken 2009.

72. Clark and Palmer 2008. This kind of "voting for peace" is common in postconflict elections (Lyons 2004, 39).

73. Palmer 2010, 291.

74. Ibid.; Stange and Patock 2010.

75. For example, ICG 2008, 2009b; World Bank 2009b.

76. CPCRS 2009a.

77. The Carter Center 2009.

78. Zaini Abdullah was formerly "foreign minister" of GAM's government-in-exile, while Muzakir Manaf had been the leader of GAM's forces on the ground in Aceh. The split first emerged in the run up to the 2006 elections when many in GAM's old guard did not back Irwandi Jusuf but another ticket that included Hasbi Abdullah, the young brother of Zaini (ICG 2006b).

79. Aspinall 2011b; ICG 2011a, 2012c.

80. ANFREL Foundation 2012.

81. Simanjuntak 2012.

82. Miller 2006, 305; McGibbon 2006.

83. One local activist told me that corruption was an "Indonesian disease" and was confident that special autonomy would lower levels of corruption. Banda Aceh, August 2005.

84. TII 2010, 15–16.

85. South Aceh, 21 April 2011.

86. Anticorruption activist, Lhokseumawe, 10 March 2011.

87. Banda Aceh, 4 March 2011.

88. Aditjondro 2007.

89. Aspinall 2009b, 11.

90. Aditjondro 2007, 18–19; World Bank 2007d.

91. Klinken and Aspinall 2011.

92. Aspinall 2009b.

93. Under national *Keppres* (Presidential Decree) 80/2003 on the procurement of goods and services, companies must be of sufficient size and have sufficient experience to bid for large contracts. Newly established GAM contractor companies do not meet these criteria, hence the need to use existing companies.

94. Activist, East Aceh, 7 March 2011.

95. Aspinall 2009b, 30.

96. Activist, North Aceh, 7 March 2011.

97. Hadiz 2010.

98. Aspinall 2009b, 3.

99. Aspinall 2005a; ICG 2005b; Barron, Clark, and Daud 2005.

100. Miller 2009.

101. Aspinall and Crouch 2003; Huber 2004.

102. Kingsbury 2006.

103. Mietzner 2009, 301.

104. Mietzner 2006, 51; Mietzner 2009, 301–302.

105. Aditjondro 2007, 14–17.

106. The MoU mandated the establishment of a Human Rights Court for Aceh (clause 2.2) and a Commission for Truth and Reconciliation (clause 2.3). The former has not been established. A Truth and Reconciliation Commission was eventually established in October 2016 but has done little since then. Aspinall 2008 discusses why there has been little progress on the human rights or justice agenda. See also Hadi 2008.

107. Aspinall 2009b, 31.

108. Expert on Aceh conflict, East Aceh, 7 March 2011. Also, NGO worker, Banda Aceh, 6 March 2011.

109. Defense and security analyst, Banda Aceh, 4 March 2011. Manaf also took one of the daughters of Sunarko, the former Indonesian military commander, as a wife.

110. ICG 2011a, 6.

111. World Bank 2008c.

112. World Bank 2008d, 2009b.

113. March 2013 discussion with Aceh conflict expert based on confidential conversations with police investigators in 2009.

114. ICG 2009b, 7.

115. Forbes Damai/DSF 2006.

116. CPCRS 2009a.

117. Barter 2011.

118. Palmer 2010; CPCRS 2009a, 2009b.

119. Interviews in Aceh, March and April 2011.

120. McGibbon 2006, 346.

121. Aspinall 2009a, 187.

122. A few weeks after the MoU was signed, I helped facilitate one of the first meetings between senior GAM leaders and local government officials to discuss plans to produce a joint information dissemination strategy for the peace agreement. I was confused when on entering the room members from each side hugged showing visible joy. It was explained to me that one of the GAM negotiators was the cousin of one of the members of the government delegation and others had been childhood friends.

123. Schulze 2007; Burke 2008.

124. World Bank 2006c.

125. World Bank 2006d.

126. World Bank 2006e, 2006f; Barron and Burke 2008, 24.

127. Fearon and Laitin 1996. Their theory is articulated in relation to ethnic violence and relations, but there is no reason why it cannot also apply to other forms of intergroup conflict.

128. As discussed below, there has been much more tolerance of smaller-scale episodic violence from both sides.

129. World Bank 2008c.

130. This was primarily through the structure of the Coordination and Communication Forum for Peace in Aceh (FKK), a government oversight body for the peace process, which had a strong presence of former military and antiseparatist group members within it. Discussions in Banda Aceh, March-April 2008.

131. World Bank 2007a.

132. Journalists, Banda Aceh, 3 March 2011; analyst of the Aceh conflict, East Aceh, 7 March 2011; Indonesia state intelligence agency officer, Banda Aceh, 4 March 2011.

133. Discussions in Aceh, 2008.

134. Schulze 2004.

135. Nessen 2006.

136. World Bank 2006a.

137. Former combatant, Southwest Aceh, January 2006. Quoted in World Bank 2006a, 17.

138. Ibid., 16.

139. Ibid., 41.

140. Of 1,024 former male combatants surveyed, 85 percent had full-time employment, 6 percent had consistent part-time/contract work, and 6 percent some part-time/contract work. The figures for civilians (n=1,794) were 78 percent, 6 percent, and 4 percent, respectively. The samples are representative for both populations and the differences are significant at the 95 percent level (Barron 2009, 22).

141. World Bank 2006a, 42.

142. World Bank 2009a, 44–45.

143. For descriptions and critical analyses of Aceh's reintegration programs, see Zurstrassen 2006; Barron 2007; Beeck 2007; ICG 2006a, 2007c; Palmer 2007; Aspinall 2008; Frodin 2008; Barron 2009; Barron and Burke 2008; and Barron, Rahman, and Nugroho 2013.

144. Barron and Burke 2008, 38. A senior GAM leader told me that there were around 30,000 GAM people in three categories: GAM in the mountains, GAM in the villages, and GAM who provided communications support (Zakaria Saman, Banda Aceh, 30 November 2006). Another assessment estimated that there were 14,300 former combatants (a figure that does not include civilian GAM), defined as those who had been in the military structure of GAM for at least a month between 1998 and 2005. Of these, less than 700, under 5 percent, were women (MSR 2009,18).

145. Academic, Banda Aceh, 4 March 2011.

146. BRA 2008.

147. World Bank 2006a, 30.

148. Ibid., 31.

149. Zurstrassen 2006.

150. ICG 2007c, 9.

151. MSR 2009, 87.

152. Barron 2008, 26–27.

153. Former AMM peace monitor, Banda Aceh, 9 March 2011.

154. East Aceh vice district head, East Aceh, 8 March 2011.

155. Academic, Banda Aceh, 4 March 2011. Interviews in North and East Aceh, March 2011.

156. State intelligence officer, Banda Aceh, 4 March 2011.

157. Interviews on Aceh's east and west coasts, March and April 2011.

158. Activist, North Aceh, 7 March 2011.

159. Ibid.

160. Schulze 2004, 12.

161. Jones 2008.

162. North Aceh, 7 March 2011.

163. Activist, Each Aceh, 9 March 2011.

164. Fieldwork on east coast of Aceh, March 2011.

165. ICG 2009b, 8.

166. Sofyan Dawood's house was attacked in April 2007. The same month a box containing an active grenade was found outside the office of Ilyas Pasee, the GAM North

Aceh district head, with a letter in Acehnese threatening him if he "continued to commit infractions in his duties." A grenade was also thrown at the house of the Lhokseumawe vice mayor (World Bank 2007b). Similar incidents continued the following month with grenades thrown at the house of the head of the Pidie district parliament, at the parliament building in Bener Meriah district, and at the offices of two subdistrict heads in Central Aceh district (World Bank 2007c). Zakaria Saman's house in Pidie district was burned in March 2012 and grenades were thrown at his residence in Banda Aceh in June 2012. There have also been attacks on KPA offices (World Bank 2008e).

167. World Bank 2007c.

168. ICG 2007c, 5.

169. ICG 2011a, 8.

170. Senior police officer, South Aceh, 21 April 2011.

171. State intelligence officer, Banda Aceh, 4 March 2011.

172. Jones 2008.

173. Newspaper journalist, Banda Aceh, 3 March 2011.

174. Former AMM peace monitor, Bangkok, November 2012.

175. State intelligence officer, Banda Aceh, 4 March 2011.

176. Acehnese working for international NGO, Aceh Besar, 6 March 2011.

177. ICG 2009b, 9–10. On Pasukan Peudeung, see World Bank 2008d: Grayman 2012; and Anderson 2013.

178. Acehnese working for international NGO, Greater Aceh, 6 March 2011.

179. World Bank 2009a.

180. Discussions with Irwandi Jusuf, Jakarta, mid-2009.

181. Activist, East Aceh, 9 March 2011.

182. Peake 2009.

183. World Bank 2006a, 25.

184. World Bank/KDP 2007, 78.

185. Ibid., 77.

186. Barron 2008, 18.

187. The return of displaced people to ethnically heterogeneous Bener Meriah and Central Aceh in late 2005, for example, raised tensions. However, these did not result in violence (World Bank 2005).

188. The World Bank's Conflict Monitoring Updates document some of these cases, which have been relatively rare compared to other types of violence.

189. ICG 2007c.

190. ICG 2009b, 2012c.

191. Three men were arrested in March 2012 for the killing, but links to senior KPA leaders were not proven (Afrida and Simanjuntak 2012).

192. ICG 2012c. The elections, which were scheduled to be held in October 2011, were postponed four times, finally taking place in April 2012. Partai Aceh wanted to ensure that Irwandi could not use the advantages that incumbency affords such as using the state apparatus for campaigning. It is also likely that some of the killings were done by the military (expert on Aceh conflict, Jakarta, 24 January 2012).

193. Of the sixteen provinces in the NVMS dataset, Aceh has the highest levels of incidents of electoral violence. Only Papua has seen more people killed in elections-related violence.

194. Thanks to Adrian Morel for this point.

195. The per capita death toll in Aceh Besar is higher than in East Aceh. However, over one-quarter of the postconflict deaths in the district were the result of police raids on a jihadi camp in early 2010, which had no link to past violence. If these are excluded, the per capita postconflict death rate is substantially higher in East Aceh.

196. MSR 2009, 18.

197. Schulze 2004, 17; Good et al. 2007, 16.

198. Good et al. 2007, 26–29.

199. Senior government leader, East Aceh, 8 March 2011; local parliament member, South Aceh, 21 April 2011.

200. A senior figure in the South Aceh contractors' association explained how elites collude to divide the contracting pie and how the entry of GAM has affected this:

"In total [in South Aceh], there are 300 local contractors. But only 10 percent of these get projects properly, based on the proper process. The rest win their contracts based on collusion. . . . KPA don't dare threaten me because I help them in solving their problems. I try to organize their share of the cake. The contractors' association receives 10 percent [of the total budget that is being contracted out]. I coordinate to give a certain percentage to KPA, a certain percentage to the district head's team, a percentage to the local parliament. [When did you make that agreement?] I tried even before KPA existed. It went well. It was against the regulation, but it did ensure the quality of projects. But now, KPA have destroyed that system" (South Aceh, 21 April 2011).

201. South Aceh, 19 April 2011. Corroborated by other interviews in South Aceh, April 2011.

202. A number of respondents in Banda Aceh and East Aceh said that Sanusi has wisdom but not authority. Former GAM combatants, they argued, wanted simple instructions and actions. Sanusi's more philosophical approach to problem solving did not go down well.

203. Former GAM negotiator, Banda Aceh, 11 March 2011.

204. Expert on Aceh conflict, Banda Aceh, 3 March 2011.

205. Expert on Aceh conflict, South Aceh, 22 April 2011.

206. Development project worker, South Aceh, 19 April 2011; local NGO worker, South Aceh, 19 April 2011.

207. Former sagoe GAM, South Aceh, 20 April 2011.

208. NGO activist, South Aceh, 19 April 2011.

209. One former combatant noted: "Overall, we're disappointed with the high rank GAM. The only shield that exists is brotherhood. If there was no brotherhood, it would be the same as in East Aceh, even if the structure was strong. . . . The sense of brotherhood is very strong here. It stops us doing violent things. For example, the current head of the local parliament, many hate him. But he has family, brothers, who make sure no violence is expressed. I am sure if there was no sense of brotherhood, that guy would be finished" (South Aceh, 20 April 2011).

210. Former combatant, South Aceh, 21 April 2011.

211. Activist, South Aceh, 19 April 2011.

212. Interviews in Manggamat and Central Kluet, South Aceh, April 2011.

213. Development project staff, South Aceh, 20 April 2011.

214. Interviews in South Aceh. Cooperatives can receive between Rp. 320,000–350,000 (US$32–35) for one gram of gold.

215. South Aceh, 21 April 2011.

216. South Aceh, 19 April 2011.

217. Former combatant and village head, South Aceh, 20 April 2011.

CHAPTER 7. WHY HAS EXTENDED VIOLENT CONFLICT NOT RECURRED?

1. One case of extended violence (the violence in West Kalimantan of early 1997) occurred before the fall of Suharto. As such, the arguments in this chapter on why extended violence occurred in the early post-Suharto era have less explanatory power for this case, although Klinken (2007, 55) argues that it occurred at a time when the New

Order regime's fragility was becoming apparent. For a full discussion of the West Kalimantan case, see Davidson 2008.

2. Bertrand 2004.

3. Ibid., 5.

4. Sidel 2006.

5. Ibid., xii.

6. Klinken 2007.

7. Ibid., 138–139.

8. Tajima 2014.

9. In 1967, the police were placed under the minister of defense and the commander of the armed forces. The police were formally separated from the military on 1 April 1999, but in practice remained part of the armed forces until 1 January 2001 (ICG 2001a). Tajima (2008) quotes Meliala (2001, 425) who observes that the police-to-population ratio of 1:1,200 in 1999 was one-fifth of that in Malaysia.

10. Honna 2003, 9.

11. For example, Anderson 2001 and Heryanto 2006.

12. Rabasa and Haseman 2002; Crouch 2007.

13. Aspinall 2005b, 44–47.

14. Hefner 2000.

15. Suryadinata 2002.

16. Honna 2003, 25.

17. Ibid., 26–35.

18. Gledhill 2012.

19. Aspinall 2005b.

20. Pepinsky 2009.

21. Honna 2003, 162.

22. Panggabean and Smith 2010; Purdey 2006.

23. Joint Fact Finding Team 1998.

24. See Schwartz 2000, 354–355; Honna 2003, chapter 7; Mietzner 2009, chapter 3; and Lee 2009.

25. Slater 2010a, 209.

26. Mietzner 2009, 134.

27. Ibid., 138.

28. Ibid., 137.

29. Crouch 2010, 251.

30. Hasan 2006, 186–190.

31. Azca 2011, 11.

32. McRae 2008, 115–119.

33. I quote at length the testimony of one Christian resident of Duma village in Galela, which saw a series of attacks by jihadis between 19 May and 19 June 2000. The final attack led to the complete destruction of the village and between 150 (Duncan 2005, 78) and 250 Christian deaths (Wilson 2008, 165). I gathered similar accounts from other residents I interviewed in Duma: "If the military were more neutral in the conflict, there would not have been as many victims . . . 19 June, the last attack, was incredible (*luar biasa*). In the preceding six months there were twenty-one attacks. The last one was on 19 June. The day before, the commander of the military *pelaton* told me that there would be an attack from the Muslims the following day. When I heard this, I said, 'You are the military. You should protect us from the attack.' But the following day the military didn't protect us. Around 10:00 a.m., they attacked Duma. In the morning, I went round the village to check conditions. I saw that every corner of the village was guarded by the military. They were also in the large field. So in my mind, it was impossible for the Muslims to attack us because there

were so many military there. If there were only a couple of military people, they could not have stopped the Muslims. But there were many of them. . . . When they attacked, the military were involved in the attack. We had no weapons. There were more than 100 victims that day. . . . We were surrounded. We could not escape. I fell down three times. There was a military person there. I called out to him. He asked me whether I was Pasukan Jihad [Muslim militiaman] or Pasukan Merah [Christian militiaman]. I said Merah. He said 'Wait' and went away, said he would call his friend. The friend he called was not military but a Pasukan Putih [Muslim militiaman]. I had a bad feeling so I moved away from where I was while the military guy went to get his friend. I fell down near my home, behind a wall. My glasses had gone so I could not see. But I kept listening to what the military and Pasukan Putih were talking about. The military guy said, 'The man was here just two minutes ago. Look for him.' The Pasukan Putih guy said, 'I'll look for him because his head is worth Rp. 50 million. It'll be paid by the Pasukan Putih in Soasio.' He said the heads of Pastor Dungir and other village leaders were worth the same. The Pasukan Putih would pay Rp. 50 million for each" (Christian resident of Duma, Galela, 13 July 2011).

34. Miller 2009, 21.

35. Kalyvas (2006), using data from the Greek civil war, shows that areas with the highest levels of insurgent control saw the least violence.

36. Miller 2009, 29.

37. On 3 May 1999, soldiers opened fire on five thousand to seven thousand villagers who were attending a GAM rally. At least 38 were killed and 115 wounded (Miller 2009, 35–36).

38. Bubandt 2008, 809–811.

39. See, for example, Aditjondro 2001; Loveband and Young 2006; and Liem Soei Liong 2002.

40. O'Rourke 2002.

41. Klinken 2007, 104.

42. In seventeen provinces for which we have data, 4,794 people were killed in violent incidents in 1999 compared to 1,720 in 1998. Of the 1998 deaths, 1,231 occurred in Jakarta with 1,193 people dying in Jakarta in May of that year.

43. Slater 2010b.

44. Aspinall 2005b.

45. Hefner 2000; Bush 2009.

46. Siegel (2001, 92) points out that the rhetorical framing of Suharto's fall as initiating a process of reformasi (reform) rather than revolution indicated a process of gradual refashioning of the political order, something incumbent elites were much more comfortable with than more rapid and power structure–altering change.

47. Crouch 2010, 21.

48. Schwartz (2000, 372) notes that for most of the political opposition, Habibie was just "a more talkative version of Suharto." He had consistently spoken of Suharto as his hero and had never articulated any other political view beyond endorsing the authoritarian New Order state.

49. Crouch 2010, 27.

50. Aspinall 2013, 31.

51. Robison and Hadiz 2004.

52. Bourchier 1999.

53. Mietzner 2009, 199.

54. Bertrand 2004, 139–140.

55. The MPR was made up of all 500 members of the lower house (the DPR) along with 135 representatives of the regions and 65 representatives of special groups.

56. Kingsbury 2005b.

57. Crouch 2010, 137.

58. Mietzner 2009, 205.

59. Ibid., 212.

60. Honna 2003, 180–184.

61. Mietzner 2009, 202.

62. In 2000, then defense minister, Juwono Sudarsono, estimated that 70 percent of defense spending came from off-budget resources (Sudarsono 2000). A large share of these resources was collected through the territorial command structure. See also Rieffel and Pramodhawardani 2007; and Mietzner 2008.

63. Following the November 1999 gathering of 500,000 people in Aceh calling for a plebiscite on self-determination, Wahid publicly stated that it was unfair that only the East Timorese should decide their political future and that a referendum on Aceh's status should also be held. Following pressure from the parliament and the military, Wahid was forced to abandon the referendum offer the following month (Miller 2009, 67).

64. Mietzner 2006, 31.

65. Crouch 2010.

66. Robison and Hadiz 2004.

67. McIntyre 2005.

68. Miller 2012; Singh 2012.

69. Mietzner 2009.

70. Sharp 2012.

71. HRW 1999; Emmerson 2000; Aspinall and Berger 2001.

72. Chauvel and Bhakti 2004.

73. Mietzner 2009, 221.

74. Simanungkalit 2002.

75. The training by the military of Laskar Jihad cadres came the month after the sacking of Wiranto. The subsequent decision to ignore the president's request to prevent Laskar Jihad departing for Ambon can be interpreted as a show of strength from the military, aggrieved at Wahid's tinkering in their affairs.

76. Mietzner 2009, 228.

77. Azca 2011, 30.

78. Schulze 2002, 67.

79. Barton 2006, 332–335.

80. ICG 2002.

81. See chapter 4.

82. Smith 2005; Davidson 2008.

83. Miller 2009, 36.

84. Ibid., 37.

85. Crouch 2010, 170–171.

86. Miller 2009, 69–70.

87. Kanmen 2001.

88. Crouch 2010, 172–173.

89. Smith 2003.

90. Crouch 2010, 61.

91. Ibid., 147–149.

92. Violence in Papua is ongoing and is sometimes viewed as being of a similar nature to the civil war in Aceh. However, Papuan violence is better characterized as being episodic than extended. NVMS data show that the largest number of people killed in any single year in the past decade in Papua and West Papua is 182 (in 2012). In contrast, thousands of people were killed each year in Aceh between 1999 and 2004. Furthermore, of the 692 people killed in Papua and West Papua between 2009 and 2012, only 83 died in separatist

incidents, just one more than died as a result of domestic violence. In contrast, 8,439 of 10,613 deaths in Aceh (80 percent) in that province's extended violence period were the result of separatist violence.

93. Mietzner 2009; Aspinall 2005c.

94. Political parties still matter because they determine who can stand for the presidency. From 2009, aspiring presidential candidates have had to secure the support of parties holding 15 percent of seats in the national parliament or who had garnered 20 percent of the popular vote. In the context of Indonesia's fragmented party system, this has meant that candidates have had to build coalitions of parties to gain nomination. Crouch (2010, 66, 74). See also Mietzner 2013.

95. Wrighter 2005.

96. Crouch 2010, 61.

97. Aspinall 2005c.

98. An assessment of the rule of law in ninety-seven countries by the World Justice Project ranked Indonesia as first among twenty-three lower middle income countries in establishing effective limits on governmental power (Asian Century Institute 2012).

99. On Yudhoyono's "rainbow cabinets," see Sherlock 2015.

100. Aspinall 2013, 10.

101. Linz 1990, 56.

102. Aspinall, Mietzner, and Tomsa 2015.

103. Mietzner 2009.

104. The TNI Act of 2004 mandated that all military businesses must be handed over to the state by 2009. However, subsequent negotiations led to the exclusion of cooperatives and foundations from the definition of military businesses. As a result, the secretary general of defense, General Sjafie Sjamsoeddin, announced that only 6 or 7 of more than 1,500 economic units under military management would be transferred (Mietzner 2009, 308). See also, Baker 2015.

105. Aspinall 2010, 24.

106. Mietzner 2009, 296.

107. Winters 2011; Aspinall and Klinken 2011. The articles in Ford and Pepinsky 2014 provide useful debates and critiques; see also Diamond 2010.

108. Hadiz 2010.

109. Aspinall 2010, 21. See also, Horowitz 2013.

110. Sukma 2010, 53.

111. Slater 2004.

112. Mietzner 2009, 298–299.

113. Miller 2009, 160.

114. Morfit 2006, 19. See also the memoir of Awaluddin (2009, 248), the chief government representative in the Helsinki negotiations. He recalls how, in response to one general continuing to express discordant views about the peace talks, Sutarto called a meeting of one hundred senior TNI officers. At the meeting he stated that if anyone in the TNI tried to stir up trouble, he would "personally place his pistol against their head and pull the trigger."

115. E-mail correspondence with Sidney Jones, 16 July 2012.

116. World Bank 2013.

117. FDI rose a record 27.2 percent from January to March 2013 compared with a year earlier and Indonesia received credit upgradings to investment status by Fitch and Moody's in late 2011 and early 2012 (Silaen and Sentana 2013).

118. McRae 2010; Aspinall 2009b.

119. From discussions with my research team in Ambon and Sidney Jones, September 2011.

120. McRae 2013.

121. The analysis is from Wilson (2013) who documents and explains the conflict in Tarakan and the security response.

122. Provinces covered are the five that that saw extended violence plus Papua and West Papua, which have seen particularly high levels of episodic violence. The argument in this section originates in Barron, Jaffrey, and Varshney 2016.

123. An intervention was defined as successful if the intervention appeared to have stopped the violence.

124. On the limited progress on police reform, see AI 2009; ICG 2012b; and Baker 2015.

125. Sukarsono (2013) argues that there has only been sanctioning of local police chiefs who have failed to effectively manage violence when there has been a high level of public pressure. He cites the case of ethnic unrest in Lampung in October 2012 and the failure of the police in Yogyakarta to protect murder suspects from being executed by soldiers in their cells. Both cases eventually led to the replacement of the local police chief, but this was only after public outcry had mounted.

126. Fearon and Laitin 2003; Weinstein 2007; Ross 2012.

127. Aspinall 2010, 34.

CONCLUSIONS

1. Kalyvas 2003.

2. It may be possible to extend my theory by focusing on how different types of goals beyond economic and political accumulation shape the instrumental use of violence, and the conditions under which these different types of goals are more or less important. This complements rather than undermines the basic approach of focusing on three sets of actors and the incentives they have for supporting violence. This is work for the future.

3. Cramer 2006.

4. Zaum and Cheng 2011.

APPENDIX

1. The United Nations Office on Drugs and Crime, for example, gathers homicide data. Information for their 2010 statistics comes from national criminal justice systems (police, prosecution, courts, and prison authorities) for 143 of 207 countries/territories, including Indonesia (UNODC 2011).

2. Sharpe 2005, 16, 19.

3. Police reported that in 2011 there were 68 murders and 64 rapes in the greater Jakarta (MetroJaya) area (Marhaenjati and Arnas 2011). The NVMS reports 328 murders in 2011 and 182 rapes that year.

4. Sharpe 2005.

5. The enumeration of the survey was completed in August 2002. Given that PODES was rolled out over a period of time, the preceding twelve months may be different for different areas.

6. Barron, Kaiser, and Pradhan 2009.

7. The PODES figures were estimates based on just one year of data. See Barron and Sharpe 2005, 8, for a discussion.

8. Vothknecht and Sumarto 2011.

9. A further 864 people were killed from violent crimes, 143 from domestic violence, and 75 from security force responses to crime or conflict. Data are for June 2004–May 2005.

10. Barron, Kaiser, and Pradhan 2009.

11. For this reason, there has been a trend toward embedding behavioral experiment games within survey instruments. Such games, however, cannot generate data on past events.

12. ITP 2010.

13. If we include violent crime, domestic violence, and security force violence, there were 19,929 violent incidents in 2009, resulting in 1,959 deaths, 14,307 injuries, and 1,493 damaged buildings. It appears that ITP use a similar inclusive definition of violence to that employed by NVMS. Their report includes a discussion of small-scale forms of violence, including routine violence and mob beatings.

14. On the Indian dataset, see Varshney 2002 and Wilkinson 2004. The tradition of using newspaper analysis to code conflict and contentious incidents goes back much further. See, for example, Snyder and Kelly 1977; and Tilly 1997b.

15. Varshney, Tadjoeddin, and Panggabean 2010. UNSFIR's first dataset included incidents of collective violence reported in two national newspapers (*Kompas* and *Antara*) for the 1990–2001 period (Tadjoeddin 2002). It soon became clear that there were considerable limitations to the data. Neither newspaper reported *any* incidents of violent group conflict anywhere in Indonesia in 1990, 1991, 1992, or 1994. One reason for these gaps was that the New Order regime, until its final years, imposed significant restrictions on national press freedoms. The press was not allowed to report on so-called "SARA" issues that could upset relations between Indonesia's many ethnic and religious groups. (SARA is an acronym for ethnic [*suku*], religious [*agama*], racial [*ras*], and intergroup [*antar golongan*] differences.) See Sen and Hill 2006.

16. UNSFIR, for example, does not record any incidents of violence in Maluku in 2003 while NVMS records 115 incidents, which led to 28 deaths.

17. Barron and Sharpe 2005.

18. Welsh 2008.

19. With the exception of East Timor. Provinces included in the version of the dataset used in this book are Aceh, East Java, West Kalimantan, Central Kalimantan, Lampung, Maluku, North Maluku, East Nusa Tenggara, West Nusa Tenggara, Papua, West Papua, South Sulawesi, Central Sulawesi, North Sulawesi, North Sumatra, and Greater Jakarta (which includes parts of Banten and West Java provinces as well as Jakarta).

20. Time periods covered vary by province. Information is only available from 2005 for Greater Jakarta (until 2012) and East Java, Lampung, West Nusa Tenggara, South Sulawesi, North Sulawesi, and North Sumatra (all until 2009, and then 2012). Full time series data are available for the six postconflict provinces plus East Nusa Tenggara, Papua, and West Papua, although there are some archive gaps for the Papuan provinces for early years. In addition, 1997 is covered for West Kalimantan Province.

21. More information on the process is provided in Barron et al. 2009. Since the publication of that working paper, some changes have been made, most notably the exclusion of nonviolent incidents from the dataset and changes in province selection.

22. A one-week training program was given to coders to learn the concepts employed, how to assign codes, etc. A 156-page manual was produced, and systematic quality control procedures included checking a large proportion of articles. For each coder, 100 percent of coded articles were checked until 95 percent accuracy was achieved. After that 10 percent of coded articles were checked. If accuracy dropped again, we returned to 100 percent checking.

23. CPCRS 2009a; Barron and Sharpe 2008.

24. Freedom House 2011.

25. Varshney 2008.

References

Acciaioli, Greg. 2001. "Grounds of Conflict, Idioms of Harmony: Custom, Religion, and Nationalism in Violence Avoidance in Lindu Plain, Central Sulawesi." *Indonesia* 72 (October): 81–114.

Acemoglu, Daron, and James A. Robinson. 2006. *Economic Origins of Dictatorship and Democracy*. Cambridge: Cambridge University Press.

Adam, Jeroen. 2008. "Forced Migration, *Adat*, and a Purified Present in Ambon, Indonesia." *Ethnology* 47 (4): 227–238.

Adam, Jeroen. 2009. "The Problem of Going Home: Land Management, Displacement, and Reconciliation in Ambon." In *Reconciling Indonesia: Grassroots Agency for Peace*, edited by Birgit Bräuchler, 138–155. London: Routledge.

Adam, Jeroen. 2010. "How Ordinary Folk Became Involved in the Ambonese Conflict: Understanding Private Opportunities during Communal Violence." *Bijdragen tot de Taal-, Land- en Volkenkunde (BKI)* 1661 (1): 25–48.

Aditjondro, George Junus. 2001. "Guns, Pamphlets and Handie-Talkies: How the Military Exploited Local Ethno-Religious Tensions in Maluku to Preserve Their Political and Economic Privileges." In *Violence in Indonesia*, edited by Ingrid Wessel and Georgia Wimhofer, 100–128. Hamburg: Abera.

Aditjondro, George Junus. 2007. "Profiting from Peace: The Political Economy of Aceh's Post-Helsinki Reconstruction." INFID Working Paper No. 3. Jakarta: International NGO Forum on Indonesian Development.

Afrida, Nani, and Hotli Simanjuntak. 2012. "Six Arrested for Election Terror in Aceh." *The Jakarta Post*, 13 March. http://www.thejakartapost.com/news/2012/03/13/six-arrested-election-terror-aceh.html (accessed 21 May 2013).

The Age. 2010. "Political Prisoner Dies as 'Truth Walks Slowly.'" 15 September. http://www.theage.com.au/world/political-prisoner-dies-as-truth-walks-slowly-20100914-15aui.html (accessed 14 May 2013).

Aguswandi and Judith Large, eds. 2008. *Reconfiguring Politics: The Indonesia-Aceh Peace Process*. London: Conciliation Resources.

Al Qurtuby, Sumanto. 2016. *Religious Violence and Conciliation in Indonesia: Christians and Muslims in the Moluccas*. London: Routledge.

Amnesty International (AI). 2004. "New Military Operations, Old Patterns of Human Rights Abuses in Aceh (Nanggroe Aceh Darussalam, NAD)." 7 October. http://195.234.175.160/en/library/info/ASA21/033/2004/en (accessed 15 October 2012)

Amnesty International (AI). 2009. *Unfinished Business: Police Accountability in Indonesia*. London: Amnesty International.

Andaya, Leonard. 1993. *The World of Maluku: Eastern Indonesia in the Early Modern Period*. Honolulu: University of Hawaii Press.

Anderson, Benedict R. O'G., ed. 2001. *Violence and the State in Suharto's Indonesia*. Ithaca, NY: Southeast Asia Program, Cornell University.

Anderson, Bobby. 2013. "Gangster, Ideologue, Martyr: The Posthumous Reinvention of Teungku Badruddin and the Nature of the Free Aceh Movement." *Conflict, Security, and Development* 13 (1): 31–56.

Andreas, Peter. 2004. "Criminalized Legacies of War: The Clandestine Political Economy of the Western Balkans." *Problems of Post-Communism* 51 (3): 3–9.

Andreas, Peter. 2008. *Blue Helmets and Black Markets: The Business of Survival in Sarajevo*. Ithaca, NY: Cornell University Press.

Anwar, Dewi Fortuna, Hélène Bouvier, Glenn Smith, and Roger Tol, eds. 2005. *Violent Internal Conflicts in Asia Pacific: Histories, Political Economies and Policies*. Jakarta: KITLV.

Aragon, Lorraine V. 2001. "Communal Violence in Poso, Central Sulawesi: Where People Eat Fish and Fish Eat People." *Indonesia* 72 (October): 45–74.

The Asia Foundation. 2016. *Sri Lanka Strategic Assessment 2016*. Colombo: The Asia Foundation.

Asian Century Institute. 2012. "Rule of Law in Asia." 4 December. http://www.asian centuryinstitute.com/politics/147-rule-of-law-in-asia (accessed 1 May 2013).

Asian Network for Free Elections (ANFREL Foundation). 2012. "Preliminary Report." 11 April. http://anfrel.org/wp-content/uploads/2012/04/Aceh-Preliminary-Report.pdf (accessed 10 December 2012).

Aspinall, Edward. 2005a. *The Helsinki Agreement: A More Promising Basis for Peace in Aceh?* Policy Studies No. 20. Washington, DC: East-West Center.

Aspinall, Edward. 2005b. *Opposing Suharto: Compromise, Resistance, and Regime Change in Indonesia*. Stanford, CA.: Stanford University Press.

Aspinall, Edward. 2005c. "Elections and the Normalization of Politics in Indonesia." *South East Asia Research* 12 (2): 117–156.

Aspinall, Edward. 2007. "The Construction of Grievance: Natural Resources and Identity in a Separatist Conflict." *Journal of Conflict Resolution* 51 (6): 950–972.

Aspinall, Edward. 2008. "Peace without Justice? The Helsinki Peace Process in Aceh." *HD Report*. Geneva: Center for Humanitarian Dialogue.

Aspinall, Edward. 2009a. *Islam and Nation: Separatist Rebellion in Aceh, Indonesia*. Stanford, CA.: Stanford University Press.

Aspinall, Edward. 2009b. "Combatants to Contractors: The Political Economy of Peace in Aceh." *Indonesia* 87 (April): 1–34.

Aspinall, Edward. 2010. "The Irony of Success." *Journal of Democracy* 21(2): 20–34.

Aspinall, Edward. 2011a. "Democratization and Ethnic Politics in Indonesia: Nine Theses." *Journal of East Asian Studies* 11: 289–319.

Aspinall, Edward. 2011b. "Aceh's No Win Election." *Inside Indonesia* 106 (October-December). http://www.insideindonesia.org/weekly-articles/aceh-s-no-win-election (accessed 8 December 2012).

Aspinall, Edward. 2013. "A Nation in Fragments." *Critical Asian Studies* 45 (1): 27–54.

Aspinall, Edward, and Mark T. Berger. 2001. "The Breakup of Indonesia? Nationalism after Decolonisation and the Contradictions of Modernity in Post-Cold War Southeast Asia." *Third World Quarterly* 22 (6): 1003–1024.

Aspinall, Edward, and Harold Crouch. 2003. *The Aceh Peace Process: Why It Failed*. Policy Studies No. 1. Washington, DC: East-West Center.

Aspinall, Edward, Marcus Mietzner, and Dirk Tomsa, eds. 2015. *The Yudhoyono Presidency: Indonesia's Decade of Stability and Stagnation*. Singapore: Institute for Southeast Asian Studies.

Aspinall, Edward, and Gerry van Klinken, eds. 2011. *The State and Illegality in Indonesia*. Leiden: KITLV Press.

Awaluddin, Hamid. 2008. "Why Is Peace in Aceh Successful?" In *Reconfiguring Politics: The Indonesia-Aceh Peace Process*, edited by Aguswandi and Judith Large, 25–27. London: Conciliation Resources.

Awaluddin, Hamid. 2009. *Peace in Aceh: Notes on the Peace Process between the Republic of Indonesia and the Aceh Freedom Movement (GAM) in Helsinki*. Jakarta: CSIS.

Axelrod, Robert. 1986. "An Evolutionary Approach to Norms." *American Political Science Review* 80: 1095–1111.

Azca, Muhammad Najib. 2004. *Security Sector Reform, Democratic Transition, and Social Violence: The Case of Ambon, Indonesia*. Berlin: Berghof Research Center for Constructive Conflict Management.

Azca, Muhammad Najib. 2006. "In Between Military and Militia: The Dynamics of the Security Forces in the Communal Conflict in Ambon." *Asian Journal of Social Science* 34 (3): 431–455.

Azca, Muhammad Najib. 2011. "After Jihad: A Biographical Approach to Passionate Politics in Indonesia." Ph.D. diss., University of Amsterdam.

Baker, Jacqui. 2015. "Professionalism without Reform: The Security Sector under Yudhoyono." In *The Yudhoyono Presidency: Indonesia's Decade of Stability and Stagnation*, edited by Edward Aspinall, Marcus Mietzner, and Dirk Tomsa, 114–135. Singapore: Institute for Southeast Asian Studies.

Barber, Richard, ed. 2000. *Aceh: The Untold Story*. Bangkok: Asian Forum for Human Rights and Development.

Barker, Joshua. 2001. "State of Fear: Controlling the Criminal Contagion in Suharto's New Order." In *Violence and the State in Suharto's Indonesia*, edited by Benedict R. O'G Anderson, 20–53. Ithaca, NY: Southeast Asia Program, Cornell University.

Barron, Patrick. 2007. "Getting Reintegration Back on Track: Problems in Aceh and Priorities for Moving Forward." Paper presented at the conference, The Peace Process in Aceh: The Remainders of Violence and the Future of Nanggroe Aceh Darussalam, Harvard University, 24–27 October.

Barron, Patrick. 2008. "Managing the Resource for Peace: Reconstruction and Peacebuilding in Aceh." In *Reconfiguring Politics: The Indonesia-Aceh Peace Process*, edited by Aguswandi and Judith Large, 58–61. London: Conciliation Resources.

Barron, Patrick. 2009. "Peace without Reintegration: Lessons for DDR Theory and Practice from Aceh." In *Small Arms Survey 2009: Shadows of War*, edited by Small Arms Survey, 248–283. Cambridge: Cambridge University Press.

Barron, Patrick. 2014. "Barriers to the Consolidation of Peace: The Political Economy of Post-Conflict Violence in Indonesia." D.Phil. diss., University of Oxford.

Barron, Patrick, with Paul Arthur and Peter Bartu. 2012. "Sub-National Violence in Middle and Higher Income Countries." Background paper for World Development Report 2011. Washington, DC: World Bank.

Barron, Patrick, Muhammad Najib Azca, and Tri Susdinarjanti. 2012. *After the Communal War: Understanding and Addressing Postconflict Violence in Eastern Indonesia*. Yogyakarta: CSPS Books.

Barron, Patrick, and Adam Burke. 2008. *Supporting Peace in Aceh: Development Agencies and International Involvement*. Policy Studies No. 47. Washington, DC: East-West Center.

Barron, Patrick, and Samuel Clark. 2006. "Decentralizing Inequality? Center-Periphery Relations, Local Governance, and Conflict in Aceh." Conflict Prevention and Reconstruction Paper No. 39. Washington, DC: World Bank.

Barron, Patrick, Samuel Clark, and Muslahuddin Daud. 2005. *Conflict and Recovery in Aceh: An Assessment of Conflict Conditions and Options for Supporting the Peace Process*. Jakarta: World Bank.

Barron, Patrick, Anders Engvall, and Adrian Morel. 2016. "Understanding Violence in Southeast Asia: The Contribution of Violent Incidents Monitoring Systems." Bangkok: The Asia Foundation.

Barron, Patrick, Sana Jaffrey, Blair Palmer, and Ashutosh Varshney. 2009. "Understanding Violent Conflict in Indonesia: A Mixed Methods Approach." Social Development Paper No. 117. Washington, DC: World Bank.

Barron, Patrick, Sana Jaffrey, and Ashutosh Varshney. 2016. "When Large Conflicts Subside: The Ebbs and Flow of Violence in Post-Suharto Indonesia." *Journal of East Asian Studies* 16 (2): 191–217.

Barron, Patrick, Kai Kaiser, and Menno Pradhan. 2004. "Local Conflict in Indonesia: Measuring Incidence and Identifying Patterns." Policy Research Working Paper No. 3384. Washington, DC: World Bank.

Barron, Patrick, Kai Kaiser, and Menno Pradhan. 2009. "Understanding Variations in Local Conflict: Evidence and Implications from Indonesia." *World Development* 37 (3): 698–713.

Barron, Patrick, and David Madden. 2004. "Violence and Conflict Resolution in Non-Conflict Regions: The Case of Lampung, Indonesia." Indonesian Social Development Papers No. 2. Jakarta: World Bank.

Barron, Patrick, Melina Nathan, and Bridget Welsh. 2005. "Consolidating Indonesia's Democracy: Conflict, Institutions and the 'Local' in the 2004 Legislative Elections." Conflict Prevention and Reconstruction Paper No. 31. Washington, DC: World Bank.

Barron, Patrick, Sri Kusumastuti Rahayu, Sunita Varada, and Vita Febriany. 2010. "Disturbing the Equilibrium: Movements Out of Poverty in Conflict-Affected Areas of Indonesia." In *Moving Out of Poverty: Rising from the Ashes of Conflict*, edited by Deepa Narayan and Patti Petesch, 290–377. Washington, DC: Palgrave Macmillan and World Bank.

Barron, Patrick, Erman Rahman, and Kharisma Nugroho. 2013. *The Contested Corners of Asia: Subnational Conflict and International Development Assistance—The Case of Aceh, Indonesia*. Jakarta/Bangkok: Asia Foundation.

Barron, Patrick, and Joanne Sharpe. 2005. "Counting Conflicts: Using Newspaper Reports to Understand Violence in Indonesia." Indonesian Social Development Papers No. 7. Jakarta: World Bank.

Barron, Patrick, and Joanne Sharpe. 2008. "Local Conflict in Post-Suharto Indonesia: Understanding Variations in Violence Levels and Forms through Local Newspapers." *Journal of East Asian Studies* 8 (3): 395–423.

Bartels, Dieter. 1977. "Guarding the Invisible Mountain: Intervillage Alliances, Religious Syncretism, and Ethnic Identities among Ambonese Christians and Moslems in the Moluccas." Ph.D. diss., Cornell University.

Barter, Shane Joshua. 2011. "The Free Aceh Elections? The 2009 Legislative Contests in Aceh." *Indonesia* 91 (April): 113–130.

Barton, Greg. 2006. *Gus Dur: The Authorized Biography of Abdurrahman Wahid*. 2d ed. Jakarta: Equinox.

Bates, Robert H. 2001. *Prosperity and Violence: The Political Economy of Development*. London: W. W. Norton.

Bates, Robert H. 2008a. *When Things Fell Apart: State Failure in Late-Century Africa*. New York: Cambridge University Press.

Bates, Robert H. 2008b. "State Failure." *Annual Review of Political Science* 11: 1–12.

Bates, Robert H., Avner Greif, Margaret Levi, Jean-Laurent Rosenthal, and Barry R. Weingast. 1998. *Analytic Narratives*. Princeton, NJ: Princeton University Press.

Bates, Robert H., Avner Greif, and Smita Singh. 2002. "Organizing Violence." *Journal of Conflict Resolution* 46 (5): 599–628.

Beeck, Christine. 2007. "Re-paving the Road to Peace: Analysis of the Implementation of DD&R in Aceh Province, Indonesia." BICC Brief No. 35. Bonn: Bonn International Center for Conversation (BICC).

Belloni, Roberto. 2008. *State-building and International Intervention in Bosnia.* London: Routledge.

Berdal, Mats. 2012. "Reflections on Post-War Violence and Peacebuilding." In *The Peace in Between: Post-war Violence and Peacebuilding*, edited by Asti Suhrke and Mats Berdal, 309–326. London: Routledge.

Berdal, Mats, Gemma Collante-Celador, and Merima Zupcevic Buzadzic. 2012. "Post-War Violence in Bosnia and Herzegovina." In *The Peace in Between: Post-war Violence and Peacebuilding*, edited by Asti Suhrke and Mats Berdal, 75–94. London: Routledge.

Berdal, Mats, and David M. Malone, eds. 2000. *Greed and Grievance: Economic Agendas in Civil Wars.* London: Lynne Rienner.

Berdal, Mats, and Dominik Zaum, eds. 2012. *Political Economy of Statebuilding: Power After Peace.* Abingdon: Routledge.

Berenschot, Ward. 2011. *Riot Politics: Hindu-Muslim Violence and the Indian State.* New York: C. Hurst.

Berkeley, Bill. 2001. *The Graves Are Not Yet Full: Race, Tribe, and Power in the Heart of Africa.* New York: Basic Books.

Bermeo, Nancy. 1992. "Democracy and the Lessons of Dictatorship." *Comparative Politics* 24 (3): 273–291.

Bertrand, Jacques. 2002. "Legacies of the Authoritarian Past: Religious Violence in Indonesia's Moluccan Islands." *Pacific Affairs* 75 (1): 57–85.

Bertrand, Jacques. 2004. *Nationalism and Ethnic Violence in Indonesia.* Cambridge: Cambridge University Press.

Besley, Timothy, and Torsten Persson. 2011. *Pillars of Prosperity: The Political Economics of Development Clusters.* Princeton, NJ: Princeton University Press.

Blattman, Christopher, and Edward Miguel. 2010. "Civil War." *Journal of Economic Literature* 48 (1): 3–57.

Bohm, C. J. 2005. *Brief Chronicle of the Unrest in the Moluccas, 1999–2005.* Ambon: Crisis Centre Diocese of Amboina.

Bourchier, David. 1990. "Crime, Law, and State Authority in Indonesia." In *State and Civil Society in Indonesia*, edited by Arief Budiman, 177–212. Clayton, Victoria: Monash University.

Bourchier, David. 1999. "Skeletons, Vigilantes, and the Armed Forces' Fall from Grace." In *The Last Days of Suharto*, edited by Edward Aspinall, Herb Feith, and Gerry van Klinken, 149–172. Clayton, Victoria: Monash Asia Institute.

Boyle, Michael J. 2012. "Revenge and Reprisal in Kosovo." In *The Peace in Between: Post-war Violence and Peacebuilding*, edited by Asti Suhrke and Mats Berdal, 95–116. London: Routledge.

Boyle, Michael J. 2014. *Violence after War: Explaining Instability in Postconflict States.* Washington, DC: John Hopkins Press.

BPS Ambon (Bureau of Statistics Ambon). 2000. *Kota Ambon Dalam Angka.* Ambon: Badan Pusat Statistik Maluku.

BPS Maluku (Bureau of Statistics Maluku). 2005. *Propinsi Maluku Dalam Angka.* Ambon: Badan Pusat Statistik Maluku.

BPS Maluku (Bureau of Statistics Maluku). 2010. *Propinsi Maluku Dalam Angka.* Ambon: Badan Pusat Statistik Maluku.

BPS Maluku Utara (Bureau of Statistics Maluku Utara). 2005. *Propinsi Maluku Utara Dalam Angka.* Ternate: Badan Pusat Statistik Maluku Utara.

BRA (Aceh Reintegration Agency). 2008. "Economic Section Update." Unpublished document. November.

Brady, Henry E., and David Collier, eds. 2004. *Rethinking Social Inquiry: Diverse Tools, Shared Standards.* Oxford: Rowman & Littlefield.

Brancati, Dawn. 2009. *Peace by Design: Managing Intrastate Conflict through Decentralization.* New York: Oxford University Press.

Brass, Paul R. 1991. *Ethnicity and Nationalism.* London: Sage.

Brass, Paul R. 1997. *Theft of an Idol: Text and Context in the Representation of Collective Violence.* Princeton, NJ: Princeton University Press.

Brass, Paul R. 2003. *The Production of Hindu-Muslim Violence in Contemporary India.* Seattle: University of Washington Press.

Bräuchler, Birgit. 2015. *The Cultural Dimensions of Peace: Decentralization and Reconciliation in Indonesia.* Basingstoke: Palgrave Macmillan.

Brown, Graham, with Christopher Wilson and Suprayoga Hadi. 2005. *Overcoming Violent Conflict.* Vol. 4. *Peace and Development Analysis in Maluku and North Maluku.* Jakarta: United Nations Development Programme.

Bubandt, Nils. 2000. "Conspiracy Theories: Apocalyptic Narratives and the Discursive Construction of 'the Violence in Maluku.'" *Antropologi Indonesia* 63: 15–32.

Bubandt, Nils. 2001. "Malukan Apocalypse: Themes in the Dynamics of Violence in Eastern Indonesia." In *Violence in Indonesia,* edited by Ingrid Wessel and Georgia Wimhofer, 228–254. Hamburg: Abera.

Bubandt, Nils. 2008. "Rumors, Pamphlets, and the Politics of Paranoia in Indonesia." *Journal of Asian Studies* 67 (3): 789–817.

Bueno de Mesquita, Bruce, Alastair Smith, Randolph M. Siverson, and James D. Morrow. 2003. *The Logic of Political Survival.* Cambridge, MA: MIT Press.

Bunte, Marco, and Andreas Ufen, eds. 2008. *Democratization in Post-Suharto Indonesia.* London: Routledge.

Burke, Adam. 2008. "Peacebuilding and Rebuilding at Ground Level: Practical Constraints and Policy Objectives in Aceh." *Conflict, Security, and Development* 8 (1): 47–69.

Burke, Adam, and Afnan. 2005. "Aceh: Reconstruction in a Conflict Environment: Views from Civil Society, Donors and NGOs." Indonesian Social Development Papers No. 8. Jakarta: World Bank.

Bush, Robin. 2009. *Nahdlatul Ulama and the Struggle for Power within Islam and Politics in Indonesia.* Singapore: Institute for Southeast Asian Studies.

Butt, Simon. 2011. *Corruption and Law in Indonesia.* London: Routledge.

Call, Charles T. 2012. *Why Peace Fails: The Causes and Prevention of Civil War.* Washington, DC: Georgetown University Press.

Call, Charles T., with Vanessa Wyeth, eds. 2008. *Building States to Build Peace.* Boulder, CO: Lynne Rienner.

Caplan, Richard. 2005. *International Governance of War-Torn Territories: Rule and Reconstruction.* Oxford: Oxford University Press.

The Carter Center. 2009. *Final Report of the Carter Center Limited Observation Mission to the April 9, 2009, Legislative Elections in Indonesia.* Atlanta, GA: The Carter Center.

Cederman, Lars-Erik, Nils B. Weidmann, and Kristian Skrede Gleditsch. 2011. "Horizontal Inequality and Ethnonationalist Civil War: A Global Comparison." *American Political Science Review* 105 (3): 478–495.

Center for Peace and Conflict Resolution Studies (CPCRS). 2009a. "Aceh Peace Monitoring Update: 1st March–30th June 2009." Banda Aceh: CPCRS, Syiah Kuala University.

Center for Peace and Conflict Resolution Studies (CPCRS). 2009b. "Aceh Peace Monitoring Update: 1st July–31st August 2009." Banda Aceh: CPCRS, Syiah Kuala University.

Chandler, David. 2006. *Empire in Denial: The Politics of Statebuilding.* London: Pluto Press.

Chandra, Kanchan. 2007. "Counting Heads: A Theory of Voter and Elite Behavior in Patronage Democracies." In *Patrons, Clients, and Policies,* edited by Herbert Kitschelt and Steven I. Wilkinson, 84–109. Cambridge: Cambridge University Press.

Chauvel, Richard. 1990. *Nationalists, Soldiers, and Separatists: The Ambonese Islands from Colonialism to Revolt, 1880–1950.* Leiden: KITLV Press.

Chauvel, Richard, and Ikrar Nusa Bhakti. 2004. *The Papua Conflict: Jakarta's Perceptions and Policies.* Policy Studies No. 5. Washington, DC: East-West Center.

Chauvet, Lisa, Paul Collier, and Håvard Hegre. 2008. "The Security Challenge in Conflict-Prone Countries." Copenhagen Consensus Conflicts Challenge paper. Web edition http://www.prio.no/CSCW/Research-and-Publications/Publication/?oid=186640 (accessed 7 October 2011).

Chesterman, Simon. 2004. *You, the People: The United Nations, Transitional Administration, and Statebuilding.* New York: Oxford.

Chesterman, Simon, Michael Ignatieff, and Ramesh Thakur. 2005. *Making States Work: State Failure and the Crisis of Governance.* Tokyo: United Nations University Press.

Chua, Amy. 2003. *World on Fire: How Exporting Free Market Democracy Breeds Ethnic Hatred and Global Instability.* New York: Doubleday.

Clark, Phil, and Zachary D. Kaufman, eds. 2008. *After Genocide: Transitional Justice, Postconflict Reconstruction, and Reconciliation in Rwanda and Beyond.* New York: Columbia University Press.

Clark, Samuel, ed. 2004. "More than Just Ownership: Ten Land and Natural Resource Conflict Case Studies from East Java and NTT." Indonesian Social Development Papers No. 4. Jakarta: World Bank.

Clark, Samuel, and Blair Palmer. 2008. "Peaceful Pilkada, Dubious Democracy: Aceh's Postconflict Elections and their Implications." Indonesian Social Development Papers No. 11. Jakarta: World Bank.

Collier, Paul. 1999. "On the Economic Consequences of Civil War." *Oxford Economic Papers* 50 (4): 168–183.

Collier, Paul. 2008. "Postconflict Economic Policy." In *Building States to Build Peace,* edited by Charles T. Call with Vanessa Wyeth, 103–117. Boulder, CO: Lynne Rienner.

Collier, Paul, and Anke Hoeffler. 2004. "Greed and Grievance in Civil War." *Oxford Economic Papers* 56 (4): 663–695.

Collier, Paul, Anke Hoeffler, and Dominic Rohner. 2009. "Beyond Greed and Grievance: Feasibility and Civil War." *Oxford Economic Papers* 61: 1–27.

Collier, Paul, Anke Hoeffler, and Mans Soderbom. 2008. "Postconflict Risks." *Journal of Peace Research* 45 (4): 461–478.

Colombijn, Freek, and Thomas Lindblad, eds. 2002. *Roots of Violence in Indonesia.* Singapore: Institute of Southeast Asian Studies.

Colson, Aurélien. 2000. "The Logic of Peace and the Logic of Justice." *International Relations* 15 (1): 51–62.

Coppel, Charles A., ed. 2006. *Violent Conflicts in Indonesia*. London: Routledge.

Coser, Lewis. 1956. *The Functions of Social Conflict*. New York: Free Press.

Cramer, Christopher. 2006. *Civil War Is Not a Stupid Thing: Accounting for Violence in Developing Countries*. London: Hurst.

Cribb, Robert. 1990. *The Indonesian Killings of 1965–1966: Studies from Java and Bali*. Melbourne: Centre of Southeast Asian Studies, Monash University.

Crouch, Harold. 2007 [1988]. *The Army and Politics in Indonesia*. Singapore: Equinox.

Crouch, Harold. 2010. *Political Reform in Indonesia after Soeharto*. Singapore: Institute for Southeast Asian Studies.

Daly, Sarah Zukerman. 2012. "Organizational Legacies of Violence: Conditions Favoring Insurgency in Colombia, 1964–84." *Journal of Peace Research* 49 (3): 473–491.

Daly, Sarah Zukerman. 2016. *Organized Violence after Civil War: The Geography of Recruitment in Latin America*. Cambridge: Cambridge University Press.

Dassen, Julie van. 2010. *Maluku Economic Recovery Program II Peace Study*. Jakarta: MercyCorps. http://www.internal-displacement.org/8025708F004CE90B/(http Documents)/719559390E0A94C5C12578000036DB53/$file/Mercy+Corps+Maluku+Positive+Deviance+Peace+Study+-+for+external+use.pdf (accessed 17 May 2013).

Davidson, Jamie S. 2008. *From Rebellion to Riots: Collective Violence on Indonesian Borneo*. Madison: University of Wisconsin Press.

Davidson, Jamie S., and David Henley. 2007. *The Revival of Tradition in Indonesian Politics: The Deployment of Adat from Colonialism to Indigenism*. London: Routledge.

Demombynes, Gabriel. 2011. "Drug Trafficking and Violence in Central America and Beyond." Background paper for the 2011 World Development Report on Conflict and Development. Washington, DC: World Bank.

D'Hondt, Laure, and M. Syahril Sangaji. 2010. "Environmental Justice in Halmahera Utara: Lost in Poverty, Interests, and Identity." Working paper, Leiden University.

Diamond, Larry. 2010. "Indonesia's Place in Global Democracy." In *Problems of Democratisation in Indonesia: Elections, Institutions, and Society*, edited by Edward Aspinall and Marcus Mietzner, 21–49. Singapore: Institute for Southeast Asian Studies.

Dominguez, Andrea. 2008. "The High Cost of Violence in Central America." http://www.comunidadesegura.org/en/STORY-High-Cost-of-Violence-in-Central-America (accessed 7 October 2011).

Doyle, Michael, and Nicholas Sambanis. 2000. "International Peacebuilding: A Theoretical and Quantitative Analysis." *American Political Science Review* 94 (4): 779–801.

Doyle, Michael, and Nicholas Sambanis. 2006. *Making War and Building Peace: United Nations Peace Operations*. Princeton, NJ: Princeton University Press.

Drexler, Elizabeth F. 2008. *Aceh, Indonesia: Securing the Insecure State*. Philadelphia: University of Pennsylvania Press.

Duncan, Christopher R. 2005. "The Other Maluku: Chronologies of Conflict in North Maluku." *Indonesia* 80 (October): 53–80.

Duncan, Christopher R. 2009. "Reconciliation and Revitalization: The Resurgence of Tradition in Postconflict Tobelo, North Maluku, Eastern Indonesia." *Journal of Asia Studies* 68 (4): 1077–1104.

Duncan, Christopher R. 2014. *Violence and Vengeance: Religious Conflict and its Aftermath in Eastern Indonesia.* Singapore: NUS Press.

Ecip, Sinansari S. 1999. *Menyulut Ambon: Kronologi Merambatnya berbagai Kerusuhan Lintas Wilayah di Indonesia.* [Setting Ambon alight: The chronology of the spread of cross-regional rioting in Indonesia]. Bandung: Pustaka Mizan.

Elbadawi, Ibrahim, Håvard Hegre, and Gary J. Milante. 2008. "The Aftermath of Civil War." *Journal of Peace Research* 45 (4): 451–459.

Ellen, Roy. 1993. "Faded Images of Old Tidore in Contemporary Southeast Seram: A View from the Periphery." *Cakalele* 4: 23–37.

Elster, John. 1989. *Nuts and Bolts for the Social Sciences.* Cambridge: Cambridge University Press.

Elster, John. 2007. *Explaining Social Behavior: More Nuts and Bolts for the Social Sciences.* New York: Cambridge University Press.

Emmerson, Donald K. 2000. "Will Indonesia Survive?" *Foreign Affairs* 79 (3): 95–106.

Erb, Maribeth, and Priyambudi Sulistiyanto, eds. 2009. *Deepening Democracy in Indonesia? Direct Elections for Local Leaders (Pilkada).* Singapore: Institute of Southeast Asian Studies.

Erikson, Mikael, and Peter Wallensteen. 2004. "Armed Conflict, 1989–2003." *Journal of Peace Research* 41 (5): 625–636.

European Union Election Observation Mission (EUEOM). 2007. "Aceh, Indonesia: Governor and Regent/Mayor Elections, Final Report." http://www.eeas.europa.eu/eueom/pdf/missions/aceh_final_report_e.pdf (accessed 21 November 2012).

Eye on Aceh. 2004. *Aceh: Logging a Conflict Zone.* Banda Aceh: Eye on Aceh.

Fearon, James D. 1995. "Rationalist Explanations for War." *International Organization* 49 (3): 379–414.

Fearon, James D. 2004. "Why Do Some Civil Wars Last so Much Longer Than Others?" *Journal of Peace Research* 41: 275–301.

Fearon, James D., and David D. Laitin. 1996. "Explaining Interethnic Cooperation." *American Political Science Review* 90 (4): 715–735.

Fearon, James D., and David D. Laitin. 2003. "Ethnicity, Insurgency, and Civil War." *American Political Science Review* 97 (1): 75–90.

Fenno, Richard. 1990. *Watching Politicians: Essays on Participant Observation.* Berkeley: Institute of Governmental Studies, University of California.

Forbes Damai/DSF. 2006. "Aceh Pilkada Dynamics Update: 5–22 December 2006." Banda Aceh: Forbes Damai/Decentralization Support Facility.

Ford, Michele, and Thomas B. Pepinsky, eds. 2014. *Beyond Oligarchy: Wealth, Power, and Contemporary Indonesian Politics.* Ithaca, NY: Cornell Southeast Asia Program Publications.

Forman, Shepard, and Stewart Patrick, eds. 2000a. *Good Intentions: Pledges of Aid for Postconflict Recovery.* Boulder, CO: Lynne Rienner.

Forman, Shepard, and Stewart Patrick. 2000b. "Introduction." In *Good Intentions: Pledges of Aid for Postconflict Recovery*, edited by Shepard Forman and Stewart Patrick, 1–34. Boulder, CO: Lynne Rienner.

Fortna, Virginia Page. 2008. *Does Peacekeeping Work? Shaping Belligerents' Choices after Civil War.* Princeton, NJ: Princeton University Press.

Fox, Sean, and Kristian Hoelscher. 2012. "Political Order, Development and Social Violence." *Journal of Peace Research* 49 (3): 431–444.

Freedom House. 2011. *Freedom of the Press 2011—Indonesia.* 23 September. http://www.unhcr.org/refworld/docid/4e7c84f81e.html (accessed 16 July 2012).

Frodin, Lina. 2008. "The Challenges of Reintegration in Aceh." In *Reconfiguring Politics: The Indonesia-Aceh Peace Process*, edited by Aguswandi and Judith Large, 54–57. London: Conciliation Resources.

Fukuyama, Francis. 2004. *State Building: Governance and World Order in the Twenty-First Century*. London: Profile Books.

Fukuyama, Francis. 2011. *The Origins of Political Order: From Prehuman Times to the French Revolution*. New York: Farrar, Straus and Giroux.

Gagnon, V. P. 1994. "Ethnic Nationalism and International Conflict: The Case of Serbia." *International Security* 19 (3): 130–166.

Galtung, Johan. 1969. "Violence, Peace, and Peace Research." *Journal of Peace Research* 6 (3): 167–191.

Gambetta, Diego. 1998. "Concatenations of Mechanisms." In *Social Mechanisms: An Analytical Approach to Social Theory*, edited by Peter Hedstrom and Richard Swedberg, 102–124. New York: Cambridge University Press.

Gates, Scott. 2002. "Recruitment and Allegiance: The Microfoundations of Rebellion." *Journal of Conflict Resolution* 46 (1): 111–130.

Gates, Scott, Håvard Hegre, Mark P. Jones, and Håvard Strand. 2006. "Institutional Inconsistency and Political Stability: Polity Duration, 1800–2000." *American Journal of Political Science* 50 (4): 893–908.

Geddes, Barbara. 2003. *Paradigms and Sand Castles: Theory Building and Research Design in Comparative Politics*. Ann Arbor: University of Michigan Press.

Geertz, Clifford. 1973. *The Interpretation of Cultures*. New York: Basic Books.

Geneva Declaration Secretariat. 2008. *Global Burden of Armed Violence*. Geneva: Geneva Declaration Secretariat.

Geneva Declaration Secretariat. 2011. *Global Burden of Armed Violence 2011: Lethal Encounters*. Geneva: Cambridge.

Ghani, Ashraf, and Clare Lockhart. 2008. *Fixing Failed States: A Framework for Rebuilding a Fractured World*. New York: Oxford University Press.

Ghobarah, Hazem Adam, Paul Huth, and Bruce Russett. 2003. "Civil Wars Kill and Maim People—Long after the Shooting Stops." *American Political Science Review* 97: 189–202.

Gledhill, John 2012. "Competing for Change: Regime Transition, Intrastate Competition, and Violence." *Security Studies* 21 (1): 43–82.

Goldstone, Jack A., Robert H. Bates, David L. Epstein, Ted R. Gurr, Michael B. Lustik, Monty G. Marshall, Jay Ulfelder, and Mark Woodward. 2010. "A Global Model for Forecasting Political Instability." *American Journal of Political Science* 54 (1): 190–208.

Good, Byron J., Mary-Jo M. D. Good, Jesse J. H. Grayman, and Matthew Lakoma. 2006. *Psychosocial Needs Assessment of Communities Affected by the Conflict in the Districts of Pidie, Bireuen and Aceh Utara*. Jakarta: International Organisation for Migration.

Good, Byron J., Mary-Jo M. D. Good, Jesse J. H. Grayman, and Matthew Lakoma. 2007. *Psychosocial Needs Assessment of Communities in 14 Conflict-Affected Districts in Aceh*. Jakarta: International Organisation for Migration.

Grayman, Jesse Hession. 2012. "Humanitarian Encounters in Postconflict Aceh, Indonesia." Ph.D. diss., Harvard University.

Gurr, Ted Robert. 1970. *Why Men Rebel*. Princeton, NJ: Princeton University Press.

Gurr, Ted Robert. 1986. "The Political Origins of State Violence and Terror: A Theoretical Analysis." In *Government Violence and Repression: An Agenda for Research*, edited by Michael Stohl and George Lopez, 45–71. New York: Greenwood Press.

The Habibie Center. 2012. "Policy Brief: Map of Violence in Indonesia (January-April 2012)." Jakarta: The Habibie Center.

The Habibie Center. 2013. "Peace and Policy Review: Map of Violence in Indonesia (September-December 2013) and Issues Raised in Nine Provinces throughout 2012." Jakarta: The Habibie Center.

Hadi, Faisal. 2008. "Human Rights and Justice in Aceh: The Long and Winding Road." In *Reconfiguring Politics: The Indonesia-Aceh Peace Process*, edited by Aguswandi and Judith Large, 66–69. London: Conciliation Resources.

Hadiz, Vedi R. 2010. *Localising Power in Post-Authoritarian Indonesia: A Southeast Asia Perspective*. Stanford, CA: Stanford University Press.

Hampson, Fen Olser. 1996. *Nurturing Peace: Why Peace Settlements Succeed or Fail.* Washington, DC: United States Institute of Peace.

Hartzell, Caroline, Matthew Hoddie, and Donald Rothchild. 2001. "Stabilizing the Peace after Civil War: An Investigation of Some Key Variables." *International Organization* 55 (1): 183–208.

Hasan, Noorhaidi. 2006. *Laskar Jihad: Islam, Militancy, and the Quest for Identity in Post-New Order Indonesia*. Ithaca, NY: Cornell Southeast Asia Program.

Hedstrom, Peter, and Richard Swedberg. 1996. "Social Mechanisms." *Acta Sociologica* 39 (3): 255–342.

Hedstrom, Peter, and Richard Swedberg, eds. 1998. *Social Mechanisms: An Analytical Approach to Social Theory*. New York: Cambridge University Press.

Hedstrom, Peter, and Lars Udehn. 2009. "Analytical Sociology and Theories of the Middle Range." In *The Oxford Handbook of Analytical Sociology*, edited by Peter Hedstrom and Peter Bearman, 25–50. Oxford: Oxford University Press.

Hefner, Robert W. 2000. *Civil Islam: Muslims and Democratization in Indonesia*. Princeton, NJ: Princeton University Press.

Hegre, Håvard, Tanja Ellingsen, Scott Gates, and Nils Petter Gleditsch. 2001. "Toward a Democratic Civil Peace? Democracy, Political Change, and Civil War, 1816–1992." *American Political Science Review* 95 (1): 33–48.

Herriman, Nicholas. 2007. "Sorcerer Killings in Banyuwangi: A Re-Examination of State Responsibility for Violence." *Asian Studies Review* 31 (1): 61–78.

Heryanto, Ariel. 2006. *State Terrorism and Political Identity in Indonesia: Fatally Belonging*. London: Routledge.

Hill, Hal, and Yogi Vidyattama. 2014. "Hares and Tortoises: Regional Development Dynamics in Indonesia." In *Regional Dynamics in a Decentralized Indonesia*, edited by Hal Hill, 68–97. Singapore: Institute of Southeast Asian Studies.

Hillman, Ben. 2012a. "Ethnic Politics and Local Political Parties in Indonesia." *Asian Ethnicity* 13 (4): 419–440.

Hillman, Ben. 2012b. "Power-Sharing and Political Party Engineering in Conflict-Prone Societies: The Indonesian Experiment in Aceh." *Conflict, Security, and Development* 12 (2): 149–169.

Hobbes, Thomas. 2008. [1651] *Leviathan*. Oxford: Oxford University Press.

Hoddie, Matthew, and Caroline A. Hartzell, eds. 2010. *Strengthening Peace in Post-Civil War States: Transforming Spoilers into Stakeholders*. Chicago: University of Chicago Press.

Hoeffler, Anke, and Marta Reynal-Querol. 2003. *Measuring the Costs of Conflict*. Washington, DC: World Bank.

Hoffman, Bert, and Kai Kaiser. 2002. "The Making of the Big Bang and Its Aftermath: A Political Economy Perspective." Paper presented at the conference Can Decentralization Help Rebuild Indonesia? Atlanta, Georgia, 1–3 May.

Honna, Jun. 2003. *Military Politics and Democratization in Indonesia*. New York: Routledge.

Horowitz, Donald L. 1985. *Ethnic Groups in Conflict*. Berkeley: University of California Press.

Horowitz, Donald L. 2001. *The Deadly Ethnic Riot*. Berkeley: University of California Press.

Horowitz, Donald L. 2013. *Constitutional Change and Democracy in Indonesia*. New York: Cambridge University Press.

Huber, Konrad. 2004. *The HDC in Aceh: Promises and Pitfall of NGO Mediation*. Policy Studies No. 9. Washington, DC: East-West Center.

Human Rights Watch (HRW). 1999. "Indonesia: The Violence in Ambon." March. http://www.hrw.org/reports/1999/03/01/indonesiaeasttimor-violence-ambon (accessed 14 May 2013).

Human Rights Watch (HRW). 2001. "Indonesia: The War in Aceh." *HRW* 13 (4). August. http://www.hrw.org/reports/2001/aceh/indacheh0801.pdf (accessed 10 December 2012).

Human Rights Watch (HRW). 2003. "Aceh under Martial Law: Inside the Secret War." *HRW* 15 (10). December. http://www.hrw.org/reports/2003/12/17/aceh-under-martial-law-inside-secret-war (accessed 17 October 2012).

Humphreys, Macartan. 2005. "Natural Resources, Conflict and Conflict Resolution: Uncovering the Mechanisms." *Journal of Conflict Resolution* 49 (4): 508–537.

Huntingdon, Samuel. 1991. *The Third Wave: Democratization in the Late Twentieth Century*. Norman: University of Oklahoma Press.

Husain, Farid. 2007. *To See the Unseen: Scenes behind the Aceh Peace Treaty*. Jakarta: Health and Hospital Indonesia.

Ignatieff, Michael. 2017. *The Ordinary Virtues: Moral Order in a Divided World*. Cambridge: Harvard University Press.

Indonesian Corruption Watch (ICW). 2009. *Hakim Karir Juara Bebaskan Terdakwa Korupsi*. Jakarta: ICW.

Indonesian Institute of Sciences, Current Asia, and the Center for Humanitarian Dialogue. 2011. *Conflict Management in Indonesia—An Analysis of the Conflicts in Maluku, Papua and Poso*. Geneva: Center for Humanitarian Dialogue.

Institut Tititan Perdamaian (ITP). 2010. *Violence Increased Dispersedly: Analysis of Variant, Pattern, and Structure of Conflict and Violence in Indonesia in 2009–2010*. http://www.peaceportal.org/documents/10156/0/Violence+Increased+Dispersedly+by+Institut+Titian+Perdamaian (accessed 12 July 2012).

International Crisis Group (ICG). 2000. "Indonesia's Maluku Crisis: The Issues." Asia Briefing No. 2. Jakarta/Brussels: ICG. 19 July.

International Crisis Group (ICG). 2001a. "Indonesia: National Police Reform." Asia Report No. 13. Jakarta/Brussels: ICG. 20 February.

International Crisis Group (ICG). 2001b. "Aceh: Why Military Force Won't Bring Lasting Peace." Asia Report No. 17. Jakarta/Brussels: ICG. 12 June.

International Crisis Group (ICG). 2001c. "Communal Violence in Indonesia: Lessons from Kalimantan." Asia Report No. 19. Jakarta/Brussels: ICG. 27 June.

International Crisis Group (ICG). 2002. "Indonesia: The Search for Peace in Maluku." Asia Report No. 31. Jakarta/Brussels: ICG. 8 February.

International Crisis Group (ICG). 2003. "Indonesia: Managing Decentralisation and Conflict in South Sulawesi." Asia Report No. 30. Jakarta/Brussels: ICG. 18 July.

International Crisis Group (ICG). 2005a. "Decentralisation and Conflict in Indonesia: The Mamasa Case." Asia Briefing No. 37. Jakarta/Brussels: ICG. 3 May.

International Crisis Group (ICG). 2005b. "Aceh: A New Chance for Peace." Asia Briefing No. 40. Jakarta/Brussels: ICG. 15 August.

International Crisis Group (ICG). 2005c. "Weakening Indonesia's Mujahidin Networks: Lessons from Maluku and Poso." Asia Report No. 103. Jakarta/Brussels: ICG. 13 October.

International Crisis Group (ICG). 2005d. "Aceh: So Far, So Good," Asia Briefing No. 44. Jakarta/Brussels: ICG. 13 December.

International Crisis Group (ICG). 2006a. "Aceh: Now for the Hard Part." Asia Briefing No. 48. Jakarta/Brussels: ICG. 29 March.

International Crisis Group (ICG). 2006b. "Aceh's Local Elections: The Role of the Free Aceh Movement (GAM)." Asia Briefing No. 57. Jakarta/Brussels: ICG. 29 November.

International Crisis Group (ICG). 2007a. "Indonesia: How GAM Won in Aceh." Asia Briefing No. 61. Jakarta/Brussels: ICG. 22 March.

International Crisis Group (ICG). 2007b. "Indonesia: Decentralisation and Local Power Struggles in Maluku." Asia Briefing No. 64. Jakarta/Brussels: ICG. 22 May.

International Crisis Group (ICG). 2007c. "Aceh: Postconflict Complications." Asia Report No. 139. Jakarta/Brussels: ICG. 4 October.

International Crisis Group (ICG). 2008. "Indonesia: Pre-Election Anxieties in Aceh." Asia Briefing No. 81. Jakarta/Brussels: ICG. 9 September.

International Crisis Group (ICG). 2009a. "Local Elections Disputes in Indonesia: The Case of North Maluku." Asia Briefing No. 86. Jakarta/Brussels: ICG. 22 January.

International Crisis Group (ICG). 2009b. "Indonesia: Deep Distrust in Aceh as Elections Approach." Asia Briefing No. 90. Jakarta/Brussels: ICG. 23 March.

International Crisis Group (ICG). 2010. "Indonesia: Jihadi Surprise in Aceh." Asia Report No. 189. Jakarta/Brussels: ICG. 20 April.

International Crisis Group (ICG). 2011a. "Indonesia: GAM vs. GAM in the Aceh Elections." Asia Briefing No. 123. Jakarta/Brussels: ICG. 15 June.

International Crisis Group (ICG). 2011b. "Indonesia: Trouble Again in Ambon." Asia Briefing No. 128. Jakarta/Brussels: ICG. 4 October.

International Crisis Group (ICG). 2012a. "Indonesia: Cautious Calm in Ambon." Asia Briefing No. 133. Jakarta/Brussels: ICG. 13 February.

International Crisis Group (ICG). 2012b. "Indonesia: The Deadly Cost of Poor Policing." Asia Report No. 218. Jakarta/Brussels: ICG. 16 February.

International Crisis Group (ICG). 2012c. "Indonesia: Averting Election Violence in Aceh." Asia Briefing No. 135. Jakarta/Brussels: ICG. 29 February.

International Displacement Monitoring Centre (IDMC). 2011. "Indonesia/Maluku and North Maluku: Support Still Needed for Thousands of People Ten Years after Their Displacement." IDMC/Norwegian Refugee Council.

Isaac, Jeffrey C. 2012. "New Approaches to the Study of Violence." *Perspectives on Politics* 10 (2): 235–241.

Jaffrey, Sana, and Dan Slater. 2017. "Violence and Regimes in Asia: Capable States and Durable Settlements." In *The State of Conflict and Violence in Asia,* edited by The Asia Foundation, 194–207. Bangkok: The Asia Foundation.

Jarstad, Anna K. 2008. "Power-Sharing: Former Enemies in Joint Government." In *From War to Democracy: Dilemmas of* Peacebuilding, edited by Anna K. Jarstad and Timothy D. Sisk, 105–133. Cambridge: Cambridge University Press.

Joint Fact Finding Team. 1998. *Final report of the Joint Fact Finding Team on 13–15 May Riot.* 23 October.

Jones, Sidney. 2008. "Keeping the Peace: Security in Aceh." In *Reconfiguring Politics: The Indonesia-Aceh Peace Process*, edited by Aguswandi and Judith Large, 72–75. London: Conciliation Resources.

Joseph, Richard A. 1987. *Democracy and Prebendal Politics in Nigeria: The Rise and Fall of the Second Republic*. Cambridge: Cambridge University Press.

Jubair, Salah 2007. *The Long Road to Peace: Inside the GRP-MILF Peace Process*. Cotabato: Institute of Bangsamoro Studies.

Jutersonke, Oliver, Robert Muggah, and Dennis Rodgers. 2009. "Gangs and Violence Reduction in Central America." *Security Dialogue* 40 (4–5): 373–397.

Kakar, Sudhir. 1996. *The Colors of Violence: Cultural Identities, Religion and Culture*. Chicago: University of Chicago.

Kaldor, Mary. 1999. *New and Old Wars: Organized Violence in a Global Era*. Cambridge: Polity.

Kalyvas, Stathis N. 2003. "The Ontology of 'Political Violence.'" *Perspectives on Politics* 1 (3): 475–494.

Kalyvas, Stathis N. 2004. "Warfare in Civil Wars." In *Rethinking the Nature of War*, edited by Jan Angstrom and Isabelle Duyvesteyn, 88–108. Abingdon, UK: Routledge.

Kalyvas, Stathis N. 2006. *The Logic of Violence in Civil War*. Cambridge: Cambridge University Press.

Kalyvas, Stathis N. 2007. "Civil Wars." In *The Oxford Handbook of Comparative Politics*, edited by Charles Boix and Susan C. Stokes, 416–434. Oxford: Oxford University Press.

Kalyvas, Stathis N. 2008a. "Promises and Pitfalls of an Emerging Research Program: The Microdynamics of Civil War." In *Order, Conflict, and Violence*, edited by Stathis N. Kalyvas, Ian Shapiro, and Tarek Masoud, 397–421. Cambridge: Cambridge University Press.

Kalyvas, Stathis N. 2008b. "Ethnicity and the Dynamics of Civil War." Paper presented at the conference Rethinking Ethnicity and Ethnic Strife. Budapest.

Kalyvas, Stathis N. 2008c. "Ethnic Defection in Civil War." *Comparative Political Studies* 41 (8): 1043–1068.

Kanmen, Douglas. 2001. "The Trouble with Normal: The Indonesian Military, Paramilitaries, and the Final Solution in East Timor." In *Violence and the State in Suharto's Indonesia*, edited by Benedict R. O'G. Anderson, 156–188. Ithaca, NY: Cornell Southeast Asia Program Publications.

Kaufman, Stuart J. 2001. *Modern Hatreds: The Symbolic Politics of Ethnic War*. Ithaca, NY: Cornell University Press.

Keen, David. 1998. "The Economic Functions of Violence in Civil Wars." Adelphi Paper No. 320. Oxford: Oxford University Press.

Kell, Tim. 1995. *The Roots of Acehnese Rebellion, 1989–1992*. Singapore: Equinox.

King, Charles. 2004. "The Micropolitics of Social Violence." *World Politics* 56: 431–455.

King, Gary, Robert O. Keohane, and Sidney Verba. 1994. *Designing Social Enquiry*. New York: Princeton University Press.

Kingsbury, Damien, ed. 2005a. *Violence In Between: Conflict and Security in Archipelagic Southeast Asia*. Singapore: Institute of Southeast Asian Studies.

Kingsbury, Damien. 2005b. *The Politics of Indonesia*. Oxford: Oxford University Press.

Kingsbury, Damien. 2006. *Peace in Aceh: A Personal Account of the Helsinki Peace Process*. Jakarta: Equinox.

Kingsbury, Damien, and Lesley McCulloch. 2006. "Military Business in Aceh." In *Verandah of Violence: The Background to the Aceh Problem*, edited by Anthony Reid, 199–224. Singapore: Institute for Southeast Asian Studies.

Klinken, Gerry van. 2000. "Ethnic Fascism in Borneo." *Inside Indonesia* 64 (June–July).

Klinken, Gerry van. 2001. "The Maluku Wars of 1999: Bringing Society Back In." *Indonesia* 71 (April): 1–26.

Klinken, Gerry van. 2007. *Communal Violence and Democratization in Indonesia: Small Town Wars.* London: Routledge.

Klinken, Gerry van. 2009. "Patronage Democracy in Indonesia." In *Rethinking Popular Representation*, edited by Olle Tornquist, Neil Webster, and Kristian Stokke, 141–159. Basingstoke: Palgrave Macmillan.

Klinken, Gerry van, and Edward Aspinall. 2011. "Building Relations: Corruption, Competition, and Cooperation in the Construction Industry." In *The State and Illegality in Indonesia*, edited by Edward Aspinall and Gerry van Klinken, 139–163. Leiden: KITLV Press.

LaFree, Gary, and Andromachi Tseloni. 2006. "Democracy and Crime: A Multilevel Analysis of Homicide Trends in Forty-Four Countries, 1950–2000." *Annals of the American Academy of Political and Social Science* 605 (1): 25–49.

Lee, Terence. 2009. "The Armed Forces and Transitions from Authoritarian Rule: Explaining the Role of the Military in 1986 Philippines and 1998 Indonesia." *Comparative Political Studies* 42 (5): 640–669.

Licklider, Roy. 1995a. *Stopping the Killing: How Civil Wars End.* New York: New York University Press.

Licklider, Roy. 1995b. "The Consequences of Negotiated Settlements in Civil Wars, 1945–1993." *American Political Science Review* 89 (3): 681–690.

Liem Soei Liong. 2002. "It's the Military, Stupid!" In *Roots of Violence in Indonesia: Contemporary Violence in Historical Perspective*, edited by Freek Colombijn and J. Thomas Lindblad, 197–226. Singapore: Institute of Southeast Asian Studies.

Lijphart, Arend. 1968. "Typologies of Democratic Systems." *Comparative Political Studies* 1 (April): 3–44.

Lijphart, Arend. 1977. *Democracy in Plural Societies.* New Haven, CT: Yale University Press.

Linz, Juan J. 1990. "The Perils of Presidentialism." *Journal of Democracy* 1 (1): 51–69.

Loveband, Anne, and Ken Young. 2006. "Migration, Provocateurs, and Communal Conflict: The Cases of Ambon and West Kalimantan." In *Violent Conflicts in Indonesia: Analysis, Representation, Resolution*, edited by Charles A. Coppel, 144–162. London: Routledge.

Lyons, Terence. 2004. "Postconflict Elections and the Process of Demilitarizing Politics: The Role of Electoral Administration." *Democratization* 11 (3): 36–62.

MacIntyre, Andrew J. 2003. *The Power of Institutions: Political Architecture and Governance.* Ithaca, NY: Cornell University Press.

Mahoney, James. 2000. "Path Dependence in Historical Sociology." *Theory and Society* 29: 507–548.

Mahoney, James, and Gary Goertz. 2006. "A Tale of Two Cultures: Contrasting Quantitative and Qualitative Research." *Political Analysis* 14: 227–249.

Mancini, Luca. 2008. "Horizontal Inequality and Communal Violence: Evidence from Indonesian Districts." In *Horizontal Inequalities and Conflict: Understanding Group Violence in Multiethnic Societies*, edited by Frances Stewart, 106–135. London: Palgrave Macmillan.

Mansfield, Edward, and Jack Snyder. 1995. "Democratization and the Danger of War." *International Security* 20 (1): 5–38.

Marhaenjati, Bayu, and Farouk Arnas. 2011. "Police Say Crime Is Down, As Are Rights Violations." *Jakarta Globe.* 31 December. http://www.thejakartaglobe. com/police-say-crime-is-down-as-are-rights-violations/488146 (accessed 14 May 2013).

Mason, T. David, and Patrick J. Fett. 1996. "How Civil Wars End: A Rational Choice Approach." *Journal of Conflict Resolution* 40 (4): 546–568.

Mason, T. David, Joseph P. Weingarten Jr., and Patrick J. Fett. 1999. "Win, Lose, or Draw: Predicting the Outcome of Civil Wars." *Political Research Quarterly* 52 (2): 239–268.

Masyrafah, Harry, and Jock M.J.A. McKeon. 2008. "Post-Tsunami Aid Effectiveness in Aceh: Proliferation and Coordination in Reconstruction." Wolfhenson Center for Development Working Paper No. 6. Washington, DC: Brookings Institute.

May, Bernhard. 2008. "The Law on the Governing of Aceh: The Way Forward or a Source of Conflicts?" In *Reconfiguring Politics: The Indonesia-Aceh Peace Process*, edited by Aguswandi and Judith Large, 42–45. London: Conciliation Resources.

McCarthy, John F. 2007. "The Demonstration Effect: Natural Resources, Ethnonationalism, and the Aceh Conflict." *Singapore Journal of Tropical Geography* 28: 314–333.

McCulloch, Lesley. 2005. "Greed: The Silent Force of the Conflict in Aceh." In *Violence In Between: Conflict and Security in Archipelagic Southeast Asia*, edited by Damian Kingsbury, 203–227. Singapore: Institute for Southeast Asian Studies.

McDonald, Terence J. 1996. *The Historic Turn in the Human Sciences*. Ann Arbor: University of Michigan Press.

McGibbon, Rodd. 2004. *Secessionist Challenges in Aceh and Papua: Is Special Autonomy the Solution?* Policy Studies No. 10. Washington, DC: East-West Center.

McGibbon, Rodd. 2006. "Local Leadership and the Aceh Conflict." In *Verandah of Violence: the Background to the Aceh Problem*, edited by Anthony Reid, 315–359. Singapore: Singapore University Press.

McIntyre, Angus. 2005. *The Indonesian Presidency: The Shift from Personal toward Constitutional Rule*. Lanham, MD: Rowman & Littlefield.

McKenna, Thomas M. 2008. *Muslim Rules and Rebels: Everyday Politics and Armed Separatism in the Southern Philippines*. Berkeley: University of California Press.

McNeish, John-Andrew, and Oscar Lopez Rivera. 2012. "The Multiple Forms of Violence in Post-War Guatemala." In *The Peace in Between: Post-War Violence and Peacebuilding*, edited by Astri Suhrke and Mats Berdal, 289–306. Abingdon: Routledge.

McRae, Dave. 2008. "The Escalation and Decline of Violent Conflict in Poso, Central Sulawesi, 1998–2007." Ph.D. diss., Australian National University.

McRae, Dave. 2010. "Reintegration and Localised Conflict: Security Impacts beyond Influencing Spoilers." *Conflict, Security, and Development* 10 (3): 403–430.

McRae, Dave. 2013. *A Few Poorly Organized Men: Interreligious Violence in Poso, Indonesia*. Leiden: Brill.

Meliala, Adrianus. 2001. "Police As Military: Indonesia's Experience." *Policing: An International Journal of Police Strategies and Management* 24 (3): 420–431.

Mietzner, Marcus. 2006. *The Politics of Military Reform in Post-Suharto Indonesia: Elite Conflict, Nationalism, and Institutional Resistance*. Policy Studies No. 23. Washington, DC: East-West Center.

Mietzner, Marcus. 2008. "Soldiers, Parties, and Bureaucrats: Illicit Fund-Raising in Contemporary Indonesia." *South East Asia Research* 16 (2): 225–254.

Mietzner, Marcus. 2009. *Military Politics, Islam, and the State in Indonesia*. Singapore: Institute of Southeast Asian Studies.

Mietzner, Marcus. 2013. *Money, Power, and Ideology: Political Parties in Post-Authoritarian Indonesia*. Singapore: Asia Studies Association of Australia/NUS Press.

Mill, John Stuart. 1872. *A System of Logic*. New York: Harper.

Miller, Michelle Ann. 2006. "What's Special about Special Autonomy in Aceh?" In *Verandah of Violence: the Background to the Aceh Problem*, edited by Anthony Reid, 292–314. Singapore: Singapore University Press.

Miller, Michelle Ann. 2009. *Rebellion and Reform in Indonesia: Jakarta's Security and Autonomy Policies in Aceh*. Abingdon: Routledge.

Miller, Michelle Ann. 2012. "Self-Governance as a Framework for Conflict Resolution in Aceh." In *Autonomy and Armed Separatism in South and Southeast Asia*, edited by Michelle Ann Miller, 36–58. Singapore: Institute of Southeast Asian Studies.

Milliken, Jennifer, ed. 2003. *State Failure, Collapse and Reconstruction*. London: Blackwell.

Morfit, Michael. 2006. "Staying on the Road to Helsinki: Why the Aceh Peace Agreement Was Possible in August 2005." Paper given at the International Conference on Building Permanent Peace in Aceh: One Year After the Helsinki Accord. Jakarta. 14 August.

Morfit, Michael. 2007. "The Road to Helsinki: The Aceh Agreement and Indonesia's Democratic Development." *International Negotiation* 12: 111–143.

Moser, Caroline O. N. 2006. "Reducing Urban Violence in Developing Countries." Policy Brief 2006–1. Washington, DC: Brookings Institute.

Mueller, John. 2004. *The Remnants of War*. Ithaca, NY: Cornell University Press.

Muggah, Robert. 2009a. "Securing the Peace: Postconflict Security Promotion." In *Small Arms Survey 2009: Shadows of War*, edited by Small Arms Survey, 218–247. Cambridge: Cambridge University Press.

Muggah, Robert, ed. 2009b. *Security and Postconflict Reconstruction: Dealing with Fighters in the Aftermath of War*. Abingdon: Routledge.

Multistakeholder Review (MSR). 2009. *Multistakeholder Review of Postconflict Programming in Aceh*. Jakarta and Banda Aceh: MSR.

Murshed, S. Mansoob, Mohammad Zulfan Tadjoeddin, and Anis Chowdhury. 2009. "Is Fiscal Decentralization Conflict Abating? Routine Violence and District Level Government in Java, Indonesia." *Oxford Development Studies* 37 (4): 397–421.

Nanere, Jan, ed. 2000. *Halmahera Berdarah: Suatu Upaya Mengungkap Keberaran*. Ambon: Yayasan Bina Masyarakat Sejahtera dan Pelestarian Alam.

Ndulu Benno J., Stephen A. O'Connell, Robert H. Bates, Paul Collier, and Chukwuma C. Soludo, eds. 2007. *The Political Economy of Economic Growth in Africa, 1960–2000*. Vol. 1. Cambridge: Cambridge University Press.

Nessen, William. 2006. "Sentiments Made Visible: The Rise and Reason of Aceh's National Liberation Movement." In *Verandah of Violence: the Background to the Aceh Problem*, edited by Anthony Reid, 177–198. Singapore: Singapore University Press.

Newman, Edward, Roland Paris, and Oliver Richmond, eds. 2009. *New Perspectives on Liberal Peacebuilding*. Tokyo: United Nations University Press.

Nordstrom, Carolyn. 2004. *Shadows of War: Violence, Power, and International Profiteering in the Twenty-First Century*. London: University of California Press.

North, Douglass C., John Joseph Wallis, and Barry R. Weingast. 2009. *Violence and Social Order: A Conceptual Framework for Interpreting Recorded Human History*. New York: Cambridge University Press.

Norwegian Refugee Council. 2002. *Profile of Internal Displacement: Indonesia: Compilation of the information available in the Global IDP Database of the Norwegian Refugee Council*. Norwegian Refugee Council/Global IDP Project.

OECD DAC. 2010. *Do No Harm: International Support for Statebuilding*. Paris: OECD DAC.

Olken, Benjamin, and Patrick Barron. 2009. "The Simple Economics of Extortion." *Journal of Political Economy* 117 (3): 417–452.

Olson, Mancur. 1965. *The Logic of Collective Action: Public Goods and the Theory of Groups*. Cambridge, MA: Harvard University Press.

O'Rourke, Kevin. 2002. *Reformasi: The Struggle for Power in Post-Soeharto Indonesia*. Sydney: Allen & Unwin.

Østby, Gudrun, Henrik Urdal, Mohammad Zulfan Tadjoeddin, S. Mansoob Murshed, and Håvard Strand. 2011. "Population Pressure, Inequality and Political Violence: A Disaggregated Study of Indonesian Provinces, 1990–2003." *Journal of Development Studies* 47 (3): 377–398.

Palmer, Blair. 2007. "The Price of Peace." *Inside Indonesia* 90 (October-December). http://www.insideindonesia.org/feature-editions/the-price-of-peace (accessed 22 November 2012).

Palmer Blair. 2010. "Services Rendered: Peace, Patronage and Postconflict Elections in Aceh." In *Problems of Democratisation in Indonesia: Elections, Institutions and Society*, edited by Edward Aspinall and Marcus Mietzner, 286–306. Singapore: Institute of Southeast Asian Studies.

Panggabean, Samsu Rizal, and Benjamin Smith. 2010. "Explaining Anti-Chinese Riots in Late 20th Century Indonesia." *World Development* 39 (2): 231–242.

Paris, Roland. 2004. *At War's End: Building Peace After Civil Conflict*. Cambridge: Cambridge University Press.

Paris, Roland, and Timothy D. Sisk. 2009. *The Dilemmas of Statebuilding: Confronting the Contradictions of Postwar Peace Operations*. Abingdon: Routledge.

Parks, Thomas, Nat Colletta, and Ben Oppenheim. 2013. *The Contested Corners of Asia: Subnational Conflict and International Development Assistance*. Bangkok: The Asia Foundation.

Peake, Gordon. 2009. "What the Timorese Veterans Say: Unpacking Security Promotion in Timor-Leste." In *Security and Postconflict Reconstruction: Dealing with Fighters in the Aftermath of War*, edited by Robert Muggah, 165–189. Abingdon: Routledge.

Peluso, Nancy Lee, and Emily Harwell. 2001. "Territory, Custom, and the Cultural Politics of Ethnic War in West Kalimantan, Indonesia." In *Violent Environments*, edited by Nancy Lee Peluso and Michael Watts, 83–116. Ithaca, NY: Cornell University Press.

Peou, Sorpong. 2012. "Violence in Post-War Cambodia." In *The Peace in Between: Post-War Violence and Peacebuilding*, edited by Asti Suhrke and Mats Berdal, 192–210. London: Routledge.

Pepinsky, Thomas B. 2009. *Economic Crises and the Breakdown of Authoritarian Regimes: Indonesia and Malaysia in Comparative Perspective*. New York: Cambridge University Press.

Petersen, Roger D. 2002. *Understanding Ethnic Violence: Fear, Hatred, and Resentment in Twentieth-Century Europe*. New York: Cambridge University Press.

Pierskalla, Jan H., and Audrey Sacks. 2017. "Unpacking the Effect of Decentralized Governance on Routine Violence: Lessons from Indonesia." *World Development* 90: 213–228.

Pierson, Paul. 2000. "Increasing Returns, Path Dependence, and the Study of Politics." *American Political Science Review* 94: 251–268.

Pinker, Stephen. 2011. *The Better Angels of Our Nature: Why Violence Has Declined*. New York: Viking.

Popkin, Samuel. 1979. *The Rational Peasant: The Political Economy of Rural Society in Vietnam*. Berkeley: University of California Press.

Posen, Barry. 1993. "The Security Dilemma and Ethnic Conflict." *Survival* 35 (1): 27–47.

Powell, Robert. 2006. "War as a Commitment Problem." *International Organization* 60 (1): 169–203.

Przeworski, Adam, and Henry Teune. 1970. *The Logic of Comparative Social Inquiry.* New York: John Wiley.

Purdey, Jemma. 2006. *Anti-Chinese Violence in Indonesia, 1996–1999.* Singapore: Singapore University Press.

Rabasa, Angel, and John Haseman. 2002. *The Military and Democracy in Indonesia: Challenges, Politics, and Power.* Santa Monica, CA: Rand Corporation.

Rachmadi, Raden, and Adida Swamurti. 2006. "Further Funds Approved." *Tempo* 44 (4). 10 July.

Raleigh, Clionadh, and Håvard Hegre. 2005. "Introducing ACLED: An Armed Conflict Location and Events Dataset." Paper presented at the Conference on Disaggregating the Study of Civil War and Transnational Violence. University of California Institute of Global Conflict and Cooperation, San Diego, CA., 7–8 March.

Raleigh, Clionadh, and Håvard Hegre. 2009. "Population Size, Concentration, and Civil War: A Geographically Disaggregated Analysis." *Political Geography* 28: 224–238.

Raleigh, Clionadh, Andrew Linke, Håvard Hegre, and Joakim Karlsen. 2010. "Introducing ACLED-Armed Conflict Location and Event Data." *Journal of Peace Research* 47 (5) 1–10.

Reid, Anthony, ed. 2006. *Verandah of Violence: the Background to the Aceh Problem.* Singapore: Singapore University Press.

Reid, Anthony. 2010. "The Aceh Conflict: A Long-Term View for Long-Term Solutions." Annex to Multistakeholder Review (MSR). *Multistakeholder Review of Postconflict Programming in Aceh.* Jakarta and Aceh: MSR. https://www. conflictanddevelopment.org/index.php?option=com_content&view=article& id=492%253AAnnexes+of+MSR+report&catid=1&lang=en (accessed 17 October 2012).

Reno, William. 2008. "Anti-corruption Efforts in Liberia: Are They Aimed at the Right Targets?" *International Peacekeeping* 15 (3): 387–404.

Restrepo, Jorge, Brodie Ferguson, Jukliana M. Zuniga, and Adriana Villamarin. 2008. "Estimating Lost Product Due to Violent Deaths in 2004." Unpublished background paper for the Small Arms Survey. Geneva: Small Arms Survey/ CERAC.

Ricklefs, M. C. 2008. *A History of Modern Indonesia Since c. 1200.* 4th ed. Stanford, CA: Stanford University Press.

Rieffel, Lex, and Jaleswari Pramodhawardani. 2007. *Out of Business and On Budget: The Challenge of Military Financing in Indonesia.* Washington, DC: USINDO and Brookings Institute Press.

Robinson, Geoffrey. 1995. *The Dark Side of Paradise: Political Violence in Bali.* Ithaca: Cornell University Press.

Robinson, Geoffrey. 1998. "Rawan Is as Rawan Does: The Origins of Disorder in New Order Aceh." *Indonesia* 66 (October): 127–156.

Robison, Richard, and Vedi R. Hadiz. 2004. *Reorganising Power in Indonesia: The Politics of Oligarchy in an Age of Markets.* London: Routledge.

Rodgers, Dennis. 2003. "Dying for It: Gangs, Violence, and Social Change in Urban Nicaragua, 1997–2002." *LSE-DESTIN Development Research Center Crisis States Programme Working Paper* No. 35. London: DRC.

Rodgers, Dennis. 2006. "The State as a Gang: Conceptualizing the Governmentality of Violence in Contemporary Nicaragua." *Critique of Anthropology* 26 (3): 315–330.

Ross, Michael L. 2004. "What Do We Know about Natural Resources and Civil War?" *Journal of Peace Research* 41 (3): 337–356.

Ross, Michael L. 2005. "Resources and Rebellion in Indonesia." In *Understanding Civil War: Europe, Central Asia and Other Regions*, edited by Paul Collier and Nicholas Sambanis, 35–58. Washington DC: World Bank.

Ross, Michael L. 2012. *The Oil Curse: How Petroleum Wealth Shapes the Development of Nations*. Princeton, NJ: Princeton University Press.

Rotberg, Robert I., ed. 2003. *When States Fail: Causes and Consequences*. Princeton, NJ: Princeton University Press.

Saideman, Stephen M., David Lanoue, Michael Campenni, and Samuel Stanton. 2002. "Democratization, Political Institutions, and Ethnic Conflict: A Pooled, Cross-Sectional Time Series Analysis from 1985–1998." *Comparative Political Studies* 35 (1): 103–129.

Sambanis, Nicholas. 2001. "Do Ethnic and Nonethnic Civil Wars Have the Same Causes? A Theoretical and Empirical Enquiry (Part 1)." *Journal of Conflict Resolution* 45 (3): 259–282.

Sambanis, Nicholas. 2002. "A Review of Recent Advances and Future Directions in the Quantitative Literature on Civil War." *Defence and Peace Economics* 13 (3): 215–243.

Sambanis, Nicholas. 2004. "What Is Civil War? Conceptual and Empirical Complexities of an Operational Definition." *Journal of Conflict Resolution* 48 (6): 814–858.

Sambanis, Nicholas, and Håvard Hegre. 2006. "Sensitivity Analysis of Empirical Results on Civil War Onset." *Journal of Conflict Resolution* 50 (4): 508–535.

Samset, Ingrid. 2012. "Sexual Violence: The Case of Eastern Congo." In *The Peace in Between: Post-war Violence and Peacebuilding*, edited by Asti Suhrke and Mats Berdal, 229–247. London: Routledge.

Sarkees, Meredith Reid. 2000. "The Correlates of War Data on War: An Update to 1997." *Conflict Management and Peace Science* 18 (1): 123–144.

Scacco, Alexandra. 2009. "Who Riots? Explaining Individual Participation in Ethnic Violence." Ph.D. diss., Columbia University.

Schelling, Thomas C. 1960. *The Strategy of Conflict*. Cambridge, MA: Harvard University Press.

Schulze, Kirsten E. 2002. "Laskar Jihad and the Conflict in Ambon." *Brown Journal of World Affairs* 9 (1): 57–70.

Schulze, Kirsten E. 2004. *The Free Aceh Movement (GAM): Anatomy of a Separatist Organization*. Policy Studies No. 2. Washington, DC: East-West Center.

Schulze, Kirsten E. 2007. "Mission Not So Impossible: The AMM and the Transition from Conflict to Peace in Aceh, 2005–2006." Working Paper No. 131. Singapore: S. Rajaratnam School of International Studies.

Schütte, Sofie Arjon. 2012. "Against the Odds: Anti-Corruption Reform in Indonesia." *Public Administration and Development* 32 (1): 38–48.

Schwartz, Adam. 2000. *A Nation in Waiting: Indonesia's Search for Stability*. 2nd ed. Boulder, CO: Westview.

Sen, Krishna, and David T. Hill. 2006. *Media, Culture, and Politics in Indonesia*. Jakarta: Equinox.

Shah, Anwar, Riatu Qibthiyyah, and Astrid Dita. 2012. "General Purposes Central-Provincial-Local Transfers (DAU) in Indonesia: From Gap Filling to Ensuring

Fair Access to Essential Public Services for All." Policy Research Working Paper No. 6075. Washington, DC: World Bank.

Sharp, Steve. 2012. *Journalism and Conflict in Indonesia: From Reporting Violence to Promoting Peace*. Abingdon: Routledge.

Sharpe, Joanne. 2005. "Using Newspapers to Monitor Conflict: Evidence from Maluku and North Maluku, Indonesia." Mimeo. Jakarta: World Bank.

Sherlock, Stephen. 2015. "A Balancing Act: Relations between State Institutions under YudhoyoNo." In *The Yudhoyono Presidency: Indonesia's Decade of Stability and Stagnation*, edited by Edward Aspinall, Marcus Mietzner, and Dirk Tomsa, 93–113. Singapore: Institute for Southeast Asian Studies.

Sidel, John T. 2006. *Riots, Pogroms, Jihad: Religious Violence in Indonesia*. Ithaca, NY: Cornell University Press.

Sidel, John T. 2008. "The Manifold Meanings of Displacement: Explaining Inter-Religious Violence, 1999–2001." In *Conflict, Violence, and Displacement in Indonesia*, edited by Eva-Lotta E. Hedman, 29–59. Ithaca, NY: Cornell University Press.

Siegel, James. 1998. *A New Criminal Type in Jakarta: Counter-revolution Today*. Durham, NC: Duke University Press.

Siegel, James. 2001. "Thoughts of the Violence of May 13 and 14, 1998, in Jakarta." In *Violence and the State in Suharto's Indonesia*, edited by Benedict R. O'G. Anderson, 90–123. Ithaca: Cornell Southeast Asia Program Publications.

Siegel, James. 2006. *Naming the Witch*. Stanford, CA.: Stanford University Press.

Silaen, Linda, and I. Made Sentana. 2013. "Indonesia Draws Record Foreign Investment." *Wall Street Journal*. 22 April.

Simanjuntak, Hotli. 2012. "Irwandi Ups his Political Ante by Forming National Aceh Party." *Jakarta Post*. 25 April.

Simanungkalit, Salomo. 2002. *Indonesia dalam Krisis, 1997–2002*. Jakarta: Penerbit Buku Kompas.

Singer, J. David, and Melvin Small. 1972. *The Wages of War, 1816–1965: A Statistical Handbook*. New York: John Wiley.

Singer, J. David, and Melvin Small. 1994. "Correlates of War Project: International and Civil War Data, 1816–1992." Ann Arbor, MI: Interuniversity Consortium for Political and Social Research. http://www.icpsr.umich.edu/icpsrweb/ICPSR/studies/9905 (accessed 28 June 2012).

Singh, Bilveer. 2012. "Autonomy and Armed Separatism in Papua: Why the Cendrawasih Continues to Fear the Garuda." In *Autonomy and Armed Separatism in South and Southeast Asia*, edited by Michelle Ann Miller, 59–76. Singapore: Institute of Southeast Asian Studies.

Sisk, Timothy D. 1996. *Power Sharing and International Mediation in Ethnic Conflicts*. Washington, DC: United States Institute for Peace.

Slater, Dan. 2004. "Indonesia's Accountability Trap: Party Cartels and Presidential Power after Democratic Transition." *Indonesia* 78 (October): 61–92.

Slater, Dan. 2010a. *Ordering Power: Contentious Politics and Authoritarian Leviathans in Southeast Asia*. Cambridge: Cambridge University Press.

Slater, Dan. 2010b. "Altering Authoritarianism: Institutional Complexity and Autocratic Agency in Indonesia." In *Explaining Institutional Change: Ambiguity, Agency, and Power*, edited by James Mahoney and Kathleen Thelen, 132–167. New York: Cambridge University Press.

Smith, Alastair, and Allan C. Stam. 2004. "Bargaining and the Nature of War." *Journal of Conflict Resolution* 48 (6): 783–813.

Smith, Anthony L. 2003. "U.S.-Indonesian Relations: Searching for Cooperation in the War Against Terrorism." *Asia-Pacific Center for Security Studies* 2 (2): 1–4.

Smith, Claire Querida. 2005. "The Roots of Violence and Prospects for Reconciliation: a Case Study of Ethnic Conflict in Central Kalimantan, Indonesia." Conflict Prevention and Reconstruction Paper No. 23. Washington DC: World Bank.

Smith, Claire Querida. 2009. "The Contested State and Politics of Elite Continuity in North Maluku, Indonesia (1998–2008)." Ph.D. diss., London School of Economic and Political Science.

Snyder, David, and William R. Kelly. 1977. "Conflict Intensity, Media Sensitivity, and the Validity of Newspaper Data." *American Sociological Review* 42: 105–123.

Snyder, Jack. 2000. *From Voting to Violence: Democratization and Nationalist Conflict.* New York: W. W. Norton.

Snyder, Richard. 2001. "Scaling Down: The Subnational Comparative Method." *Studies in Comparative International Development* 36 (1): 93–110.

Spector, Bertram I. 2011. *Negotiating Peace and Confronting Corruption: Challenges for Postconflict Societies.* Washington, DC: United States Institute for Peace.

Spyer, Patricia. 2002. "Fire without Smoke and Other Phantoms of Ambon's Violence: Media Effects, Agency, and the Work of Imagination." *Indonesia* 74 (October): 21–36.

Stange, Gunnar, and Roman Patock. 2010. "From Rebels to Rulers and Legislators: The Political Transformation of the Free Aceh Movement (GAM) in Indonesia." *Journal of Current Southeast Asian Affairs* 29 (1): 95–120.

Staniland, Paul. 2012. "States, Insurgents, and Wartime Political Orders." *Perspectives on Politics* 10 (2): 243–264.

Stedman, Stephen John. 1997. "Spoiler Problems in Peace Processes." *International Security* 22 (2): 5–53.

Stedman, Stephen John, Donald Rothchild, and Elizabeth M. Cousens, eds. 2002. *Ending Civil Wars: The Implementation of Peace Agreements.* Boulder: Lynne Rienner.

Stewart, Frances, ed. 2008. *Horizontal Inequalities and Conflict: Understanding Group Violence in Multiethnic Societies.* Houndmills: Palgrave Macmillan.

Stewart, Rory. 2011. "The Plane to Kabul." In *Can Intervention Work?* edited by Rory Stewart and Gerald Knaus, 1–89. New York: W. W. Norton.

Stone, Lawrence. 1979. "The Revival of Narrative." *Past and Present* 18: 3–24.

Straus, Scott. 2006. *The Order of Genocide: Race, Power, and War in Rwanda.* Ithaca, NY: Cornell University Press.

Sudarsono, Juwono. 2000. "The Military and Indonesia's Democratic Prospects." Transcript of Remarks at the United States-Indonesia Society Open Forum, Washington, DC 11 April.

Suhrke, Astri. 2012. "The Peace in Between." In *The Peace in Between: Post-War Violence in Between: Post-war Violence and Peacebuilding*, edited by Astri Suhrke and Mats Berdal, 1–24. Abingdon: Routledge.

Suhrke, Astri, and Mats Berdal, eds. 2012. *The Peace in Between: Post-war Violence and Peacebuilding.* Abingdon: Routledge.

Suhrke, Astri, and Ingrid Samset. 2007. "What's in a Figure? Estimating Recurrence of Civil War." *International Peacekeeping* 14 (2): 195–203.

Sukarsono, Achmad. 2013. "Oversight Needed to Make Police Accountable." *Jakarta Globe.* 3 May. http://www.thejakartaglobe.com/opinion/oversight-needed-to-make-police-accountable/ (accessed 6 May 2013).

Sukma, Rizal. 2004. *Security Operations in Aceh: Goals, Consequences, and Lessons.* Policy Studies No. 3. Washington, DC: East-West Center.

Sukma, Rizal. 2010. "Indonesia's 2009 Elections: Defective System, Resilient Democracy." In *Problems of Democratisation in Indonesia: Elections, Institutions, and Society*, edited by Edward Aspinall and Marcus Mietzner, 53–74. Singapore: Institute for Southeast Asian Studies.

Sulaiman, M. Isa. 1997. *Sejarah Aceh: Sebuah gugatan terhadap tradisi*. Jakarta: Pustaka Sinar Harapan.

Sulaiman, M. Isa. 2006. "From Autonomy to Periphery: A Critical Evaluation of the Acehnese Nationalist Movement." In *Verandah of Violence: The Background to the Aceh Problem*, edited by Anthony Reid, 121–148. Singapore: Singapore University Press.

Suryadinata, Leo. 2002. *Elections and Politics in Indonesia*. Singapore: Institute for Southeast Asian Studies.

Swedish Ministry of Foreign Affairs. 2006. *Stockholm Initiative on Disarmament, Demobilisation, and Reintegration: Final Report*. Stockholm: Ministry of Foreign Affairs.

Tadjoeddin, Mohammad Zulfan. 2002. "Anatomy of Social Violence in the Context of Transition: The Case of Indonesia." Working Paper 02/01. Jakarta: UN Support Facility for Indonesian Recovery.

Tadjoeddin, Mohammad Zulfan. 2014. *Explaining Collective Violence in Contemporary Indonesia: From Conflict to Cooperation*. New York: Palgrave Macmillan.

Tadjoeddin, Mohammad Zulfan, Anis Chowdhury, and S. Mansoob Murshed. 2011. "Routine Violence in Java, Indonesia: Neo-Malthusian and Social Justice Perspectives." In *Climate Change, Human Security, and Violent Conflict*, edited by Jürgen Scheffran et al., 632–650. Germany: Springer.

Tadjoeddin, Mohammad Zulfan, and S. Mansoob Murshed. 2007. "Socioeconomic Determinants of Everyday Violence in Indonesia: An Empirical Investigation of Javanese Districts, 1994–2003." *Journal of Peace Research* 44 (6): 689–709.

Tajima, Yuhki. 2004. "Mobilizing for Violence: The Escalation and Limitation of Identity Conflicts: the Case of Lampung, Indonesia." Indonesian Social Development Papers No. 3. Jakarta: World Bank.

Tajima, Yuhki. 2008. "Explaining Ethnic Violence in Indonesia: Demilitarizing Domestic Security." *Journal of East Asian Studies* 8 (3): 451–472.

Tajima, Yuhki. 2012. "The Institutional Basis of Intercommunal Order: Evidence from Indonesia's Democratic Transition." *American Journal of Political Science* 57 (1): 104–119.

Tajima, Yuhki. 2014. *The Institutional Origins of Communal Violence: Indonesia's Transition from Authoritarian Rule*. New York: Cambridge University Press.

Tambiah, Stanley. 1996. *Levelling Crowds: Ethnonationalist Conflicts and Collective Violence in South Asia*. Berkeley: University of California Press.

Taylor, Michael. 1982. *Community, Anarchy, and Liberty*. Cambridge: Cambridge University Press.

Tempo. 2011. "Feeding at the Regional Trough." *Tempo*, 27 July–2 August (English edition).

Thelen, Kathleeen. 2003. "How Institutions Evolve: Insights from Comparative Historical Analysis." In *Comparative Historical Analysis in the Social Sciences*, edited by James Mahoney and Dietrich Rueschemeyer, 208–240. Cambridge: Cambridge University Press.

Tilly, Charles. 1975. "Reflections on the History of European State-Making." In *The Formation of National States in Western Europe*, edited by Charles Tilly, 3–83. Princeton, NJ: Princeton University Press.

Tilly, Charles. 1992. *Coercion, Capital, and European States*. London: Blackwell.

Tilly, Charles. 1995. "To Explain Political Processes." *American Journal of Sociology* 100: 1594–1610.

Tilly, Charles. 1997a. "Means and Ends of Comparison in Macrosociology." *Comparative Social Research* 16: 43–53.

Tilly, Charles. 1997b. "Parliamentarization of Popular Contention in Great Britain, 1758–1834." *Theory and Society* 26 (2/3): 245–273.

Tilly, Charles. 2003. *The Politics of Collective Violence*. New York: Cambridge University Press.

The Timor-Leste Commission for Reception, Truth and Reconciliation (CAVR). 2005a. *Chega! The Report of the Commission for Reception, Truth and Reconciliation in Timor-Leste (CAVR)*. Dili: CAVR. http://www.cavr-timorleste.org/chegaFiles/finalReportEng/07.2-Unlawful-Killings-and-Enforced-Disappearances.pdf (accessed 14 May 2013).

The Timor-Leste Commission for Reception, Truth and Reconciliation (CAVR). 2005b. *Conflict-Related Deaths in Timor-Leste 1974–1999*. Dili: CAVR. http://www.cavr-timorleste.org/updateFiles/english/CONFLICT-RELATED%20DEATHS.pdf> (accessed 14 May 2013).

Tindage, Rudy W. 2006. *Damai yang Sejati: Rekonsiliasi di Tobelo, Kajian Teologis dan Komunikasi*. Jakarta: Yakoma PGI.

Toft, Monica Duffy. 2003. *The Geography of Ethnic Violence: Identity, Interests, and the Indivisibility of Territory*. Princeton, NJ: Princeton University Press.

Toft, Monica Duffy. 2010. *Securing the Peace: The Durable Settlement of Civil Wars*. Princeton, NJ: Princeton University Press.

Tomagola, Tamrin Amal. 2000. "The Bleeding Halmahera of the North Moluccas." Paper presented at the first annual meeting of Asian Studies, Oslo, Norway, 5 June.

Tomsa, Dirk. 2009a. "Local Elections and Party Politics in a Postconflict Area: The Pilkada in Maluku." Indonesian Studies Working Paper No. 8. Sydney: University of Sydney.

Tomsa, Dirk. 2009b. "Electoral Democracy in a Divided Society: The 2008 Gubernatorial Election in Maluku, Indonesia." *South East Asia Research* 17 (2): 229–259.

Tomsa, Dirk. 2015. "Toning Down the 'Big Bang': The Politics of Decentralisation during the Yudhoyono Years." In *The Yudhoyono Presidency: Indonesia's Decade of Stability and Stagnation*, edited by Edward Aspinall, Marcus Mietzner, and Dirk Tomsa, 155–174. Singapore: Institute for Southeast Asian Studies.

Transparency International Indonesia (TII). 2010. *Survei Barometer Korupsi Aceh*. Jakarta: Transparency International Indonesia.

Trijono, Lambang. 2001. *Keluar dari Kemelut Maluku: Refleksi Pengalaman Praktis Bekerja untuk Perdamaian Maluku*. Yogyakarta: Pustaka Pelajar.

Tunny, M. Azis. 2006. "Ambon Terrorist Jailed, Supporters Run Amok." *Jakarta Post*. February 21.

United Nations Disarmament, Demobilization, and Reintegration Resources Centre (UNDDR). 2006. *Integrated Disarmament, Demobilization, and Reintegration Standards*. New York: UNDDR.

United Nations Office on Drugs and Crime (UNODC). 2011. *Global Study on Homicides 2011: Trends, Context, and Data*. Vienna: UNODC.

Uvin, Peter. 1998. *Aiding Violence: The Development Enterprise in Rwanda*. West Hartford: Kumarian Press.

Van Evera, Stephen. 1997. *Guide to Methods for Students of Political Science*. Ithaca, NY: Cornell University Press.

Varshney, Ashutosh. 2002. *Ethnic Conflict and Civil Life: Hindus and Muslims in India*. New Haven: Yale University Press.

Varshney, Ashutosh. 2003. "Nationalism, Ethnic Conflict, and Rationality." *Perspectives on Politics* 1 (1): 85–99.

Varshney, Ashutosh. 2007. "Ethnicity and Ethnic Conflict." In *The Oxford Handbook of Comparative Politics*, edited by Charles Boix and Susan C. Stokes, 274–295. Oxford: Oxford University Press.

Varshney, Ashutosh. 2008. "Analyzing Collective Violence in Indonesia: An Overview." *Journal of East Asian Studies* 8 (3): 341–360.

Varshney, Ashutosh, and Joshua R. Gubler. 2012. "Does the State Promote Communal Violence for Electoral Reasons?" *India Review* 11 (3): 191–199.

Varshney, Ashutosh, Mohammad Zulfan Tadjoeddin, and Rizal Panggabean. 2010. "Patterns of Collective Violence in Indonesia." In *Collective Violence in Indonesia*, edited by Ashutosh Varshney, 19–50. Boulder, CO: Lynne Rienner.

Vel, Jacqueline. 2001. "Tribal Battle in Remote Island: Crisis and Violence in Sumba (Eastern Indonesia)." *Indonesia* 72 (October): 141–158.

Vothknecht, Marc, and Sudarno Sumarto. 2011. "Beyond the Overall Economic Downturn: Evidence of Sector-specific Effects on Violent Conflict from Indonesia." DIW Discussion Papers No. 1105. Berlin: German Institute for Economic Research.

Wagner, R. Harrison. 1994. "Peace, War, and the Balance of Power." *American Political Science Review* 88 (3): 593–607.

Walsh, Jason. 2013. "15 Years after Good Friday Agreement, an Imperfect Peace in Northern Ireland." *Christian Science Monitor*. 10 April. http://www.csmonitor.com/World/Global-News/2013/0410/15-years-after-Good-Friday-Agreement-an-imperfect-peace-in-Northern-Ireland (accessed 10 May 2013).

Walter, Barbara F. 2002. *Committing to Peace: The Successful Settlement of Civil Wars*. Princeton: Princeton University Press.

Walter, Barbara F. 2004. "Does Conflict Beget Conflict? Explaining Recurring Civil War." *Journal of Peace Research* 41 (3): 371–388.

Walter, Barbara F. 2009a. "Bargaining Failures and Civil War." *Annual Review of Political Science* 12: 243–261.

Walter, Barbara F. 2009b. *Reputation and Civil War: Why Separatist Conflicts Are So Violent*. Cambridge: Cambridge University Press.

Walter, Barbara F. 2010. "Conflict Relapse and the Sustainability of Postconflict Peace." Background paper for the World Development Report 2011. Washington, DC: World Bank.

Weber, Max. 1946. "Science as a Vocation." In *From Max Weber: Essays in Sociology*, edited by H. H. Gerth and C. Wright Mills, 129–156. New York: Oxford University Press.

Weinstein, Jeremy M. 2005. "Resources and the Information Problem in Rebel Recruitment." *Journal of Conflict Resolution* 49 (4): 598–624.

Weinstein, Jeremy M. 2007. *Inside Rebellion: The Politics of Insurgent Violence*. Cambridge: Cambridge University Press.

Welsh, Bridget. 2008. "Local and National: Keroyakan Mobbing in Indonesia." *Journal of East Asian Studies* 8 (3): 473–504.

Wilkinson, Steven I. 2004. *Votes and Violence: Electoral Competition and Ethnic Riots in India*. Cambridge: Cambridge University Press.

Wilson, Chris. 2005. "The Ethnic Origins of Religious Conflict in North Maluku Province, Indonesia, 1999–2000." *Indonesia* 79 (April): 69–91.

Wilson, Chris. 2008. *Ethno-Religious Violence in Indonesia: From Soil to God*. London: Routledge.

Wilson, Chris. 2011. "Provocation or Excuse? Process-Tracing the Impact of Elite Propaganda in a Violent Conflict in Indonesia." *Nationalism and Ethnic Politics* 17 (4): 339–360.

Wilson, Chris. 2013. "'Ethnic Outbidding' for Patronage: The 2010 Riots in Tarakan, Indonesia." *Southeast Asia Research* 21 (1): 105–129.

Wilson, Ian. 2010. "The Rise and Fall of Political Gangsters in Indonesian Democracy." In *Problems of Democratisation in Indonesia: Elections, Institutions and Society*, edited by Edward Aspinall and Marcus Mietzner, 199–218. Singapore: Institute for Southeast Asian Studies.

Winters, Jeffrey A. 2011. *Oligarchy*. New York: Cambridge University Press.

Wolf, Eric R. 1964. *Anthropology*. Englewood Cliffs, NJ: Prentice Hall.

Wolf, Eric R. 1999. *Envisioning Power: Ideologies of Dominance and Crisis*. Berkeley: University of California Press.

Wood, Elisabeth J. 2003. *Insurgent Collective Action and Civil War in El Salvador*. New York: Cambridge University Press.

Woodward, Susan L. 2002. "Economic Priorities for Successful Peace Implementation." In *Ending Civil Wars: The Implementation of Peace Agreements*, edited by Stephen John Stedman, Donald Rothchild, and Elizabeth M. Cousens, 183–214. Boulder, CO: Lynne Rienner.

World Bank. 2003. "Decentralizing Indonesia: A Regional Public Expenditure Review Overview Report." East Asia Poverty Reduction and Economic Management Report No. 26191-IND. Washington, DC: World Bank.

World Bank. 2005. "Aceh Conflict Monitoring Update: 1st–31st December 2005." Banda Aceh: World Bank/DSF.

World Bank. 2006a. *GAM Reintegration Needs Assessment: Enhancing Peace through Community-level Development Programming*. World Bank: Jakarta.

World Bank. 2006b. *Aceh Public Expenditure Analysis: Spending for Reconstruction and Poverty Reduction*. Jakarta: World Bank.

World Bank. 2006c. "Aceh Conflict Monitoring Update: 1st–28th February 2006." Banda Aceh: World Bank/DSF.

World Bank. 2006d. "Aceh Conflict Monitoring Update: 1st–31st March 2006." Banda Aceh: World Bank/DSF.

World Bank. 2006e. "Aceh Conflict Monitoring Update: 1st–30th April 2006." Banda Aceh: World Bank/DSF.

World Bank. 2006f. "Aceh Conflict Monitoring Update: 1st–31st May 2006." Banda Aceh: World Bank/DSF.

World Bank. 2007a. "Aceh Conflict Monitoring Update: 1st–31st January." Banda Aceh: World Bank/DSF.

World Bank. 2007b. "Aceh Conflict Monitoring Update: 1st–30th April." Banda Aceh: World Bank/DSF.

World Bank. 2007c. "Aceh Conflict Monitoring Update: 1st–31st May." Banda Aceh: World Bank/DSF.

World Bank. 2007d. "Aceh Conflict Monitoring Update: 1st–30th September." Banda Aceh: World Bank/DSF.

World Bank. 2008a. *Aceh Poverty Assessment 2008: The Impact of the Conflict, the Tsunami and Reconstruction on Poverty in Aceh*. Jakarta: World Bank.

World Bank. 2008b. *Aceh Economic Update: October 2008*. Jakarta/Banda Aceh: World Bank/Bank Indonesia/Multi-Donor Fund.

World Bank. 2008c. "Aceh Conflict Monitoring Update: 1st January–29th February 2008." Banda Aceh: World Bank.

World Bank. 2008d. "Aceh Conflict Monitoring Update: 1st–30th September 2008." Banda Aceh: World Bank.

World Bank. 2008e. "Aceh Conflict Monitoring Update: 1st October–30th November 2008." Banda Aceh: World Bank.

World Bank. 2008f. *Indonesia Public Expenditure Review—Spending for Development: Making the Most of Indonesia's New Opportunities*. Jakarta: World Bank.

World Bank. 2009a. *Aceh Growth Diagnostic: Identifying the Binding Constraints to Growth in a Postconflict and Post-Disaster Environment*. Jakarta: World Bank.

World Bank. 2009b. "Aceh Conflict Monitoring Update: 1st December 2008–28th February 2009." Banda Aceh: World Bank.

World Bank. 2010. *Pengelolaan Keuangan Daerah dan Pelayanan Publik di Provinsi Seribu Pulau*. Jakarta: World Bank.

World Bank. 2011a. *World Development Report 2011: Conflict, Security and Development*. Washington, DC: World Bank.

World Bank. 2011b. *Crime and Violence in Central America: A Development Challenge*. Washington, DC: World Bank.

World Bank. 2011c. Presentation 'Review of Aceh's Special Autonomy Fund Management and Expenditures Utilization'. Jakarta, 16 November.

World Bank. 2012. Subnational dataset. Unpublished.

World Bank. 2013. *Indonesia Economic Quarterly (March): Pressures Mounting*. Jakarta: World Bank.

World Bank/KDP. 2007. *2006 Village Survey in Aceh: An Assessment of Village Infrastructure and Social Conditions*. Banda Aceh/Jakarta: World Bank/ Government of Indonesia.

World Health Organisation (WHO). 2002. *World Report on Violence and Health*. Geneva: WHO.

Wrighter, Selina. 2005. "Questions of Judgment: The New Constitutional Court Combines Law and Politics." *Inside Indonesia* 81 (Jan-March).

Zartman, I. William. 1995. *Elusive Peace: Negotiating an End to Civil Wars*. Washington, DC: Brookings Institution Press.

Zaum, Dominik, and Christine Cheng, eds. 2011. *Corruption and Postconflict Peacebuilding: Selling the Peace?* Abingdon: Routledge.

Zurstrassen, Matthew. 2006. "An Evaluation of BRA Support to Former Combatants." Unpublished World Bank evaluation report for BRA.

Index

Aceh, 124–159
  community support for violence in,
    152–153
  consequences for large-scale violence in,
    130, 142–144; lack of, for small-scale
    violence, 150–151, 158
  extended violence in, 52, 54tab, 61tab,
    125–128, 169, 223n26
  peace agreement (MoU), 56, 128–129,
    130–131, 132, 134–135, 143, 150,
    237n106
  peaceful alternatives in, 130–142
  postconflict violence in: levels and forms,
    55–56, 57tab, 58tab, 62–63, 62tab,
    63tab, 124, 129, 135–136, 137, 143, 149,
    153, 154, 154tab, 195; motivations for,
    144–151, 158–159
  resources awarded to violence perpetrators
    in, 130–132, 137–139, 140, 146–148;
    signaling of, 144, 146–149, 151, 158–159;
    attempts to disconnect, 124, 130
Aceh Besar, 61tab, 239n195
ACLED database, 217n71
adat (traditional unwritten laws), 83, 84, 116,
  117, 121, 232n70
Agas, 228n86
Albar, Muhammad, 106–107, 114, 121, 232n64
Ambon
  extended violence in, 2, 61, 61tab, 65, 66–67,
    223n26
  population profile, 224n6, 224n31, 224n32
  postconflict violence in: levels and forms,
    62, 62tab, 63tab, 67–68; riots, 1–2, 68,
    76–77, 93–94, 185–186
AMM (Aceh Monitoring Mission), 143
Andili, Bahir, 98, 99, 114
Andili, Syamsir, 119
APKLI Maluku, 75
Armaiyn, Thaib, 98, 99, 101, 107, 114–115, 120
Aspinall, Edward, 78, 127, 139, 173, 190
asymmetrical wars, 215n38
Attamimi, Ustadz Mohammad, 71
Australian embassy bombing, 55
Axelrod, Robert, 47

Bali bombing, 55
bargaining, 28–31, 32, 33, 41
Bates, Robert H., 218n73
Berdal, Mats, 9–10
Bermeo, Nancy, 44–45
Bertrand, Jacques, 162
Besley, Timothy, 34
Bireuen, 61tab
BKO forces, 76, 77, 94
Blattman, Christopher, 10, 13
Bosnia, 12, 30, 36
Brancati, Dawn, 220n58
Brass, Paul R., 29, 219n29
Bräuchler, Birgit, 31, 228n94

casualties. *See* death rates
Cederman, Lars-Erik, 32
Central America, 4, 213n14
central elites
  forms of violence and, x, 37–41, 42fig,
    169–170, 188
  motivations: for peace, 181–184; for
    violence, 47, 170–180, 189, 195–196
  See also military; state
Central Kalimantan, 54, 54tab, 55, 57tab, 58tab
Central Maluku, 61, 61tab, 62, 62tab, 63tab,
  67–68, 74–75, 223n26
central state. *See* state
Central Sulawesi, 54, 54tab, 55, 57tab,
  58tab, 168
Christian-Muslim relations. *See* religious
  groups
civil wars
  asymmetrical *vs.* symmetrical, 215n38
  Central American, 4, 213n14
  collaborating to profit from, 30–31
  definitions, 19, 21tab, 215n39
  episodic violence during, 216n55
  regional variations in impacts of, 10–11,
    223n26
  scholarship on, 5, 8, 9, 10, 12–14
  secessionist, 2, 11, 14
  state fragility, link to, 34, 220n46, 220n49
  See also Aceh: extended violence in

CPSIA information can be obtained
at www.ICGtesting.com
Printed in the USA
BVHW032217140319
541611BV00011B/12/P

9 781501 735448